VICTORIA
& VANCOUVER ISLAND

Help Us Keep This Guide Up to Date

Every effort has been made by the authors and editors to make this guide as accurate and useful as possible. However, many things can change after a guide is published—establishments close, phone numbers change, hiking trails are rerouted, facilities come under new management, etc.

We would love to hear from you concerning your experiences with this guide and how you feel it could be made better and be kept up to date. While we may not be able to respond to all comments and suggestions, we'll take them to heart and we'll also make certain to share them with the authors. Please send your comments and suggestions to the following address:

The Globe Pequot Press
Reader Response/Editorial Department
P.O. Box 480
Guilford, CT 06437

Or you may e-mail us at:

editorial@globepequot.com

Thanks for your input, and happy travels!

HILL GUIDES™ SERIES

SIXTH EDITION

VICTORIA
& VANCOUVER ISLAND

*A Personal Tour of
an Almost Perfect Eden*

KATHLEEN THOMPSON HILL
AND GERALD N. HILL

INSIDERS' GUIDE®

GUILFORD, CONNECTICUT
AN IMPRINT OF THE GLOBE PEQUOT PRESS

The prices and rates listed in this guidebook are in Canadian dollars and were confirmed at press time. We recommend, however, that you call establishments before traveling to obtain current information.

To buy books in quantity for corporate use
or incentives, call **(800) 962–0973**
or e-mail **premiums@GlobePequot.com.**

Maps by Clover Point Cartographics, Victoria, B.C.
Illustrations by Mauro Magellan
Photos by Kathleen Hill and Gerald Hill, except for chapter head photos courtesy of Tourism Victoria, Port Hardy by Bob Carver, Chesterman Beach by Wickaninnish Inn, and Aerie courtesy of Aerie Resort. In chapter 8, "History of Victoria and Vancouver Island," all illustrations are photocopied archival photographs from B.C. Archives & Records, Province of B.C., Canada, except as noted.

ISSN 1546-6302
ISBN 978-0-7627-4564-7

Manufactured in the United States of America
Sixth Edition/First Printing

For

**Erin and Mack,
again, and again,**

Still hoping that they will
eventually love
British Columbia
as we do

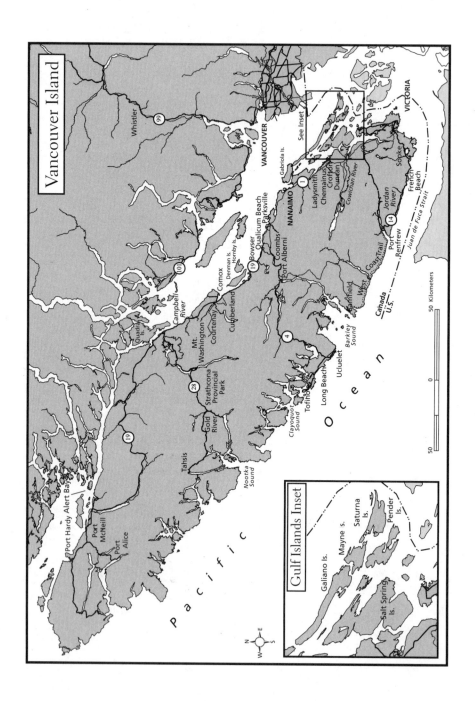

Vancouver Island

Whistler

VANCOUVER

Gabriola Is.

See Inset

NANAIMO

Ladysmith
Chemainus
Crofton
Duncan
Cowichan River

Qualicum Beach
Parksville
Bowser
Coombs
Port Alberni

Denman Is.
Hornby Is.

Comox
Courtenay
Cumberland
Mt. Washington

Campbell River

Quadra Is.

Strathcona Provincial Park

Gold River

Tahsis

Nootka Sound

Port Hardy Alert Bay

Port McNeill

Port Alice

Bamfield

Barkley Sound

Ucluelet

Long Beach

Tofino

Clayoquot Sound

West Coast Trail

Canada
U.S.

Jordan River

Port Renfrew

French Beach

Sooke

VICTORIA

Juan de Fuca Strait

P a c i f i c   O c e a n

50   0   50   Kilometers

Gulf Islands Inset

Galiano Is.

Mayne s.

Saturna Is.

Pender Is.

Salt Spring Is.

N
W   E
S

Contents

Preface   ix

CHAPTER 1: USING YOUR HILL GUIDE TO VICTORIA AND VANCOUVER ISLAND   1
    Basic Facts   2
    How to Be a Visitor and Not a Tourist in Victoria   6
    Terms of Endearment—A Glossary   8

CHAPTER 2: GETTING HERE AND GETTING AROUND   11
    Getting Here   11
    Getting Around Once You're Here   17

CHAPTER 3: NEIGHBORHOODS OF GREATER VICTORIA   25
    Downtown Victoria   28
    Special Streets of Downtown Victoria   70
    Residential Neighborhoods   123
    Significant Others   132
    Things You Really Should See   144
    Where to Stay   154

CHAPTER 4: EXPLORING OUTSIDE VICTORIA   159
    Victoria to Sidney   159
    Victoria to Port Renfrew   169
    Port Renfrew   183

CHAPTER 5: UP ISLAND   187
    Victoria to Nanaimo   187
    Nanaimo to Port Hardy   215
    Nanaimo to Tofino   227

CHAPTER 6: THE OTHER ISLANDS   243
  Gulf Islands   243
  Discovery Islands   256

CHAPTER 7: OUTDOOR THINGS TO DO   261
  Biking   261
  Diving   261
  Fishing   264
  Golf   266
  Hiking   269
  Kayaking and Canoeing   269
  Kid Stuff   271
  Skiing   271
  Swimming   272
  Walking (and Other) Tours   272
  Whale Watching   273

CHAPTER 8: HISTORY OF VICTORIA AND VANCOUVER ISLAND   275

CHAPTER 9: LIST OF LISTS   323
  Antiques Shops   323
  Bookstores   324
  Galleries   326
  Laundromats   327
  Nightlife/Music   327
  Pharmacies   329
  Popular Bus Destinations   329
  Restrooms   331
  Theaters   332

CHAPTER 10: ANNUAL EVENTS AND FESTIVALS   335
  Greater Victoria, Sooke, Duncan, Cowichan Valley   335
  Nanaimo to Port Hardy, Port Alberni, West Coast   340

Index   343
About the Authors   355

Preface

We firmly believe that we need to live in a place for a while in order to write about it clearly and accurately enough to give our readers the best possible mental and emotional picture of it before they visit. That way we can save you time and grief and provide you with sufficient information to make good choices, still find adventure, and maximize your enjoyment.

Jerry's older adult children, Megan and David, have lived in British Columbia since high school, and both graduated from the University of Victoria. Megan manages budgets and contracts for British Columbia and lives in Victoria with her husband, John Albright, and son, Sam; David and his wife, Deidre Matheson, live and work in Victoria with their son, Thomas, and daughter, Talia. It is because of them that we first came to Victoria and fell in love with the city. Now we live here as much as we can and co-taught U.S. politics at the University of Victoria and at the University of British Columbia in Vancouver for several years.

We do not presume to judge which of anything is the best. We simply tell you which places are our favorites, because you might have different tastes. When we say "one of our favorites," it means all the adult Hills love it. When a place is tagged as one of Kathleen's, Jerry's, Megan's, or David's favorites, it will give you a hint of to whom it appeals, and perhaps a generational difference of opinion. But then Kathleen and Jerry have their favorite toy stores, too. Instead of categorizing places as inexpensive to expensive, we simply tell you what things cost so that you can make your own judgment based on your budget. With this edition we include even more small wineries, organic food growers and producers, organic bakeries, cheese makers, and specialty food shops.

Where else in the world can you enjoy Canadian urbanity with fine wines and restaurants, shops, museums, and theater, and in five minutes be at the beach or in thirty minutes be deep in the rain forest? Still wondering? Turn the pages and explore Victoria and Vancouver Island with us.

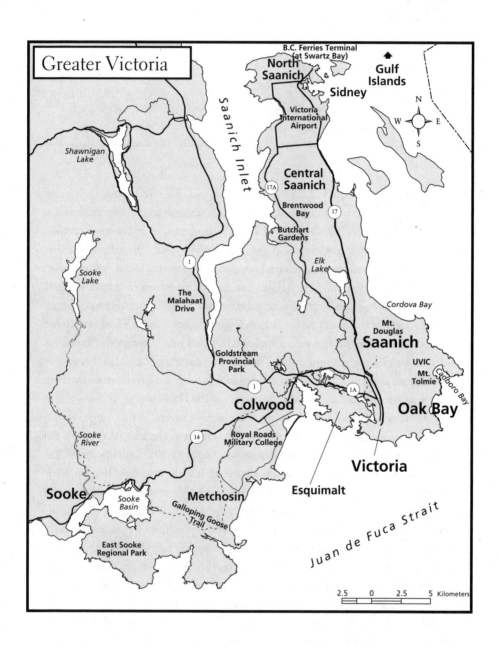

Greater Victoria

B.C. Ferries Terminal
(at Swartz Bay)

North
Saanich

Gulf
Islands

Sidney

Victoria
International
Airport

N
W   E
S

Saanich Inlet

Shawnigan
Lake

Central
Saanich

17A

Brentwood
Bay

Butchart
Gardens

Elk
Lake

Sooke
Lake

The
Malahaat
Drive

Cordova Bay

Mt.
Douglas

Saanich

UVIC
Mt.
Tolmie

Cadboro Bay

Goldstream
Provincial
Park

1

Colwood

1A

Oak Bay

Sooke
River

14

Royal Roads
Military College

Victoria

Esquimalt

Sooke

Sooke
Basin

Metchosin

Galloping Goose
Trail

Juan de Fuca Strait

East Sooke
Regional Park

2.5   0   2.5   5 Kilometers

1

Using Your Hill Guide to Victoria and Vancouver Island

W hat do Steve Nash, twice Most Valuable Player in the National Basketball Association, Nelly Furtado, winner of Grammy, World Music, and many other awards for performances and albums, and Diana Krall, two-time Grammy award-winning jazz musician have in common?

Answer: They are all from Vancouver Island. Nash came to Victoria from South Africa as a small child when his parents, who were Caucasian, decided they did not want their child growing up in the apartheid culture. Furtado, whose parents emigrated from the Azores, was born in Victoria. Krall was born in Nainamo, where she began playing jazz piano and singing in local restaurants when she was fifteen. This guide will help you learn much about Victoria and Vancouver Island and its pleasant people, famous or not.

Whether you are a first-time visitor or a lifelong resident, this guide is organized to help you maximize your pleasure, starting with this chapter's section on "Basic Facts," such as health care, weather, and money exchanges.

The "Getting Here and Getting Around" chapter lays out the most effective ways to travel in Victoria and around the island, including economies, car rentals, bus routes, sightseeing, ferries, tours, scooters, and walking.

Step-by-step guidance through each of the different neighborhoods, up each side of the streets to restaurants, stores, and special places in natural walking patterns, including "Antique Row" along Fort Street, is given in the "Neighborhoods of Greater Victoria" chapter.

This chapter's "Significant Others" section leads you to restaurants and interesting destinations outside the normal tourist routes, helping you to zero in on many places of culture and enjoyment.

The "Exploring Outside Victoria" chapter takes you up the Saanich Peninsula to Sidney and westward along the island coast to Sooke and, if you're adventurous, as far as rugged Port Renfrew. We have added a new listing of organic farms so you can experience U-picking if you want to try it.

The chapter "Up Island" provides details of a tour northward through the totem pole town of Duncan, past the murals of Chemainus, on to Nanaimo, Courtenay, Campbell Bay, and Port Hardy. At Parksville we direct you over the mountains to Port Alberni and the beaches of Ucluet and Tofino ("tough town"). The traveler is guided through spectacular forests and ends up at the dramatic beaches and colorful villages.

"The Other Islands" chapter helps you explore where arts, solitude, fishing, water sports, and nature meet off the east coast of Vancouver Island.

Details on the opportunities to enjoy year-round golf, stunning whale watching, boating, hiking, biking, and some of the world's finest fishing are provided in the "Outdoor Things To Do" chapter.

Our "History of Victoria and Vancouver Island" chapter traces the lively story of the city and island, including the First People, explorers, frontier struggles, progress, and colorful characters.

The "List of Lists" chapter lays out checkoffs to make your time in Victoria and the Island most effective and enjoyable. Pick your favorite pleasures—antiques, bookstores, galleries, nightlife/music, and theaters, or your special needs—Laundromats, pharmacies, bus destinations, and restrooms.

Our chapter "Annual Events and Festivals" helps you plan and schedule visits to the many lively spectacles and celebrations.

Welcome to what colonial governor Sir James Douglas called "the perfect Eden."

BASIC FACTS

One fact that most Americans and other non-Canadians find nearly impossible to comprehend is that Victorians are the most considerate and pleasant people you may ever encounter. This calls for a cultural adjustment, so be forewarned.

Remember to check your guns at the border. Canadians don't allow them or any other weapons in—including pepper spray.

We are happy to report that smoking is no longer allowed in public buildings, including restaurants and bars. A few restaurants with patios or sidewalk tables allow smoking.

Basic medical insurance costs each adult British Columbian about $54 per month for one person, $96 for two (straight or gay), and $108 for a family of three or more, with no deductibles and no "preexisting conditions." Health care premiums doubled after former Liberal B.C. Premier Gordon Campbell cut provincial taxes right after he took office in 2001.

Community is important here. The government actually subsidizes artists and writers, poets, and publishers, although federal and provincial governments are cutting back on those grants.

Local drivers are courteous and generous with their time. They actually stop to let you merge into their lanes and stop for pedestrians approaching the curb to cross the street.

Most speed limits and distances in Canada are posted in kilometers, with a few around Victoria in miles also. A kilometer is $^6/_{10}$ mile. Remember: 50 gets you 30, 80 gets you 50, 100 gets you 60, and 120 gets you a $100 fine. It's okay to turn right on a red light after stopping. If you drive without insurance and get caught, you're off to jail.

If you don't like the weather, wait twenty minutes. The weather in Victoria is the best in Canada, which is why Canadians known as snowbirds come here in the winter. It rarely snows in Victoria—about as often as it does in San Francisco. But it has snowed here recently. In 1996–97 there was enough snow to make Victorians and visitors wish city mothers and fathers hadn't sold the city snowplows!

Temperatures in Canada are given in Celsius, which, by whatever formula you think you remember, never seems to translate correctly to Fahrenheit. For a rough approximation double the figure for Celsius, subtract a few degrees (the greater the temperature, the more you subtract), and add the result to 32°F. For accuracy multiply Celsius by 9, divide by 5, and add 32. Thus 10°C is 50°F, 20°C is 68°F, 25°C is 77°F, and so on.

Victoria's worst weather month is January, when the temperature averages 38°F or 3°C with sixteen rainy days. It gradually warms each month. While the averages are only 62°F and 17°C in July and slightly lower in August, there are many days in both months that are warm and even hot by California standards.

It rains only about 29 inches annually in Victoria, less than half what Vancouver city gets. The storms roll in from the Pacific, blow right by Victoria, up against the mountains around Vancouver, and dump there. For weather updates call (250) 656–3978; for marine weather, (250) 656–7515.

Victorians dress less formally than eastern Canadians and regard the slightest glimmer of sun-generated warmth as permission to break out in Bermuda shorts and tennies. Subtle natural colors dominate, and Victorians spot Americans partly by their loud colors and voices.

Homelessness and panhandling are increasing here. You see more of both in the summer months when the weather is pleasant and people in need are out in the open more.

Locals often drink bottled or filtered water, although we have drunk tap water throughout the island with no uncomfortable results.

Victoria has quickly become much more conscious of the needs of persons in wheelchairs and is moving rapidly to make things accessible. We tell you which facilities are accessible. More than half of Victoria buses are accessible. Call B.C. Transit (250–382–6161) to check on which buses are and when they come.

Generally Victoria is a tolerant city. We find nearly all businesses in Victoria are gay friendly; some are gay owned.

Differences and diversities are encouraged because Canada lives by the *mosaic principle,* in which all kinds of people are expected to live and work together with pride, instead of the U.S. melting pot, into which everyone is supposed to dive and come out as alike as possible.

Here is a rundown of other basic facts that you should find useful:

Money. Banks and ATMs are the best places to exchange currency because you get the best exchange rate. The exchange rate varies, but you will get approximately $1.05 Canadian for $1.00 U.S. Many businesses on Vancouver Island take American dollars but give you change in Canadian currency, including a slight charge for doing you the favor. Money exchange shops have the poorest exchange. *All prices quoted in this book are in Canadian dollars and are subject to change.*

Shopping. Business hours vary in Victoria by season. Shops along Government Street and the rest of the downtown area generally open at 10:00 A.M. and close at 6:00 P.M. during summer season, while some shops selling T-shirts and other souvenirs stay open later. In fall and winter, most shops close at 5:00 P.M.

Emergencies. Call 911.

Eyeglass repair. There are loads of eyeglass places on Douglas Street between Broughton and Fisgard, as well as in the Bay Centre mall and on Fort Street.

Medical care. You can walk into any doctor's office labeled as a clinic or walk-in clinic or a hospital emergency room and get treatment. Non-Canadians usually have to pay for the doctor's services and then recover the amount from their insurance company.

Hospitals. Royal Jubilee Hospital, 1800 Fort Street, (250) 370–8000, emergencies, (250) 370–8212; Victoria General Hospital, 35 Helmcken Road, (250) 727–4212, emergencies, (250) 727–4181.

Hot lines. Emotional crises center: (250) 386–6323; help line for children: 0 and ask for Zenith 1234; poison control center: (250) 595–9211; sexual assault center: (250) 838–3232; British Columbia road conditions: (250) 380–4997; SPCA (animals): (250) 385–6521.

Library. Greater Victoria Public Library (250–382–7241) has its main entrance on Blanshard Street, but the library extends through the block to Broughton, where there is a parking garage right next door to the entrance. This is one of the busiest and most exciting libraries we have ever seen. Children and teen sections are on the first floor.

Liquor stores. Hard liquor is sold primarily at government liquor stores or at stores adjacent to or within hotels. Hours vary by location. Most open at 10:00 or 11:00 A.M. and close between 6:00 and 11:00 P.M. On Friday nights many stay open late. Taxes keep prices high. Legal drinking age is nineteen. Driving drunk sends you to jail. Period. Three drunk-driving offenses and Canadians have their licenses withdrawn for life; foreigners are kicked out of the country.

In 2003 B.C. Premier Gordon Campbell pleaded, "no contest" to drunk driving (very) in Maui, Hawaii, paid his substantial fine, refused treatment, and lived happily ever after, suspending government employees accused of similar offenses.

Newspapers. Victoria's local daily, the *Times-Colonist,* comes out every morning; the weekly television schedule is in the Friday edition. The what's-happening newspaper is *Monday Magazine,* which comes out on Thursday, of course. There are several alternative and neighborhood papers, which are great sources for up-to-date local information. The national *Globe and Mail* (www.globeandmail.com) is the Canadian equivalent of the *New York Times.* Its Saturday edition is big, and it also puts out a weekly export edition that we find extremely informative.

Pharmaceuticals. You can get anything here that you can get in the United States and more. Most over-the-counter medications made in the United States are also made in Canada. Aspirin, its substitutes, and even toothpaste cost less than in the United States (see the List of Lists chapter for pharmacies).

Taxes. Oh yes. Everyone pays 7 percent provincial sales tax (PST) and another 7 percent goods and services federal tax (GST). GST and PST taxes do not apply to groceries or essential cosmetics such as soap, toothpaste, and shampoo. Clothing (even backpacks) for children younger than age sixteen is PST exempt. Visitors from outside Canada can get the GST part refunded by filling out a Visitor Tax Refund form available at most stores.

HOW TO BE A VISITOR AND NOT A TOURIST IN VICTORIA

Residents of Victoria and Vancouver Island are remarkably nice to visitors and tourists. They know and respect the fact that tourists bring a large portion of Victorians' income with them, and they want to make parting with money as enjoyable and as painless for visitors as possible. Try to make payment in Canadian currency by exchanging at banks before venturing out. Use a nonbank commercial currency exchange only if you are desperate.

A political note: According to polls, most Canadians do not believe in the United States' invasion of Iraq, and some support Canada's role in Afghanistan.

We have heard firsthand stories from British Columbia residents about getting jeered in Washington State because of their B.C. license plates and for not supporting the invasion of Iraq.

Despite all this, Canadians are still gracious, warm, and welcoming to most Americans.

Modulate your voices, wait your turn, and tone down the clothes. Generally everyone strolling up and down Government Street in shorts is a tourist. If you want to fit in, dress as if you are going to work in informal clothes. If you don't care—don't.

Wearing Victoria T-shirts may give you away as a tourist, although you will see many residents of Victoria and Vancouver Island wearing shirts and caps supporting the Vancouver Cannucks ice hockey team or the University of Victoria (UVic) Vikes or boasting that they completed a local marathon. It's best to buy your shirts on the island and then wear them back home.

Canadians rarely throw paper, garbage, or drink containers in the street or on public property. We once watched a street clown admonish an American boy who had tossed a candy bar wrapper on the sidewalk on Government Street. The clown suggested so politely to the young man that he pick it up and dispose of it properly that the kid didn't get it. After five or six tries, the clown finally convinced the boy that he should put the paper in the can next to him. His parents were, fortunately, sensitive enough to be embarrassed.

Learn to speak Canadian. Many English words have different meanings for Canadians and Americans. "Terms of Endearment—A Glossary" will help you understand and fit in. Some of the differences will tickle your funny bone.

Return the extreme courtesy that Victorians extend to each other and to you.

Terms of Endearment— A Glossary

aboriginals: *natives who inhabited North America before white people arrived; Indians*

B.C.: *British Columbia*

bill: *the charges presented to you at a restaurant*

brown bread: *whole-wheat bread*

bum: *one's bottom or rear end*

buns: *rolls, as in breakfast rolls or rolls on which sandwiches are served*

busker: *a person who performs independently outdoors to entertain the public and thrives on gratuities*

cheque: *a check, such as a bank check or paycheck*

chips: *french fries*

cutlery: *silverware; forks, knives, and spoons; utensils*

elastics: *rubber bands*

English Canadian: *one whose first language is not French*

esthetician: *beautician*

European: *white people, presumed by natives to be of European descent*

family name: *maiden name*

First Peoples: *original inhabitants of North America before white people arrived; Indians*

First Nations: *same as First Peoples, more politically correct since the late 1990s*

flat bread: *from First Peoples' tradition, similar to pizza*

fuel: *gasoline*

fully licensed: *licensed to serve hard liquor, beer, and wine*

heritage: *historic; e.g., a heritage house*

Interior: *the part of British Columbia east of the Coast Mountains; e.g., east of Vancouver city*

interpretive center, tour, etc.: *spoken guide or explanation*

licensed premises: *bar or restaurant that serves beer and wine (see fully licensed)*

lineup: *a waiting line or queue*

lounge: *bar where alcohol is served*

Lower Mainland: *all the population centers within 100 miles of the Canada–U.S. border; in British Columbia, specifically from the Canada–U.S. border to Whistler Resort*

mum: *mom, mother*

parkade: *parking garage*

pension: *pay one receives from a former employer; the government check seniors receive, like U.S. Social Security*

poutine: *a Quebec-origin concoction of french fries, white cheese curds, and gravy*

return: *round-trip*

serviettes: *table napkins*

suite: *apartment, condominium, or office space*

sweets: *desserts and pastries*

till: *cash register*

UBC: *University of British Columbia (Vancouver)*

UVic: *University of Victoria (Victoria)*

up island: *any part of Vancouver Island north of Greater Victoria*

Van Isle: *Vancouver Island*

washroom: *bathroom or restroom*

wharfinger: *the person who manages a marine wharf or marina*

wicket: *bank teller's window; upright sticks behind a batter in cricket that the batter has to keep the ball from hitting*

08/18

12:45 p.m. crossing — To CANADA!

cool, overcast morning, but gradually
clearing to a bright silver. NO GLARING
SUN, THANK GOODNESS. Sun did come out
halfway through the crossing and was soft
and diffused. First part of the crossing was
a little rough, and I couldn't walk
around the deck; Inside at the table was
a little too much swaying for my comfort.
It smoothed out after about 45 minutes; When
the sun came out and we neared Vancouver Island
everything was so beautiful, soft queen-blue
hills and blue, blue, water. Arrived Victoria
at 2:30 p.m. - We left Port angeles at 1:15,
They were running late! Coho - Black Ball!
other than that, and the snippy lady at the
ticket window, it was a pleasantly-run operation.

2

Getting Here and Getting Around

It's easy to get to Victoria and Vancouver Island by air or ferry. Lots of airlines fly to Seattle and Vancouver, and then you can fly or take a ferry to Victoria.

GETTING HERE

By Air

You have three choices: fly to Vancouver and transfer to a bus and ferry, fly to Vancouver and transfer to another plane, or fly to Seattle and transfer to another plane or take a ferry. Be sure to compare ticket prices to Seattle and Vancouver, because at certain times of the year airlines' competitive rates may influence your decision.

Fly to Vancouver and take the bus and ferry to Victoria. If the airfares of the moment allow you to do so, we recommend you fly to Vancouver International Airport (YVR) and then connect by Pacific Coast Lines (PCL) bus to B.C. Ferries to Victoria, or simply fly connecting flights all the way to Victoria.

Our favorite airline to Vancouver is Air Canada, which acquired Canadian Airlines. The staff treats passengers gently and with good humor, and they actually still offer snacks, with sandwiches for sale, whereas United Airlines from San Francisco to Vancouver offers absolutely no food whatsoever.

PCL runs several buses daily directly from the Vancouver airport onto the B.C. ferry and into downtown Victoria. Generally they leave the airport at 7:45 A.M. and every two hours after that until 7:45 P.M. Walk outside the luggage and immigration floor to the center island and wait for the PCL bus. Call (604) 662–8074 in Vancouver or (250) 385–4411 in Victoria or visit www.pacificcoach.com for information and en route pickup reservations.

The PCL buses drive right onto the front of the ferry, you get off and go upstairs for a meal if you wish, and then you get back on the same bus and complete the trip into Victoria. You can also get off at Swartz Bay (where the ferries dock on Vancouver Island) and connect to ferries to other islands. All this costs $42.50 one way or $83.00 round-trip from Vancouver Airport. It's $37 each way and $72 round-trip from Vancouver Depot (Pacific Central Station), and prices fluctuate slightly with B.C. Ferries' charges.

If your airport arrival does not coincide with these bus departures, walk outside the terminal and catch the van/bus to the Pan Pacific Hotel ($8). At the hotel, go in the front door and turn immediately left to the PCL ticket desk, where you can leave your baggage until your bus arrives. The Pan Pacific has an espresso cart in the lobby, a lounge and restaurant, a more formal dining room, and the Suehiro Restaurant. Oh yes, and a 200-foot waterslide for the kids.

B.C. Ferries sails its pleasant car ferries hourly both ways between Vancouver (Tsawwassen) and Victoria (Swartz Bay) from 7:00 A.M. to 10:00 P.M. from late June until early September, and on uneven hours in winter. The trip takes one hour and thirty-five minutes, and slightly longer during fuel price crises. You can also board as a walk-on passenger, or with a bike or motorcycle. Fares vary by season, size of vehicle, and number of passengers. Every trip we make we marvel at how those ferries float with loaded lumber trucks, new-car transport trucks, and several tourist buses on board.

We recommend the Pacific Island Buffet, if your ferry has one, as transition sustenance, especially if you are extremely hungry. Buffet staff will answer all questions on food ingredients. Meals range from $14 to $20 (less for children) depending on time of day and day of week and now include salmon, dim sum, yellow squash, chicken tarragon, and Thai specialties. Desserts are to die for.

The large ferries also have snack bars with hot and cold foods, as well as cafeterias catered by White Spot restaurants, Canadian hamburger legends, and healthier Bread Garden sandwiches and decent salads.

B.C. Ferries, 1112 Fort Street, Victoria V8V 4V2; (250) 386–3431 or (888) 223–3779; Fax: (250) 381–5452; www.bcferries.com.

Fly to Vancouver, and then fly to Victoria. You have several options for flying on to Victoria from Vancouver:

Helijet Airways (in Vancouver: 604–273–4688 or 800–665–4354; www.helijet .com) flies Sikorsky S76 or S61 helicopters from the Vancouver International Airport for $114–$199. In Victoria Helijet flights land at and leave from 79 Dallas Road (Ogden Point) near where cruise ships dock. Helijet makes the thirty-five-minute flights more than twenty times daily, with four round-trips on weekends.

Harbour Air Shuttle (in Victoria: 250–384–2215; in Vancouver: 604–688–1277; 800–665–0212; www.harbourair.ca or www.harbour-air.com) flies deHavilland DHC-2 and DHC-3 nine- and sixteen-seat floatplanes between Vancouver and Victoria Harbours (ten round-trips weekdays and four on weekends). The thirty-five-minute flights cost $120 one way plus tax on every flight.

West Coast Air (in Vancouver: 604–606–6888; in Victoria: 250–388–4521 or 800–347–2222; www.westcoastair.com) flies eighteen-seat deHavilland Twin Otter floatplanes and a Vistaliner. You may also charter the Vistaliner for flights around B.C.'s south coast and Gulf Islands. There are fifteen thirty-five-minute flights each way weekdays on the hour and some half hours. In February 2005 West Air opened its terminal in downtown Vancouver at 1075 West Waterfront Road. West Coast lands in the Inner Harbour between Broughton and Courtney Streets, about 2 blocks from the Fairmont Empress Hotel. Fare: $119 each way plus tax.

Air Canada JAZZ (604–273–2464 or 250–360–9074; www.flyjazz.com) is the Air Canada connector for major airlines that fly direct into Vancouver from San Francisco, Los Angeles, Chicago, New York, Ottawa, Toronto, and Montreal. It makes eight flights daily from Vancouver to Victoria on Dash 100 or Dash 300 planes carrying thirty-seven or forty-eight passengers and landing at Victoria International Airport. (See the following section on transportation from the airport.)

Fly to Seattle and fly to Victoria. You have several options for continuing your trip by air if you choose to land at Seattle/Tacoma Airport (SeaTac):

Horizon Air (800–547–9308; www.horizonair.com) flies from Seattle to Victoria International Airport and back six times daily, with direct flights to Victoria taking about thirty-five minutes. From Victoria to Seattle, Horizon stops in Port Angeles or Bellingham, Washington, for U.S. Customs, making these trips about one hour and fifteen minutes. Fare: $113–$216 plus tax.

Kenmore Air (866–435–9524, U.S. and Canada; Seattle: 425–486–1257; www.kenmoreair.com) makes three seaplane flights daily from Seattle to Victoria ($152 each way, $184 round-trip, $190–$231 round-trip on certain flights). In the summer Kenmore provides scheduled shuttle vans from Seattle/Tacoma Airport to its departure point, Seattle's downtown Lake Union (950 Westlake Avenue North). If you plan to take Kenmore from Seattle to Victoria outside of May–Labor Day (early September), you can either call a shuttle (about $20) on arrival at the baggage claim area at SeaTac or take a cab (about $30).

Kenmore's flight from Lake Union to Victoria takes about fifty-five minutes and deposits you in the Inner Harbour at 1234 Wharf Street between Broughton and Courtney Streets, about 1 block from the Fairmont Empress Hotel. The schedule varies wildly by season, but basically there are several flights every day both ways.

Transportation from Victoria International Airport. Once at Victoria airport, excellent airporter service is available to get you downtown and to your hotel. **AKAL Airport Shuttle Bus** provides daily service every half hour from 4:00 A.M. to 7:00 P.M. to and from Victoria International Airport and all hotels, motels, and downtown. The trip from Victoria International Airport takes about one hour.

AKAL Airport Shuttle Bus (250–386–2525 or 877–386–2525; Fax: 250–386–2526; www.victoriaairportshuttle.com). Fares: adults $15–$20 (outside downtown), groups $10–$13 each person, groups of five or more $8 each, children under five free.

If you're part of a group of three or more, you might want to consider a taxi. Taxi fares from the airport, which is near Sidney, to downtown Victoria are about $40. Your options: Victoria Taxi, (250) 383–7111; Empress Taxi (including Yellow Cab, with a large fleet of hybrid vehicles), (250) 381–2222; and Blue Bird Cabs, (250) 384–1155 or (800) 665–7055.

By Water—Ferries from Washington and Vancouver, B.C.

Victoria Clipper's high-speed catamarans are the quickest and most efficient ferries to Victoria, making the trip in about three hours. Now **Victoria Clipper** has outdone itself with a turbojet that skims the water between Seattle and Victoria in one and three-quarters hours. No automobiles on board. Meals may be ordered at your seat. Both catamarans and turbojets leave Seattle's Pier 69 at 7:30 or 8:30 A.M. daily, with additional turbojet sailings in the summertime. Some early sailings follow a scenic route through the San Juan Islands, including a stop in Friday Harbor.

Victoria Clipper (206–448–5000 [U.S.]; 250–382–8100 [Canada]; www.victoriaclipper.com). $65–$140 per person round-trip. Group, senior, and children's discounts are available. The Victoria Clipper's schedule is confusing because at some times of the year it changes every two weeks and varies according to turbo vs. nonturbo hydroplanes. Be sure to call for current departure times and fares.

Black Ball Transport runs the *Coho* ferry between Port Angeles, Washington, and Victoria, B.C., several times daily. Since increased security at the border check at the Peace Arch south of Vancouver, we highly recommend traveling on the *Coho.* Traveling to or from Port Angeles, you wind along the lovely Olympic Peninsula from either near Olympia or Tacoma, hence avoiding the traffic jams possible through Seattle.

Check in at the tiny Port Angeles–Victoria Tourist Bureau (360–452–1223) right beside the ferry dock for loads of excellent advice on where to have lunch, where to stay, and even how to make reservations for accommodations in Victoria. Be sure to browse in the pier shops and galleries, downstairs and on the mezzanine, where there is also an excellent coffee bar.

The number of trips the *Coho* makes practically varies by month, with no service during the first two weeks in February, so be sure to call or to check its Web site for the latest details. Fares are around $44.00 for a car and driver, plus $11.50 for each additional passenger. Motorcycles are $25.00, sidecar $13.50 extra (helmets required in B.C.), and bikes are $5.25 (helmets required also).

Black Ball Transport Inc. Coho ferry: Port Angeles, Washington: 101 East Railroad Avenue, Port Angeles 98362, (360) 457–4491, Fax: (250) 457–4493; Victoria: 430 Belleville Street (near Parliament building), Victoria V8V 1W9, (250) 386–2202, Fax: (250) 386–2207; www.cohoferry.com.

Charcoal-Grilled Seafood Steaks

Hegg & Hegg fish cannery, Port Angeles, Washington. Courtesy of National (U.S.) Federation of Fishermen/Washington Sea Grant

2 lb. fish steaks, fresh or frozen
$1/2$ cup oil
$1/4$ cup lemon juice
2 tsp. salt
$1/4$ tsp. white pepper
dash liquid hot-pepper sauce
paprika
citrus sections or cut fruit pieces

Thaw frozen fish steaks, cut to serving size, and place on greased grill. Combine remaining ingredients, except paprika. Baste fish with sauce and sprinkle with paprika. Cook about 4 inches from moderately hot coals for eight minutes. Baste again and sprinkle with paprika, turn over, and cook for seven to ten minutes longer or until fish flakes easily when tested with a fork.

Serves six.

By Train

Leaving from the United States, **Amtrak,** the national railroad system, runs its Coast Starlight from Los Angeles up the West Coast, the Empire Builder from Chicago across the top of the United States, and Pioneer from Chicago through Utah to Portland, Oregon. They all get you to Seattle, from which a high-speed train whisks you to Vancouver in about four hours. From there you can take a B.C. ferry, or fly, to Victoria.

> *Amtrak (800–USA–RAIL). All Amtrak trains are wheelchair accessible. The train from Seattle to Vancouver leaves at 7:45 A.M. and arrives at 11:40 A.M.*

From train to ferry. Pacific Coach Lines (604–662–8074 in Vancouver; 250–385–4411 in Victoria) will take you from Vancouver's Civic Central Station to B.C. Ferries for $10–$30 each way depending on age and season (round-trip is slightly less than double), right onto the ferry and into Victoria. Coaches leave every two hours from 5:45 A.M. to 7:45 P.M.

If you'd like to depart from Canada, **VIA Rail Canada** comes straight (well, not exactly) across Canada, and at Jasper, Alberta, you can go southwest to Vancouver and make connections to Victoria. The train arrives in Vancouver at 8:30 A.M. Friday, Sunday, and Tuesday. Pacific Coach Lines buses will again transport you from the train station onto the B.C. ferry and into downtown Victoria.

> *VIA Rail Canada (www.viarail.ca) suggests travelers in the United States call a travel agent. In Canada VIA Rail has separate phone numbers for each province and some cities, so look it up or call information for the number. In Canada VIA Rail has a TDD line for the hearing impaired: (800) 268–9503 everywhere except in the Toronto area, where it is (800) 368–6406.*

By Water — Boat

Yacht enthusiasts can dock at many harbors on Vancouver Island. Since Victoria's Inner Harbour has a three-day maximum stay in front of the Fairmont Empress Hotel, many people dock at marinas on the eastern side of the island, such as Oak Bay Marina and Sidney.

Port Sidney Marina offers all services and the proximity of a resort town with fine shops and restaurants as well as a complimentary shuttle bus during the summer to Victoria and the Butchart Gardens. Port Sidney Marina features twenty-four-hour customs check-in, concierge services, transient berths to 140 feet length, dockominium sales, annual moorage, laundry, garbage, pump-out, boat repairs, parking, ice, power, water, cable, washrooms and showers, carts, affordable fishing charters, whale watching, a well-stocked marine supply store, and Sidney Harbour Shuttles for waterfront and pub tours and shopping.

Local bus No. 70 (Pat Bay Highway) goes to downtown Victoria, and bus No. 75 goes to the Butchart Gardens and then on to Victoria. You can catch both at the corner of Beacon Avenue and Fifth Street in Sidney.

Port Sidney Marina, 9835 Seaport Place, Sidney, BC V8L 4X3; (250) 655–3711; Fax: (250) 655–3771; VHF channel 68; www.sidney.ca. Rates vary by season and boat length. Register with dock attendant for day moorage. Monthly rates off-season only.

Oak Bay Marina is an elegant full-service marina barely on the eastern side of Vancouver Island and therefore protected from some weather, with magnificent views of the Haro Strait and Mount Baker. Showers and laundry facilities are available.

Oak Bay Marina also offers boat rentals and sailing charters, nature cruises, and fishing charters. Annual moorage: $8.20 per foot per month; transient moorage: from $1.25 per foot, per night, up to 70 feet. Reservations strongly advised.

Oak Bay Marina, 1327 Beach Drive, Victoria V0S 2N4; (250) 598–3369; Fax: (250) 598–1361; VHF channel 68; www.oakbaymarina .com. Bus 2. Hours: 6:00 A.M.–10:00 P.M. daily in summer.

Victoria Inner Harbour Marina, call Marilyn or Michael at (250) 388–6466 or (250) 208–6466 at 1810B Store Street, Victoria V8T 4R4, or check boating radio at frequency VHF channel 73.

GETTING AROUND ONCE YOU'RE HERE

Once you're here, you have several options for getting around Victoria and the surrounding area. The cheapest and best means of transport are your feet. If you are capable, the city is small enough that all you need are good walking shoes to see the real Victoria.

Buses

Of course, you probably won't want to walk to all the sites all the time. B.C. Transit's **Victoria Regional Transit System** is the best we've ever been on. Buses are clean and graffiti-free. The front seats are reserved for seniors or people with disabilities. Nearly half of Victoria's buses are wheelchair accessible. Nearly all evening and weekend bus service is accessible; at rush hour, about half the buses are accessible.

Bus drivers graciously answer your questions without making you feel like an idiot and help you with the correct change if you get confused. Generally, young people give up their seats for seniors. What's more, the buses are on time and comfortable!

> *Victoria Regional Transit System (250–382–6161, twenty-four-hour information line; www.bctransit.com). Fares for one zone: $2.25; seniors $1.40 and kids under six free. Pick up the bus schedule, known as the Rider's Guide, for a full and easily understandable schedule, including accessibility information. See the list of buses for popular destinations in chapter 9.*

Other buses. Several other companies also provide bus transportation in Victoria and on Vancouver Island. For information on all buses, in Victoria call (250) 385–4411; in Vancouver call (604) 662–8074. Also call these numbers for pickup at certain locations. Here is some information on the specific companies:

Pacific Coach Lines (700 Douglas Street; 250–385–4411; www.pacificcoach .com) is the easiest way to get from Victoria to Vancouver (on the Lower Mainland) by public transportation. Its buses take you from the depot at Douglas and Belleville or pick you up at many other spots. Buses run every two hours in winter and every hour in summer, as do the ferries.

Laidlaw (700 Douglas Street; 250–388–5248; www.greyhound.ca) delivers people and packages all over Vancouver Island. Laidlaw buses are your best bet for getting to the far reaches of the island without a car. They provide carefree passage through some of the most beautiful and dramatic scenery in North America, including examples of ancient forests and blatant clear-cutting.

Bus Tours

Gray Line of Victoria starts tours in front of the Fairmont Empress Hotel and will pick you up at your hotel at no added charge if you call. Grand City and Craigdarroch Castle Tour (adults $22, children $12), one of its most popular tours, takes in the best of Victoria's lovely homes and gardens, points of historic interest, the city center, Chinatown, Antique Row, the exclusive Uplands and Oak Bay residential areas with their luxurious gardens, Victoria Golf Club, Beacon Hill Park, and spectacular views of Washington's Olympic Mountains and the Strait of Juan de Fuca. It also includes a stop at Oak Bay Marina to view wild seals, visit the gift shop, or enjoy a snack or beverage. The Grand City Drive tour is also offered in combination with other destinations.

Other representative Gray Line tours include Butchart Gardens and Butterfly Gardens (adults $59, juniors $48, and children $23). Check the Gray Line Web site for the whole list of tours, including carriages, trolleys, and dinner excursions.

Gray Line of Victoria, 700 Douglas Street, (250) 388–6539 or (800) 667–0882; www.grayline.ca/victoria. Gray Line tours run from April or May 1 through mid-September or November, depending on the tour.

Oak Bay Explorer transports guests from the *Coho* ferry on Belleville Street and many hotels and the Fairmont Empress Hotel to art galleries, historic sites, and Oak Bay. The tour is excellent, only $2, and you can get on and off. Available Monday–Saturday.

Taxis

Taxis in Victoria are all reliable and clean. Most do personalized sightseeing tours, many for a fixed, agreed-in-advance fee. Major companies include the following:

Victoria Taxi: (250) 383–7111 downtown, (250) 383–1515 Oak Bay, (250) 381–2030 Gordon Head.

Empress Taxi or Yellow Cab (hybrid vehicles): (250) 381–2222, (250) 381–2242.

Blue Bird Cabs, Ltd.: (250) 384–1155, (800) 665–7055.

AllStar Taxi: (250) 475–2511.

Empire Taxi: (250) 383–8888 downtown, (250) 384–2511 Gordon Head, (250) 381–1121 Oak Bay.

Automobiles

With Victoria's excellent public transportation system, and if you are able to walk freely, you rarely need a car except to go out of town. Driving a car in Victoria is a refreshing experience since Victorians are polite in everything, including driving.

Lots of locals ride bikes around town and want to share Victoria's narrow streets. Please use extra caution when passing cyclists, turning, opening your car door, or pulling away from the curb.

Whenever a person appears to be approaching a curb to cross the street, *stop* and let him or her cross, whether a crosswalk is there or not.

Watch the one-way street signs—those in Victoria don't make much sense. Several in a row go the same direction down to Wharf Street. It's hard to learn to get around by car—another reason we encourage walking if you are capable.

Oh yes, Victorians will stop dead to let you enter their lane of traffic, on a city street or on a highway. In order to preserve their dignity and sanity, please go when they motion you to.

Car rental agencies. Victoria and Victoria International Airport have the major automobile-rental agencies as well as some minor and innovative ones.

Many used-car companies and automobile dealerships rent the cars on their lots, so inquire at those located on outer Government and Douglas Streets. Reservations are suggested for cars in Victoria.

Avis Rent-A-Car, 2G-1001 Douglas, (250) 386–8468; at the airport, (250) 656–6033.

Budget Rent-A-Car, 727 Courtney (downtown), (250) 953–5300; at the airport, (250) 656–3731.

Enterprise Rent-A-Car, 2507 Government, (250) 475–6900; at the airport, (250) 656–4808 or (800) 325–8007.

Hertz Rent-A-Car, downtown, (250) 360–2822; at the airport, (250) 656–2312.

National, 767 Douglas, (250) 386–1213 or (250) 386–1828; at the airport, (250) 656–2541.

Parking. While some people lament parking difficulties in downtown Victoria, we have never found a problem. Certain shopping times make things more complicated, like Saturday and Sunday, of course. The city of Victoria runs several parking garages (parkades); a few are privately run. Many downtown businesses will provide one-hour, free-parking validation stickers for city-operated parkades. Just ask the staff in any shop you're in.

Downtown Parkades

Broughton Street between Broad and Douglas.

Broughton between Douglas and Blanshard (near the library).

Fort Street, 1 short block off Wharf on Langley.

View Street has three: between Government and Douglas, between Douglas and Blanshard, and between Blanshard and Quadra.

Johnson Street has three: across from Market Square below Government Street, between Douglas and Blanchard, and between Blanshard and Quadra.

Chinatown Parkades

Pandora, between Store Street and just up from Market Square below Government Street and on.

On Fisgard Street at Store Street, up Fisgard toward Government, or on Fisgard behind City Hall near Douglas Street.

Carriages and Pedal Cabs

Picturesque horses and carriages are used for touring rather than for transportation from one place to another. While some people object strongly to the inhumanity of driving the horses to work this hard, others delight in the experience. We have seen only one horse bolt from sudden fear, break free of its harness, and gallop down the street into oncoming traffic. The carriages gather at the horses' feed and watering spot in the street just west of the Parliament buildings and south of the Royal Victoria Wax Museum. The carriages and drivers range from casual and smallish to big and formal—something for everyone.

Kabuki Kabs (250–385–4243; www.kabukikabs.com) are pedicabs that will pick you up anywhere downtown and take you anywhere downtown. Their healthy-looking drivers are always fun to talk or listen to. Pedicabs usually board passengers at the Inner Harbour on the water side of Government Street across from the Fairmont Empress Hotel.

Kabuki Kabs offers a wide range of tours based on $1.00/minute for one to two people and $1.50/minute for three to four people, with tours of the Inner Harbour ranging from fifteen to thirty minutes. Some operators have developed specialized tours such as cyclist Freddie Kruger's (yes!), a $300 tour from the Fairmont Empress Hotel to Butchart Gardens, special architecture or church tours, and heritage home tours.

Heritage Tours and Daimler Limousine Service (713 Bexhill Road, 250–474–4332; www.islandnet.com/~daimler/) takes you on a luxurious tour of the city in a British Daimler limousine. For only $62 per hour per carload, up to six passengers can see Victoria, the Butchart Gardens, and Craigdarroch Castle or just about anything else. What a way to go!

Kabuki Kab

Tallyho Carriage Tours (180 Goward Street, 250–514–9257 or 866–383–5067; www.tallyhotours.com) takes you on horse-drawn carriage tours of the Inner Harbour, Government Street, Beacon Hill Park, James Bay, Dallas Road and the beach, Thunderbird Park, and heritage homes, including Emily Carr's residences. Tallyho operates from March to September and begins its tours from Belleville and Menzies Streets or from the front of the Fairmont Empress Hotel. Traditional Tallyho wagons accommodate up to twenty adults, while private Central Park–style carriages seat up to ten. Informed guides accompany the tours. Fares: Short and Sweet Tour (15 minutes): $40 per carriage; Waterfront Tour (30 minutes): $80 per carriage; Beacon Hill Park Tour (45 minutes): $120; Deluxe Tour (60 minutes): $160 per carriage on up to $240 for 100 minutes.

Sightseeing Ferries

The little green and yellow ferries of **Victoria Harbour Ferries,** which bills itself as "the tour you can get off of," will take you on "hops" between various points in the harbor, full forty-five-minute tours of the Gorge and Inner Harbour, or a romantic thirty-minute moonlight cruise. In summer, a couple can rent the ultimate ferry as a bed-and-breakfast overnight cruise. Wow!

Victoria Harbour Ferries, (250) 708–0201; www.harbourferry.com.
Inner Harbour ferries depart every twelve minutes, and the Gorge tours

Sightseeing ferries

leave every fifteen to twenty minutes from 11:00 A.M. to 4:00 P.M. Fares: $20 adults and $10 children for the Inner Harbour tour, and $20 adults, $18 seniors, and $10 children for the Gorge tour. Harbour ferries sail beginning mid-March, with the full schedule afloat May 1.

Sightseeing by Train

The **E & N** (Esquimalt & Nanaimo) runs its lovingly restored two-car Malahat back and forth between Victoria (east end of the blue bridge at 450 Pandora and Wharf Streets, 250–383–4324; www.tourismvictoria.com/content/En/281.asp) and Nanaimo and Courtenay, with as many stops along the way as passengers call out. The yellow train's red leather seats let you bask and take in the sights with plenty of leg room. No food or beverages are served on the two-and-a-half-hour trip, so bring yours along. Stops include Duncan, Chemainus, Nanaimo, Cassidy, Qualicum Beach, Mount Washington, and Courtenay.

Scooters and Bicycles

Scooters are popular with visitors for venturing to beaches and the outer reaches of town, but operate them cautiously.

Bicycles are an even more popular mode of transportation in Victoria and on Vancouver Island. Island highways often have bike lanes, but the roads to Tofino and Port Renfrew are a little hairy where the edges have fallen down the cliffs into the water. Plan for climbs on many routes. You can easily ride around Victoria with only slight inclines if you plan well. Helmets are required by British Columbia law.

You can **rent scooters or bicycles** at the following spots:

Cycle B.C.–Victoria (747 Douglas Street, 250–380–2453; www.cyclebc.ca) rents bicycles, scooters, and motorcycles.

Harbour Rentals (811 Wharf Street, 250–995–1661; Fax: 250–386–3370; www .cycletreks.com) rents Rocky Mountain bikes, kids' bikes, tandems, trailers, and in-line skates during the summer season only.

Sports Rent (1950 Government Street, 250–385–7368; www.sportsrentbc.com) rents bikes and equipment year-round for roads and trails, including hybrid, moderate terrain, technical, and advanced mountain bikes in a variety of frame sizes. It offers higher-end popular in-line skates with full protection padding, group and private lessons, canoes, kayaks, water skis, surfing gear, mountain climbing and camping equipment, plus winter skis and snowboards. Reservations suggested. Rates differ depending on length of rental, ranging from $20 to $100.

3

Neighborhoods of Greater Victoria

I n a society where community is extremely important, neighborhoods form and are formed by the focus of community identity. Some neighborhoods attract people of like backgrounds or ethnic and national origins. Others attract people of common interests and attitudes, or people who just like the view.

Most visitors see only downtown Victoria, including the Inner Harbour, Old Town, Chinatown, and maybe James Bay. Other neighborhoods well worth seeing are Fairfield, Oak Bay Village, Cook Street Village, Fernwood, Rockland, and Fisherman's Wharf.

Then there are all those other places many tourists never reach but should if there's time: Sidney, twenty minutes northeast of Victoria; Sooke, forty minutes west of Victoria, Port Renfrew, another ninety minutes west; and the up-island communities of Duncan, Chemainus, Nanaimo, Quallicum Beach, Courtenay, Campbell River, Port Hardy, Port Alberni, Ucluelet, and Tofino. These are all small to medium towns with distinct characters, some stemming from the original countries of their founding parents.

Some neighborhoods and settlements are more British than others, some more earthy than others, and some more interesting.

We will now take you on a tour of Victoria and Vancouver Island, neighborhood by neighborhood, so that you can discover it yourself and maximize your enjoyment.

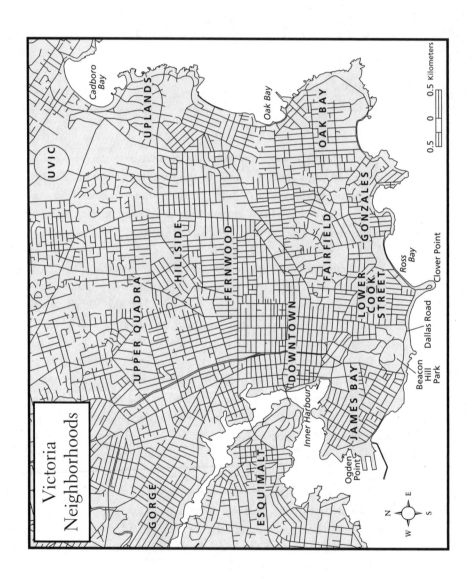

Victoria
Neighborhoods

Cadboro Bay

UPLANDS

UVIC

Oak Bay

OAK BAY

HILLSIDE

FERNWOOD

UPPER QUADRA

GONZALES

FAIRFIELD

Ross
Bay

Clover Point

DOWNTOWN

LOWER
COOK
STREET

Dallas Road

GORGE

ESQUIMALT

Inner Harbour

JAMES BAY

Beacon
Hill
Park

Ogden
Point

N
W   E
S

0.5   0   0.5 Kilometers

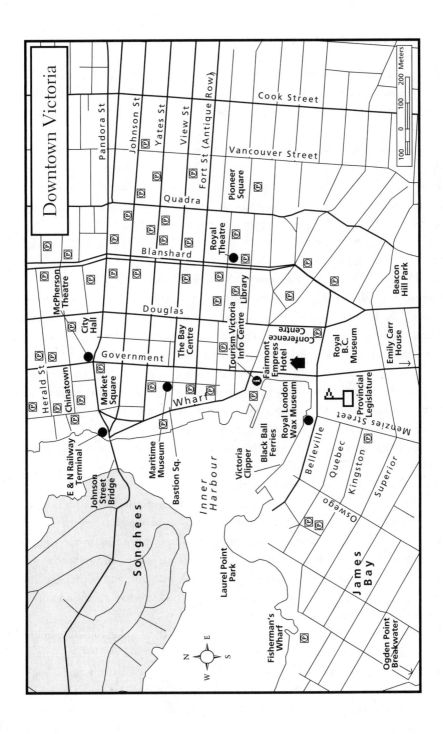

Downtown Victoria

Cook Street

Pandora St

Johnson St

Yates St

View St

Fort St (Antique Row)

Vancouver Street

Quadra

Pioneer Square

Royal Theatre

Blanshard

Douglas

McPherson Theatre

City Hall

Library

Tourism Victoria Info Centre

Conference Centre

Beacon Hill Park

Chinatown

Herald St

Government

The Bay Centre

Fairmont Empress Hotel

Royal B.C. Museum

Emily Carr House

Market Square

Wharf

Royal London Wax Museum

Provincial Legislature

Menzies Street

E & N Railway Terminal

Maritime Museum

Bastion Sq.

Black Ball Ferries

Victoria Clipper

Belleville

Quebec

Oswego

Kingston

Superior

Johnson Street Bridge

Songhees

Inner Harbour

Laurel Point Park

James Bay

Fisherman's Wharf

Ogden Point Breakwater

N
W   E
S

Meters
100   0   100   200

DOWNTOWN VICTORIA

Begin at the Inner Harbour, at or near the Fairmont Empress Hotel or the many nearby hotels and motels. By nature, we would start somewhere else just because *everyone* starts here, but we're going to conform this once just to help you out. (You're welcome.)

Baskets of gorgeous, cheerful, tasteful flowers hang from all the light posts downtown in the spring and summertime. They are everywhere. No one we know has ever seen anyone water them or trim the flowers. If you do, let us know. In the winter, the flowers are replaced with attractive pine arrangements. Every spring the chamber of commerce sponsors a flower count, and each year Victorians try to produce more blossoms than the year before. The count is currently in the billions. All for your pleasure and theirs, of course.

Do go right over to the **Tourism Victoria Centre** (812 Wharf Street at Government, 250–382–2127; www.tourismvictoria.com), a short tower overlooking the Inner Harbour. This art deco tower was built in 1931 for an anticipated seaplane base in the harbor. When the base wasn't developed, the building was used for years as an automobile service station.

Tourism Victoria's staff will answer almost any question you can imagine, make reservations for you, find you a place to stay or dine, sell you tickets for performances or native salmon barbecues, and let you take hundreds of brochures on almost any interest you might want to explore on Vancouver Island.

Before you get distracted by the commanding edifices of the Parliament buildings and the Fairmont Empress Hotel, take a deep breath and look around at what's here: the **Inner Harbour** itself.

This is the *new* Inner Harbour created in 1905. Originally a bridge was built in 1859 to link Parliament to downtown. Then a causeway was constructed to keep the water away so that fill could be dumped to create a site for the Canadian Pacific Railway to build its luxury Empress Hotel, now a Fairmont property. The hotel, built on 2,680 gumwood pilings sunk into goo and bedrock, constantly sinks into the silt ever so slightly, causing the Canadian Pacific and others to shore it up and redecorate.

The cement railing along the sidewalk above the three-sided causeway holds up people as well as plaques memorializing ships' captains and war heroes. At the top of the southern stairway down to the causeway, you will usually find a bagpiper playing for a living next to a totem pole, which recently received a face-lift, fodder for a photo epitomizing two of the tiles in Canada's great cultural mosaic.

The causeway below is not easily wheelchair accessible. At the far northern end, past Milestones restaurant and cafe, is a steep slope driveway from Wharf Street. A wheelchair can be brought down in a car to the causeway level, and there is a slightly steep ramp behind the Royal London Wax Museum on Belleville Street.

There are rewards at the bottom. A young local sells espresso drinks from a cart at the southern end. In the middle of the causeway you can walk right down the gangplank and up to visiting yachts, often having fun conversations with their passengers. Artists and other hopefuls sell their art, while

Two cultures meet at the Inner Harbour

musicians of many proficiencies play guitars, saxophones, and banjos for whatever your generosity will allow you to contribute.

Enjoy a stroll and a beverage, and bask in this rarefied atmosphere reminiscent of the banks of Paris's Seine, but with clean air.

A visit to the causeway at night is a must for cheap fun and entertainment. Mostly talented buskers entertain nightly in the summer, with juggling comedians (or comedic jugglers) stealing most of the attention. These entertainers must obtain approval and licenses from the city of Victoria. Please do make a donation into their passed hats in return for enjoying their talents.

This is where you board **Victoria Harbour Ferries,** "the tour you can get off of." We usually shun touristy experiences and try to live as locals in the places we visit or stay in, but this is terrific, and locals commute on these little boats.

We selected the **Gorge Tour,** which includes Banfield and Gorge Parks and **Point Ellice House,** an Italianate villa featuring an unusually interesting collection of Victoriana, high tea (reservations a must), and light lunches. This is easily the prettiest way to reach the house, the other being from Bay Street and north on Pleasant Street, ½ block through industrial Victoria.

Many locals believe this is the best tea in Victoria, along with that at the James Bay Tea Room, and it's far less expensive than the one at the Fairmont Empress Hotel. There's a little chill in the garden after three, so plan to go for tea earlier. The breeze comes off the water, and large arbutus trees shade the garden, which, of course, is actually an asset on hot days.

Capt. James Cook presides over Victoria's Inner Harbour

Point Ellice House was built in time for the Peter O'Reilly family to buy it and give birth to second daughter, Kathleen, there on New Year's Eve, 1867. The O'Reillys added on to both their seven-room cottage and to their family, resulting in a rambling 4,000-square-foot house and four children. Kathleen lived there all her life and died there in 1945. Many locals believe her ghost is still there and appears frequently.

The O'Reillys did much of the gardening at Point Ellice House themselves, and fortunately they catalogued and wrote about many of the plantings and flowers. But by the early 1900s the gardens had become an overgrown mess. In the mid-1960s, their grandson, John, and his wife, Inez, began the restoration and replanting that is still going on today, and they lived in the house until 1975.

Among the interesting stuff you can see here: "Kings Border" pattern Minton china from England, porcelain place cards, chairs with removable wicker backs to keep the heat off the backs of people seated near the fire, a large Albion Iron Works range dated 1889, a rare 1897 copper water heater, Victorian cooking implements such as jelly bags to strain cows and calves foot jelly, butter molds, and assorted food grinders.

Afternoon tea includes freshly baked scones and Devonshire cream and is served 11:00 A.M.–4:00 P.M.

Point Ellice House, 2616 Pleasant Street, (250) 380–6506; www.point ellicehouse.ca. Admission to house, including the tour: $6; afternoon tea and house tour: $22. Children 5–12 $3 tour, $11 tea and tour. Hours: May 1–mid-September, daily noon–5:00 P.M., last house tour at 4:30 P.M. If you go by car rather than ferry, head north on Government, west on Bay, then right on Pleasant. By bus: Bus 14 Craigflower.

The majestic English lady facing the Inner Harbour looking ever so slightly imposing is the **Fairmont Empress Hotel.** With its hat and veil straightened for the foreseeable future, its sensible shoes and straight legs shored up again, it is now, thank heavens, sinking more slowly toward China. Do not try to enter through the front door; i.e., up the obvious front stairs entrance, which used to serve as just that. Go to the left and enter where you see cars dropping off people and doormen opening the door to the reception lobby. You can also enter from Douglas Street through the Victoria Conference Centre or at the hotel's south end across from the Royal British Columbia Museum.

Owned by the Canadian Pacific, the Empress is currently managed by the Fairmont Hotel group. The original lobby, where tea is served, is up the circular stairway. The Garden Cafe is downstairs, as is Kipling's, which serves an excellent buffet at breakfast, lunch, and dinner, as well as Sunday brunch.

Francis Rattenbury designed the original center block of the Empress, which opened in 1908. More wings were added in 1910, 1913, and 1929 (a good year!), doubling the size of the hotel. When the Canadian Pacific shored up the old lady and put on her face in 1989, a recreation center, swimming pool, and the reception lobby, where you should start, were added.

It is the restored old center of the hotel that you must see to appreciate Victoria's heritage. On your way to the tea lobby, you will see the warmly elegant oak-paneled dining room and the lobby lounge. Once you get to the tea lobby, notice the inlaid hardwood floors, for decades protected by a thick covering of carpet, which muffled sounds as if in a living room. The decor is elegant English staid.

Jeans, shorts, sweats, and T-shirts are not allowed at tea.

Tea, please

Victoria is the ideal place to sample your first English tea or enjoy your customary indulgence, depending upon your background and experience. With few exceptions, tea is not a snooty ritual here. Rather, it is a friendly, celebratory break in your day.

"Afternoon tea" or "light tea" are nearly the same thing, meant to be an interlude between meals. "High tea" or "full tea" might replace your evening meal.

The lighter, less expensive tea often includes small sandwiches, scones, clotted cream, jams, berries, and coffee or tea. The heavier high tea includes more varieties of the above, plus English trifles. A more expensive tea does not necessarily mean a better tea.

For an authentic English experience, try any of the following places. Beginning in the Inner Harbour area, these tearooms then fan outward geographically. Reservations are recommended.

Fairmont Empress Hotel *(721 Government Street, 250–389–2727 or 250–384–8111; www.fairmont.com/empress) offers Victoria's most famous tea experience. In the summer, book reservations three days ahead. If you don't want to indulge here, at least walk through the hotel in the afternoon to catch a glimpse. A strict dress code is enforced in the Tea Lobby: no jeans, sports clothes, or sport shoes. Considering ambience, decorum, and service, this is the ultimate tea in Victoria, for a mere $44–$55 depending on the month.*

Murchie's *(1110 Government Street, 250–383–3112; www.murchies.com) is officially a "cappuccino and dessert bar" but sells most of the components of a good tea at its counter. You can easily have a scone with preserves and clotted cream with coffee or tea for less than $5 and sit indoors or outdoors at green tables along the sidewalk.*

James Bay Tearoom and Restaurant *(332 Menzies Street, 250–382–8282; www.jamesbaytearoomandrestaurant.com) is just a block beyond the southwestern back corner of the Parliament buildings. A favorite of locals and visitors alike for value and friendliness; daily afternoon high tea served for only $12.75, and high tea on Saturday and Sunday afternoons* is $16.00, with "Kid's Tea" available. Also serves kippers or bangers and eggs, steak and kidney pie with ale gravy, Welsh rarebit on toast, full breakfast, and lunch.

Blethering Place Tearoom & Restaurant *(2250 Oak Bay, 250–598–1413; www.thebletheringplace.com) is a cozy, comfortable tearoom in Oak Bay Village frequented by locals. Teas are served from 11:00 A.M. to 7:00 P.M., or any other time if you ask. Light tea, $14.95, full tea, $16.95, or you can assemble your own for less than $6.00. Bus 1 Willow or 2 Oak Bay.*

At **Point Ellice House** *(2616 Pleasant Street, 250–387–4697; www.pointellicehouse.ca), a heritage (historic) home, teas are served outside on the lawn, where you sit in white wicker furniture while overlooking the Gorge. It's one of the best teas in Victoria, with afternoon tea and house tour at $18. Bus 14 Craigflower or Harbour Ferries' Gorge Tour.*

Four Mile Roadhouse *(199 Island Highway, View Royal; 250–479–2514) is a pleasant old home, restaurant, and pub where you can sample teas at $12.95; real Devonshire cream $1.95 extra. Serves 2:00–5:00 P.M. daily.*

Adrienne's Tea Garden *(5325 Cordova Bay Road, Saanich; 250–658–1535; www.adriennesteagarden.com), in the Mattick's Farm complex, offers high tea for $15.95 during the summer.*

Butchart Gardens *(800 Benvenuto Avenue, Central Saanich; 250–652–4422; www.butchartgardens.com) serves extensive afternoon tea for $24.75, or you can assemble parts of tea at its other facilities. Bus 75.*

Point-No-Point Resort *(1808 West Coast Road, River Jordan; 250–646–2020; www.pointnopoint.com) is well worth the beautiful trip by car out to this cozy home-turned-fine-restaurant-and-resort, nestled in tall trees and overlooking the water, for afternoon tea at $13, or for lunch or dinner.*

White Heather Tea Room *(1885 Oak Bay, 250–595–8020) is Agnes Campbell's lovely Scottish tearoom with made-from-scratch soups, tea sandwiches, delicate shortbreads, scones, and miniature tarts. At once elegant, casual, and hilarious. Set teas from the Wee Tea ($8.00–$14.00) to the Big Muckle Giant Tea ($32.95 for two people) are offered, or put together your own combination. Hours: 9:30 A.M.–5:00 P.M. Tuesday–Friday, 8:30 A.M.–5:00 P.M. Saturday.*

The Fairmont Empress Hotel and the active Inner Harbour in summer

The Fairmont Empress serves afternoon tea in the lobby to nearly 80,000 people a year, so reservations are a must. High tea is a meal. Afternoon tea, which is served here, is meant as a snack to tide you over until dinner, although it certainly could serve as a meal. Each offering is served to be tasted and digested, not to be chowed down.

Afternoon tea at the Empress usually includes crumpets with honey; scones with Devonshire cream and strawberry preserves; berries with Chantilly cream; cucumber, watercress, and egg salad sandwiches (our favorite); salmon and cream cheese pinwheels; lemon rolls; black currant tartlets; and the Empress's own tea blend served in a silver teapot.

Be sure to check out the stained-glass dome of the Palm Court, just before the Crystal Ballroom, with its ten huge crystal chandeliers reflecting on the mirrored ceiling.

Beyond and east of the tea lobby and toward Douglas Street, you will find the famous Bengal Lounge, originally the hotel's library, built in 1912. It is worth walking into the Bengal Lounge just to experience the deep warmth of the decor and atmosphere, the Indian-style ceiling fans, the tiger-skin wall hanging, and an exotic or customary beverage. You may also stay for curry or other Indian dishes, fish and chips, or other interesting light fare.

Past the Bengal Lounge toward Douglas Street, you will find the conservatory and its tropical plants (are they producing enough oxygen for the whole building?) and one entrance to the Victoria Conference Centre. You can also exit through the courtyard to the south and walk to the bus station and to the Royal British Columbia Museum.

Fairmont Empress Hotel, 721 Government Street, (250) 389–2727; www.fairmont.com/empress. Reservations for afternoon tea should be made three or four days in advance.

The **Old Spaghetti Factory,** at 703 Douglas Street, is a great casual restaurant for lunch or dinner for the whole family. Lunch and children's menu items are all less than $9, and you can also enjoy a wide range of pastas and steaks. All entrees include soup or salad, garlic bread, coffee or tea, and spumoni ice cream and range from spaghetti and tomato sauce ($9.25) to baby back ribs ($16.75) at dinner, with luncheon specials all under $10.00. The first Old Spaghetti Factory in Canada opened in March 1970 in Vancouver's Gastown.

Old Spaghetti Factory, 703 Douglas Street, (250) 381–8444; www.old spaghettifactory.ca. Hours: 11:30 A.M.–10:00 P.M. Monday–Thursday, 11:30 A.M.–11:00 P.M. Friday–Saturday, 11:30 A.M.–9:00 P.M. Sunday. Fully licensed. Mostly wheelchair accessible. Credit cards: Visa, Master-Card, American Express.

Across the intersection of Douglas and Belleville Streets, you will see a huge native carving facing northeast on the **Mungo Martin House** (Wawadit'la), a tribute to the internationally renowned aboriginal artist (1881–1962). Mungo Martin House serves as a training center for young aboriginal artists, who learn their traditional craft with mentors such as Martin's grandson, famed artist Tony Hunt. The house was entrusted to the Royal British Columbia Museum by Kwakwaka'wakw chief Mungo Martin, who also oversaw the house's construction beginning in 1952–53.

Helmcken House, at Douglas and Belleville Streets, is Victoria's oldest home, built in 1852. Dr. John Sebastian Helmcken had it built for his bride, Cecilia, daughter of governor James Douglas, on an acre given to the newlyweds by Douglas.

Mungo Martin House

The stereo-taped tour (included in admission price) allows you to hear "the good doctor" describe what Victoria was like in the good old days, Cecilia recount her life as a pioneer mother, and Aunt Dolly reveal why she left her father's room untouched as a shrine to his memory after he died in 1920. Upstairs you can see Dr. Helmcken's famous medical collection.

In December, Helmcken House puts on its Christmas programs, first for schoolchildren, and then from December 21–31 for the rest of the world. Experience the spirit of giving by walking into a play of characters dressed and acting the parts of an 1899 family Christmas. Helmcken House is part of the Royal British Columbia Museum Corporation.

> ***Helmcken House,*** *Douglas and Belleville Streets, (250) 361–0021 or (250) 387–4697; www.heritage.gov.bc.ca/helmcken.htm. Admission is included in the Royal British Columbia Museum ticket price. Wheelchair accessible first floor only. Ramp is at the east end of Royal British Columbia Museum.*

While in this neighborhood, you must visit the **Royal British Columbia Museum,** without a doubt the most people-friendly state or provincial museum we have seen. Before you even get inside the museum's doors you can buy great coffee and snacks from outdoor vendors to sustain you inside. Or you can visit the Museum Cafe, which, lucky us, is run by Willie's Bakery. At the cafeteria-style cafe you can select hot lunches or sandwiches and famous pastries, as well as excellent teas and coffees and sit inside or out. If you can, avoid normal noonish lunchtime, because it gets very crowded. The cafe is 100 percent nonsmoking.

In the main floor lobby, you buy your tickets, check your coat and/or umbrella, get information, and find washrooms, including a special accessible washroom. The other great temptation is the Royal Museum Shop, which is loaded with books on every British Columbia subject imaginable, from cookbooks and history to First Peoples studies and fish, as well as fabulous native jewelry and other artifacts.

Elevators and escalators are toward the rear of the building.

On the second floor you find a variety of permanent exhibits—*Open Ocean, Living Land, Living Sea, Mammoths,* and *Coastal Forest* among them—as well as temporary galleries of special exhibits. Wheelchair-accessible washrooms are also on this floor.

The third floor has must-sees for all ages. There are galleries on recent histories, and an Old Town with so much atmosphere and societal relics that you might want to live in those "good old days," whenever they were. You can sit down and watch old Charlie Chaplin movies and wait in an old train station replica for the train to come by. The Chinatown exhibit is hauntingly accurate with little peekaboo alleys. The galleries devoted to the First Peoples are an enlightening experience, and the Totem Gallery is breathtaking. The third-floor mezzanine (which is not wheelchair accessible) has more recent history and First Peoples galleries, as well as special exhibits.

Each year the Royal British Columbia Museum also hosts special landmark exhibits, which often go on to major cities throughout the world. One such recent exhibit was the fabulous *Titanic* Artifact Exhibition, which ran through October 2007. National Geographic's IMAX Theater is an absolute must-see for families.

As you leave the museum, check out the replica of a ceremonial longhouse in Thunderbird Park next to the museum entrance—a great learning and sensitivity experience. Take a walk around this forest of totem poles.

Thunderbird Park, downtown Victoria

Royal British Columbia Museum, *675 Belleville Street, (250) 356–RBCM (7226) or (888) 447–7977; Fax: (250) 387–5674; www.royal bcmuseum.bc.ca. Hours: 9:00 A.M.–5:00 P.M. daily except Christmas and New Year's Day. Admission: adults $14.00, IMAX film $10.50, combo $22.50; seniors or youth $9.50, IMAX $8.25, combo $17.75; children 3 to 5 free to museum, IMAX $5.00; family $33.70, IMAX $32.50, combo $70.00. Public and accessible restrooms on the first three floors.*

One of the most stately of Canada's edifices, the **Parliament** building, at 501 Belleville Street, has become a world-famous symbol of Victoria, the capital of British Columbia. How many provinces or states can you think of that have their capitals offshore? Perhaps this is just symbolic of British Columbia's and Victoria's different-from-the-rest-of-Canada nature.

Parliament is the building with 3,330 light bulbs burning around its exterior to create one of the most beautiful nighttime sights anywhere.

The provincial legislature actually meets here in the second-floor chamber designed by Francis Rattenbury to resemble the British Parliament; it was completed in 1897 to commemorate Queen Victoria's diamond jubilee. The legislative chamber aisle is just wide enough to make it impossible for two swords to reach across from opposing sides. Handy! Notice the throne slightly above the other leaders' seats, kept properly just in case the queen shows up. This is an important place because the legislature makes decisions that guide the provincial government, which is the largest employer in Victoria.

For the easiest entry go to the east end of the main building, where there are just three or four stairs, compared to the imposing staircase at the front. The hallways are lined with fascinating historic photos and Rattenbury's architectural drawings. Attentive guards and other staff are extremely helpful in answering questions and directing you to the next free tour. You are also encouraged to join tours already in progress.

On the second floor you can see the legislative chamber, worth the trip even if parliament is not in session. You will see photos of all B.C. premiers and notable Canadian women, the famous stained-glass window ("The Jubilee Window") depicting the original B.C. coat of arms (before Queen Victoria's foreign office insisted it be changed so it wouldn't look as if the sun were setting on the British Empire), and photos and memorabilia of British royal visits.

British Columbia's Parliament building during the Symphony Splash

The Jubilee Window in the British Columbia Parliament Building

You can watch the seventy-five members in action from public galleries when they are in session, but that is somewhat hard to predict. Normally they meet from sometime in early spring to sometime in early summer, and sometimes they don't. If they are meeting, catch the action between 2:00 and 2:30 P.M. when they indulge in the British traditional question period during which members can ask the premier or cabinet members questions directly. Americans might find this a refreshing approach.

> *Parliament, 501 Belleville Street, (250) 387–3046 for private or group tour arrangements. Hours: 8:30 A.M.–5:00 P.M. daily except statutory holidays. Admission: free. Restrooms, which are a half floor above and below the first floor, are not wheelchair accessible, though the building is. The wheelchair entrance is from Government Street; take ramp to basement and follow signs to elevator.*

Across Belleville Street is the **Royal London Wax Museum.** Originally the Canadian Pacific Railway's marine terminal building, it was Vancouver Island's equivalent of Ellis Island and most visitors' entrance to Victoria until 1965. One of the last of Francis Rattenbury's and P. L. James's collaborations, this 1924 neo-classic structure with Ionic columns was the first Victoria building to employ precast concrete.

The museum houses 250 wax figures depicting the famous and infamous from history and show business (some looking like death not yet warmed over). The royal family forms an interesting group, while Princess Diana has been moved around to the royals' back side so that you see her at the end of your main-floor tour. Try the Chamber of Horrors downstairs, which you "enter at your own risk!" Young children and the fainthearted may pass right by to Storybook Land, the Garden of Literature featuring Charles Dickens, Rudyard Kipling, Mark Twain, and many other literary guests, before they move on to Frozen in Time, in which the challenge of finding the Northwest Passage is told in a multimedia theater format. In the Galaxy of Stars, you will meet Charlie Chaplin, John Wayne, Marilyn Monroe (with that famous white dress blowing up), Clint Eastwood, Goldie Hawn, Christopher Reeve, and many others. Don't miss the Crown Jewels' Treasury.

Royal London Wax Museum, 470 Belleville Street, (250) 388–4461; www.waxmuseum.bc.ca. Hours: 9:00 A.M.–5:00 P.M. October 1–mid-May; 9:00 A.M.–9:00 P.M. mid-May–August 31; 9:00 A.M.–7:00 P.M. September. Admission: adults $10, seniors $9, military $8, students ages thirteen to nineteen or with university ID $7, children $5, disabled $3 with no charge for attendant, family package $27, special group rates. Museum and restrooms wheelchair accessible.

The **Undersea Gardens,** at 490 Belleville, offers a wonderfully real and fantasy experience for all ages, featuring at least 5,000 kinds of marine life from salmon to ferocious-looking wolf-eels, prehistoric sturgeon, brilliant red snapper, white and crimson anemones, and the world's largest octopus. There are continuous shows with scuba divers feeding fish and entertaining people. Part of the Oak Bay Marine Group, this exhibit actually floats, and you can't miss it in the water opposite the Parliament buildings, or from anywhere in the Inner Harbour for that matter.

Undersea Gardens, 490 Belleville Street, (250) 382–5717; www.pacific underseagardens.com. Hours: winter 10:00 A.M.–5:00 P.M.; summer 9:00 A.M.–8:00 P.M. Admission: adults $9.50, seniors $8.50, children ages five to eleven $5.50, children under five free. Not wheelchair accessible.

No restrooms, but we suggest public washrooms in Coho Ferry Terminal west of the Royal London Wax Museum.

Miniature World (649 Humboldt) is located at the north end of the Fairmont Empress Hotel. Billed as "the Greatest Little Show on Earth" and "Little People's Wonderful World of Smallness," this is a terrific show for collectors and children of all ages. While the exhibit emphasizes historic war scenes, there is lots more to see.

Inside you can see "the world's smallest operational sawmill," which took eleven years to build; the "world's largest dollhouse," circa 1880, with fifty rooms furnished in unusually exquisite detail; and the great Canadian railway model as part of one of the world's largest model railways, which winds its way through replicas of Canada's ten provinces. Take in the Wonderful World of the Circus, including the Grand City Parade, Big Top, Wild Beasts, and "death-defying high wire acts." Guaranteed educational and fun entertainment.

Miniature World, 649 Humboldt Street, (250) 385–9731; Fax: (250) 385–2835; www.miniatureworld.com. Hours: summer daily 8:30 A.M.– 9:00 P.M., winter 10:00 A.M.–5:00 P.M. Admission: adults $9, youths $8, children $7, families with three or more and seniors get 10 percent discount. Building, but not restrooms, wheelchair accessible. Credit cards: Visa, MasterCard, American Express.

At 633 Humboldt you'll find the classic **Charles Dickens Pub.** This elegant English-style pub with cheerful dark decor features Canadian and British beers, whiskies, and prices lower than those in the Fairmont Empress Hotel. Some locals hang out here. Live entertainment on weekends.

Charles Dickens Pub, 633 Humboldt Street, (250) 361–2600. Hours: 11:00 A.M.–midnight daily. Wheelchair accessible. Credit cards: Visa, MasterCard, American Express, enRoute, Diners.

The nearby **Pescatore's Fish House & Grill** is believed by some to be the finest fish restaurant in Victoria. It certainly is the most lively and hip in decor, ambience, staff, and creative cuisine. Diego Rivera/Frida Kahlo–style murals and paintings decorate the walls, huge fans hang from the ceiling and turn romantically slowly, and menus are available in Japanese, German, French, and English.

Pescatore's offers a set menu as well as ultrafresh shellfish and other specials written on a blackboard over the bar. Those might include Prince Edward Island mussels, Queen Charlotte Island manilla clams, Nova Scotia deep-sea lobster, and Vancouver Island Dungeness crab—possibly the best in the world.

Lunch may include a Caesar salad with blackened salmon ($15.00); seafood salad with scallops, tiger prawns, crab, calamari, and shrimp ($16.00); crab and lobster canneloni ($14.95); halibut burgers ($10.95); a beef burger with crab and béarnaise sauce ($10.95); and a New York steak sandwich with sautéed mushrooms ($13.95). Dinner adds a few entrees and about $5 to the lunch selections.

> *Pescatore's Fish House & Grill, 614 Humboldt Street, (250) 385–4512; Fax: (250) 385–5562; www.pescatores.com. Hours: summer 11:30 A.M.–11:00 P.M. Monday–Saturday, 5:00–11:00 P.M. Sunday. Winter earlier closing. Wheelchair accessible. Credit cards: Visa, MasterCard, American Express, Diners.*

Sydney Reynolds, on the corner, is one of Victoria's best chinaware shops. Located ideally for tourists, it was originally a saloon in 1908, a bank in 1909, and it became a shop in 1929. You can easily find several selections of teacups and saucers from $14.95, mint trays from $14.95, and Woodburns chocolates for only $1.25, as well as more expensive collectors' china, including Lladro and Lomonosov porcelain dolls, St. Petersburg and Ukrainian dolls, Spode, Waterford, Belleek, flower faeries, and pewterware.

> *Sydney Reynolds, 801 Government Street, (250) 383–2081; www .sydneyreynolds.com. Hours: 9:00 A.M.–9:00 P.M. Monday–Saturday, 10:00 A.M.–7:00 P.M. Sunday. Wheelchair accessible. Credit cards: Visa, MasterCard, American Express. Japanese spoken.*

The sidewalk tables at **Sam's Deli** have the best view of the Inner Harbour at the lowest price in town, even though we hate to tell too many people this. Sam's friendly and gracious young staff begs you not to feed the birds that flitter in for your yummy crumbs.

Local businesspeople and government workers come here for daily lunch specials, chicken potpie, spinach lasagne with salad, or a half tuna sandwich with thick, chunky clam chowder, particularly in the winter when fewer visitors are around. We find the shrimp sandwich irresistible and unequaled anywhere. It's so big we share it, sometimes accompanied by a Caesar salad. It's a good 1½ inches thick with shrimp, lettuce, alfalfa sprouts, avocado, tomato, and lettuce on brown, white, or rye, all for $8.25. Other usual deli meats are available, plus bagels with lox. Try the asparagus sandwich, too.

Each sandwich is made as you order it at the counter, and the maker asks you ingredient by ingredient if you want that, a little more, teensy bit less, Dijon or regular mustard, on and on. The line might go all the way out into the street, but you and your sandwich are still special and the most important for now. How these servers retain their cool is beyond us. But then, they're Canadian.

Vancouver natives Bruce and Barbara Housser opened Sam's in 1976 and have been running it ever since, even though the fabulous Rogers' Chocolates up the street bought Sam's in November 2004. They find and employ the best of university students year-round, whether business warrants it or not, and we should support them for this sensitivity. One of our favorite spots.

Sam's Deli, 805 Government Street, (250) 382–8424; www.sams deli.com. Hours: Monday–Saturday 7:30 A.M. on, Sunday from 9:00 A.M. Wheelchair accessible. Restrooms at back left, not the cleanest, but handy. Credit cards: Visa, MasterCard.

Spirit of Victoria is the most elegant souvenir shop on Government Street, featuring special Roots/Victoria shirts and hats including a combo pack for $19.99, food samples, island chutney, nautical ship models, bedding, and film.

Spirit of Victoria, 811 Government Street, (250) 383–7233. Hours: 10:00 A.M.–10:00 P.M. daily. Downstairs wheelchair accessible. Will accept foreign currencies and give U.S. change for U.S. dollars. Credit cards: Visa, MasterCard, American Express, JCB.

As of press time, **Oh Gelato!** was working to open a new imported and Canadian chocolate and other candy store at 905 Government Street. Oh Gelato!'s original store is up the street at 1013 Government (see later write-up).

While somewhat visitor-oriented, **Stone's Fine Jewellery** does lots of business with locals also. Their presentation and display of jewelry is most peaceful, elegant, and unpretentious, with something for everyone. Stone's features B.C. and Chinese jade, pink and gray stones, and fine fiery opals, as well as more expensive, quality jewels. Prices range from $29 to $18,000.

Stone's Fine Jewellery, 911 Government Street, (250) 383–0062. Hours: summer 8:00 A.M.–9:00 P.M., winter 9:00 A.M.–6:00 P.M. Wheelchair accessible. Credit cards: Visa, MasterCard, American Express, Diners, JCB. Japanese, French, and German spoken.

If you are a chocolate fan, lover, junkie, or aholic, an absolute must-visit is **Rogers' Chocolates.** No question. Period. Particularly for the chocolate creams.

In business in Victoria for more than one hundred years, Rogers' chocolates have been enjoyed by various residents of both the White House and Buckingham Palace. Savor one of their fabulous chocolate creams, filled with a multitude of flavors from mandarin orange to peppermint, raspberry, coffee, or more chocolate, for just $2.50, tax included. They're big enough to share.

Rogers' products range from the creams and chocolate-coated ginger to Victoria truffles, creams miniatures, milk chocolate almond brittle, thin mints, candied nutcorns, and even dark and light (not meant as low-fat) fruitcakes. Available in combo packs, some with Murchie's teas and coffees, all can be ordered by mail.

Fine points: The Queen Ann Revival–style Rogers Building is a heritage building designed in 1903 by architects Thomas Hooper and Edward Watkins under direction of Charles Rogers, the store's eccentric founder. Keep your eyes open for the resident ghost.

Rogers' Chocolates, 913 Government Street, (250) 384–7021 or (800) 663–2220; Fax: (250) 384–5750; www.rogerschocolates.com. Hours: Sunday–Wednesday 9:00 A.M.–7:00 P.M., Thursday–Saturday 9:00 A.M.–9:00 P.M. Wheelchair accessible. Credit cards: Visa, MasterCard, American Express.

Stormtech & Edinburgh Tartan Shop, 921 Government Street, offers a large range of Canadian products, including B.C. jade animals, weatherproof jackets and hats, performance apparel, umbrellas (great in an emergency), Canadian sweaters (we have bought several here over the years), gifts, and an interesting native art gallery upstairs on the balcony that wraps around the walls of the store. You can also buy English toffees, Scottish shortbread, maple syrup, smoked Pacific salmon, and even moccasins.

Stormtech & Edinburgh Tartan Shop, 921 Government Street, (250) 953–7790. Hours: 8:00 A.M.–11:00 P.M. daily. Wheelchair accessible. Credit cards: Visa, MasterCard, American Express, Diners, JCB. Japanese spoken.

Lush, a branch of a successful English fresh, handmade cosmetics company, has turned this corner into a downtown hot spot. *Time Out* says "entering Lush is like

Victoria's oldest brick building, 1001 Government Street

having sex." Not so sure that's true, but the soothing aromas and spoons to scoop all-natural cosmetics into your own container or cutting off your own chunk of herbal soap do lead to romantic and self-indulgent fantasies. Many of the products look, feel, and smell good enough to eat, or at least salivate over.

> **Lush,** *1001 Government Street, (250) 384–LUSH; www.lush.com. Hours: 9:30 A.M.–6:00 P.M., Friday and Saturday until 7:00 P.M., Sunday 11:00 A.M.–6:00 P.M., open later in summer. Wheelchair accessible. Credit cards: Visa, MasterCard, American Express.*

Artisan Wine Shop offers tastes of and sells wine of the Mark Anthony Wine Group, which means all the wines displayed are from the same company under different labels. These include Mission Hill, Wild Horse Canyon, Rigamarole, Fork in the Road, Sonora Ranch, and many others.

Nibbles available include Monet crackers and dips and sauces, with some wine books and a Mission Hills video playing in the back mini-theater.

Artisan Wine Shop, 1007 Government Street, (250) 384–9995; www .artisanwineshop.ca. Hours: 10:00 A.M.–7:00 P.M., later Thursday and Friday and in summer. Wheelchair accessible. Credit cards: Visa, Master-Card, American Express.

Old Time Deli is a handy inexpensive deli with wireless and computer rentals and a slightly funky ambience. Lots of lox and bagels, wraps, pannini, Montreal smoked brisket, pastas, breakfast sandwiches until 11:00 A.M., and pizzas. Old Time's specialty is Callebaut Chocolate Fondue for two or more with fresh fruit and lady fingers ($7.95 per person) or cheese fondu with eight European cheeses, white wine, and kirsch.

Old Time Deli, 1009 Government Street, (250) 483–5483. Hours: 8:30 A.M.–8:00 P.M. Wheelchair accessible. No credit cards.

In this block former mega-landlords John and Bill Gidden have the slick and slightly plastic **Oh Gelato!,** at which a hilarious clownlike mannequin named "Jennie Gelato" greets you. Enjoy sixty-six terrific gelato flavors and Italian sodas.

Oh Gelato!, 1013 Government Street, (250) 381–1448. Hours: 9:00 A.M.– 11:00 P.M. Sunday–Thursday, 9:00 A.M.–11:30 P.M. Friday–Saturday; shorter hours in winter. Wheelchair accessible. No credit cards.

Irish Linen Stores, a traditional Irish linen store here since 1910, has almost too-Irish shamrock bow ties, linen pincushions, hankies, crocheted doilies and place mats, dainty white aprons, printed tea towels, and handwoven scarves.

Fine points: 1017 and 1019 Government Street are part of the Galpin Block, constructed in 1884.

Irish Linen Stores, 1019 Government Street, (250) 383–6812. Hours: summer 9:00 A.M.–7:00 P.M., winter 9:00 A.M.–5:30 P.M. Wheelchair accessible. Credit cards: Visa, MasterCard, American Express, JCB.

Birks Jewellers offers the most elegant of jewelry, along with engraving, appraisals, replating, and restyling at several locations.

Birks Jewellers, 1023 Government Street, (800) 682–2622; www .birks.com. Hours: 9:00 A.M.–9:00 P.M., winter 9:00 A.M.–6:00 P.M.

Wheelchair accessible from Government Street. Credit cards: Visa, MasterCard, American Express, Diners, Discover, JCB.

What is now the the **Bay Centre** started life as Eaton Centre, which ran into the ground via fourth-generation Eatons. Sears bought it and failed, and the renowned Bay (Hudson's Bay Corporation) stepped in and saved the entire mall. This is a multilevel mall covering the entire block between Government, Fort, Douglas, and View Streets. This redevelopment project, completed in 1990, keeps the mall downtown. The Bay houses more than one hundred stores, some excellent and some predictable. On extremely rainy days it seems as if half of Victoria hangs out here.

Clean public restrooms, elevators, and telephones are located on the ground floor, halfway between the Government and Douglas Street sides. If you enter from Fort Street, they are almost straight ahead.

The Bay Centre also has a Smithsbooks bookstore and a food court that offers the usual sandwiches and hamburgers, plus Greek, Japanese, and Korean foods.

Bay Centre, Fort, Douglas, and View Streets. Hours: 9:00 A.M.–9:00 P.M. Wheelchair accessible. Credit cards: acceptance varies by store.

Earl's, a Canadian umbrella drink and casual dining chain, took over the prime real estate formerly occupied by Elephant & Castle and closed its restaurant near the new Save-On arena.

Earl's is not inexpensive, but it is usually lots of fun. Specialties include a warm turkey and Gouda sandwich ($11.00), spicy Thai green curry ($15.00), Santa Fe chicken sandwich ($14.00), jerk chicken with tropical fruit salsa ($17.00), cedar-planked salmon ($19.00), braised Australian lamb shank ($22.00), and espresso flake gelato cake ($6.50). Also expect burgers and sandwiches, ribs, chicken, and steaks, with dinner entrees under $30.

Earl's, 1199 Government Street, (250) 381–1866; www.earls.ca. Hours: 11:30 A.M.–midnight daily. Fully licensed. Wheelchair accessible. Credit cards: Visa, MasterCard, American Express.

New Balance Shoes, a spin-off of Victoria's Frontrunners community-minded running and walking shoe store, and an expensive locally owned Levi's store are housed in the marvelously cavernous Royal Bank building on Government between View Street and Trounce Alley. W. & J. Wilson, Polo Ralph Lauren, and Eddie Bauer are all in the same block.

Cross View Street and continue on Government to **W. & J. Wilson Clothiers Since 1862.** This wonderful and warm store, in an 1870s building that was renovated in 1912 as an example of Edwardian simplicity, has wood paneling and thick carpets and is the oldest family-owned clothing store in Canada. Tom and Kathy Thompson and Lisa and Scott are the current generations managing Wilson's, with the charm and delight that only proud family members can muster.

Mum goes to Europe and imports the clothes herself. Her taste is classic exquisite, and ranges from Geiger and Bianca from Germany to Castleberry and Rodier, Burberry and Mansfield coats, Tilley hats, and Cambridge and Austin Reed clothes.

Be sure to visit their Adventure Clothing shop, featuring Liberty of London and Tilley Endurables, at Fort and Broad Streets, opposite the south side entrance to the Bay Centre.

W. & J. Wilson Clothiers, 1221 Government Street, (250) 383–7177. Hours: 9:30 A.M.–5:30 P.M. Monday–Saturday, 11:00 A.M.–4:00 P.M. Sunday. Wheelchair accessible. Credit cards: Visa, MasterCard, American Express, JCB.

Roots, at 1227 Government Street, provided all those sleek-looking sports clothes for Canada's 1998 Winter Olympics athletes as well as 2002 Winter Olympic clothes for Canadian, British, and U.S. teams. It specializes in made-in-Canada sweat suits and other athletic clothing, denim, soft leather shoes and boots for adults and kids, and leather bags and jackets. In 1973 owners Don Green and Michael Budman designed a shoe called the "Negative Heel," like a 1960s earth shoe, for ultimate walking comfort. We have bought boots, sandals, and loafers here and find them, along with our Hush Puppies and Doc Martens, to be the most comfortable shoes we've ever worn. Lots of Olympic and post-Olympic gear here. One of our favorites.

Roots, 1227 Government Street, (250) 383–4811; www.roots.ca. Hours: 9:30 A.M.–6:00 P.M. Monday–Saturday, noon–5:00 P.M. Sunday. Wheelchair accessible. Credit cards: Visa, MasterCard, American Express.

Sasquatch Trading Company Ltd. offers an unusually good collection of Cowichan art crafts, including masks, and 1,500 genuine Cowichan sweaters bought directly from the reserve. You'll also find smoked salmon, leather gloves, suede vests, slippers and moccasins, drums, carvings, and cowhide rugs.

Sasquatch Trading Company Ltd., 1233 Government Street, (250) 386–9033; www.cowichantrading.com. Hours: summer 8:30 A.M.–9:00 P.M. daily, winter 8:30 A.M.–5:30 or 6:00 P.M. Wheelchair accessible. Credit cards: Visa, MasterCard, American Express, Diners, Carte Blanche, JCB.

Street fills the need for a hot teenagers' and early twenties' boutique with great back-to-school sales if you time it right. Fashion labels include Levi's, Ikeda, Guess, Big Star, Esprit, Razzy, Diesel, London's Pepe Jeans, and Joe Boxer.

Street, 1241 Government Street, (250) 383–0424. Hours: summer 9:30 A.M.–9:00 P.M., winter 9:30 A.M.–6:00 P.M. Wheelchair accessible. Credit cards: Visa, MasterCard, American Express.

Pacific Trekking, 1305 Government Street, is one of the best places for people who walk, hike, and travel to find quality outdoor travel gear. This is an unusually welcoming and friendly store where you are greeted at the door, and there is an information counter to the right of the door where you can ask questions ranging from hiking trails and climate to the location of the nearest restroom.

Pacific Trekking's clothes are suited to serious outdoors activities or everyday wear. You will find a huge supply of Gore-tex products (both sold and repaired here), tents, boots, a kids' room, an upstairs trail center, a great travel book selection, and entire rooms devoted to boat and rain gear. Assistance is available in every room.

Pacific Trekking, 1305 Government Street, (250) 388–3976; www .trailspace.com. Hours: 10:00 A.M.–6:00 P.M. Monday–Saturday, noon– 5:00 P.M. Sunday. First floor is wheelchair accessible. Credit cards: Visa, MasterCard, American Express, JCB.

Christmas runs year-round at the **Original Christmas Village,** where there is an emphasis on German and former Soviet Union national decorations like Ukrainian dolls and ornaments.

Owner Falk Reinhold, who imports directly and tries to keep prices low, seeks to blend the feel of Germany's Christkindl market with the charm of Victoria. While inside, you may feel as if you've taken a quick trip to Bavaria.

Fine points: This store has an extremely strict policy with children, so read the many signs carefully to find out your responsibilities.

Original Christmas Village, 1323 Government Street, (250) 380–7522. Hours: 9:00 A.M.–5:30 P.M. daily. Street floor is wheelchair accessible but crowded. Credit cards: Visa, MasterCard, American Express.

Cross Government Street toward the west and walk down the other side, and you'll come to **Cowichan Trading Company,** one of a group of privately owned stores that sells authentic Cowichan products. This one has the usual tourist souvenirs and some interesting additions, such as soapstone and an extensive choice of Cowichan sweaters, hats, masks, aprons, and pot holders, as well as Canadian windsocks and native handcarvings. You can get Cowichan knitting wool for $7.50 (eight ounces) and rabbit pelts for less than $6.00.

Fine points: The building numbered 1316–1328 on Government Street was built between 1879 and 1888, originally in Victorian style, but later "modernized" with stucco.

Cowichan Trading Company, 1328 Government Street, (250) 383–0321; www.cowichantrading.com. Hours: summer 9:00 A.M.–9:00 P.M. daily, winter 9:30 A.M.–5:30 P.M. daily. Wheelchair accessible from two doorways. Credit cards: Visa, MasterCard, American Express, enRoute, JCB.

We think **Kaboodles** is one of the most fun shops in Victoria. It's primarily a kids' toy store that appeals to grown-ups, and the skillful and artful displays tempt any age. Kites, windsocks, Legos, Gund bears, Thomas the Tank, games, bubbles, stickers, Mr. Bean, and Brio goodies will lure you right in. We all need bubbles in our lives. Voted Best Independent Toy Store three consecutive years.

Kaboodles, 1320 Government Street, (250) 383–0931. Hours: 9:30 A.M.–6:00 P.M. Monday–Saturday, noon–5:00 P.M. Sunday, later in summer. Wheelchair accessible. Credit cards: Visa, MasterCard, American Express.

Roberta's Hats may be our favorite fun hat store anywhere. Young saleswomen wearing hats, natch, make you feel special and can always find a hat that's you. This is one hat store where you won't feel self-conscious.

Roberta's has everything from Australian Outback hats to berets and fake leopard skin, plus kids' hats. Don't let the men stand outside—they'll like this one 'cause there's something for them, too. The ladies at Roberta's take hats seriously and do hat reblocking and cleaning, a rarity these days.

Roberta's Hats, 1318 Government Street, (250) 384–2788. Hours: 10:00 A.M.–5:30 P.M. Monday–Saturday, noon–5:00 P.M. Sunday. Wheelchair accessible. Credit cards: Visa, MasterCard, American Express.

Seed of Life Natural Foods is a small, good, solid natural foods store with a whole wall of vitamins and supplements, and some metaphysical books.

Seed of Life Natural Foods, 1316 Government Street, (250) 382–4343. Hours: 9:00 A.M.–6:00 P.M. Monday–Saturday, noon–5:00 P.M. Sunday. Wheelchair accessible. Credit cards: Visa, MasterCard.

You will indeed have **Sweet Memories** after trying Connie and Shukry Regep's goodies. The Regeps, who are originally from Michigan and Czechoslovakia, respectively, have developed a popular spot.

You can watch Connie baking waffle cones in the front window, after which you have to go in and see what else they have made: their own ice cream and frozen yogurt. The Regeps make such personalized flavors as tin roof, moose trader, turtle (caramel pecans and chocolate), caribou caramel (caramel ripple with chocolate caramel cups), orange creamsicle (remember 50/50s?), and chocolate banana.

There are no seats here. The best you can do is to lean your fanny against the brick windowsill in front or walk around with your treat.

Fine points: Sweet Memories has been voted the best yogurt and hard ice-cream shop in Victoria by locals several times, and the building was originally part of the 1892 New England Hotel, designed by John Teague, architect of City Hall.

Sweet Memories, 1312 Government Street, (250) 383–1312. Hours: summer noon–9:00 or 10:30 P.M. ("as long as there are people out there"), winter noon–5:30 P.M. Closed Christmas through February. Wheelchair accessible. Credit cards: none.

Command Post Militaria & Antiques sells and pays cash for German and Nazi military paraphernalia and sells British and Canadian military and mounted police medals, along with patches, navy ship hats, uniforms, knives, and old flags. Since moving from a previous location, it appears to be emphasizing antiques and dolls rather than the Nazi stuff, although a sign in the window begs for German World War II supplies. Tells you something.

Command Post Militaria & Antiques, *1306 Government Street, (250) 383–4421. Hours: 9:00 A.M.–5:00 P.M. daily. Wheelchair accessible. Credit cards: Visa, MasterCard.*

Fields Shoes is a great store for no-fuss, real work, and cowboy boots for both workers and cowboys as well as for hip teens and others. Brands include Caterpillar, Boulet western boots, Ecco, Birkenstock, and Timberland. You'll also find motorcycle boots, and some belt buckles. Even men will like this store. It makes you want to touch the good-smelling leather.

Fine points: The building was erected in 1891 by the Canadian Pacific Railway and designed by Thomas Hooper.

Fields Shoes, *1300 Government Street, (250) 388–5921. Hours: 10:00 A.M.–6:00 P.M. Monday–Saturday, closed Sunday. Wheelchair accessible. Credit cards: Visa, MasterCard.*

Starbucks bought the more elegant Torrefazione Italia at 1234 Government. Starbucks are multiplying faster than people in Victoria; you will find them easier than you might want to.

The **Irish Times** is the hot spot on Government Street at Bastion Square. Penny Farthing Pub publican/owner Matt MacNeil branched out to this new location where Polo Ralph Lauren was and turned the elegant store into a gorgeous, bustling pub that features pub grub about as good as it comes.

Crowded all the time, the Irish Times, named for Ireland's biggest newspaper, offers exceptional light meals at average prices. Standouts include Stilton Spuds, potato skins filled with bacon and Stilton blue cheese ($8.99); cornmeal-dusted oysters with Guinness aioli and shoestring potato bread crisps ($9.99); crab and hand-peeled shrimp cakes ($9.99); Irish potato flat bread with Cashel blue cheese (the best) butter sauce ($6.99); and the already famous Irish Times Oyster Bake ($11.99–$16.99).

There are lots of salads, including a Celtic Cobb salad with bacon, eggs, avocado, and chunky Irish blue cheese dressing with wild spring salmon, New York strip loin, or grilled chicken breast ($13.99); a Bailey's marinated chicken and Brie salad ($10.99); and a terrific Guinness and crab bisque or clam chowder. Oyster and Guinness stew or original Irish stew are less than $13. You can also get a wide range of sandwiches, such as a fresh crab and Guinness cheddar burger ($14.99), a fresh crab and Brie panini ($11.99), oyster po' boy, and even a garden burger, as well as pizzas and pastas.

Other specials include corned beef and cabbage ($16.99–$21.99), shepherd's pie ($12.99), steak and Guinness potpie with Canadian beef ($13.99), or a Guinness-braised lamb shank ($17.99–$23.99). Their fish and chips comes in either wild red spring salmon or halibut, both from the Queen Charlotte Islands. Cortez Island oysters and chips ($13.99) are divine.

Irish Times, 1200 Government Street, (250) 383–7775; www.victoria pubcompany.com. Hours: 11:00 A.M.–1:00 A.M. daily. Fully licensed. Wheelchair accessible. Credit Cards: Visa, MasterCard, American Express.

Bastion Square, to the west of Government Street, is a pedestrian mall that connects to View Street east of Government.

At 50 Bastion Square, the **Re-Bar** serves "modern [read healthy, vegetarian] cuisine" and is extremely popular with locals for its seasonal and regional cuisine at breakfast, including scrambled eggs or omelets between $8.00–$9.50, and at lunch for sandwiches or salads (and terrific quesadillas). Funky with wild colored walls, Re-Bar also has an excellent fresh juice bar featuring exotic fruit and vegetable juices, baked goods, Northwest's best coffees, dinner, and Sunday brunch, all cafeteria-style. We highly recommend Re-Bar's *Re-Bar Modern Food Cookbook*!

Re-Bar, 50 Bastion Square, (250) 361–9223; www.rebarmodernfood .com. Hours: 8:30 A.M.–9:00 P.M. Monday–Saturday, Friday and Saturday until 10:00 P.M., 8:30 A.M.–3:30 P.M. Sunday. Not wheelchair accessible. Credit cards: none. Beer and wine.

At the **Maritime Museum of British Columbia,** 28 Bastion Square, you can see many interesting examples of the ships and discoveries that are important parts of British Columbia's history.

In the museum's cavernous halls you'll see a full-scale model of the stern of Captain Cook's ship; the dugout *Tilicum* with cabin and sail in which John Claus Voss sailed around the world from Oak Bay between 1901 and 1904; a model of the *Beaver;* a set of three chronometers; and *Trekka,* the smallest (20 feet, 6 inches) sailboat to circle the globe (1955–59). Maps, equipment, an 1847 photo of the Songhee war party, and a feast of other memorabilia delight history and maritime fans.

Fine points: Originally the Provincial Court House built in 1889 where the old city jail once stood and public hangings took place, this building, designed by H. O. Tiedman and Francis Rattenbury, became the Maritime Museum in 1965.

Maritime Museum of British Columbia, 28 Bastion Square, (250) 385–4222; Fax: (250) 382–2869; www.mmbc.bc.ca. Hours: 9:30 A.M.–4:30 P.M. daily September 16–June 14; 9:30 A.M.–5:30 P.M. daily June 15–September 15. Admission: adults $8, seniors older than sixty-five and students $5, children ages six to eleven $3, under age six free, families $20. Wheelchair accessible. Credit cards: none.

Back in a cozy European-feeling corner of Bastion Square are the Blue Carrot Café, serving Mexican wraps, salads, chili, and breakfast all day, and the Greek Porto Souvlaki restaurant.

Stroll down the rest of Bastion Square toward the stairs, and then we'll bring you back up the south side.

Notice Burnes House, 18–26 Bastion Square, which was built in 1887 as a reputable hotel. It also served as a brothel and a warehouse.

Entrance to Bastion Square at Government Street

D'Arcy's Pub, 15 Bastion Square, formerly known as Harpo's, the Planet, and Liquid, is a Victoria musical landmark where Jimi Hendrix, B. B. King, Jann Arden, Jeff Healey, and the Crash Test Dummies have all performed. This popular incarnation of a recycled rock club on Bastion Square is run by the Irish pub D'Arcy McGee's, which is located just downstairs facing Wharf Street and the water of the Inner Harbour. Live local and touring bands Sunday–Wednesday, DJs Thursday–Saturday.

Fine points: This is the oldest steel-framed building in Victoria.

D'Arcy's Pub, 15 Bastion Square, (250) 385–5333. Hours: 9:00 P.M.–2:00 A.M. Monday–Thursday, 8:00 P.M.–2:00 A.M. Friday–Saturday, 8:00 P.M.–midnight Sunday. Not wheelchair accessible. Credit cards: Visa, MasterCard, American Express.

Anthony's Old Time Portraits is lots of fun if you want to dress up in old-timey costumes for a quickie photo—ready in five minutes. You can fulfill a fantasy of looking like a gangster or moll, pioneer, Charlie Chaplin, Royal Canadian Mounted Police, or a Victorian lady or gentleman.

Anthony's Old Time Portraits, 19 Bastion Square, (250) 383–2290. Hours: noon–6:00 P.M. daily. Credit cards: Visa, MasterCard.

Camille's Fine West Coast Dining, below 45 Bastion Square, offers a splendid romantic dining experience featuring the best of local wild game, including ostrich and venison; local crab cakes; duck confit salad ($9); fillet of wild salmon ($25); green curry seafood claypot ($24); breast of Cowichan Bay chicken ($26); rack of venison ($32); breast of duck ($27); and a great West Coast bouillabaisse ($23). David Mincey and Paige Robinson have earned an international reputation for elegant dining in a warm setting and for using the best local and organic ingredients. We prefer the entry-level room, surrounded by wine bottles. With more than 150 wine selections, the staff's wine knowledge is excellent, and the desserts are worth succumbing to.

Camille's Fine West Coast Dining, below 45 Bastion Square, (250) 381–3433; www.camillesrestaurant.com. Hours: dinner 5:30–10:00 P.M. Not wheelchair accessible. Credit cards: Visa, MasterCard, American Express. Fully licensed.

Green Curry

David Mincey of Camille's Fine West Coast Dining, Victoria

3 bunches cilantro, leaves only
4 large shallots
1 oz. fresh ginger, peeled
10 small cloves garlic
3 tbsp. soy sauce
2 tbsp. lemon juice
½ lb. fresh basil
1 tbsp. cumin
2 medium jalapeños, seeded
4 cans coconut milk

Puree all ingredients except coconut milk in food processor until fine. Add mixture to the coconut milk in pot and whisk well. Reduce by half over medium heat.

Note from David: "We use this sauce in our claypot dish with grilled seafood, Shanghai noodles, and Asian greens. It also makes a great pasta sauce or sauce for prawns, chicken, or any vegetarian stir-fry."

Garrick's Head Pub, an old-fashioned British-style pub, is part of the Bedford Hotel, with patio tables facing Bastion Square. Sandwiches, meat pies, hamburgers, fish and chips, and daily specials make up Garrick's better-than-usual pub grub, mostly less than $8. Great variety of ales and beers. Friendly and fun hangout.

Fine points: The 1885 building was originally the law office of Theodore Davie, who was B.C. premier 1892–95.

Garrick's Head Pub, 69 Bastion Square, (250) 384–6835; www.bedford regency.com. Hours: 11:00 A.M.–11:00 P.M. Monday–Tuesday, 11:00 A.M.–1:00 A.M. Wednesday–Saturday, 10:00 A.M.–10:00 P.M. Sunday. Wheelchair accessible through Bedford Hotel. Credit cards: Visa, Master-Card, American Express.

Sesame-Citrus Dressing

David Mincey of Camille's
Fine West Coast Dining, Victoria

Some of the ingredients are available at import and specialty food shops.

$\frac{1}{2}$ cup fresh orange juice concentrate

1 cup lime juice

$\frac{1}{2}$ cup balsamic vinegar

$\frac{1}{2}$ cup brown sugar

2 tbsp. Ketjap Manis

1 tsp. Sambal Oelek

1 tbsp. grainy Dijon mustard

$\frac{1}{4}$ cup chopped cilantro

2 tbsp. sesame oil

$\frac{1}{4}$ cup soy sauce

3 cups olive oil

Blend all ingredients in a blender except olive oil. When blended, slowly add oil to mixture while blending some more, until thick.

Note from David: "This does make a lot of dressing, but it keeps for weeks in the fridge. We use this in our famous Warm Duck Salad, tossed with baby greens, fresh ginger, orange segments, and hot confit of duck. It works with many types of salad—try with fresh tomatoes, shrimp or pan-seared scallops, bacon, bell peppers, etc."

Go up around the corner of Government Street and to the right into **Breeze,** a hip, popular clothing store featuring sample sales, Esprit clothes, watches, sunglasses, good deals on Hush Puppies shoes in several colors, Unlisted bags, Calvin Klein, and Hot Sox. This place is always busy with the young and young at heart.

Breeze, 1150 Government Street, (250) 383–8871. Hours: summer 10:00 A.M.–10:00 P.M. Monday–Saturday, noon–8:00 P.M. Sunday; winter 10:00 A.M.–6:00 P.M. Monday–Saturday, noon–6:00 P.M. Sunday. Wheelchair accessible. Credit cards: Visa, MasterCard, American Express.

Elegant **Old Morris Tobacconist,** purveyors of "smokers requisites since 1892," sells Cuban cigars, both those made totally in Cuba and those made in Canada

from Cuban tobacco. Americans who may or may not believe in doing bus
with Cuba flock to this store to buy what is contraband in their country. C
Morris also sells house blends, private blends, and personal blends (at your
request), as well as a fine selection of pipes for all seasons.

As you enter the shop, notice the burning flame in the center of the room,
and don't walk into it. Green tile floors, a heavy wood look, toy airplane mobiles,
a portrait of Queen Elizabeth behind the cash register, and English chocolates all
combine to give you a unique experience.

Even if you, like us, do not endorse the use of tobacco in any form, you
might want to visit this store just to see the well-preserved architecture. There's
also a good variety of newspapers available at the door.

Fine points: Built in 1882, the building was redesigned by Thomas
Hooper in 1909 to provide founder E. A. Morris with Edwardian "restrained elegance."

*Old Morris Tobacconist, 1116 Government Street, (250) 382–4811;
www.oldmorris.com. Hours: 9:00 A.M.–6:00 P.M. daily, until 9:00 P.M.
Friday, noon–5:00 P.M. Sunday summer. Wheelchair accessible. Credit
cards: Visa, MasterCard, American Express.*

In business since 1894, **Murchie's Tea and Coffee** at 1110 Government, with a
tea and coffee store next door where you can buy tins and gift packages, is the
ultimate tea destination of British Columbia. You can rely on Murchie's to sell
the best of everything. We take many late afternoon rests and sustenances here,
preferably at the outdoor tables if the weather allows.

In the tearoom you can enjoy everything from orange or currant scones with
clotted cream and jam to sandwiches, salads, and daily specials such as vegetarian or meat lasagna. Biscotti and special teatime-size sweets and tarts tempt
locals as well as visitors. Espresso drinks and a full range of teas, including a few
decaffeinated, warm the soul. Murchie's does not sell decaf coffee, although it
claims its coffee has only 30 percent of the caffeine of regular coffee.

Here's the routine: You stand in line to place your order. (Don't be discour-
aged, the line moves fast.) There's a second line at the far end of the counter. Go
directly there. If you are in a hurry, try the ready-made tuna, egg salad, or turkey
sandwiches priced at less than $6. The Greek salad is especially good.

Local ladies often come for their afternoon tea and sit on the mezzanine
(two steps up), while visitors like to people-watch at the front. An extremely

ir experience. Get on the mailing list. Restrooms are
at the back of the tearoom. Turn left at the bottom

retail shop offers loose fair trade teas, teapots, cozies,
bottle of Mexican vanilla at $19.95.

Fine points: The 1907 building, designed by William R. Wilson, is
beautifully preserved.

*Murchie's Tea and Coffee, 1110 Government Street, (250) 383–3112;
www.murchies.com. Hours: 9:00 A.M.–6:00 P.M. Monday–Wednesday,
9:00 A.M.–9:00 P.M. Thursday–Friday, 8:00 A.M.–6:00 P.M. Saturday–
Sunday. Partly wheelchair accessible (restrooms wheelchair accessible from
Langley Street). Credit cards: Visa, MasterCard.*

Munro's Books, 1108 Government Street, is a book lovers' heaven, plain and
simple. The heritage building's warm hardwood floors immediately set the quiet
tone for what's ahead: the ultimate book experience. Even if you rarely buy books,
come on in here, and you will love it.

Special large sections featuring Canadiana, Victoria, and Vancouver Island
are to the left of the door; cooking and travel are farther back on the left; and a
fantastic children's reading room hides at the left back. Politics, philosophy, and
everything else work their way up the right side of the store. This is a great place
to pick up Canadian cookbooks.

Owner James Munro is usually there working alongside the staff. A leading
figure in Victoria known for his generous support of the arts, historic preservation, and the environment, he treats his staff and books as gently and respectfully
as he does the environment.

Be sure to notice Carole Sabiston's fabulous banners hanging on the walls,
the larger of which are titled *The Four Seasons Suite.* Carole's textile assem-
blages appear throughout Canada, the United States, and the United Kingdom. She is a member of the Royal Canadian Academy of Arts and has
received the prestigious Saidye Bronfman Award for excellence in the arts. In
1992 she received the order of British Columbia. Coincidentally, she is married to Jim Munro.

Terrific sale tables occupy the center of the store toward the back. We always
find something irresistible here.

Munro's Books and Murchie's Tea and Coffee on Government Street

Fine points: The building was designed by Thomas Hooper and built as the Royal Bank in 1909–10. When James Munro renovated it in 1984, he uncovered and retained the original plaster ceiling.

Munro's Books, *1108 Government Street, (250) 382–2464 or (888) 243–2464; Fax: (888) 382–2832; www.munrobooks.com. Hours: 9:00 A.M.–6:00 P.M. Monday–Wednesday and Saturday, 9:00 A.M.–9:00 P.M. Thursday–Friday, 9:30 A.M.–6:00 P.M. Sunday. Wheelchair accessible, although ramp is a little steep. Credit cards: Visa, MasterCard, American Express, JCB.*

James Bay Trading Company, 1102 Government Street, is a somewhat upscale souvenir shop with attractive sweaters, leathers, slippers, caps, and much more. Leather fanny packs start at $50, ladies' leather gloves at $59, indigo leather backpacks at $260, and beautiful Cowichan-style blue or green and beige sweaters at $177. Check out the duck decoys and native jewelry, as well as packaged smoked salmon, maple sugar, and film.

Fine points: James Bay is housed in the Lascelles-Southgate Building erected in 1869, with the second story and tower added in 1887.

James Bay Trading Company, 1102 Government Street, (250) 388–5477. Hours: 9:30 A.M.–10:00 P.M. Monday–Saturday, 9:30 A.M.– 8:00 P.M. Sunday. Wheelchair accessible. Credit cards: Visa, MasterCard, American Express, JCB.

Seeing Is Believing moved here from the Bay Centre with its load of tourist-oriented, whimsical "possible gifts for impossible people." You will find car dice, games, wild lamps, Ravensburger puzzles, Pokémon shirts, and many other unbelievable objects of fancy.

Fine points: Between 1885 and 1987 this was the Bank of British Columbia, designed by Warren Williams, architect of the Dunsmuir Craigdarroch Castle. Famed poet Robert Service ("The Shooting of Dan McGrew") once worked for the bank and lived upstairs.

Seeing Is Believing, 1020 Government Street, (250) 382–8578. Hours: 9:00 A.M.–9:00 P.M. daily. Not wheelchair accessible. Credit cards: Visa, MasterCard, American Express.

Out of Ireland, possibly our favorite store, has been creating nurturing, stylish fabrics in Ireland since 1723, and now they are available in Victoria, thank heavens, god, and goddess.

Therese Palmer and her husband, Perry Foster, reopened the store here with Irish flare and fun, as usual. Therese makes her own buying trips to her native Ireland and carries only the best, and at reasonable prices. Perry plays in the Victoria Symphony and occasionally organizes a Celtic concert.

We find some of the most beautifully feminine Irish women's clothing here, such as capes, coats, jackets, and skirts, and men's Irish tweed jackets and hats, as well as handwoven mohair blankets and scarves. Waterproof coats and waxed cotton jackets run $99, and you can find authentic Aran knit sweaters here for $99—the best price anywhere. A definite must.

Out of Ireland, 1012 Government Street, (250) 389–0886. Hours: summer 9:00 A.M.–9:00 P.M. Monday–Saturday, 10:00 A.M.–8:00 P.M. Sunday; winter 9:00 A.M.–5:30 P.M. Monday–Saturday, noon–5:00 P.M. Sunday. Wheelchair accessible. Credit cards: Visa, MasterCard, American Express.

Moose Crossing has thousands of hilarious and prank magnets, glow-in-the-dark stuff, and R. C. M. P. (Royal Canadian Mounted Police) collectibles.

Moose Crossing, 1010 Government Street, (250) 381–9945. Hours: summer 9:00 A.M.–11:00 P.M. daily; winter 10:00 A.M.–6:00 P.M. Sunday–Thursday, 10:00 A.M.–8:00 P.M. Friday–Saturday. Wheelchair accessible. Credit cards: Visa, MasterCard, American Express, JCB.

Hill's Native Art has a marvelous collection of truly authentic First Peoples' crafts, wood arts, drums, and colorful shirts, which make fabulous gifts. The sales staff is knowledgeable and answers dumb questions graciously, thank heavens.

Hill's Native Art, 1008 Government Street, (250) 385–3911; www .hillsindiancrafts.com and www.hillsnativeart.com. Hours: 9:00 A.M.– 7:00 P.M. Wheelchair accessible. Credit cards: Visa, MasterCard, American Express, JCB.

Artina's Jewellery is an exquisite gallery shop of tasteful native and British Columbia silver and jewelry and whimsical, colorful ceramic necklaces by Libby Nicholson.

Artina's Jewellery, 1002 Government Street, (250) 386–7000. Hours: 9:30 A.M.–5:30 P.M. daily. Wheelchair accessible. Credit cards: Visa, MasterCard, American Express, JCB.

Locally owned **Island Spirit** sells some of the best quality souvenirs in town, as well as disposable cameras, candles, real Butchart Gardens calendars and books in several languages, the ever-present sweat clothes, and interesting British Columbia jade.

Island Spirit, 910 Government Street, (250) 281–3711; Fax: (250) 381–4430. Hours: 8:30 A.M.–6:00 or 9:00 P.M. Wheelchair accessible. Credit cards: Visa, MasterCard, American Express.

West Pacific Traders is a high-quality, pleasant souvenir shop down some stairs below sidewalk level with lots of the usual, plus Rogers' chocolates, Tilley hats (you must have one), and cold drinks.

West Pacific Traders, 910 Government Street, (250) 381–4001. Hours: summer 8:00 A.M.–11:00 P.M., winter 9:00 A.M.–9:00 P.M. Not wheelchair accessible. Credit cards: Visa, MasterCard, American Express, Discover, JCB, Diners.

If you are in need of immediate sustenance, feet rest, a fancy drink, or a meal slightly more elegant than Sam's Deli, cross Humboldt with the light to **Milestone's.** While this popular restaurant has one of the absolute best views in Victoria, it even has excellent food and young local staff. Amazing!

This is the ultimate umbrella-drink spot in town. Horrendous pink and orange alcoholic margaritas or daiquiris and Long Island or Eclectic iced tea snow cones come in actual fish bowls, usually with more than one straw.

Milestone's specializes in tasty pastas ($8.95 and up) and salmon but also has burgers ($7.95), salads, good steaks, Kobe beef meat loaf, and daily specials.

The outdoor cafe downstairs (open only in warm months) is right on the Inner Harbour Causeway facing the Fairmont Empress Hotel and Parliament buildings, and it costs slightly less than the upstairs dining room. We have been extremely happy with their very local fish and huge chips ($10.95) and a Caesar salad ($9.95; with chicken or shrimp, add $2.95), splitting both. Not your healthy meal prize, but great fun.

> *Milestone's, 812 Wharf Street, (250) 381–2244. Hours: 11:00 A.M.–10:00 P.M. Monday–Thursday, 11:00 A.M.–11:00 P.M. Friday, 10:00 A.M.–11:00 P.M. Saturday, 9:00 A.M.–10:00 P.M. Sunday including brunch. Dining room not wheelchair accessible, but downstairs cafe on the causeway is, from Wharf Street. Credit cards: Visa, MasterCard, American Express, Diners. Fully licensed.*

A stroll along **Wharf Street**'s 5 short blocks can fill a whole morning or afternoon, or you can just cover a few blocks and get the flavor (although you might miss some of the colorful shops). We'll take you up the east side of the street and then back down the water side.

Nautical Nellies Restaurant & Oyster Bar is a surprisingly good tourist-oriented restaurant with an excellent fillet of salmon burger or halibut clubhouse ($9.98) including soup or salad, ten oyster selections, white truffle fries ($6.00), clams, calamari ($10.00), pastas, burgers, oyster shooters in vodka and Tabasco ($3.98), aged steaks ($23.00–$36.00), whole Dungeness crab ($35.00), and Nova Scotia lobster ($43.00). The view of the Inner Harbour is terrific from here.

> *Nautical Nellies Restaurant & Oyster Bar, 1001 Wharf Street at Broughton, (250) 380–2260; www.nauticalnelliesrestaurant.com. Hours:*

winter 11:00 A.M.–10:30 P.M., summer until 11:30 P.M. Fully licensed. Wheelchair accessible. Credit cards: Visa, MasterCard, American Express.

A branch of the **Keg Steakhouse & Bar,** this one is elegant and offers great, slightly expensive steaks cooked to perfection from blue rare to "Chicago style," pastas, and sirloin or salmon Caesar salads, burgers, wraps, potpies, and ribs. A few outdoor tables have been added to take advantage of the spectacular Inner Harbour view.

Fine points: Just up the block from Keg are J. R.'s India Curry House, Siam Thai, and Koto Japanese restaurants, offering interesting ethnic alternatives in case the steak house doesn't appeal to you.

Keg Steakhouse & Bar, 500 Fort Street at Wharf, (250) 386–7789; www.kegsteakhouse.com. Hours: 4:30–10:30 P.M. Fully licensed. Partly wheelchair accessible. Credit cards: Visa, MasterCard, American Express.

D'Arcy McGee's, a somewhat jazzed up Irish pub, has a fabulous Inner Harbour view and offers Irish and Canadian beers and ales, Irish pub grub, and the required good fish and chips. Music on weekends.

D'Arcy McGee's, 1127 Wharf Street, (250) 380–1322; Fax: (250) 380–1335. Hours: 11:00 A.M.–10:00 P.M. weekdays and until midnight on weekends. Fully licensed. Wheelchair accessible. Credit cards: Visa, MasterCard, American Express.

Garlic lovers' delights at the **Garlic Rose** range from breakfast—muffins ($3.50), omelets ($7.50), and waffles ($5.95)—to burgers (including the Garlic Rose with garlic and herbs for $8.50), and salads, pizzas, shellfish, Mediterranean spiced fish, kabobs, and steaks. There's also a full vegetarian menu.

Spicy Honey Walnuts

Nautical Nellies Restaurant & Oyster Bar, Victoria

4 cups walnut pieces
2 oz. butter, melted
4 oz. honey
1 oz. water
2 tbsp. prepared Cajun spice

Melt butter in heavy-bottomed sauté pan. Add walnuts and toast lightly. Add the honey and toss to coat nuts. Add the water and continue cooking until water is evaporated. Sprinkle Cajun spice over the nuts and toss to coat. Turn onto baking sheet and cool. Enjoy alone or tossed in a salad.

Owner Moses Hanna has lived in forty countries and now says he has settled in heaven—Victoria. You get lots of food, no matter what you order. Service is sometimes slow and nonchalant. Superb view from outside tables in good weather.

Fine points: From here to 1213 Wharf Street is the Reid Block, completed in 1863.

Garlic Rose, 1205 Wharf Street, (250) 384–1931. Hours: summer 8:30 A.M.–midnight or so, winter 8:30 A.M.–10:00 P.M. Fully licensed. Wheelchair accessible. Credit cards: Visa, MasterCard.

Tattoo Zoo specializes in piercing and tattooing of all kinds. Several binders of plastic-coated pages allow you to select a design if you don't have your own. Options range from native to Celtic (which amazingly resemble each other), plus lots of hooded sweats and T-shirts. Personal note: We were treated with respect and politeness by the young staff.

Tattoo Zoo, 1215 Wharf Street, (250) 361–1952. Hours: 11:00 A.M.–6:00 P.M. Monday–Saturday, noon–4:00 P.M. Sunday. Wheelchair accessible. Credit cards: Visa, MasterCard.

For a quick lunch, snack, or dinner, try **Lola's Pizza.** This hip pizza place offers vegetarian options, gluten-free pizza, and pizza by the slice, delivers whole pizzas, and recycles all cans and bottles near the door. Fifteen-inch pizzas are only $10.00 plus $1.50 per topping; 18-inchers start at $13.00.

Fine points: 1215–1219 Wharf Street was built in 1891 by James Yates.

Lola's Pizza, 1219 Wharf Street, (250) 389–2226. Hours: 11:00 A.M.–3:00 A.M. Monday–Saturday, 11:00 A.M.–1:00 A.M. Sunday. Wheelchair accessible. Credit cards: none.

Cross Wharf Street toward the water, and we will continue back on the water side of the street at **Chandler's Seafood Restaurant.** This elegant, impressive restaurant with its rich dark wood interior is right next door to the Victoria Regent Hotel. It has been voted Best of the City seafood restaurant for several years.

Chandler's outdoor decks nearly hang over the water, enabling you to see, hear, and feel seaplanes arriving from Washington and Vancouver. This is a great place to soak up old Victoria.

Some of the excellent dishes you might try include seafood chowder ($8.00); smoked salmon ($10.00); local halibut six ways ($19.00–$29.00); Dungeness crab cakes ($12.00); Atlantic lobster; clams and mussels ($19.95); salmon cakes ($8.95); and chicken ($14.95–$19.95). Wild local Red Coho salmon runs from $19 to $29, while a whole Dungeness crab goes for $35. Chandler's Feast combinations run from $48 for one person to $109 for two.

Fine points: The 1896 building was commissioned by James Yates, a Hudson's Bay Company carpenter who started a bar and made a fortune. It was first used to wholesale liquors, cigars, and blankets to Yukon miners and later served as a ship chandlery until 1979.

Chandler's Seafood Restaurant, 1250 Wharf Street at the bottom of Yates Street, (250) 385–3474; www.chandlersseafood.com. Hours: 5:00–10:00 P.M. daily. Partly wheelchair accessible. Credit cards: Visa, MasterCard, American Express, enRoute.

The Victoria Regent Hotel is convenient for commuters and visitors from Vancouver or Seattle because seaplanes land practically off the deck. Many rooms include kitchens, and continental breakfast is included. (See "Where to Stay.")

Global Currency Exchange, at 1208 Wharf Street (250–398–0520), offers convenient but expensive money exchange, so if you can hold off, wait until you get to a bank for a better rate.

Fine points: Global's building was constructed in 1882 for Roderick Finlayson, who built Fort Victoria; the Finlayson Building was divided into shops in 1944.

A cozy, quickie cafe, the **Blue Carrot Café** is part of a group of eateries that also includes the Wharfside Eatery. This one is inexpensive: great sandwiches at $4.95 or Black Forest ham and asparagus at $5.95; pizzas such as Canadian back bacon, shrimp, and scallops from $5.95 to $6.95; huge homemade cookies; Island-grown meats and vegetables; and Salt Spring certified organic coffee.

Blue Carrot Café, 1208 Wharf Street, (250) 360–1808. Hours: summer 7:00 A.M.–6:00 P.M., winter 7:00 A.M.–3:00 P.M. Not wheelchair accessible. Credit cards: Visa, MasterCard, American Express.

The **Wharfside Eatery & Decks** is a favorite local hangout for lunch, afternoon tea ($14.95), or after work. Lots of young people come here for a good beer. The decor will cheer you just for its humor with huge hanging fake flowers, Spanish tile floors, ceiling fans, and a wooden cutout of Nasty Jack with his theoretical pirate patch.

The Wharfside features a daily light lunch at $7.95 in addition to its full-range menu of burgers made with Alberta grain–fed beef, filet of salmon burgers, pastas, salads, seafood, pizza from its wood-burning oven, and chicken that will please you and the kids. The beautiful enclosed deck faces the Inner Harbour water for gorgeous year-round dining or drinking. Umbrellas for shade upon request.

Wharfside Eatery & Decks, 1208 Wharf Street, (250) 360–1808; www .wharfsideeatery.com. Hours: 11:30 A.M.–midnight daily, afternoon tea 2:00–5:00 P.M. Fully licensed. Wheelchair accessible. Credit cards: Visa, MasterCard, American Express.

We now continue on to **Store Street,** which is practically an extension of Wharf Street, and in 1 block several business establishments are actually part of **Market Square.** Here they are.

Cafe Mexico, 1425 Store Street, serves Mexican food in a fun, colorful, and appropriately raunchy atmosphere. You'll also find calamari, carne chipotle, and tortillas filled with prawns, scallops, and mushrooms with white wine sauce, sour cream, and avocado. And, yes, burgers ($10–$20). Cafe Mexico boasts "no lard, no MSG."

Cafe Mexico, 1425 Store Street, (250) 386–5454. Hours: 11:30 A.M. on Sunday–Thursday, 11:30 A.M.–midnight Friday–Saturday. Beer and wine. Wheelchair accessible. Credit cards: Visa, MasterCard, American Express, Diners.

Muffet & Louisa is the ultimate kitchen store with a fun, cheerful ambience. Its original store is in Sidney. Bed, bath, and dining items are also sold. Enjoy the culinary paintings of Shawn Shepherd.

Muffet & Louisa, 1437 Store Street, (250) 382–3201 or (866) 382–3201; Fax: (250) 382–3205; www.muffetandlouisa.com. Open 10:00 A.M.–6:00 P.M. daily. Wheelchair accessible. Credit cards: Visa, Master-Card.

The corner of Store and Pandora Streets is **Goodfellow's Cigars Ltd.,** a cigar emporium and smoking room that appears to do very well with its special-interest audience. Smokers may enjoy the smoking area where people come to puff billows, lick their lips, and enjoy their habit, often newly acquired.

Most of the cigars here are Cuban, but some are made in Canada of Cuban tobacco. Make very sure you are getting specifically what you expect. Brands you might recognize include Cohiba, Partages, Romeo y Julietta, and Bolivar.

Goodfellow's Cigars Ltd., 1441 Store Street, (250) 385–2772; Fax: (250) 383–0822; www.goodfellascigarshop.com. Not wheelchair accessible. Credit cards: Visa, MasterCard, American Express, JCB.

While you are in the neighborhood, be sure to drop by Swans at the corner of Pandora Street (1 block south of Fisgard) and Store Street (which continues to Wharf Street on the west side of Market Square). This is a neatly restored heritage building that houses a pleasant small hotel, pub and brewery, restaurant, an excellent wine and beer shop, and a nightclub. **Swans Cafe & Pub** is an extremely popular thirtysomethings hangout, with Caesar salads, huge burgers and fries, piled-high nachos, local halibut and chips, shepherd's pie, and occasionally a lowish-fat chicken taco tostada, other salads, breakfast wraps, and stir-frys. In-house brewed ales are the best, of course. Food prices are reasonable. Ask for a window table for best view (the Gorge is across Store Street) and people-watching. Swans's founder died a few years ago and left this whole restaurant-hotel-brewery-nightclub complex to the University of Victoria. Swans's Wild Saffron restaurant features "progressive West Coast cuisine." Swans Brewpub was awarded "National Brewpub of the Year" in 2006.

Swans Cafe & Pub, 506 Pandora Street, (250) 361–3310; www.swans hotel.com. Hours: 11:00 A.M.–2:00 A.M. Wheelchair accessible. Credit cards: Visa, MasterCard, American Express.

You can park at Pandora and Store Streets for $1.50 in quarters for three hours.

Fran Willis Gallery and the Store Street Studios offer a variety of work from local artists and gifts.

We enjoy the **Sour Pickle Cafe,** a cafe with Mount Royal bagels, healthy muffins, huge sandwiches, juices, and organic coffee, with breakfast or lunch starting at $2.99. Some sidewalk tables.

> *Sour Pickle Cafe, 1623 Store Street, (250) 384–3593. Hours: 7:30 A.M.–11:30 P.M. Wheelchair accessible. Credit cards: none.*

Susan Toby's and Maria Henson's **Insideout Home and Garden Ltd.** offers a charming and earthy array of home accessories with a twist. Perfect lamps (for Kathleen's taste), furniture, native paddles, children's furniture and accessories, bedding, cribs, and elegant wrought-iron bistro sets abound.

> *Insideout Home and Garden Ltd., 1627 Store Street, (250) 388–0661; Fax: (250) 388–0662; www.insideoutvictoria.com. Hours: 9:30 A.M.– 5:30 P.M. Monday–Saturday, 11:00 A.M.–5:00 P.M. Sunday. Wheelchair accessible. Credit cards: Visa, MasterCard.*

SPECIAL STREETS OF DOWNTOWN VICTORIA

This walk will take you up and down the charming streets that run east and west and across Government Street all the way to Chinatown. We will also guide you through Antique Row, Chinatown, Old Town, and Market Square.

The first street you come to going north (up) Government Street is Courtney. Up to the right are several sources of food. On the left side going up you will see the **Bun Shop,** where great, inexpensive sandwiches served on soft panini-style buns/rolls are perfect to take on picnics, ferry rides, and tours. The red chairs and white tables out on the sidewalk mark the spot. The Bun Shop serves salmon, tuna, egg salad, ham, turkey, cheeses, and salads, all for less than $5.50. Next door you can get twenty-four flavors of local Dairyland ice cream.

> *Bun Shop, 600 Courtney Street, (250) 385–3511. Hours: summer 7:30 A.M.–9:00 P.M., ice-cream parlor open until 11:00 P.M.; winter 7:30 A.M.–5:00 P.M. Wheelchair accessible. Credit cards: Visa, MasterCard.*

Just a block off the beaten track, **Hugo's Grill and Brewhouse** has converted itself from an ultraelegant steak house to a terrific grill with its still-fabulous steaks and eight great pizzas (about $11.00), excellent lunches from a lamb

burger with Brie ($12.95) to wild salmon spinach salad ($9.95), pastas from pri-
mavera ($12.95) to smoked chicken linguine, AAA beef stroganoff ($15.95), and
various seafood dishes. Appetizers include Indian spring rolls, crab cakes, crispy
calamari, and pan-fried Fanny Bay oysters. Soups and salads are always good
with real green goddess among dressing choices, and then you can get into the
divine steaks (up to $42.95), spring salmon, chicken, and mixed grill.

At lunch you can try a cranberry turkey burger ($9.95), or their spectacular
Hugo burger or halibut burger ($9.25), all of which come with choice of salads
or pommes frites. Their pub and brewhouse are right up Courtney Street. Lots
of fun, friendly staff led by manager Michele Linley, and great food all around.
A la carte brunch on Sunday.

Hugo's brewpub is one of the most popular in Victoria.

Hugo's Grill and Brewhouse, 625 Courtney, (250) 920–4844; Fax:
(250) 920–4842. Hours: 11:00 A.M. on. Fully licensed with their brews
on tap. Partly wheelchair accessible. Credit cards: Visa, MasterCard,
American Express.

Across Courtney Street, Harbour Sweets offers candies, Harbour Cones sells ice
cream and smoothies, and Le Soleil makes custom jewelry.

Eagle Feather is a unique enterprise of gallery manager Shirley Blackstar,
who shows forty Vancouver Island First Nations artists' work and even has traditional carvers working on-site daily. Enjoy masks, drums, fabulous silver and
gold jewelry, baskets, and prints from Nuu-chah-nulth (Nootka), Kwak-
wakawaku, and Haida custom artists and craftspeople.

Eagle Feather, 904 Gordon Street, (250) 388–4330; Fax: (250)
388–4328; www.eaglefeathergallery.com. Hours: 10:00 A.M.–5:30 P.M.
daily. Wheelchair accessible. Credit cards: Visa, MasterCard, American
Express.

If you want to try Vietnamese food, you might walk around the corner to Langley Street and the best Victoria has to offer, **Le Petit Saigon,** an authentic Vietnamese experience with exotic full carnivore and vegetarian menus and
interesting spring rolls, all with Chinese and French influences.

Le Petit Saigon, 1010 Langley Street, (250) 386–1412. Hours: lunch
11:00 A.M.–2:00 P.M., dinner from 5:00 P.M. Fully licensed. Wheelchair
accessible. Credit cards: Visa, MasterCard, American Express.

Just up from the corner is **Valhalla Pure Outfitters Factory Outlet,** 615 Broughton. This Canadian company's ultralight outdoor gear is made in British Columbia. The quality is top of the line, and the prices reflect the workmanship. You can get hiking boots, Teva sandals, Valhalla packs, Eco clothes of recycled material, and sleeping bags. Valhalla also features a wide array of gear for rock and ice climbing.

Fine points: There's a parking garage here on Broughton and Broad Streets.

Valhalla Pure Outfitters Factory Outlet, 615 Broughton Street, (250) 360–2181 or (888) 551–1859; www.vpo.ca. Hours: 9:30 A.M.–6:00 P.M. Monday, 9:30 A.M.–9:00 P.M. Tuesday–Saturday, 10:00 A.M.–6:00 P.M. Sunday. Wheelchair accessible. Credit cards: Visa, MasterCard, American Express, Diners, JCB.

For a near-European experience, duck into **Chocolatier Bernard Callebaut,** an elegant Belgian candy store with shiny copper and brass counters. Bernard Callebaut chocolates are well known throughout Canada (there are also stores in the States, in Seattle and in Phoenix). Forty-seven varieties of handmade chocolates are made weekly with fresh cream, butter, chocolate, and no preservatives.

Chocolatier Bernard Callebaut, 623 Broughton Street, (250) 380–1515; http://bernard-callebaut.com. Hours: 9:30 A.M.–5:30 P.M. Monday–Saturday, noon–4:00 P.M. Sunday. Wheelchair accessible. Credit cards: Visa, MasterCard, American Express, Diners.

It's worth the trip another block up Broughton to the **Greater Victoria Public Library.** This fabulous library, built in 1980, has active children's and teens' sections to the right of the entrance, excellent card and computer catalogues, and a most hospitable staff. The espresso cart in the courtyard is quite good.

Greater Victoria Public Library, 735 Broughton Street, (250) 384–3182. Hours: 9:00 A.M.–6:00 P.M. Monday, Wednesday, Friday, Saturday; 9:00 A.M.–9:00 P.M. Tuesday, Thursday. Wheelchair accessible.

Café Madrid offers a little spice to Victoria's culinary life in this tiny restaurant that features a short menu of paella of the day ($8.75), three tapitas (sort of a sampler) including croquette, Spanish omelet, a turnover, Picasso salad, paella, and crunchy bread ($8.25), bocatas (pannini) with distinct Spanish twist ($6.50), salads such as the Picasso (our favorite), which is a combo of potato, tuna, egg, carrots, olives, peas, green beans, corn, asparagus and mayo ($4.25), soup of the day ($4.25), Salt Spring Island organic coffee drinks, and a Saturday tapas brunch ($10.00). Worth a try.

Café Madrid, 762 Broughton Street, (250) 386–1176. Hours: 11:30 A.M.–4:00 P.M. Tuesday–Wednesday, 11:30 A.M.–9:00 P.M. Thursday–Friday, 11:30 A.M.–9:00 P.M. Saturday. No credit cards.

If you don't want to go up a block to the library, cross Broughton and start at the far end of the block. **Tony's Trick & Joke Shop,** at 688 Broughton, is a don't-miss spot. Magicians/owners Tony and Ann Eng truly are "In Business For Fun." While they do a land-office business supplying professional magicians' needs, the place is a town headquarters for every kid and grown-up fascinated by illusion and fantasy.

Tony's Trick & Joke Shop, 688 Broughton Street, (250) 385–6807; www.magictrick.com. Hours: 10:00 A.M.–5:30 P.M. Monday–Saturday, noon–4:00 P.M. Sunday. Wheelchair accessible. Credit cards: Visa, MasterCard.

Hime Sushi hosts many Japanese visitors and local businesspeople who pack in for the reasonable daily lunch specials from $6.45 to $8.45, the Bento lunch box specials at $8.25, and sushi plates, which may combine New York steak, teriyaki, and tempura. Slow, seven-course dinners are only $19.95.

Hime Sushi, 680 Broughton Street, (250) 388–4439. Hours: 11:30 A.M.–9:00 P.M. Monday–Saturday. Sake, beer, wine. Wheelchair accessible. Credit cards: Visa, MasterCard, American Express, enRoute, JCB.

Broughton Street Café-Deli is a cheerful new addition to the inexpensive casual dining scene, with loads of sandwiches including hot and cold Montreal smoked meats, Black Forest ham, chicken salad, tuna and egg salad, marinated tofu sandwiches, daily soups, gluten-free offerings, and made-before-your-eyes peanut butter cookies and butter tarts, everything under $8. Brijitte and Brent Laing serve fair-trade certified organic coffees, and they have used clever decor with window scenes painted on the old walls to totally remake a space formerly occupied by the provincial driving license office.

Broughton Street Café-Deli, 648 Broughton Street, (250) 380–9988; http://pw.engl.uvic.ca/~deli/. Hours: 7:00 A.M.–4:00 P.M., later in summer. Wheelchair accessible. No credit cards.

The **Wine Barrel,** 644 Broughton, is a friendly and interesting wine and wine accessories shop started by Dr. Wilf Krutzmann, a veterinarian who preferred to cheer people more than animals gradually and who recently sold his shop to Bruce Stuart. Here you can buy from a great selection of B.C.'s VQA (Vintners Quality Alliance) best wines at winery prices.

Wilf and now Bruce provide a place to get wine information from all over the world as well as wineglasses; gourmet goods to serve with wine, such as Gigi biscotti; Cuisine Perel chocolate sauces; wine soup; wine racks, Riedel glassware and corkscrews; Schoffeitt spices; organic Kicking Horse coffee; and gift wrap.

Until a few years ago, one could not sell wine in British Columbia unless one's store was actually attached in some way to a government liquor store. After a long, public struggle with the government, Wilf finally triumphed and obtained one of the few private wine shop licenses in June 1998. Victoria mayor Bob Cross cut the ribbon at the broadly publicized reopening of the Wine Barrel as a wineshop actually selling wine. Bruce continues to carry a complete selection of B.C. wines and conducts fabulous and informative Friday evening wine tastings. One of our favorite places.

Wine Barrel, 644 Broughton Street, (250) 388–0606; www.thewine barrel.com. Hours: 10:00 A.M.–7:00 P.M. Monday–Saturday; noon–5:00 P.M. (sometimes later) Sunday. Wheelchair accessible. Credit cards: Visa, MasterCard, Diners, enRoute.

Details is an old-feeling boutique where Barbara Reed features Italian and French provincial place mats; bed, bath, and home accessories; a four-poster bed; jeweled picture frames; and many feminine-pleasing accoutrements.

Details, 618 Broughton Street, (250) 995–2095; Fax: (250) 995–2025. Hours: 10:00 A.M.–6:00 P.M. daily winter, 9:00 A.M.–8:00 P.M. summer. Not wheelchair accessible. Credit cards: Visa, MasterCard.

Ebizo Sushi, a popular local hangout at lunchtime, serves an extensive sushi menu and lunch specials such as lemongrass chicken at $8.95 with soup, rice, and condiments, or beef or salmon teriyaki at $8.95. Many locals say this is the best sushi in Victoria.

Ebizo Sushi, 604 Broughton Street, (250) 383–3234. Hours: lunch 11:30 A.M.–3:00 P.M. Tuesday–Saturday; dinner 5:00–9:30 P.M. Tuesday–

Thursday, 5:00–10:00 P.M. Friday and Saturday. Sake, beer, wine. Some tables wheelchair accessible. Credit cards: Visa, MasterCard.

Whale Store offers killer whale and marine life–watching tours and "anything you can think of with whales on it." Look for whale-decorated aprons, boxer shorts, towels, photos, shirts, and much more.

Whale Store, 602 Broughton Street, (250) 383–ORCA; www.ocean explorations.com. Hours: summer 8:00 A.M.–9:00 P.M. daily, winter 11:00 A.M.–5:00 P.M.; reservations 7:00 A.M.–11:00 P.M. Wheelchair accessible. Credit cards: Visa, MasterCard, American Express, JCB.

Go back a short block to **Broad Street,** one of our favorites. Its old-world ambience and the quality boutiques and restaurants make it a true pleasure to visit, both here and on the other side of the Bay Centre. We'll begin on the west side of Broad Street, south of the Bay Centre.

Simply the Best Fine Clothing & Accessories does not overstate this elegant European boutique with the best clothing *and* the best pen collection in western Canada. Clothing labels include Nautica, Breitling, the Paul & Shark Yachting line, Calvin Klein, handpainted ties to $500, and $150 cashmere socks.

But it's the pens that grab you, ranging in price from $30 to $100,000. Feast your eyes and wallets on Montegrapas, Omas, Lamy, Aurora, Pelikan, and Rotiring. And don't forget your raincoat with zip-out opossum lining. Watch makers include Porsche, Breitling, and Phillippe.

Simply the Best Fine Clothing & Accessories, 1008 Broad Street, (250) 386–6661. Hours: 9:30 A.M.–6:00 P.M. Monday–Saturday, Sunday close to Christmas. Wheelchair accessible. Credit cards: Visa, MasterCard, American Express, JCB.

Winchester Galleries features contemporary Canadian and historical paintings including Canada's Group of Seven, Ann Savage, David Milne, F. S. Coburn, Goodbridge Roberts, and William Kurelek. The company's main gallery is located at 2260 Oak Bay Avenue.

Winchester Galleries, 1010 Broad Street, (250) 286–2773; www .winchestergalleriesltd.com. Hours: 10:00 A.M.–6:00 P.M. Wheelchair accessible. Credit cards: Visa, MasterCard, American Express.

On the east side of Broad Street, still south of the Bay Centre, we'll start with **Flowers on Top,** a fabulous downtown florist with flowers displayed on the sidewalk, bringing cheer to everyone, even on a gloomy day. Victorians love giving flowers to each other and themselves.

> *Flowers on Top, 1005 Broad Street, (250) 383–5262. Hours: when you see the flowers out. Wheelchair accessible. Credit cards: Visa, MasterCard.*

One of Victoria's most popular restaurants and watering holes is **Pagliacci's,** at 1011 Broad. Howie Siegel, his brother David, and Alan Difiori (thank heavens someone was Italian!) opened this magnetic, charismatic, Jewish–Italian–Brooklyn–San Francisco restaurant in 1979 because they couldn't find cappuccino or cheesecake after a Sunday movie.

Thousands of Victorians and visitors rejoice at their good luck. This place is so popular that they don't take reservations; you just line up on the sidewalk, patiently. Good conversation usually mingles, focaccia bread passes, and occasionally a surprise beverage shows up in coffee cups.

Pagliacci's is always the place we go for our first and last nights in Victoria. It's that good and that much fun. Besides, it's our kids' favorite.

At dinner, everything is good, some things creamier and garlickier than others. The names of menu highlights get you laughing before you even order: the Toots Shor New York steak, the Mae West, Prawns Al Capone, Girl from Ipanoodle, and the Hemingway Short Story. Their queen of dishes is pasta with mushrooms, artichokes, Cajun spices, and cream at $17.95. Good wine list.

At lunch the same menu is available, including a "bottomless bowl of soup" ($5.95) and a new salmon fillet

Pagliacci's Famous Tomato Sauce

Pagliacci's, Victoria

1 tbsp. garlic
$^1/_4$ cup olive oil
1 100 oz. tin crushed tomatoes
8 oz. tin tomato paste
10 oz. tomato puree
$1^1/_2$ tsp. fennel seed
1 tbsp. chopped fresh basil or 1
    tsp. dried basil
2 tsp. black pepper
1 tbsp. salt
$^1/_2$ tsp. chiles, crushed
2 tbsp. sugar
2 tbsp. parsley

Sauté garlic in olive oil. Add crushed tomatoes, tomato paste, tomato puree. Season with fennel seed, basil, black pepper, salt, crushed chiles, sugar, and parsley. Bring to simmer. Cook for two hours.

salad. There are booths if you need one, and tables get moved out of the front window at about 9:00 P.M. to make room for the band Sunday–Wednesday. The music is always highest quality, fun, and local. One of our favorites.

> ***Pagliacci's,*** *1011 Broad Street, (250) 386–1662. Hours: lunch 11:30 A.M.–3:00 P.M.; tea, espresso drinks, and sweets 3:00–5:00 P.M.; dinner 5:30–10:00 P.M. Fully licensed. Wheelchair accessible. Credit cards: Visa, MasterCard.*

Local **Adventure Clothing, Ltd.,** an elegant activewear outpost of J. Wilson, is a great addition to this block. Adventure offers Tilley Endurables and Liberty of London among other brands.

> ***Adventure Clothing, Ltd.,*** *1015 Broad Street, (250) 384–3337 or (877) 381–3337; E-mail: sean@islandnet.com. Hours: 9:30 A.M.–5:30 P.M. Monday–Saturday, 11:00 A.M.–4:00 P.M. Sunday. Not wheelchair accessible. Credit cards: Visa, MasterCard.*

This brings you to Fort Street and the Bay Centre mall across Fort. We'll now proceed down the north side of Fort across Government to Wharf Street, then return up the south side back to Government.

   Koto House, a Japanese restaurant and sushi and salad bar, features traditional Japanese and American foods. Beautifully displayed specialty dishes include obento, tofu tempura, and salmon katsu. There are fifteen to twenty main courses at dinner, and ten to thirteen sashimi varieties, all including soup, salad, and rice.

> ***Koto House,*** *510 Fort Street, (250) 382–1514. Hours: lunch 11:30 A.M.–2:00 P.M. daily; dinner 5:00–9:30 P.M. Sunday–Thursday and 5:00–10:00 P.M. Friday–Saturday. Fully licensed. Wheelchair accessible. Credit cards: Visa, MasterCard, American Express.*

Siam Thai Restaurant is a convenient Thai restaurant with interesting dishes such as garlic pepper pork at $8.95 or Pad Talay with prawns, squid, scallops, fish, and veggies in oyster sauce at $13.95. There's an entire vegetarian menu such as hot and spicy vegetarian noodles with egg, vegetables, and tofu at $7.95.

> ***Siam Thai Restaurant,*** *512 Fort Street, (250) 383–9911. Hours: lunch 11:30 A.M.–2:00 P.M.; dinner 5:00 P.M. on. Fully licensed. Wheelchair accessible. Credit cards: Visa, MasterCard, American Express.*

Now we're back to Government Street. Cross it and continue up the south side of Fort. This block has interesting boutiques and galleries, and Antique Row begins 2 blocks east of here. Fort Street is now one way up (east).

A good first stop, at least to look, is **Baden-Baden,** a "casual, classic European elegance" boutique that features German designers and German imports. The owners go to Germany and buy directly, in the style of that famous resort of Baden-Baden. Their wares include beautiful blouses, shirts, jackets, and sweaters.

> *Baden-Baden, 611 Fort Street, (250) 380–1063. Hours: 9:30 A.M.–5:30 P.M. Monday–Saturday. Wheelchair accessible. Credit cards: Visa, Master-Card, American Express.*

Lens & Shutter is absolutely the most convenient camera shop to fill all your camera, film, and developing needs. They have everything, including one-hour developing services; batteries; used cameras and lenses; filters from most manufacturers, such as Nikon, Leica, Minolta, and Vivitar; and bags and cases of all sizes.

> *Lens & Shutter, 615–617 Fort Street, (250) 383–7443; www.lensand shutter.com. Hours: 9:30 A.M.–5:30 P.M. Monday–Saturday. Wheelchair accessible. Credit cards: Visa, MasterCard, American Express.*

Next door, **Knightsbridge Gift Shops Ltd.** is a classic gift shop featuring knick-knacks and Limoges porcelain.

> *Knightsbridge Gift Shops Ltd., 623 Fort Street, (250) 385–1312; www .moorcraft.com. Hours: 9:30 A.M.–5:30 P.M. Monday–Saturday, 11:00 A.M.–5:00 P.M. Sunday. Wheelchair accessible. Credit cards: Visa, Master-Card.*

At the **Golden Chopsticks Restaurant,** with its clean, sparkling interior, exciting lunch specials range from $6.95 to $9.95, including soup, and dinner may include the usuals plus chop suey, deep-fried garlic spare ribs, Szechuan everything, pepper and salt squid or bean curd, and Ma Po Tofu. Family dinners for up to six people, including deliveries to downtown hotels, are $47.95.

> *Golden Chopsticks Restaurant, 627 Fort Street, (250) 388–3148. Hours: 10:00 A.M.–9:00 P.M. Monday–Saturday, 11:00 A.M.–9:00 P.M. Sunday. Fully licensed. Wheelchair accessible. Credit cards: Visa, MasterCard.*

Scaramouche Gallery is a gift shop and gallery where you might find turquoise jewelry, glassware, Nova Scotia seagull pewter, local pottery, native art, Robin Righton's raku pottery, and loads of cat things.

> *Scaramouche Gallery, 635 Fort Street, (250) 386–2215. Hours: summer 9:00 A.M.–9:00 P.M.; winter 9:00 A.M.–6:00 P.M., Sunday 10:00 A.M.–5:00 P.M. Wheelchair accessible. Credit cards: Visa, MasterCard, American Express, Diners, Discover, JCB.*

Tired feet ought to stop at **Footloose Leathers,** where the emphasis is on "shoes that are good for your feet." Keith and Kirsten Greiner sell comfortable shoes such as Gage-Cole, Birkenstock, Mephisto, Ecco, Doc Martens, Australian boots, and John Fleuvogs, as well as orthopedic shoes that look and feel good. Keith also makes custom shoes personally. One of Kathleen's favorites.

> *Footloose Leathers, 637 Fort Street, (250) 383–4040; www.footloose shoes.com. Hours: 9:30 A.M.–5:30 P.M. Monday–Saturday, 11:00 A.M.– 5:00 P.M. Sunday, later in summer and holiday season. Not wheelchair accessible. Credit cards: Visa, MasterCard.*

Paboom is a gallery of wild modern home accessories, such as standing candelabra, see-through flower place mats ($1.95), day-glo flower pots, and mod kitchen utensils—all at great prices.

> *Paboom, 641 Fort Street, (250) 380–0020. Hours: 10:00 A.M.–6:00 P.M. Monday–Wednesday and Saturday, 10:00 A.M.–9:00 P.M. Thursday– Friday, 11:00 A.M.–5:00 P.M. Sunday. Wheelchair accessible. Credit cards: Visa, MasterCard.*

As you cross Broad Street, notice that the Bay Centre takes up the block to the left with some stores we will explore on our way back down Fort Street.

Be sure to visit **Alcheringa Gallery,** the best and most expensive native arts gallery in Victoria. It features tribal art from the Canadian Northwest coast, the island of New Guinea, and aboriginal Australia. B.C. First Peoples artists whose work you usually find here include Robert Davidson, Reg Davidson, Richard Hunt, Tony Hunt, Corrine Hunt, and several other Hunts. Masks, posters, books, and prints are all available from $100 to $10,000. You are welcome to come in, browse, sit on benches, read, contemplate, and learn.

A Haunted City

"Victoria is a haunted city," said the late Robin Skelton, emeritus professor from University of Victoria, poet, and coauthor of A Gathering of Ghosts.

A woman in a flowing white dress haunts Oak Bay Golf Course. In early evening she walks across the course; later in the evening she is seen staring out to sea. She first appeared in 1936, shortly after the strangling murder of Doris Gravlin, a nurse found buried in a sand trap on the course. Suspicion fell on her husband, Victor, a local newspaper reporter who drowned himself while the police were investigating. Doris appears always to young couples walking on or driving by the golf course and usually disappears in a dwindling pool of light. The sightings occur about twice a year and have been reported by responsible, nonhysterical couples.

Several tourists visiting the Point Ellice House have thanked the management for the pleasant woman (always in a blue dress) who gave them directions when there were no docents on duty. Others have reported being scolded by an ethereal woman who ordered them to leave the premises, including two young nurses who camped out one night. The descriptions match that of a younger beautiful Kathleen O'Reilly, the party-loving daughter of Peter and Caroline O'Reilly, born there in 1867. She passed up numerous eligible suitors and returned after World War I to live in the house until her death in 1945, lonely and unhappy. It was rumored that this ghost story was cooked up by family members trying to promote the house as a tourist attraction, but the reports of visitations continued after it was sold to the province in 1974.

The ancient Tod farmhouse has its specter, an Indian woman in chains. James Dunsmuir's mansion at Hatley Park (Royal Roads University) is visited by the spirit of a little old lady. A bearded man in a long greatcoat appears some October mornings sitting on the curb outside the McPherson Theatre. To believers he is called "the Frenchman" because in the 1880s a young French-

man was shot dead, supposedly in an argument during a
poker game held after hours in
the area. Legend has it that
youthful Alexander Duns-
muir of the coal company was
present, and to cover up both
the murder and scandal, the
body was placed sitting on the
curb, propped against a tree.
Dissatisfied that his death
was unsolved, the Frenchman
returns to haunt the scene.

Tombstones at Ross Bay Cemetery

One ghost was the busy resident of the upstairs office of world-famous
Rogers' Chocolates on Government Street. Quite regularly lights and the radio
went on when no one was present, and footsteps going up and down the stairs
and moving about were heard by employees working late in the store. The
eccentric candy maker, Charles Rogers, and his wife, Leah, lived upstairs in
what is now the office for about fifteen years. Charles Rogers died in 1927 still
heartbroken over the suicide of their only son in 1903. His wife sold the business and then gave the fortune to her church and other charities, finally living
in abject poverty in a small James Bay house with no electricity until her death
at eighty-eight in 1958. She was buried at Ross Bay Cemetery but was so poor
there was no money for a headstone. The restless phantom of the offices soon
arrived. Convinced that Leah's spirit might be angry that she had no grave
marker, the Rogers' Chocolates Company bought a headstone for Leah Rogers'
grave. Apparently satisfied, the ghost no longer visits the store.

Fine points: This is one of Victoria's oldest buildings, which opened in 1879 as a grocery store.

Alcheringa Gallery, 665 Fort Street, (250) 383–8224; www .alcheringa-gallery.com. Hours: 9:30 A.M.–5:30 P.M. Monday–Saturday, noon–5:00 P.M. Sunday. Wheelchair accessible. Credit cards: Visa, Master-Card, American Express.

Do not miss **Interactivity Games,** which has wonderful stuff for kids of all ages. Buy a biosphere just like the one taken on a Russian space shuttle or Total yo-yos like the ones Tommy Smothers uses from $5 to $150. A gigantic collection of jigsaw puzzles attracts serious puzzle fans. Magnificent chess sets, enormous kites, game books, and origami paper are also for sale. One of Jerry's favorites.

Interactivity Games, 667 Fort Street, (250) 480–3979. Hours: 10:00 A.M.–5:00 P.M. Monday–Saturday, noon–5:00 P.M. Sunday (until 8:00 or 9:00 P.M. in summer). Wheelchair accessible. Credit cards: Visa, Master-Card.

As you cross Douglas Street, a rather wide street, you approach the part of Fort Street that is marked on city street signs as Antique Row, even though there aren't any antiques for another block. Antique Row has many other interesting shops and restaurants, which we will help you explore.

If you need those photos done now, **One-Hour Photo Express** is truly a one-hour film development place. Services include passport photos, negative prints from slides, and camera repairs. They also sell batteries and accessories.

One-Hour Photo Express, 705 Fort Street, (250) 389–1984. Hours: 8:30 A.M.–5:00 P.M. Monday–Saturday. Wheelchair accessible. Credit cards: Visa, MasterCard, American Express, JCB.

Eyecatching **Amos & Andes Imports** offers eclectic ethnic handmade clothing and bags, including Ecuadorian sweaters, dresses, and shirts; some loose or plus sizes; Asian Creations; and Caribbean Pacific labels, all with some humor.

Amos & Andes Imports, 795 Fort Street, (250) 480–5183; www.amos andandes.com. Hours: 10:00 A.M.–5:30 P.M. daily. Wheelchair accessible. Credit cards: Visa, MasterCard, American Express.

Antique Row

Now cross Blanshard and enjoy the real **Antique Row.** Any of the antiques deal-ers will give you a copy of their brochure, *Victoria's Antique Shops.*

Special Teas is a fabulous-smelling importer, shipper, and retailer of 250 teas from around the world. Owner Irene Drmla offers tastes, whiffs, and tea leaf readings; sells to bed-and-breakfasts and restaurants throughout the West Coast; and will send your order by mail once you are hooked.

> *Special Teas, 803 Fort Street, (250) 386–8327; Fax: (250) 386–8329; www.specialtea.com. Hours: 10:00 A.M.–5:00 P.M. Monday–Wednesday, 10:00 A.M.–6:00 P.M. Thursday–Saturday, noon–4:00 P.M. Sunday. Wheelchair accessible. Credit cards: Visa, MasterCard, American Express.*

MVP Sports Cards serves as a hangout for sports fans of all ages and sexes and sells sports hats, cards, Christmas ornaments, wall clocks, novelty phones, and everything you can imagine connected to hockey, baseball, basketball, and foot-ball, plus NASCAR memorabilia. Posted prices include the 7 percent GST.

> *MVP Sports Cards, 807 Fort Street, (250) 380–1958. Hours: 9:00 A.M.–5:30 P.M. Monday–Saturday, noon–4:00 P.M. Sunday and holi-days. Wheelchair accessible. Credit cards: Visa, MasterCard.*

AAA Stamp, Coin, Jewellery Inc. and **Century Antiques and Collectibles,** 809–811 Fort Street, feature estate jewelry, worldwide coins, placer gold, and an eclectic mix of silver, porcelain, dolls, toys, and collectibles.

> *AAA Stamp, Coin, Jewellery Inc., 809 Fort Street, (250) 384–1315. Century Antiques and Collectibles, 811 Fort Street, (250) 361–2677.*

Recollection Antique and Collectibles Mall represents seventy-five antiques dealers of all tastes and price ranges.

> *Recollection Antique and Collectibles Mall, 817A Fort Street, (250) 385–1902. Hours: 10:00 A.M.–5:00 P.M. Monday–Saturday, noon–4:00 P.M. Sunday. Wheelchair accessible. Credit cards: Visa, MasterCard, American Express.*

At **Pacific Antiques,** Leonard Clarke specializes in wonderful conversation as well as eighteenth- and nineteenth-century English, Irish, and Oriental furniture, silver, glass, and porcelain. He also has 450 pieces of British brass cabinet hardware. Clarke, who has lived in Canada for more than twenty years, has joined with **Wendy Russell Jewellery** in this charming location.

> *Pacific Antiques and Wendy Russell Jewellery, 829 Fort Street, (250)*
> *388–5311; www.pacificantiques.com. Hours: 9:30 A.M.–5:30 P.M. daily.*
> *Wheelchair accessible. Credit cards: Visa, MasterCard, American Express.*

Van Isle Coin & Stamp is just what it says, specializing in buying and selling gold wafers, Krugerrands, maple leafs, collector coins, stamp supplies, junk silver coins, and silver bars.

> *Van Isle Coin & Stamp, 831 Fort Street, (250) 382–6331. Hours: 9:00*
> *A.M.–5:00 P.M. Monday–Saturday. Wheelchair accessible. Credit cards:*
> *Visa, MasterCard.*

Angela Fashions offers cramped but intriguing displays of dramatically feminine dresses and shoes intended for weddings, bridal parties, mothers of the bride, and formal wear. Smartly, for everyone's sake, there is a children's play center in the corner.

> *Angela Fashions, 833 Fort Street, (250) 480–0114; www.angelafashions*
> *.com. Hours: 10:00 A.M.–5:00 P.M. Monday–Saturday. Wheelchair accessible. Credit cards: none.*

Arca Nova is David Newberry's extension of his late cousin, Fred Newberry's, shop. David has added collectibles, affordable prints, and reproductions to the handcrafted decoys, English and Oriental antiques, collectors' pieces, silver, china, and art deco.

> *Arca Nova, 835 Fort Street, (250) 383–6540. Hours: 11:00 A.M.–5:00*
> *P.M. Monday–Saturday. Wheelchair accessible. Credit cards: Visa, MasterCard, American Express.*

At **Romanoff & Co. Antiques,** 837 Fort Street, Paul Freeman and Brandi Roth represent a new generation of antiques dealers with pizzazz and flair. The store's plum walls, lighted glass display cases, and carved wooden chairs make it one of the most warm and elegant places in the area.

Romanoff's features china dolls, silver, art glass, bronzes, estate jewelry, paintings, historical prints, ancient coins, watches, and artifacts. Paul's brother

Ian Freeman owns Penny Black Antiques, Stamps & Coins, and his parents own the 1800 Shop next to Penny Black, both on Langley behind Murchie's Tea and Coffee.

Romanoff's has added more Tuskers Collectible Toys ("sold to help African wildlife"), Steiff bears, mechanical toys, and collectors' toys from around the world. Romanoff's toy sales support the David Sheldrick Wildlife Trust. Paul's old English sheepdog, Winston Gallagher Romanoff, is a neighborhood favorite.

Romanoff & Co. Antiques, 837 Fort Street, (250) 480–1543. Hours: 10:30 A.M.–5:30 P.M. Monday–Saturday in summer, or by appointment. Wheelchair accessible. Credit cards: Visa, MasterCard, American Express.

Britannia & Co. Antiques has some prestigious pieces, specializing in Great Britain and Empire coins and stamps, paper money, watches, and "things with a history."

Britannia & Co. Antiques, 828 Fort Street, (250) 480–1954. Hours: 10:30 A.M.–5:30 P.M. Monday–Saturday. Wheelchair accessible. Credit cards: Visa, MasterCard, American Express.

Voted Best Lunch by *Victoria News* readers, the woman-owned **Blue Fox Cafe** at 919 Fort is colorful, cheerful, and terrific. Megan and her then week-old son came here for her "coming out" lunch. And, of course, she ran into friends.

Lunch ranges from lush burgers to creamy shrimp Caesar salad and everything in between. Their potatoes are exceptional. Good espresso drinks. David thinks the gigantic homemade veggie burgers are the best in town, while Jerry goes gaga over the seafood club sandwich (smoked salmon and shrimp).

Breakfast may be the best in town also, with the omelets rivaled only by those at John's Place. Pancakes with fruit are humongous, yogurt and fruit likewise, toast may be on their homemade bread (yes!), and cinnamon rolls to die for, all reasonably priced. Kathleen thinks the veggie omelet is the best anywhere.

There's usually a line outside on weekends, and it's nearly impossible to get in between noon and 1:00 P.M., but it's worth the wait, honest. The menu is written on most walls in primary colors plus some, and the chintz tablecloths' colors cover the spectrum, superimposed with Far Side cartoons at each place. One of our favorites.

Blue Fox Cafe, 919 Fort Street, (250) 380–1683. Hours: 7:30 A.M.– 4:00 P.M. Monday–Friday, 8:00 A.M.–4:00 P.M. Saturday, 9:00 A.M.–

3:00 P.M. Sunday. Beer and wine. Wheelchair accessible. Credit cards: Visa, MasterCard.

After you pass the office buildings at the Vancouver Street corners, you will be on the busiest block of Antique Row.

Old 'n' Gold purchases and sells jewelry, watches, clocks, collectibles, and a few antiques.

Old 'n' Gold, 1011 Fort Street, (250) 361–1892. Hours: 10:00 A.M.–5:00 P.M. Monday–Saturday. Not wheelchair accessible. Credit cards: Visa, MasterCard, American Express.

Food lovers must at least go into **Captain Cook's Bakery Ltd.,** a great bakery with fine hot and cold deli foods at the back counter, including flatbreads (pizza), stuffed peppers, meats and vegetables, Greek salad, tortellini, fruit, coleslaw, meat and cheese pasta salads, meat pies, salamis, and daily specials. A huge range of breads from ryes and raisin breads to twists, sweet and sourdough, and traditional European breads tempts, as well as sweets and pastries galore. Often voted Victoria's Best Donut Shop, Captain Cook's also has a full-service restaurant upstairs with a huge wall and ceiling mural depicting Captain Cook's adventures.

Sometimes you need to take a number, because this place buzzes. Tearoom and restrooms are upstairs, too. Victorians hang out with tea, lunch, or coffee at ample outside tables. Try the low-fat muffins or an apple fritter with coffee ($1.99). One of Kathleen's favorites.

Captain Cook's Bakery Ltd., 1019 Fort Street, (250) 386–4333. Hours: 6:30 A.M.–6:30 P.M. Monday–Saturday. Beer and wine (upstairs restaurant). Outside and main level wheelchair accessible, upstairs is not. Credit cards: Visa, MasterCard.

Jean Hutton Custom Framing truly does do "framing with a flair" as advertised. The shop frames everything either plainly or ornately and sells fine-art reproductions, posters by interesting artists from David Hockney to Paul Klee, and food posters, too.

Jean Hutton Custom Framing, 1031 Fort Street, (250) 382–4493. Hours: 10:00 A.M.–5:00 P.M. Monday–Saturday. Wheelchair accessible. Credit cards: Visa, MasterCard.

Vancouver Island Soup, located in the MOSAIC building, makes soup—surprise! The MOSAIC is a former union hall converted to a condominium complex with retail shops on the street floor. The terrific Chronicles of Crime mystery bookstore, Skandia Jewelry, and the Med Grill have opened and cheer up this building.

Roger's Juke Box Records sticks with oldies. Classic 33 rpm albums are stacked in cartons inside the store, and 50-cent album crates line the sidewalk in front. A 1960s-feeling kinda place.

Roger's Juke Box Records, 1071 Fort Street, (250) 381–2526. Hours: 10:00 A.M.–5:30 or 6:00 P.M. daily. Wheelchair accessible. Credit cards: Visa, MasterCard.

Avalon Restaurant is a slightly funky little restaurant with all-day breakfast, homemade oaten bread, and strawberry-rhubarb-ginger jam, with local artists' work, such as wacky wall clocks and mirror creations, on the walls. Full breakfasts range from lighter fare (starting at $5.55) to "The Cure": two eggs, two slices of bacon, two sausages, ham, grilled mushrooms, sliced tomatoes, cottage potatoes, toast, juice, and coffee ($18.95 for two). Other options include low-carb breakfast wraps and eggs Benedict.

Lunch includes several salads, quesadillas, burgers, wraps, fajitas, and a pierogi platter of eight potato and cheddar cheese–filled dumplings sautéed with bacon and onions, served with soup or salad ($8.25).

Avalon Restaurant, 1075 Fort Street, (250) 385–2129. Hours: 8:00 A.M.–2:30 P.M. daily. Ten percent off for students on Monday, for everyone with coupon from take-out menu Monday–Friday. Wheelchair accessible. Credit cards: Visa, MasterCard, American Express.

J & J Watch And Clock Repair has a surprisingly interesting collection of new and old wall clocks, pocket watches, and wristwatches. Watchmaker Canh N. Ho repairs all clocks with a smile and will change a watch battery while you wait.

J & J Watch And Clock Repair, 1046 Fort Street, (250) 361–4480. Hours: 9:30 A.M.–5:30 P.M. daily. Wheelchair accessible. Credit cards: Visa, MasterCard.

Charles Baird Antiques is a welcome addition to Antique Row. A venture into this beautiful, narrow shop (8½ feet wide) is an elegant treat, as is Charles Baird's sense of humor.

> *Charles Baird Antiques, 1044A Fort Street, (250) 384–8809. Hours: 9:00 A.M.–5:00 P.M. Monday–Saturday, closed Sunday. Wheelchair accessible. No credit cards, "but will accept checks, small children, dogs, old autos."*

In **Vanity Fair Antique Mall,** forty antiques dealers sell their collections and provide an interesting experience and hours of entertainment. Everything is here. We have found exceptional books and old kitchen utensils, dolls, memorabilia, china, spoons, and more in rooms and rooms of great stuff and artwork. Victorians regularly vote this place Best Antique Shop.

> *Vanity Fair Antique Mall, 1044 Fort Street, (250) 380–7274; www.vanityfairantiques.com. Hours: 10:00 A.M.–5:30 P.M. Monday–Saturday, 11:00 A.M.–4:00 P.M. Sunday. Wheelchair accessible. Credit cards: Visa, MasterCard.*

At **Domus Antica Galleries,** Helga Past specializes in eighteenth- and nineteenth-century furniture, porcelain, glass, paintings, brass, and pewter. You must see the copper collection!

> *Domus Antica Galleries, 1038–1040 Fort Street, (250) 385–5443. Hours: 10:30 A.M.–5:00 P.M. daily. Wheelchair accessible. Credit cards: Visa, MasterCard, American Express.*

Not Just Pretty is a fabulous new shop featuring earth-conscious clothing made of organic cotton, Tencel, or organic silks; organic bath and perfume lines; and soy candles. Not Just Pretty's bags are even made from recycled billboards! Pam Skelton and her family moved to Victoria from New York City in 1971, and she opened the Vegetable Restaurant, the first vegetarian restaurant in Victoria (now gone), as she resumed teaching for thirty years in Victoria schools.

> *Not Just Pretty, 1036 Fort Street, (250) 414–0414. Hours: 10:00 A.M.–6:00 P.M. daily. Wheelchair accessible. Credit cards: Visa, MasterCard, American Express.*

Plenty Epicurean Pantry is where environmentally ethical Trevor Walker sells loads of organic and ethnic specialty foods, including many from British Columbia; organic and fair-trade teas and hard-to-find spices; herbs; mushrooms; cheeses; soaps; pottery; chocolates; and books. A good place for foodies to get lost in a cozy shop.

> *Plenty Epicurean Pantry, 1034 Fort Street, (250) 380–7654; www .epicureanpantry.ca. Hours: 10:00 A.M.–6:00 P.M. Monday–Wednesday, 10:00 A.M.–7:00 P.M. Thursday–Saturday. Wheelchair accessible. Credit cards: Visa, MasterCard.*

Shabby Tiques features shabby chic estate linens and new linens, all in pink, red, and white. Nia DaCosta Reis opened Shabby Tiques, appropriately, on Valentine's Day.

> *Shabby Tiques, 1032 Fort Street, (250) 386–1177. Hours: 10:00 A.M.– 5:00 P.M. Monday–Saturday, noon–4:00 P.M. Sunday. Wheelchair accessible. Credit cards: Visa, MasterCard.*

Sally Bun, a spinoff of the Sally Cafe, is ideally convenient for shoppers and local workers alike. Here you can enjoy light snacks, including dim sum–style buns filled with sun-dried tomatoes, artichokes, and pesto; pizza makings; chocolate; mushrooms; or daily surprises. Soup and salad attract lots of locals, as do the coffee and outrageous cinnamon buns, splitable for two for breakfast.

> *Sally Bun, 1030 Fort Street, (250) 360–1889. Hours: 10:00 A.M.–5:00 P.M. Monday–Saturday. Wheelchair accessible. Credit cards: Visa, Master-Card.*

Applewood Antiques features a true emporium of great collectibles, restorations, solid wood period furniture, fine art, distinctive antiques, and old photos, including some by Man Ray.

> *Applewood Antiques, 1028 Fort Street, (250) 360–1889. Hours: 10:00 A.M.–5:00 P.M. Monday–Saturday. Wheelchair accessible. Credit cards: Visa, MasterCard.*

The best Chinese restaurant in Victoria is, indisputably, **J & J Wonton Noodle House** at 1012 Fort. This is the most creative Chinese cuisine we have ever experienced. The entire kitchen is glassed in so you can watch the cooks, a restaurant fad rarely indulged in by Chinese restaurants. Co-owner/chef Joseph Wong spent months in China learning more exciting cooking techniques and specialty dishes.

Of course, noodles are the focus, as in soups, meins, and funs. Try the daily luncheon specials. Lunch costs from $6.95 up, and delightful dinner dishes range from $3.95 to $13.95. Full vegetarian menu available at all times, including vegetables and tofu with black bean sauce ($9.95). Air-conditioned. Be sure to try the ginger-garlic fried chicken! One of our favorites.

J & J Wonton Noodle House, 1012 Fort Street, (250) 383–0680; www .jjnoodlehouse.com. Hours: 11:00 A.M.–2:00 P.M., 4:30–8:30 P.M. Tuesday–Saturday. Beer and wine. Wheelchair accessible. Credit cards: Visa, MasterCard, American Express, JCB.

Wedged between two of Victoria's best restaurants is an interior design and home accessory studio called **Room by Room by Room,** which has elegant funk from picture frames to candle lamps and soji screens.

Room by Room by Room, 1010B Fort Street, (250) 388–6780. Hours: 10:00 A.M.–5:00 P.M. Monday–Saturday. Wheelchair accessible. Credit cards: Visa, MasterCard.

Da Tandoor, lauded by many as Victoria's best Indian restaurant, features vegetarian, poultry, lamb, seafood, and Tandoori kabobs. We have tried many dishes here and all were excellent, but one or two have been slightly dry. Da Tandoor also sells Indian and Pakistani jarred foods and chutneys.

Da Tandoor, 1010 Fort Street, (250) 384–6333. Hours: dinner after 5:00 P.M. daily. Beer and wine. Wheelchair accessible. Credit cards: Visa, MasterCard. Reservations recommended.

Cafe Brio is one of the best restaurants in Victoria, and for good reason. Co-owner Greg Hays started the renowned Herald Street Caffé and sold it in 1992. With food philosopher Silvia Marcolini he redid the Marina Restaurant and later opened Cafe Brio. Cafe Brio is now a restaurant where chefs go for something special, and Herald Street Caffé is closed.

Cafe Brio gets all of its poultry products from Lyle and Fiona Young in Cowichan Bay, who have received SPCA awards for humane treatment of livestock. All of their beef is from Alberta and is AAA grade or better.

A new feature at Cafe Brio is their three-course Chef's Dinner every evening for $28 (must be seated by 6:15 P.M.). This real deal may include local oysters or endive salad; crispy chicken confit or spot prawn, clam, and halibut ragoût; and dessert choices may include vanilla bean crème brûlée or hazelnut cake with espresso ice cream.

Chef Laurie Munn makes fabulous soups, house-made sausage, the best crispy roasted sweetbreads ($15), grilled quail ($16), and fresh-made pastas ($10–$24).

Main dishes include rib eye steak with herb buttered frites ($38–$43 for two), Dungeness crab–wrapped halibut ($29), Cowichan Bay Farm chicken breast with mascarpone potato purée ($29), organic Sloping Hills Farm heritage breed pork ($26), or osso buco ($28), with accompaniments $7 extra. Cafe Brio's menus always suggest a wine to be paired with every dish and offer several ports, grappas, and six single-malt scotches.

Cafe Brio, 944 Fort Street, (250) 383–0009; www.cafe-brio.com. Hours: dinner daily from 5:30 P.M. Fully licensed. Wheelchair accessible. Credit cards: Visa, MasterCard, American Express.

Pacific Editions exhibits, distributes, and sells the best of Northwest Coastal native fine art and limited-edition prints, silver objects, and jewelry. Custom framing is also available here. Artists represent several styles from Gitxsen Wet'-suwet'en, Haida, Kwakwaka'wakw, Nisga'a, Nuu-chah-Nulth, Ojibway, Salish, Tlingit, and Tsimshian nations.

Pacific Editions, 942 Fort Street, (250) 388–5233; www.pacific editions.ca. Hours: 9:30 A.M.–5:00 P.M. Monday–Saturday. Credit cards: Visa, MasterCard.

Catchily named **Senzushi** is said by many to be the best sushi restaurant in Victoria. You will also enjoy its attractive decor.

Senzushi, 940 Fort Street, (250) 385–4320. Hours: 11:00 A.M.–10:00 P.M. Monday–Saturday. Beer and wine. Wheelchair accessible. Credit cards: Visa, MasterCard.

Lund's Auctioneers & Appraisers is a great place to find treasures, including fine-art estate sales and collectibles. Some galleries buy furniture here, then repaint and resell it. Auctions take place weekly on Tuesday at 1:00 and 7:00 P.M. You may preview the next week's sale goods Saturday from 10:00 A.M. to 4:00 P.M., Monday from 9:00 A.M. to 6:00 P.M., and Tuesday from 9:00 A.M. until sale time.

Lund's Auctioneers & Appraisers, 926 Fort Street, (250) 386–3308 or (800) 363–5863; www.lunds.com. Hours: see above. Wheelchair accessible. Credit cards: Visa, MasterCard.

Cross Quadra to the **SpiceJammer.** Some locals think this is the best Indian restaurant around, serving a variety of foods. East Africa natives Amin and Bilkiz (Billie) named their restaurant after the first ship that brought spices to Victoria, via a journey similar to their own. At lunch, sandwiches are all three-tiered, such as a BLT with soup and tossed salad for $6.50. At dinner have Tandoori kabobs ($9.95), Vindaloo chicken ($13.95), spinach curry ($11.95), or clay oven–cooked chicken tikka ($12.95). Samosas vary by filling, including vegetarian. The menu makes easy sense, and the food and decor are just as straightforward. One of Megan's favorites.

SpiceJammer, 852 Fort Street, (250) 480–1055; www.spicejammer .com. Hours: 11:30 A.M.–2:30 P.M., 5:00–9:00 P.M. Monday–Friday; noon–3:00 P.M., 5:00–10:00 P.M. Saturday. Fully licensed. Wheelchair accessible. Credit cards: Visa, MasterCard.

Miroirs is an elegant shop that features "the most beautiful mirrors in the world," meaning a few antiques and hundreds of Canadian reproductions of classic European mirrors. John Doyle has created a pleasant ambience with Oriental rugs and warm red walls.

Miroirs, 832 Fort Street, (250) 361–3382; cell: (250) 216–7820; E-mail: sales@miroir.com. Hours: 11:00 A.M.–5:00 P.M. daily. Wheelchair accessible, but tight. Credit cards: Visa, MasterCard.

The **Flag Shop,** 904 Gordon Street, is part of a chain that manufactures and sells flags of all nations and makes them for personal or public causes and beliefs. It also sells pins, crests, patches, and decals. Truly a fun place to explore and temporarily transport yourself elsewhere. Don Flynn, Jim Webb, and Jim and Chantal answer questions most graciously.

Flag Shop, 904 Gordon Street, (250) 382–3524 or (800) 665–3996; www.flagshop.com/victoria. Hours: 9:00 A.M.–5:30 P.M. weekdays, 10:00 A.M.–4:00 P.M. Saturday. Not wheelchair accessible. Credit cards: Visa, MasterCard, American Express.

At **Mirage Design** (830 Fort Street) imaginative Rob Bond features dramatic reproduction furniture and furnishings, including antique brass from Italy, bronze, and silver. As an interior and exterior designer, Rob entertains here and at his **Mirage Home & Garden** (822 Fort Street), both with his exciting personality and his sensational merchandising, which appears to be a jumbled museum of fantastic home and garden accessories, including candles. Check out both shops.

> *Mirage Design and Mirage Home & Garden, 830 and 822 Fort Street, (250) 382–4831. Hours: 11:00 A.M.–5:00 P.M. daily. Wheelchair accessible but very tight. Credit cards: Visa, MasterCard, American Express, Diners.*

Go in to experience **Classic Silverware** in the Chelsea Building. In contrast to some other antiques shops, this one's sign welcomes you and means it: WE'RE OPEN. FEEL FREE TO COME IN AND BROWSE.

Margaret Kuyvenhoven and Ita Laninga specialize in discontinued silverplated flatware at affordable prices, vintage linens, lace, old baptismal gowns, tablecloths, and bedding and are contemplating moving across the street. A friendly place.

> *Classic Silverware, 826 Fort Street, (250) 383–6860. Hours: 10:00 A.M.–5:00 P.M. Monday–Saturday. Wheelchair accessible. Credit cards: Visa, MasterCard.*

Cairo Coffee Merchants, a designer coffee bean (roasted daily) boutique, also carries proper teapots, mugs, packaged spices, Bombay chutneys, and imported teas. You can mix your own tea blends.

> *Cairo Coffee Merchants, 774 Fort Street, (250) 386–3937. Hours: 9:00 A.M.–5:30 P.M. Monday–Saturday. Wheelchair accessible. Credit cards: none.*

Be sure to try **New Saigon Vietnamese Restaurant** unless you are MSG sensitive. Clean and pleasantly decorated with Vietnamese prints and live plants, New Saigon offers truly authentic Vietnamese cuisine, such as grilled garlic meatballs with meat brochette and rice sticks ($5.75), fish hot pot ($10.95), pork hot pot marinated in fish sauce with caramel sauce ($8.95), noodle soups, and green papaya salad ($5.50).

New Saigon Vietnamese Restaurant, 772 Fort Street, (250) 385–5516. Hours: 11:00 A.M.–3:00 P.M., 5:00–9:00 P.M. Monday–Saturday. Liquor not served. Wheelchair accessible. Credit cards: Visa, MasterCard, enRoute, American Express.

Locals come to **Patisserie Daniel** daily for exceptional salads and lunches, pastries, cakes, low-fat goodies, vegetable crostini, tomato rosemary flatbread, and dressings made with peach vinegar. One of our favorites.

Patisserie Daniel, 768 Fort Street, (250) 361–4243. Hours: 8:00 A.M.–5:30 P.M. Monday–Friday, 9:30 A.M.–5:30 P.M. Saturday. Wheelchair accessible. Credit cards: Visa, MasterCard.

Women will have a pleasant surprise at **B.C. Shavers & Hobbies,** a wonderful emporium of things traditionally masculine: shaver (and hair dryer) repair; sharpening of knives, scissors, and tools; scale model trains and race cars; air brushes; compressors; paints; metal detectors; model boats and planes; and electric shavers. It also sells a huge collection of puzzles and railroad books, X-acto craft tools, and collectibles. A good place to break the molds, so to speak. One of our favorites.

B.C. Shavers & Hobbies, 742 Fort Street, (250) 383–0051; www.bc shaver.com. Hours: 9:00 A.M.–5:30 P.M. Monday–Thursday, Saturday; 9:00 A.M.–9:00 P.M. Friday. Wheelchair accessible. Credit cards: Visa, MasterCard, American Express.

At **Russell Books,** Diana and Russell del Pol and daughter hold forth at their 9,000-square-foot, three-floor book emporium with remarkable collections of calendars (Marilyn Monroe fans, run!); cards; new, used, and antiquarian books; and historic prints and posters. Browsers of all stripes are welcomed by a member of the family, which includes adult children Andrea, Brandon, Sean, and Chad. One of Jerry's favorites.

Russell Books, 734 Fort Street, (250) 361–4447; www.russellbooks.com. Hours: 9:00 A.M.–5:30 P.M. Monday–Saturday, noon–5:00 P.M. Sunday. Wheelchair accessible. Credit cards: Visa, MasterCard, American Express.

Unless you think you're only going to tempt yourself, be sure to take a number the minute you walk into the **Rhineland Bakery.** The deep, fully packed meat pies, cookies, breads (including chipmunk health bread, made with wheat, oats, flax, barley, and sunflower seeds), and gorgeous sweets for all occasions make you want to stay.

Rhineland Bakery, 730 Fort Street, (250) 383–9725. Hours: 7:00 A.M.–5:30 P.M. Monday–Friday, 7:30 A.M.–5:30 P.M. Saturday. Wheelchair accessible. Credit cards: Visa, MasterCard.

How do Victorians survive? **Dutch Bakery & Coffee Shop,** another successful sweet shop, tempts the browsing weary with homemade chocolates, pastries, meat pies (from $1.55), buttery cookies ($2.70 a dozen), and wedding and birthday cakes made the same day you order. Breakfasts until 12:30 P.M.

Dutch Bakery & Coffee Shop, 718 Fort Street, (250) 385–1012. Hours: 7:30 A.M.–5:30 P.M. Tuesday–Saturday. Wheelchair accessible. Credit cards: none.

Stevenson's Shoe Clinic calls itself "the essential Birkenstock repair center" (although others do it). Mephisto, Clark, Rockport, Ecco, and Timberland shoes and Samsonite luggage all are fixed here happily and promptly.

Stevenson's Shoe Clinic, 714 Fort Street, (250) 383–8615. Hours: 8:00 A.M.–5:30 P.M. Monday–Friday, 8:45 A.M.–5:00 P.M. Saturday. Wheelchair accessible. Credit cards: Visa, MasterCard.

La Cache is a super-feminine boutique that makes even tomboys feel girly, with lots of print dresses for little girls, mothers, and grandmothers; children's and adult bedding; dishes; jewelry; gifts; curtains; and other home accessories.

La Cache, the Bay Centre at Fort Street entrance, (250) 384–6343; www.lacache.com. Hours: 9:30 A.M.–6:00 P.M. Monday–Saturday. Wheelchair accessible with inside ramp. Credit cards: Visa, MasterCard, American Express.

Scallywags is an elegant children's boutique (yes, it's the same as the one in the Fairmont Empress Hotel) featuring children's clothes, dolls, teddy bears, and stuffed dolls galore. Go in just for the fun of it.

Scallywags, 624 Fort Street, (250) 360–2570; www.scallywags-island .ca. Hours: 9:30 A.M.–5:30 P.M. Monday–Saturday, 10:00 A.M.–5:00

P.M. Sunday, later in summer and holiday season. Wheelchair accessible. Credit cards: Visa, MasterCard.

If you want to explore more of the Bay Centre, go ahead. We're going to continue. View Street runs east and west right outside the northern doors of the Bay Centre. Many of the shops on the north (non–the Bay Centre) side of View Street below Broad also face on Trounce Alley, which you must explore. This private street, designed and developed by Thomas Trounce, used to be closed off once a year to keep it from technically becoming a public way.

This side of Trounce Alley was built in 1889 by developer/architect Thomas Trounce. It has served as a bank, YMCA, and Victoria Stock Exchange. A duplicate building across the alley burned down in 1910.

The **Tapa Bar,** a delightfully Spanish reworking of Vin Santo Urban Bistro, offers tapas and entrees from Four Bean Salad with salted cod, calamari fritos ($7), Bisteck Madagascar ($12), swordfish cebiche ($3), or mussels, chicken, and chorizo fondue to pastas and thin-crust pizza. A pitcher of sangria is only $14. Green and white checked cloths cover outdoor tables while bold paintings hang on mustard walls inside.

Tapa Bar, 620 Trounce Alley, (250) 383–0013. Hours: 11:30 A.M.– 10:00 P.M. Monday–Thursday, 11:30 A.M.–midnight Friday–Saturday. Full bar. Wheelchair accessible. Credit cards: Visa, MasterCard, American Express.

Visit **All in Bloom** for the cheer, as well as for the home and garden accessories. Shelagh Macartney owns and hosts this boutique, chock-full of the perfect sun/shade hat, smocks, gifts with a floral theme, books, unique papers and cards, ribbons, gardening tools and gloves, teensy rubbed-color plant pots from $7.95 to $13.95, and mosaic-covered vases. Don't miss the Near Naked Man ironing-board cover (Kathleen bought two), sushi candles, and Virgin and Slut soaps and lip balm.

Just as important, Shelagh's shop is the hilarious communications community/ social center for a whole segment of Victoria. Even if you don't need anything, go in just to enjoy her and her customers.

All in Bloom, 616 Trounce Alley, (250) 383–1883. Hours: 10:00 A.M.–5:30 P.M. Monday–Saturday, noon–4:00 P.M. Sunday. Wheelchair accessible. Credit cards: Visa, MasterCard, American Express, and "no library cards," says Shelagh.

Instinct Art and Gifts offers New Age spiritual gifts, incense, tapes, and books with interesting native and Celtic jewelry in a very peaceful and nonaggressive atmosphere. Dumb questions answered graciously here.

> *Instinct Art and Gifts, 622 View Street, (250) 388–5033. Hours: 10:00 A.M.–5:30 P.M. Monday–Saturday, noon–5:00 P.M. Sunday. Wheelchair accessible. Credit cards: Visa, MasterCard.*

We're now at Broad Street, north of the Bay Centre.

On the back (north) side of the Bay Centre, facing View and Broad Streets, food lovers absolutely must visit the Tuscan Kitchen and Haute Cuisine Cookware.

Gerri and Mauro Schelini's **Tuscan Kitchen** specializes in Italian food stuffs; majolica and rustica ceramics; tools; gadgets; Röste, All Clad, and Peugeot pots and pans; Dean & DeLuca herbs and spices; sauces and olive oils; Mario Batali cookware and kitchen utensils; MAC knives; confections; twenty balsamic vinegars; and loads of Italian cookbooks.

> *Tuscan Kitchen, 653 View Street, (250) 386–8191; www.thetuscan kitchen.com. Hours: 9:30 A.M.–6:00 P.M. and later Monday–Saturday, 11:00 A.M.–5:00 P.M. Sunday. Wheelchair accessible. Credit cards: Visa, MasterCard.*

A must-stop is the **West End Gallery,** at the northeast corner of View and Broad. West End Gallery features Canadian artists and hosts the annual Canadian Glass Show, featuring the work of more than sixty artists. Try to see the work of Grant Leier and Barton Nixie.

> *West End Gallery, 1203 Broad Street, (250) 388–0009; Fax: (250) 388–0099; www.westendgalleryltd.com. Hours: 10:00 A.M.–5:30 P.M. Monday–Friday, 10:00 A.M.–5:00 P.M. Saturday, noon–4:00 P.M. Sunday and holidays. Not wheelchair accessible. Credit cards: Visa, MasterCard.*

Haute Cuisine Cookware is Victoria's best kitchen accessories shop and one of the most enjoyable, period. Stephanie Clark has assembled the finest of everything: Le Creuset, Emile Henry porcelain cookware, iron grills, loads of peppermills (including brass), woks (12 inches–30 inches)—including the largest wok and peppermill on the island—Martha Stewart parody books, magnetic poetry for your fridge, Bodum coffee presses, aprons, place mats, napkins, the perfect garlic press and wine bottle openers, a superior selection of cookbooks, tea kettles, and designer teapots. One of our favorites.

Braciole del Vinaio

Tuscan Kitchen, Victoria

(Author's note: Vin Santo or another sweet dessert wine is key to this recipe!—Kathleen Hill)

For the meat:
6 veal cutlets
1 tbsp. unsalted butter
A drop of Vin Santo or other sweet dessert wine

For the toasts:
6 slices day-old Tuscan bread
Milk
Flour
Freshly grated Parmesan cheese
Pepper
Drops of Vin Santo or other sweet dessert wine

For the mushrooms:
3 oz. fresh mushrooms, brushed clean with a cloth and sliced
2 tbsp. olive oil
$1/2$ clove garlic, minced
Drops of Vin Santo or other sweet wine

Dip the slices of bread in milk, dredge them with flour, and then cover in grated Parmesan cheese.

In a skillet large enough for the meat slices to lie flat, cook them in the butter, turning them once or twice and sprinkling them with a few drops of Vin Santo or other dessert wine. While the meat is cooking, sauté the bread on both sides, and sprinkle it with a couple drops of Vin Santo.

While all this is going on, heat the olive oil in a pot, add the mushrooms and garlic, sauté the mushrooms, and add a few drops more of Vin Santo when finished.

Place slices of bread on plates, lay slices of meat over them, and spoon mushrooms over both. Add pepper to taste. Serves 6.

Haute Cuisine Cookware, 1210 Broad Street, (250) 388–9906. Hours: 10:00 A.M.–6:00 P.M. Monday–Saturday. Wheelchair accessible, but be careful. Credit cards: Visa, MasterCard.

We usually check in at the **Vitamin Shop,** a health shop to end them all, featuring 4,000 items of everything you need away from home or at home: vitamins, Natural Factors, Good Health Guides, Quest, Nature's Way, Herbal Select teas, Gaia herbs, and consultations.

Vitamin Shop, 1212 Broad Street, (250) 386–1212; www.canadian vitaminshop.com. Hours: 9:00 A.M.–6:00 P.M. Monday–Friday, 9:30 A.M.–5:30 P.M. Saturday, 11:00 A.M.–5:00 P.M. Sunday. Wheelchair accessible. Credit cards: Visa, MasterCard.

Locals like **Eugene's Greek Restaurant on Broad,** which offers dining inside or at a couple of sidewalk tables, plus takeout. Because of its business-area location, cafeteria-style service is quick whether you order souvlaki, gyros, spanakopita, tiropita, Greek salad, or baklava. You can also get comfort foods such as chicken pie for $3.50 and "criss cut" fries at $2.25. Souvlaki (kabobs) pork is only $5.50 and lamb $5.75. Go to the counter in back and order your food. The food and decor are simple, good, and direct. One of David's favorites.

Eugene's Greek Restaurant on Broad, 1280 Broad Street, (250) 381–5456. Hours: 8:00 A.M.–8:00 P.M. Monday–Friday, 10:00 A.M.–8:00 P.M. Saturday. Beer and wine. Wheelchair accessible. Credit cards: Visa, MasterCard.

Universal Tattoo is the oldest tattoo studio in Victoria (more than twenty-five years) and offers Celtic, tribal, native, military, portrait, family crest, fix-up, custom, and esoteric tattoos. You can keep environmentally sound by paying an extra $100 to use vegetable-based inks. Just to keep you happy while you wait, Zain and Gary have pool tables and pinball machines.

Universal Tattoo, 1306 Broad Street, (250) 382–9417; www.universal tattoos.com. Hours: 11:00 A.M.–7:00 P.M. daily. Wheelchair accessible. Credit cards: Visa, MasterCard.

Cross Yates Street, and in the next block of Broad you'll come to **Sun & Surf Swimwear,** dudes' and dudettes' headquarters. Hot stuff for surfing, which you can do here, believe it or not. You'll find Billabong; Mr. Zogs; Sex Wax (calm down, parents); skateboards; Redsand, O'Neill, and Speedo swimsuits; wet suits; surfer, body, and bowling magazines; and Frisbees. Cool sunglasses.

> *Sun & Surf Swimwear, 1314 Broad Street, (250) 920–5511. Hours: 10:00 A.M.–6:00 P.M. Monday–Thursday, Saturday; 10:00 A.M.–8:00 P.M. summer Fridays; 11:00 A.M.–5:00 P.M. Sunday. Partly wheelchair accessible. Credit cards: Visa, MasterCard, American Express.*

Bonnie and Mick Grunwald's **Rising Star Bakery & Cafe** used to produce all the delightfully light breads for afternoon tea at both the Fairmont Empress Hotel and Point Ellice House. While this funky Jewish bakery is not strictly kosher, this is a health-foods cafe despite the huge, fluffy cinnamon buns; focaccia Mexican (an ethnic confusion that works); soups; sandwiches; teas; and coffees.

> *Rising Star Bakery & Cafe, 1330 Broad Street, (250) 388–9411. Hours: 7:00 A.M.–7:00 P.M. Monday–Friday, 8:00 A.M.–4:00 P.M. Saturday– Sunday. Wheelchair accessible. Credit cards: none.*

Robinson's Outdoor Store has completed a major makeover and update under third-generation-owner Gayle Robinson, who has brightened up the store and the stock with the latest in outdoor equipment and fashion with great success. It's fun just exploring in this shop, even if you aren't an outdoorsy person. At "the last stop on the way to your next great adventure," find fishing equipment, shoes, socks, yoga everything, crab traps, and all you need for backpacking, hiking, and climbing.

> *Robinson's Outdoor Store, 1307 Broad Street, (250) 385–3429 or (888) 317–0033; www.robinsonsoutdoors.com. Hours: 10:00 A.M.–6:00 P.M. Monday–Saturday, 11:00 A.M.–4:00 P.M. Sunday. Wheelchair accessible. Credit cards: Visa, MasterCard.*

Now we're back at Yates. Up Yates from Broad, on your left (north side), you will find Lyle's Place and the English Sweet Shop. **Lyle's Place** is definitely the hip place for new and used CDs, cassettes, DVD rentals, posters, T-shirts, concert tickets, and to find out what's happening.

> *Lyle's Place, 770 Yates Street, (250) 382–8422; www.members.shaw.ca/ lyles.place. Hours: 10:00 A.M.–6:00 P.M. Monday–Saturday, noon–5:00 P.M. Sunday. Wheelchair accessible. Credit cards: Visa, MasterCard.*

Two highlights of Yates Street for sugar lovers with an affinity for traditional British candies are the English Sweet Shop and the British Candy Shoppe.

The **English Sweet Shop** is the self-claimed "sweetest shop in town since 1932." This old-fashioned English candy shop also claims to carry "the largest selection of imported toffees and sweets in the Northwest." They also carry British groceries such as chutneys and sauces, biscuits, cream of tomato soup, Devon custard, Marmite, and mushy peas.

> *English Sweet Shop, 738 Yates Street, (250) 382–3325 or (800) 848–1533; www.englishsweets.com. Hours: 9:30 A.M.–5:30 P.M. daily. Wheelchair accessible. Credit cards: Visa, MasterCard.*

A block down Yates Street (on the other side), the **British Candy Shoppe** is an extremely up-to-date, colorful, and vibrant British import candy shop where locals and visitors of British origin line up for their favorite comfort candies from home, some even waiting for just the right-shaped jelly bean expected in on a certain day. You simply select your candy bar, biscuits, or loose candy from huge glass jars, pay, and reminisce to your heart's and dentist's content.

> *British Candy Shoppe, 635 Yates Street, (250) 382–2634. Hours: 9:30 A.M.–5:30 P.M. daily. Wheelchair accessible. Credit cards: Visa, MasterCard.*

If you cross Yates at Broad and want to go down Yates, on the south side is Silverwood.

Silverwood is a direct-import shop featuring masks, mirrors, jewelry, sculpture, and incense from Thailand, Bali, Indonesia, and India.

> *Silverwood, 619 Yates Street, (250) 389–6119. Hours: 10:00 A.M.–6:00 P.M. Monday–Saturday, 11:00 A.M.–5:00 P.M. Sunday. Wheelchair accessible. Credit cards: Visa, MasterCard.*

Azuma Sushi features the freshest ingredients on display. Elegant and simple. Bento boxes at $11.95.

> *Azuma Sushi, 615 Yates Street, (250) 382–8768; www.azumasushi .com. Hours: 11:00 A.M.–9:30 P.M. daily. Beer, sake, wine. Wheelchair accessible. Credit cards: Visa, MasterCard.*

Cross Yates. If you love or even like the smell of leather, **Leather World** is it. Handmade belts, soft backpacks, barrettes, purses, fanny packs, silver-spiked black leather collars, string ties, and wallets, much of which is made here. You will also find 1,500 different styles of belt buckles, from Harley-Davidson and BSA to personal names, or with cars, fishing, and Canadian themes. One of our favorites.

> *Leather World, 610 Yates Street, (250) 388–7825. Hours: 9:30 A.M.–5:30 P.M. daily. Wheelchair accessible. Credit cards: Visa, MasterCard.*

Bernstein & Gold is one of the most elegant and least snobbish shops selling European home furnishings, table linens, and fine china. Beautiful.

> *Bernstein & Gold, 608 Yates Street, (250) 384–7899; www.bernstein andgold.com. Hours: 10:00 A.M.–5:30 P.M. Monday–Saturday, noon–5:00 P.M. Sunday. Wheelchair accessible. Credit cards: Visa, MasterCard, American Express.*

Cross Government Street on Yates, you will again pass Fields Shoes, and then go down the north side of Yates. There is a parking garage on the south side of Yates.

Receptor Shoes is Fields Shoes's jazzy working-shoe store for the twenty-first century.

> *Receptor Shoes, 576 Yates Street, (250) 382–3226. Hours: 9:30 A.M.–6:00 P.M. Monday–Saturday. Credit cards: Visa, MasterCard, American Express.*

Fields Shoe Outlet at 574 Yates offers a good selection of inexpensive one- or two-year-old styles.

Steamer's Pub serves as a gathering place for local twenty-, thirty-, and fortysomethings with loads of excellent local beers; great food, including huge salads from $2.95, tasty pastas, and fish and chips, all at great prices; plus sidewalk table seating in good weather. Good Canadian rock and Celtic bands play here frequently. Pool tables in the back. A favorite.

> *Steamer's Pub, 570 Yates Street, (250) 381–4340. Hours: 11:30 A.M. on daily. Fully licensed. Mostly wheelchair accessible. Credit cards: Visa, MasterCard.*

Hughes Ltd., an elegant, with-it clothes boutique for men and women, features designers Lida Baday, Cole Haan, Ron et Normond of Vancouver, Gerard Dapel,

Ike & Dean, J. Lindeberg, Dibari, Sara Pacini, Nougat, Martinique, Sandwich, Tombolini, and InWear. You must venture upstairs to a theatrical-feeling space with high ceilings in what was once the Majestic Theatre.

Hughes Ltd., *564 Yates Street, (250) 381–4405; www.hughesclothing .com. Hours: 10:00 A.M.–5:30 P.M. Monday–Saturday, noon–5:00 P.M. Sunday. Downstairs is wheelchair accessible. Credit cards: Visa, Master-Card, American Express.*

Don't miss Victoria's finest men's couture clothing boutique, **Outlooks for Men.** Dale Olsen's shop is the place to play pool and get the latest men's fashions at Victoria prices. A limited stock of high-quality labels such as Hugo Boss, Orange Label, Z Zegna, Jack Victor, Strellson, Signum, Omega, Oliver & James, Melting Pot, Horst, Ballin, Swiss Army, and Mezzrow draws locals and visitors of all ages and lifestyles. One of David's favorites.

Outlooks for Men, *554 Yates Street, (250) 384–6121; www.outlooksfor men.ca. Hours: 10:00 A.M.–5:30 P.M. Monday–Thursday, 10:00 A.M.–8:00 P.M. Friday, noon–4:00 P.M. Sunday. Wheelchair accessible. Credit cards: Visa, MasterCard, American Express, Diners.*

Lots of local government workers and businesspeople drop into **Ferris' Grill** to get food to go or lunch on the deck in back, where there's a seafood barbecue every Sunday from noon to 10:00 P.M. Blood-red walls with bold paintings, rough plank floors, a narrow wooden bar, white oak tables and chairs, a potted cactus on each table, and stained-glass windows give the partial feeling of a true pub. Try Cajun prawns ($13), Indonesian chicken ($13), jambalaya ($16), oysters every which way, burgers, and flat breads. Tom and Sandy Ferris started a Pug Rescue organization in Western Canada and now have pug parties at the restaurant!

Fine points: Built in the 1850s, this was the first masonry building on Yates Street. The founder, James Webster, was shot dead in 1862 when the killer mistook him for someone else.

Ferris' Grill, *536 Yates Street, (250) 360–1824; www.ferrisoysterbar .com. Hours: 11:30 A.M.–10:00 P.M. Monday–Thursday, Sunday; 11:30 A.M.–11:00 P.M. Friday–Saturday. Fully licensed. Wheelchair accessible. Credit cards: Visa, MasterCard.*

Upstairs Gallery is an upstairs gallery and public meeting space called a "gallery, studio, venue, loft."

As you reach the lower end of Yates Street, you get into Old Town Victoria. As you cross Waddington Alley, you will come upon the **Victoria International Hostel,** a clean, cheerful hostel welcoming all ages with some private rooms; 110 beds from $17.00–$20.00 for members to $21.28–$24.28 for nonmembers. You can also get tourist information from a friendly host at the hostel.

Victoria International Hostel, 516 Yates Street, (250) 385–4511 or (888) 883–0099; www.hihostels.ca. Hours: twenty-four hours. Partly wheelchair accessible. Credit cards: Visa, MasterCard. One hundred percent nonsmoking and nondrinking.

At **Restaurant Matisse,** John Phillips and David Reimneitz have re-created a little bit of Paris right here in Victoria and are members of the prestigious Chaine des Rôtisseurs. Enjoy Atlantic lobster bisque ($10.00); the excellent bouillabaise of local fish, crab, and other shellfish in a pernod broth ($31.00); the steak tartare ($13.50); fillet of beef Bordelaise ($29.00, add $10.00 for fresh foie gras and truffles); slow-roasted duckling ($26.00); or venison Grand Vebeur in a rich port reduction ($31.00). Don't miss the crème brûlée or tarte tatin ($8).

Restaurant Matisse, 512 Yates Street, (250) 480–0883; www.restaurant matisse.com. Hours: 5:30–10:00 P.M. Wednesday–Sunday. Fully licensed. Wheelchair accessible. Credit cards: Visa, MasterCard, American Express.

At the **Reef,** owners Simon Cotton and Liz da Mata have brought a little piece of the West Indies to Victoria, and are we ever thankful! Great music, including reggae, dance hall, dub, and urban hip-hop DJ music Friday and Saturday.

Chef Jeff Weatherhead creates terrific plantain chips, curried mango and sweet potato soup, chana—a warm curried chickpea salad with West Indian flatbread, and jicama salad for starters. At lunch a rasta rap consists of jerk tofu wrapped in a roti shell; jerk chicken or jerk pork on Jamaican sweet coco buns come with great coleslaw; and the creole snapper burger lights up the senses. Ackee and salt fish, Jamaica's national dish, combines fruit and salt cod for a tasty mess resembling scrambled eggs. All under $10.00, with sides up to $1.50.

At dinner try the Reef Caesar, squash fritters of Trinidadian pakora, West Indian curries, Bajan fried chicken with gravy and coleslaw ($15), yellowfin tuna ($12), or a steak Castro grilled with rum fire ($17). We like the St. Bart's lamb shank braised in red coconut curry with mashed potatoes and slaw ($14). Great

Jicama Salad: Beets, Orange on Exotic Greens with Pineapple Habanero Vinaigrette

Chef Jeff Weatherhead of
the Reef restaurant, Victoria

FOR THE PINEAPPLE HABANERO VINAIGRETTE

1 bunch cilantro

1 fresh habanero chile, minced (do not touch your eyes after touching
   habanero chile)

$1/3$ cup fresh orange juice

4 tbsp. fresh lime juice

2 tbsp. extra-virgin olive oil

4 oz. fresh minced pineapple

Mix all ingredients and set aside.

FOR THE SALAD

1 jicama

3 beets, peeled, boiled, and cut into slices

2 fresh oranges, peeled, seeded, and sliced

organic mixed greens

Remove skin of jicama, and cut jicama into matchstick slices. Combine the matchstick-sliced jicama with some of the vinaigrette and marinate for 10 minutes. Then stack jicama onto mixed greens, and arrange sliced beets and oranges around the jicama for great color. Pour the rest of the vinaigrette over the beets, oranges, and greens. Chef Weatherhead says, "Yum yum!" So do we.

kids menu. The Reef offers twenty-one premium rums, several tequilas and excellent whiskies, and fresh, nonalcoholic, house-made ginger beer, all reasonably priced. Check out the mosaics in the restrooms.

Reef, 533 Yates Street, (250) 388–JERK; www.thereefrestaurant.com. Hours: 11:00 A.M.–midnight Sunday–Wednesday, 11:00 A.M.–1:00 A.M. Thursday–Saturday. Fully licensed. Wheelchair accessible. Credit cards: Visa, MasterCard.

The Reef is just up the street from **Periklis Restaurant,** at 531 Yates. Periklis offers authentic Greek cuisine, featuring lamb, steak, chicken, ribs, seafood, souvlaki, dolmadakia, taramosalata and pita, Greek salata, and special Greek combinations. Weekend nights Greek and belly dancers perform with an occasional appearance by Zorba and the Bad Greeks.

Owner/manager Paul Vasilakopoulos and family have been here for more than a quarter century "so we must be doing something right." In keeping with Periklis the Greek's political nature, Periklis the Restaurant is frequented by B.C. politicians, such as former premier Mike Harcourt.

Periklis Restaurant, 531 Yates Street, (250) 386–3313. Hours: lunch 11:30 A.M.–5:00 P.M. Monday–Friday, dinner 5:00–11:00 P.M. daily. Fully licensed. Wheelchair accessible. Credit cards: Visa, MasterCard, American Express.

We are now going to explore Johnson Street, but first, turn into Waddington Alley, the only street in Victoria with wood-block paving. In an even smaller alleyway off Waddington, between Yates and Johnson, you'll find **Il Terrazzo Ristorante,** best known as just Il Terrazzo. It is worth finding as it is part of the world-rated Chaine des Rotisseurs. The menu is available in English, French, German, and Japanese.

The decor is novella Italian Canadian with bright colors, bright people, big plants, lots of windows, and a cheerful outdoor feeling indoors. Il Terrazzo's food is excellent West Coast Italian and was voted Best Italian Restaurant 1995–2002.

Try the Fisherman's Soup with prawns, mussels, and clams ($11.95) or an artichoke bottom stuffed with salmon and crab meat, baked in the wood-burning oven ($12.95). Seven-inch pizzas are $14.95–$15.95. At dinner we had mouth-watering chicken breast stuffed with prawns and crab ($24.95). There was also char-broiled veal tenderloin with shallots, green peppercorns, and Marsala wine demi-glace ($26.95), Australian rack of lamb encrusted with Dijon mustard ($36.95), and osso buco with wild mushrooms and saffron risotto ($24.95). The pastas and wine list are both excellent, and lunch includes many specials under $12. One of our favorites.

Il Terrazzo Ristorante, 555 Johnson Street, (250) 361–0028; www .ilterrazzo.com. Hours: lunch 11:30 A.M.–3:30 P.M. and dinner from 5:00 P.M. daily. Fully licensed. Wheelchair accessible. Credit cards: Visa, MasterCard, American Express, Diners Club.

We will now take you up both sides of **Johnson Street,** which is one way up (east).

Willie's Bakery bakes organic bread and other goodies for its parent, the group that includes Il Terrazzo and Pescatore's. The made-from-scratch soups and sandwiches are fabulous deals at about $6 to $8. Kathleen loves the Pacific clubhouse with wild salmon, tuna, avocado, and sprouts ($9.00), and other sandwiches such as the free-range chicken clubhouse ($8.75); the smoked turkey and cranberry chutney; and the grilled Havarti and cheddar, peppers, and sun-dried tomato pesto ($6.95). Sample the excellent coffees, salads such as roasted portobello mushroom, and baked goods, and try to get there in time to enjoy the popular pan au chocolat. Full creative breakfasts, such as poached eggs and chorizo and house-made granola, are under $10. Don't miss one of our favorites, and the bed-and-breakfast upstairs.

Fine points: This little Italianate building was erected in 1887 for baker Louis Wille (sic).

Willie's Bakery, 537 Johnson Street, (250) 381–8414; www.isabellas bb.com/willies/. Hours: 7:00 A.M.–6:00 P.M. Monday–Thursday, open at 8:00 A.M. but close later Friday and Saturday. Beer and wine. Wheelchair accessible. Credit cards: Visa, MasterCard, American Express.

Bliss Clothing Co. caters to the eighteen–to–thirty-five age group with Mexx, Dis, Dex, Quick Reflex, Hot Kiss, XOXO, and Hollywood labels, and some jewelry. Check it out, whatever your age, just for fun.

Bliss Clothing Co., 545 Johnson Street, (250) 386–8606. Hours: 10:00 A.M.–6:00 P.M. Monday–Saturday, noon–5:00 P.M. Sunday. Wheelchair accessible but tight. Credit cards: Visa, MasterCard.

Hemp & Co. offers some great, sturdy, Canadian-made, environmentally friendly clothes, including hats, pants, and shirts, as well as hemp bags, hemp soap, shampoo, and other body-care products. Tempting.

Hemp & Co., 547 Johnson Street, (250) 383–4367. Hours: 10:00 A.M.– 5:00 P.M. Monday–Saturday, 11:00 A.M.–5:00 P.M. Sunday. Wheelchair accessible. Credit cards: Visa, MasterCard, American Express.

Still Life sells fun vintage, used, and new clothing, with something for almost everyone, including Diesel, Nudie, Trovata, J Brand, Corpus, Twelfth Street, Joe's Jeans, and Loom State labels.

> *Still Life, 551 Johnson Street, (250) 386–5655. Hours: 10:30 A.M.–6:00 P.M. Monday–Saturday, close at 5:00 P.M. Sunday. Wheelchair accessible. Credit cards: Visa, MasterCard.*

Calibre for Men carries Firetrap, Puma, Matinique, and Bertoni labels, while **Graciella Shoes** features fashionable women's styles from Steve Madden, Miss 60, Tano bags, and other hip shoes.

Rap and New Age music junkies will love **Boomtown,** which sells new and used, with even some rentals.

> *Boomtown, 561 Johnson Street, (250) 380–5090. Hours: 10:00 A.M.– 6:00 P.M. Monday–Wednesday, until 7:00 P.M. Thursday–Friday, 1:00–8:00 P.M. Saturday. Not wheelchair accessible. Credit cards: Visa, MasterCard, American Express.*

Julia Bump's store motto is "Why be normal?" and at **Zydeco** you'll see what she means. This delightfully wacky shop offers the unusual from all over the world: literary best-sellers *Roadkill Cookbook* and *What Bird Did That?*; the born-again Christian car-magnet fish with "Darwin" in it; hard-to-get Ray Troll fishing shirts from Alaska with artwork and titles like "Twist and Trout"; Betty Boop dolls; "cramp-relieving bubble bath"; and a bonanza of Christmas stocking stuffers or party favors. Locals also shop here, for good reason.

> *Fine points:* The building dates from 1879.

> *Zydeco, 565 Johnson Street, (250) 592–6308. Hours: 10:00 A.M.–5:30 P.M. daily. Wheelchair accessible. Credit cards: Visa, MasterCard.*

Zinnia World Notions is an interesting little shop full of unusual imported jewelry, Oriental rugs recycled into pillows, oils and perfumes, and teas from India, all at reasonable prices. Owner Dustin Hanoski traveled to Asia and Mexico gathering handmade crafts and has taken great care to make sure artists and craftspeople are not ripped off in the selling process.

> *Zinnia World Notions, 569 Johnson Street, (250) 385–9915; www .zinnia.ca. Hours: 10:00 A.M.–5:30 P.M. Monday–Saturday, noon–5:00*

P.M. Sunday. Wheelchair accessible. Credit cards: Visa, MasterCard, American Express.

Saltspring Soapworks brings thirty kinds of fabulous handmade soaps from Salt Spring Island, plus natural pumice stone (lava rock), natural nail brushes, kiddies' soaps, Baby Cakes cleansing bars, aromatherapy, foot care, sensual body care, lavender, and a free scrub demonstration.

Saltspring Soapworks, 575 Johnson Street, (250) 386–7627; www.salt springsoapworks.com. Hours: 10:00 A.M.–5:30 P.M. Monday–Saturday, 11:00 A.M.–4:00 P.M. Sunday. Wheelchair accessible. Credit cards: Visa, MasterCard.

The young merchants on this block of Johnson Street search for a label for the many green and organic stores here. Many feature hemp and eco-friendly clothing and natural body-care products.

Flavour offers retro and vintage clothing, custom T-shirts, video games, hats, lots of leather jackets, western shirts, cowboy boots, belt buckles, funky sunglasses, and attitude.

Flavour, 581 Johnson Street, (250) 380–3528. Hours: 10:00 A.M.– 6:00 P.M. daily. Wheelchair accessible but crowded aisles. Credit cards: Visa, MasterCard, American Express.

Directly across Johnson Street from Waddington Alley and Willie's Bakery is **Market Square,** which is now a huge, restored complex of forty-plus small shops and restaurants with distinct personalities, many on Johnson and Pandora Streets. Try everything in Market Square, if you have time. Created in the 1970s from old Victorian structures, Market Square's core buildings included the Grand Pacific Hotel (also known as Russ House and later Drake Hotel) at the corner, dating from 1879, and the Scott & Peeden Building next door on Store Street, erected in 1896. Tenants included houses of prostitution, saloons, gunsmiths, and an opium factory.

Robyn Burton's **Dig This—Gifts and Gear for Gardeners** is an original gardeners' paradise with plants, soil, nutrients, quality tools, and garden furniture. With a slogan of "adopt a plant," the fun staff also sells raucous gardeners' T-shirts. With a horticulturist on duty, Dig This offers complete support service for city gardeners. And from this therapy a beautiful plant grows! Check out their organic plant seeds from Seeds of Change and Garden Path Seeds of Victoria. Be sure to say hello to the lovely lady perched on the bench in front of the store!

Dig This—Gifts and Gear for Gardeners, 128–560 Johnson Street, (250) 385–3212; E-mail: digthis@telus.net. Hours: 9:30 A.M.–5:30 P.M. Monday–Saturday, noon–5:00 P.M. Sunday. Not wheelchair accessible. Credit cards: Visa, MasterCard.

Dannsu Gifts is a treasure trove of exotic artwork, carvings, masks, furniture, jewelry, miniature collectibles, tapestries, and clocks, all imported by owner Frank Liu and son and manager, Darryl, from their native Malaysia. The Lius also import collectibles from Indonesia, Nepal, India, Pakistan, and other Far Eastern sources. Darryl says prices range from "40 cents to a couple of thousand dollars," and we treated each other to masks from Dannsu as anniversary presents one year.

Dannsu Gifts, 574 Johnson Street, (250) 383–8128; Fax: (250) 383–8089; www.dannsu.com. Hours: 10:00 A.M.–6:00 P.M. daily. Wheelchair accessible. Credit cards: Visa, MasterCard, American Express.

Now walk into giant **Market Square** and explore its many levels. Be sure to notice the new mural down the stairway by Chris Johnson of the Chippewas of the Nawash Band.

Woofles—A Doggy Diner is a miniscale gourmet doggie-treat shop with wheat-free pizza bites, carob-dipped hearts, and Chateau Woof de Pup bottles of goodies. Dogs welcomed.

Woofles, 560 Johnson Street, (250) 385–WOOF. Hours: 10:00 A.M.–6:00 P.M. daily. Wheelchair accessible. Credit cards: Visa, MasterCard.

Don't miss **Foxglove Toys,** where Marga Konig carries giant kites, Thomas the Train pieces of all sorts, and other fabulous toys. Children of all ages will enjoy it.

Foxglove Toys, 560 Johnson Street, (250) 383–8852; Fax: (250) 474–6359; E-mail: foxglovetoys@hotmail.com. Hours: 10:00 A.M.–5:00 P.M. daily. Wheelchair accessible. Credit cards: Visa, MasterCard.

People walk or ride from all over town to get to **Green Cuisine,** a totally vegetarian restaurant with a hot buffet, salad bar, in-house organic bakery, juices, and espresso drinks (made with soy milk if you prefer). You go through the buffet line and pay for your food by weight. Could be cleaner!

Green Cuisine, 560 Johnson Street (lower level), (250) 385–1809. Hours: 10:00 A.M.–8:00 P.M. daily. Wheelchair accessible by elevator. Credit cards: Visa, MasterCard, American Express.

New England Square actually faces Pandora Avenue while still part of Market Square, with an abundance of New England antiques and reproductions, pewter, hand-woven fabrics, wrought iron, Shaker wooden boxes, and milk paint, all inspired by owners Michael and Shirley McBride's twelve years in Boston. Great furniture and a few old home accessories, some of which may fit in your suitcase.

New England Square, 560 Johnson Street, Suite 152, (350) 384–5777; www.newenglandsquare.com. Hours: 10:00 A.M.–6:00 P.M. daily. Partly wheelchair accessible. Credit cards: Visa, MasterCard, American Express.

Back out on Johnson Street, the next store you come to is **Jeune Brothers Outdoor Equipment,** one of Victoria's best outdoor equipment stores, carrying Sierra Designs, North Face, rentals, tents, kayaks, and a great selection of travel guides. Its store next door, Jeune Brothers Tent and Awning, Ltd. (250–385–7751), sells canvas of all sizes and colors (even to cover your yacht), boat toppings, lawn swings, and a few flags. These two stores cover many of your leisure-time needs.

Jeune Brothers Outdoor Equipment, 570 Johnson Street, (250) 386–8778. Hours: 10:00 A.M.–6:00 P.M. daily. Opens earlier on weekends. Wheelchair accessible. Credit cards: Visa, MasterCard, American Express.

After you cross Government Street going up (east), you come to an exceptionally good block for kids, starting with **Olde Towne Shoe Repair,** with the DOC MARTENS FIXED sign in the window. Mike Waterman, a former banker who ditched that profession more than twenty years ago to "do his own thing" and work with his hands, is a native Victorian who loves to talk to his customers while he works. In his whopping 356-square-foot shop he will repair your leather purse on the spot or explain the anatomy of Doc Martens shoes and actually fix them, saving Doc lovers hundreds of dollars. Mike also fixes cracked soles of Birkenstocks and Rockports. One of Jerry's favorites.

Olde Towne Shoe Repair, 605 Johnson Street, (250) 386–8333. Hours: 9:00 A.M.–5:30 P.M. Monday–Friday. Wheelchair accessible. Credit cards: none.

A hit in Victoria is the vegan **Lotus Pond Vegetarian Restaurant.** Try Shiitake Delight, a dish of lightly battered shiitake mushrooms sautéed in spicy basil sauce ($12.95); Lemon Mock Chicken ($10.95); soups and noodle dishes; and wheat-free selections. Several Buddhist and Chinese publications on sale. Lunchtime natural vegan buffet, where your food is weighed and costs $1.39 per one hundred grams (about a quarter pound), and dim sum menu. Voted Best Vegetarian Menu by *Victoria News* readers.

> *Lotus Pond Vegetarian Restaurant, 617 Johnson Street, (250) 380–9293. Hours: 11:00 A.M.–9:00 P.M. Tuesday–Sunday. Wheelchair accessible. Free delivery; discount for pick-up orders. Credit cards: Visa, Master-Card.*

At **Snowden's Books** Jerry Snowden sells his well-established and incredible collection of new and used paperback books, computer games, magazines, mysteries, sci-fi, literature, romance, kids' hockey stories from the 1950s, and back issues of *Playboy, Penthouse, Road & Track, Conan,* and *Celebrity Sleuth,* all at discount prices. Buy five paperbacks, get one free. Great place to find a cheap read.

> *Snowden's Books, 619 Johnson Street, (250) 383–8131; www.snowdens .bc.ca. Hours: 10:00 A.M.– 5:00 P.M. daily, half day on Monday. Wheelchair accessible. Credit cards: Visa, MasterCard.*

Dark Horse Books has, primarily, books on witchcraft, Wicca, science fiction, and fantasy, both new and used, mostly paperbacks. Heaven if those are your interests.

> *Dark Horse Books, 623 Johnson Street, (250) 386–8736; E-mail: drkhors@shaw.ca. Hours: 10:00 A.M.–6:00 P.M. Wednesday–Saturday, noon–5:00 P.M. Sunday. Wheelchair accessible. Credit cards: Visa, Master-Card.*

Games Workshop is a Warhammer strategy-game and war games shop.

> *Games Workshop, 625 Johnson Street, (250) 361–1499. Hours: 10:00 A.M.–6:00 P.M. Monday–Wednesday, 10:00 A.M.–9:00 P.M. Thursday–Saturday, noon–5:00 P.M. Sunday. Wheelchair accessible. Credit cards: Visa, MasterCard, American Express.*

Curious Comics and Image is a terrific comic-book store with great posters and action figures, lots of books about comics, DC comics, Star Wars, Lord of the Rings, and comics T-shirts. It also sells computer games.

> *Curious Comics and Image, 631 Johnson Street, (250) 384–1656. Comic hotline: (250) 384–1053; www.curious.bc.ca. Hours: 9:30 A.M.–6:00 P.M. Monday–Saturday, 11:00 A.M.–5:00 P.M. Sunday. Wheelchair accessible. Credit cards: Visa, MasterCard.*

Legends is a great comic-book store on what might be called Comics Row. Legends specializes in unusual back issues, independent local "zines," and comics that go with game sets. Lots of fun to browse and chat.

> *Legends, 633 Johnson Street, (250) 388–3696. Hours: 10:30 A.M.–5:00 P.M. Monday–Thursday, until 6:30 P.M. Friday, 10:00 A.M.–6:00 P.M. Saturday, noon–5:00 P.M. Sunday. Wheelchair accessible. Credit cards: Visa, MasterCard, American Express.*

Old Nick's Emporium opened, appropriately, on April Fools' Day 2001 and has never looked back. Originally printing special-order T-shirts in the back room, the company now employs several people in a warehouse in Esquimalt to produce concert T-shirts for some of the world's best bands. A local attraction are its T-shirts and mugs that feature the mug shot of B.C. Premier Gordon Campbell as he was booked into jail for drunk driving in Maui, Hawaii. Old Nick's does special-order T-shirts for anyone and sells smoking equipment as well. A trip back to the 1960s and 1970s.

> *Old Nick's Emporium, 639 Johnson Street, (250) 382–6423; Fax: (250) 382–6403; www.oldnicks.com. Hours: 11:00 A.M.–6:00 P.M. daily. Wheelchair accessible. Credit cards: Visa, MasterCard.*

You will find even more comics at **Yellow Jacket Comic Books & Toys,** which has all current comics galore and life-size Star Wars cardboard cutouts for $34.95. Another kids' heaven.

> *Yellow Jacket Comic Books & Toys, 649 Johnson Street, (250) 480–0049. Hours: 9:30 A.M.–5:30 P.M. Monday–Saturday, 11:00 A.M.–5:00 P.M. Sunday. Wheelchair accessible. Credit cards: Visa, MasterCard.*

Walk from Johnson Street through Market Square to Pandora Avenue. Pandora Avenue has become much more interesting, particularly from a culinary standpoint.

Global Village Store is run by a nonprofit society and buys only from fairtrade co-ops and village craftspeople and growers in Peru, Guatemala, Argentina, Ethiopia, Kenya, India, Indonesia, Cambodia, Thailand, and Vietnam. Try the fair-trade chocolates, coffee, and tea, and great bags, wraps, and yo-yos, among other trinkets. Profits from the store go back to the villages from which the products come.

Global Village Store, 535 Pandora Avenue, (250) 380–1530. Hours: 10:00 A.M.–5:00 P.M. Monday–Saturday. Not wheelchair accessible. No credit cards.

Just up the street from Global Village is Solstice Café, a comfy coffeehouse featuring organic fair-trade coffees, sandwiches, and the occasional pizza.

Mo:Lé restaurant serves friends, hipsters, and everyone else, although the first two categories are most welcomed. Dishes include products from local and organic farms sure to please carnivores as well as vegans and raw foodies, all served in fun whimsical decor against historic brick walls.

Breakfast and lunch feature eggs all ways, sprouted organic buckwheat cacao crunch, tofu scrambles, huevos rancheros, salads of smoked tuna, Caesar salad with sun-dried black olives and avocado, a pro vita meal, free range chicken taco salad, a yam wrap, a chicken sandwich, BLT or grilled veggie sandwiches, coconut curry, macaroni and cheese, and organic beef burgers, with everything under $15.

Dinner gets more restaurantlike with small plates of polenta chips, marinated raw veggie ratatouille (both $8). Medium plates ($14) include braised organic short ribs, pastas, peas and cheese risotto, raw pizza, free range chicken, and eight varieties of dinner salads.

Large plates vary from Thai coconut broth mussels with Asian vegetables and organic brown Basmati rice or rice noodles ($16) or a stuffed pepper ($18) to local lingcod ($19), roasted free range chicken leg ($21), or organic Ranchland New York strip loin ($26).

Music nightly.

Mo:Lé, 554 Pandora Avenue, (250) 385–6653; www.molerestaurant .ca. Hours: 8:00 A.M.–3:00 P.M. and 5:30–9:30 P.M. daily. Beer and wine (licensed). Wheelchair accessible. Credit cards: Visa, MasterCard.

Habit is possibly the most hip new coffeehouse in Victoria, where Shane Deveraux and friends have brought their restaurant and other experience to create coffee drinks right next door to Mo:Lé. These people really care about and dote over every single cup of coffee. Girlfriends bring their knitting to chat and sip and knit together. Books and laptops abound, and hospitality oozes. A habit it might become!

We are glad to see such creative culinary enterprises upgrade this block!

Habit, 552 Pandora Avenue, (250) 704–8304. Hours: 8:00 A.M.–9:00 or 10:00 P.M. daily. Wheelchair accessible. Credit cards: Visa, MasterCard.

Chinatown

Now we come to Victoria's 1-block **Chinatown.** The ornate, elegant Gate of Harmonious Interest, built in 1882 and restored and lovingly painted in 1996–97, marks your official entry into the area.

While Victoria's Chinatown is small by San Francisco or Vancouver standards, it is intense, colorful, vibrant, and growing, along with Victoria's and Vancouver's Chinese immigrant populations. Many Hong Kong Chinese moved to Vancouver before China's takeover of Hong Kong from the British. Victoria's Chinatown is still the hub of the Chinese community, who shop here and in a few stores adjoining the recognized center.

Hours: Most shops and restaurants in Chinatown stay open as long as there are customers, so we cannot be specific; they like to keep flexible. Many of them do not have telephones or listed phone numbers, and few take credit cards.

The first store on the left, at Government and Fisgard, is **Quonley's Gifts and Grocery.** Beach mats (two for $2.99) and back scratchers ($1.29) on the sidewalk outside immediately signal Chinatown. Inside you will find lovely wind chimes, lacquered boxes, Chinese and Japanese traditional shoes and slippers, and basic groceries. China tea sets, incense, best-deal rice bowls, and Chinese and Japanese candies are complemented by Anglo foods such as ice-cream cones and sandwiches to go.

Fine points: There is a public telephone in the pagoda on the sidewalk here.

Gate of Harmonious Interest, Chinatown, Fisgard Street

Quonley's Gifts and Grocery, *1628 Government Street, (250) 383–0623. Wheelchair accessible.*

Jia Hua Trading offers great, cheap veggies, imported Chinese delicacies, and smelly dried fish. *Wheelchair accessible.*

The **Jan K Company,** 555 Fisgard, is the cleanest, best grocery store (and more) in Chinatown. Displays of Chinese vegetables such as choy sum, gai lan, yu choy, eggplant, kohlrabi, snow peas, and surian (a soft Thai pineapple-like fruit) beckon you from the sidewalk. Inside, at least eight varieties of dried mushrooms and seaweed, rice bowls (as low as 99 cents), canned and dried imported Asian foods galore, tofu, dried pea snacks, waters, juices, and candies grab your money. *Mostly wheelchair accessible.*

We find the **Chinatown Trading Company** to be a fabulous emporium of Chinese imports. The abundance, good taste, variety, and display of world imports here is astounding. Great inexpensive souvenirs and Christmas stocking stuffers, home accessories, embroidered flower bun warmers at only $2.99, hundreds of teapots, kitchen utensils, madras bedspreads, baskets, papier-mâché, chimes, more baskets, and even rugs fill this historic building's maze of rooms.

In a display case toward the back you can see a rare private collection of actual Chinese workers' artifacts, including dominoes, work and play tools, lanterns, and books from the original Chinatown. Peek into the old-time gambling/ banking center hidden in the corner.

Chinatown Trading Company, 551 Fisgard Street, (250) 381–5503. Mostly wheelchair accessible. Credit cards: Visa, MasterCard.

The last room of the Chinatown Trading Company exits onto Fan Tan Alley, which we will visit as soon as we complete our trip down this side of Fisgard and come back up the other side.

Fan Tan Cafe is a small restaurant that does a nice job catering to visitors with its good Hong Kong cuisine, hamburgers for kids (or anyone else) in a pinch, combination plates, and great prices. Lunch is served until 4:30 P.M. A Victoria *Times-Colonist* restaurant reviewer named Fan Tan one of her top ten restaurants, although we find the food to be inconsistent (dinner $11–$12). Enjoy the red and black Miro-like interior and paintings, and the starry lights in the ceiling.

Fan Tan Cafe, 549 Fisgard Street, (250) 383–1611. Hours: noon–2:30 A.M. Monday–Saturday, noon–9:00 P.M. Sunday. Fully licensed. Wheelchair accessible. Credit cards: Visa, MasterCard, American Express.

Moon Key Groceries offers Chinese foods, dishes, kitchen equipment, sauces, and jillions of Chinese noodle varieties and candies with a new historic plaque on the building.

Moon Key Groceries, 545 Fisgard Street, (250) 384–3742. Hours: 10:00 A.M.–5:00 P.M. Wednesday–Sunday. Wheelchair accessible. Credit cards: Visa, MasterCard.

A large Chinese clientele frequents **Kimbo Restaurant,** a Chinese family-style restaurant with Formica tables and padded chrome chairs. Worth a try.

Kimbo Restaurant, 543 Fisgard Street, (250) 383–5251. Fully licensed. Wheelchair accessible. Credit cards: Visa, MasterCard.

Fan Tan Gallery is a cozy non-Chinese emporium of home-decor accessories with a collection of pillows, baskets, handmade rugs of all sizes from Turkey and India, local furniture, and Mexican pots. The house cat might surprise you by staying asleep in the folded rugs. If you are thinking of buying a rug here, be sure to ask if it is colorfast, and listen carefully to the answer.

Fan Tan Gallery, 541 Fisgard Street, (250) 382–4424. Hours: 10:00 A.M.–5:30 P.M. Monday–Saturday, noon–4:00 P.M. Sunday and holidays. Entry floor is wheelchair accessible. Credit cards: Visa, MasterCard.

Dale's Gallery is another non-Chinese gallery of beautifully tasteful prints and watercolors by local artists such as Elizabeth Griffiths and Brian Crovet, plus framing and painting conservation services, cards, and graphic design.

Dale's Gallery, 537 Fisgard Street, (250) 383–1552. Hours: 10:00 A.M.–5:30 P.M. Monday–Saturday, noon–4:00 P.M. Sunday. Wheelchair accessible. Credit cards: Visa, MasterCard, American Express.

The **Chinese-Canadian Cultural Association** at 535 Fisgard serves as a community center of sorts and is generally closed to the non-Chinese public. Photos of Mao Zedong, founder of the People's Republic of China, and former Canadian prime minister Pierre Elliott Trudeau still hang on the walls.

Fine points: The building was constructed in 1901 by Lee Cheong and Lee Wong with an elegant facade and a passageway to tenements in back.

Bean Around the World is an excellent Anglo coffeehouse at the end of this group of buildings. Popular with real coffee lovers, Bean serves only organic coffee and is gay friendly. Lots of friendly characters work and gather here, for chocolate mousse or coconut cream pie and Italian ice creams.

Bean Around the World, 533 Fisgard Street, (250) 386–7115. Hours: early to late.

Tamami Sushi majors in sushi and teriyaki specialties such as salmon or New York steak, with combination plates ($13.95–$17.95) available.

Tamami Sushi, 509 Fisgard Street, (250) 382–3529. Hours: 11:30 A.M.–2:30 P.M. and 5:00–10:00 P.M. Tuesday–Saturday, 5:00–10:00 P.M. Sunday. Wheelchair accessible. Credit cards: Visa, MasterCard.

The Bubble Tea Place offers faddish bubble teas, including taro, red bean, and other exotic flavors, as well as beads, loose teas, furniture, leather bags, hemp shirts, chocolates, and scarves.

The Bubble Tea Place, 532 Fisgard Street, (250) 391–8960. Hours: 10:00 A.M.–7:00 P.M. daily. Wheelchair accessible. Credit cards: Visa, MasterCard.

Eastern Food Market has improved tremendously recently. Chinese delicacies, baskets, teas, chopstick sets, bowls, Chinese snacks, vases, and cooking utensils are worth a visit.

Eastern Food Market, 534 Fisgard Street, (250) 383–7388. Wheelchair accessible. Credit cards: Visa, MasterCard.

At **Don Mee's Seafood Restaurant** (upstairs) the word *Chinese* is left out of the name but probably is assumed. This is the most elegant Chinese restaurant in town, featuring traditional Cantonese- and Szechuan-style seafood, chicken, and beef, and a traditional dim sum lunch daily. Live, swimming lobsters and crabs greet you and await your order. The family dinners start at $13.95 per person. Climb the stairway to the second-floor entrance. Free delivery after 5:00 P.M.

Don Mee's Seafood Restaurant, 538 Fisgard Street (upstairs), (250) 383–1032. Hours: 10:00 A.M.–10:00 P.M. daily, dim sum served 10:00 A.M.–3:00 P.M. Fully licensed. Not wheelchair accessible. Credit cards: Visa, MasterCard, American Express, Diners.

Tradewinds is a small Chinese import shop with lots of miniatures, teacups, and personal soaps.

Tradewinds, 544 Fisgard Street, (250) 381–5422. Wheelchair accessible. Credit cards: Visa, MasterCard.

Hunan Village Cuisine offers wake-you-up Hunan-style hot and peppery cuisine (heat can be altered) featuring seafood such as local oysters, crab, cod in season, and duck. Lunch ranges upward from $6.45, dinner from $8.45, and combination dinner from $11.95. Free delivery within 6 miles, which most hotels and motels are.

Hunan Village Cuisine, 546 Fisgard Street, (250) 382–0661. Beer and wine. Wheelchair accessible. Credit cards: Visa, MasterCard, American Express.

Kwong Tung Seafood Restaurant serves Hong Kong–style Cantonese and Szechuan cuisine with dim sum served daily. Lunch combination plates range from $7.25, dinner from $12.95, and group meals from $6.95 for two or more. Fresh crab. Free delivery after 5:00 P.M. within 4 miles.

Kwong Tung Seafood Restaurant, 548 Fisgard Street (upstairs), (250) 381–1223. Hours: lunch and dim sum 11:00 A.M.–3:00 P.M., dinner from 5:00 P.M. Beer and wine. Not wheelchair accessible. Credit cards: Visa, MasterCard, American Express.

Fisgard Market is a small, traditional Chinese full-service grocery with cold Chinese drinks and Chinese specialties such as vegetables, mangoes, papayas, coconut milk, and cold drinks.

Fisgard Market, 550 Fisgard Street, (250) 383–6969. Wheelchair accessible.

Loi Sing Restaurant & BBQ Bakery is a small, local, Formica-table Chinese restaurant frequented by local Chinese and neighborhood workers, and it sometimes has cooked poultry and pork hanging in the window.

Fine points: Originally the Chinese Benevolent Association building (designed by John Teague in 1885), it was later the first Chinese school, replaced by a cigar factory.

Loi Sing Restaurant & BBQ Bakery, 560 Fisgard Street, (250) 388–6968. Hours: 10:00 A.M.–8:30 P.M. Monday–Saturday, 10:00 A.M.– 6:45 P.M. Sunday. Beer and wine. Wheelchair accessible. Credit cards: none.

Mild Chinese cuisine catering to North American tastes is the focus at **Foo Hong Chop Suey.** Lots of chop suey and chow mein; lunch specials from $4.75 and dinner for less than $8.00.

Original Chinese school on Fisgard Street

Foo Hong Chop Suey, 564 Fisgard Street, (250) 386–9553. Hours: 11:30 A.M.–3:00 P.M., 4:30–9:00 P.M. Thursday–Tuesday. Beer and wine. Wheelchair accessible. Credit cards: none.

Ocean Garden Restaurant serves bland Cantonese and Szechuan specialties including fresh oysters, crabs, and clams in season; lunch specials from $4.95 for veggie combos or $5.50 with some meat; special dinners for two from $17.50. Lots of Chinese and other locals eat here daily. Free delivery; discount if you pick up and take out.

Ocean Garden Restaurant, 568 Fisgard Street, (250) 360–2818. Hours: 11:30 A.M. on daily. Beer and wine. Wheelchair accessible. Credit cards: Visa, MasterCard.

Now walk ½ block back down the south side of Fisgard to **Fan Tan Alley.** Like Waddington and Trounce Alleys, Fan Tan Alley was cut through the block to provide "street" frontage for more buildings. New owner and civic leader William J. Mac-Donald created the alley in 1881. Some of the buildings along here date from the 1880s, including an opium factory that remained legal until 1907.

Between 1912 and 1920 Chinese owners hired architects and replaced older structures with the current brick buildings, most housing retail stores on the ground floor and tenements above. Obviously sunlight and fresh air were not considerations. At its narrowest point the alley is only 4 charming feet wide. Fan Tan, by the way, is a Chinese gambling game.

Heart's Content is a happening boutique/shop that feels

Fan Tan Alley

like London-west, featuring jazzy hip clothes, including an excellent supply of
Doc Martens shoes and boots, Ray Troll T-shirts at $24, well-priced skirts and
dresses, and fun sun hats. One of our favorites.

> *Heart's Content, 18 Fan Tan Alley, (250) 380–1234. Hours: 11:00
> A.M.–5:30 P.M. daily. Wheelchair accessible. Credit cards: Visa, Master-
> Card.*

Dragon Song Music Company is a fascinating home to historic, ethnic,
acoustic, and imported musical instruments. Oriental rugs accentuate displays of
African and Celtic Bodhran drums, as well as old sound equipment.

> *Dragon Song Music Company, 16 Fan Tan Alley, (250) 385–4643.
> Hours: 10:00 A.M.–6:00 P.M. daily, closed 12:30–1:00 P.M. for lunch.
> Wheelchair accessible. Credit cards: Visa, MasterCard.*

At the **New Town Barber** an ancient Chinese gentleman and, occasionally, a
younger man cut hair the old-fashioned way, slowly, and in an ancient building,
and usually for Asian clients.

> *New Town Barber, 10 Fan Tan Alley, (250) 382–3813. Hours: 9:30
> A.M.–5:00 P.M. or whenever a barber happens to be there. Wheelchair ac-
> cessible. Credit cards: none.*

We visit the **Turntable** to scan the fabulous collection of high-quality old
records, CDs, and tapes from George Carlin to Elvis and Frank Sinatra, plus
every acid rock and rap available. Psychedelic and current concert posters paper
the ceiling and walls in the little space left. Gary Anderson and friends will play
anything you bring up to the counter. They also stock an interesting small collection of Celtic and Canadian Celtic music. One of our favorites.

> *Turntable, 3 Fan Tan Alley, (250) 382–5543. Hours: 10:00 A.M.–5:30
> P.M. (sometimes later) daily. Not wheelchair accessible. Credit cards: Visa,
> MasterCard, American Express.*

For a new or familiar experience, stop in at **Triple Spiral Metaphysical,** the ultimate cozy source of metaphysical and pagan supplies, from incense and candles
to books, tapes and CDs, jewelry, cards, fabulous paintings and collages, drums,
scented oils, and ritual tools. Previous owner Alison Skelton, daughter of the late
witch and poet Robin Skelton, sold the store to Phylis Everlie Songhurst, C.P.A.,

a Wicca priestess of Thirteenth House Mystery School. Triple Spiral also offers astrologic readings by e-mail.

> ***Triple Spiral Metaphysical,*** *3 Fan Tan Alley, (250) 380–7212; www .triplespiralmetaphysical.com. Hours: 11:00 A.M.–5:00 P.M. daily. Readings by appointment. Not wheelchair accessible. Credit cards: Visa, Master-Card.*

Turtle Express is an interesting, cozy southeast Asian import shop you shouldn't miss. It features original handcrafted jewelry, handpainted material, gorgeous sarongs ($20), and accessories.

> ***Turtle Express,*** *3 Fan Tan Alley, (250) 384–2227. Hours: 11:00 A.M.–5:30 P.M. daily. Not wheelchair accessible. Credit cards: Visa, Master-Card, American Express.*

Whirled Arts features imports from Central and South America, including bags, clothing, and chatchkas, and holds candlewax readings.

> ***Whirled Arts,*** *3 Fan Tan Alley, (250) 386–2787. Hours 10:00 A.M.– 6:00 P.M. daily. Not wheelchair accessible. Credit cards: Visa, Master-Card, American Express.*

RESIDENTIAL NEIGHBORHOODS

Now we begin our look at neighborhoods beyond the downtown area, starting with James Bay.

James Bay. James Bay was originally named for governor James Douglas, who built his home and lived there in the 1850s. James Bay itself included the area where the Inner Harbour and the Fairmont Empress Hotel now stand, since the bay was filled in during 1903–4. Most of the flat part was Beckley Farm, once producer of vegetables for Victoria and now remembered in name almost solely as a pleasant retirement home.

Today James Bay includes the Parliament buildings and waterfront; everything south to Dallas Road, including Ogden Point, where cruise ships and the Royal Victoria ferry dock, and over to Beacon Hill Park; the James Bay Inn at 270 Government Street and Emily Carr's home at 207 Government Street; and the community center of James Bay on Menzies Street. Many Victorian homes remain and are worth a drive or carriage tour. Almost all of the waterfront along Dallas Road and Beacon Hill Park is wheelchair accessible.

In James Bay village, at the intersection of Menzies, Simcoe, and Toronto Streets (1 block west and 3 blocks southwest of the Fairmont Empress Hotel), you will find a government liquor store, a small shopping center with beautifully expanded Thrifty Market, a barber, a Starbucks, and a cleaners. Don't miss Cup a Joe, across Toronto downstairs from the drugstore and the Bank of Montreal, for great breakfast and lunch from $2.95 on up.

At this intersection enjoy the Bent Mast, a neighborhood bar/restaurant/ hangout; the James Bay Coffee & Books for excellent scones and humongous cinnamon buns (white or whole wheat), Internet access, and coffees and teas; a Laundromat right next door so that you can enjoy coffee while you do your laundry; a lovely flower shop; and, of course, fish and chips and burgers; and Coast Capital Savings. The James Bay Tearoom and Restaurant is also in James Bay at 332 Menzies Street.

Heron Rock Bistro has hugely uplifted the James Bay culinary scene at the west end of James Bay Square. Drew Moffatt and Ben Peterson renovated the space to include a jazzy casual cafe in the front that's separated by a bar island from the linen tablecloth dining room in the back. Diners share the same menu throughout the place, which is frequented by visitors as well as neighborhood seniors. Whether you're a first-timer or a regular, ordering a coffee or a full-course meal, you'll receive the same attentive service.

Heron's French fries have been voted #2 Best Fries on Vancouver Island, so we went for the works with garlic. They came out slightly clumpy, but maybe it was a fluke of the weather.

At lunch, sandwich and quiche specials might include Dungeness crab and shrimp cakes ($11), baked French onion soup ($6), poutine of Comox cheese curds, house gravy and hand-cut fries (a Canadian favorite) ($8), house pâté of duck confit, calf's liver, and pork shoulder and belly ($10), crôques madame and crôques monsieur grilled sandwiches, veggie and beef burgers, and organic Metchosin lamb burger.

Dinner options expand to include sesame crusted local tuna loin ($20), Pacific sablefish ($22), steamed local mussels and fries ($18), a vegetarian plate or Portobello mushroom Wellington ($19), pastas, and local organic chicken.

Heron offers "Nightly Frugal Feasts" at $10 for main course only or $14 for soup or salad, nightly special main course, and dessert.

Live blues and jazz on Friday at 8:00 P.M.

Heron Rock Bistro, #4-435 Simcoe Street at Croft, (250) 383–1545. Hours: 9:00 A.M.–9:00 P.M. Sunday–Thursday, 9:00 A.M.–10:00 P.M. Friday–Saturday. Fully licensed. Wheelchair accessible. Credit cards: Visa, MasterCard, American Express.

Cook Street Village. Cook Street Village is on—surprise—Cook Street, a few blocks east of Beacon Hill Park. Like many Victoria neighborhood villages, it primarily supplies locals with foods and flowers, as well as more mundane necessities. Huge chestnut trees canopy the street and set the cozy mood.

The 300 block of Cook Street hosts dueling coffee chains, with relatively local Moka House on the east side and Starbucks directly across the street, both enjoying regulars. Moka House has music some nights and generally healthier food, including fabulous sandwiches and pastries. On the Starbucks side, PicAFlic rents movies and videos and has an unusual collection of foreign films.

Lifestyle Markets is an oasis of organic groceries, including coffees, pastries, and diet supplements.

Kay's Korner at 337 Cook (250–386–5978) features collectibles and "experienced goods" and a sense of humor. A great place for experienced treasures.

The Cook Street Market Place, 333 Cook, sells groceries and many other things worth investigating. World of Flowers is here, and Valerie Engel's Bubby Rose, for challah buns, whole-wheat sticky buns, and other irresistables. The Village Card Shoppe (250–383–1943) sells charming cards and notes, knickknacks, and lottery tickets and offers full postal services. The Beagle Pub, at the corner of Cook and Oxford Streets, is the most beautiful neighborhood pub in Victoria. Also check out Rosie's Diner at 253 Cook.

Be sure to drop in to the excellent Fairfield Bookshop for the best in used books, and check out Surroundings next door, one of our favorites, for restored local antiques and imported furnishings.

On the west side of Cook at number 252, Cook Street Fish and Chips (250–384–1856) serves a breakfast special all day for $3.45 and a lunch special salmon sandwich with soup or fries for $4.95. It also has outdoor seating. Starbucks serves its usual great coffees and munchies.

Wine lovers should check out Cook Street Village Wines at 242 for B.C. wines and ice wines, as well as local entertainment from Glenn Barlow, Richard Pyatt, and Ian Sutherland. Booster Juice offers quality health drinks and panini sandwiches.

Bubby Rose's Bakery & Café opened in September 2006 and was immediately inundated with loyal and new fans. A slightly larger cafe than its small site farther down Cook Street, Bubby Rose's bakes here and offers a few comfy tables in a bright and colorful atmosphere, which can be important in Victoria much of the year.

Valerie and Mark Engels' cinnamon rolls, sticky buns, chocolate croissants, and artisan breads are to die for, including those on the day-old rack near the door. Other faves include carrot cake, fruit crumble, flourless dark chocolate torte, bran muffins, vegan and wheat-free Bubbymores with peanuts, cranberry spelt muffins, butter tarts, and chocolate chunk cookies.

Lunch brings soups, quiches, roasted veggie or veggie pâté sandwiches, bagels with smoked salmon, and egg salad and other sandwiches, mostly for under $5.

Bubby Rose's Bakery & Café, 1022 Cook Street, (250) 472–8229; www .bubbyrosesbakery.com. Hours: 8:00 A.M.–6:00 P.M. Monday–Saturday, 9:00 A.M.–5:00 P.M. Sunday. Wheelchair accessible. Credit cards: Visa, MasterCard, American Express.

Fairfield. Fairfield is a pleasant residential neighborhood that was cut from governor James Douglas's Fairfield Farm. It extends from the eastern side of Beacon Hill Park to Gonzales Bay and includes Ross Bay Cemetery between Fairfield and Dallas Roads. Many Arts and Crafts–style houses remain on Trutch Street. It's worth a trip to see, especially in April when the Yoshina cherry trees blossom with an abundance of soft pink pompons.

Fairfield Plaza on Fairfield Road has a collection of food places such as Nature's Fare, where you can stock up on organic foods and bread from the Italian Bakery, and Bagga Pasta.

Fernwood. The Fernwood neighborhood focuses on its center at Fernwood Road and Gladstone Avenue, and when you get there, you'll see why. It looks and feels like a small English village with a very un-square square that has several vacant storefronts, unfortunately. Named for Fernwood Manor, the first Victoria mansion built outside of the James Bay area in 1860, it was once the 300-acre estate of Benjamin Pearse. Now younger people are renovating older homes, and the neighborhood has an almost secret, with-it sense of self and eccentricity since the addition of a great Corner Café coffeehouse, a tapas and wine bar, and Freedom Kilts.

Freedom Kilts Company is a fun and interesting bright light in the "new" Fernwood, where Steve Ashton and Bobbie Williams recently relocated their custom kilt making business from their dining room. They make loads of custom and practical kilts, from baggy to dress, and kilt accessories, adapting to fashion with khaki cargo pockets almost wherever you want them, and tartans. The coffee is always on and there are cookies in the jar, so stop by and learn a lot.

A former helicopter pilot and yacht designer, Ashton started to make kilts as a self-proclaimed "retirement business," which has now projected into one of the largest kilt-making businesses in the world. But it is still homey and comfy.

Freedom Kilts Company, 1311 Gladstone Avenue, (250) 386–KILT. Hours: 10:00 A.M.–6:00 P.M. Tuesday–Saturday. Credit cards: Visa, MasterCard, American Express.

The **Belfry Theatre,** at 1281 Gladstone Avenue (250–385–6815), was built around 1890 and was once the Emmanuel Baptist Church. Originally formed on a 1974 six-month government grant to help three people develop a theater company, the Belfry (no bats, we hope) is now one of Canada's premier small theaters.

Across Fernwood and beside the Belfry Theatre is Gladstone Square, which feels European, complete with gazebo and kiosk, Front Row Video with a full range of movies and cult classics, Gordies Music, and a tattoo parlor.

Oak Bay Village. Oak Bay Village is a truly self-sufficient village community with its own town council. It includes what used to be the Uplands Farm and the Tod Farm, the latter of whose house stands today. When 243 property owners in Oak Bay petitioned the city of Victoria to be annexed in 1906, they were turned down, and later that same year Oak Bay incorporated as a city.

Oak Bay is known for gentility, British influence, nice weather, a beautiful marina, its village center, large Edwardian-style homes, the Oak Bay Beach Hotel, and the Marina Restaurant complex. We strongly encourage you to take a bus tour or car through the area and sample neighborhood living. (Bus 1 Willow or 2 Oak Bay.)

Belfry Theatre, Fernwood

Fine points: You can take the Oak Bay Explorer bus from Belleville Street or in front of the Fairmont Empress Hotel.

Now we will take you through the attractions of Oak Bay and down its main street, coincidentally called Oak Bay.

Ottavio Italian Bakery & Delicatessen reopened at this location at Oak Bay and Monterey, along with Winchester Gallery. Co-owners Monica Pozzolo and Andrew Moyer offer a few outdoor terrace tables and more indoor cafe space than its original spot down the street. Ottavio still produces the best hand-rolled Italian breads in town, along with Italian and French import foods, cured meats and olives, 240 artisanal cheeses, and their own house-made gelato made with locally grown fruit and organic milk, even in the form of gelato sundaes.

Now you can order lunch or snacks such as muffaletta, carciofo, Melanzana, salmon, peperonata, or meat panini ($5.75). Additional grilled panini flavors include "Primavera," with artichoke hearts, Brie, basil pesto, and red onion; the "Alpino," with braised fennel, caramelized onion, Qualicum raclette cheese, and herb and spinach pesto; or Black Forest Schinkenspeck ham with organic Emmentaler cheese and greens (each $6.50). A kids' grilled cheese is only $3, with an extra 25 cents for Italian ham.

Other great choices include daily soups, salads, a torte with salad, antipasto, and San Pellegrino soft drinks and mineral water, and Illy coffees.

Ottavio hosts five annual events: A Day in France, Festa Italiana, Spanish Day, Oktoberfest, and The Big Cheese Cut.

Ottavio Italian Bakery & Delicatessen, 2272 Oak Bay Avenue, (250) 592–4080; www.ottaviovictoria.com. Hours: 8:00 A.M.–6:00 P.M. Tuesday–Saturday, 10:00 A.M.–6:00 P.M. Sunday. Beer and wine. Credit cards: Visa and MasterCard.

One highlight experience of Oak Bay for visitors is the **Blethering Place Tearoom & Restaurant** (2250 Oak Bay, 250–598–1413; www.thebletheringplace .com). Loads of locals frequent this cozy and comfortable Tudor-style tearoom with teas served from 11:00 A.M. to 7:00 P.M. or just about any other time if you ask. Light tea is $14.95 and afternoon tea is $15.95. Lunch and dinner are also served, including bangers and mash ($10.95), British India curry ($15.95), turkey dinner ($15.95), liver and onions ($14.95), and steak and kidney pie ($14.95).

Right around the corner from the Blethering Place, eaters and food lovers must check out Colin Campbell Village Butcher and Oak Bay Seafoods Fresh

Basic Risotto with Parmigiano

Ottavio Italian Bakery & Delicatessen, Victoria

8 cups chicken or vegetable stock
2 tbsp. unsalted butter or olive oil
1 medium yellow onion or 4 large shallots, finely chopped
2½ cups Arborio rice
Salt
½ cup white wine (optional), added to stock before simmering
125 grams (1 cup) grated Parmigiano-Reggiano cheese, plus extra for serving
2 more tbsp. unsalted butter

Bring stock with wine to a boil and immediately reduce to a simmer. Put 2 tbsp. butter or olive oil in a heavy-bottomed sauté pan over medium heat. When butter is hot, add onion and cook until translucent, stirring for about 3 minutes. Raise heat to high and add rice. Stir vigorously for about 1 minute. Immediately reduce heat to low and add two to three more ladles of stock, stir, and season with salt. Adjust heat to low so stock is barely bubbling.

In about 2 minutes the rice will appear dry with air pockets in a creamy wet surface. Add another ladleful of simmering stock and stir in briefly. If rice is sticking to pan, add more stock or reduce heat. Add salt as needed.

Rice should be at tender-but-not-firm stage in 18 to 20 minutes, but it should not get hard or mushy. Risotto is done when you decide one more ladleful will make it perfect. Remove pan from heat. Add Parmigiano-Reggiano and stir it in vigorously. When the risotto takes on a satiny sheen, add 2 tbsp. butter and stir in. Cover and let rest for 1 minute.

Serve on warm plates and grate more cheese over each serving. You might want to add variations such as Gorgonzola, porcini or other mushrooms, squash, sweet fennel, saffron, or prosciutto. Serves 6 as entree, more as side dish.

Fish & Game (back behind the butcher shop). Colin Campbell personally cuts, ages, and sells exquisite meats and poultry ranging from game hens and Scotch eggs to baron of beef, and Tuxford and Tehbutt cheeses. Fresh Fish & Game offers salmon pâté, smoked pheasant sausage, venison pepperoni and sausage, and venison and maple breakfast sausage, to say nothing of the freshest fish around.

Blethering Place Tearoom & Restaurant

Tucked downstairs in Monterey Mews between the provisions shops and the tearoom are Upstairs Downstairs, selling dollhouses and everything a collector could want; and the Celtic Cottage, with Irish and Scottish foods, candies, and Celtic jewelry.

In the same building but back on Oak Bay Street, Side Street Studio showcases 175 B.C. artists, and Nushin Boutique has another shop featuring elegant European clothes. At the Grafton Bookshop, Jill Grafton serves as a community secondhand and antiquarian bookstore for what she calls "a reading neighborhood." Grafton Bookshop is a must-visit for book lovers. Wonderful! Oak Bay Books is a small, charming, local, very independent bookstore.

Rogers' Tudor Sweet Shoppe features Rogers' famous chocolates, British specialty sweets, and Jackson's of Piccadilly teas. Check out Ivy's Bookshop, a rare surviving, competing, and charming independent local bookstore. Try Penny Farthing Olde English Pub, which really looks like one and provides an elegant pub ambience with excellent fish and chips, all-day breakfast, and other great pub grub.

Cross Oak Bay Street to the Athlone Court complex at Oak Bay and Hampshire Road. Here you will also find the Hampshire Grill, Fairway Market, and Timeless Toys.

For a light, inexpensive lunch, try Side Street Bistro on Hampshire Road off Oak Bay for excellent soups, small pizzas, sushi, and whole-grain sandwiches.

The **White Heather Tea Room** on Oak Bay is where you can either indulge in lunches of a "sconewish," a cheese and chive scone filled with chicken, egg salad, or cream cheese and roasted peppers, with soup or salad ($6.95); salads; or tea choices.

White linen tablecloths and serviettes and Oriental rugs set the tone for your tea and White Heather's humor, from the Wee Tea at $8.75 to the Not So Wee Tea ($13.25) and the Big Muckle Giant Tea ($32.95) for two people. Don't miss the Welsh cakes cooked to order on the grill from 2:00 to 4:00 P.M. at only $1.50 for four "cakes." Remember the chicken a la king from your youth? It's here ($7.95)!

White Heather Tea Room, 1885 Oak Bay, (250) 595–8020. Hours: 9:30 A.M.–5:00 P.M. Tuesday–Friday, 8:30 A.M.–5:00 P.M. Saturday. Wheelchair accessible. Credit cards: Visa, MasterCard.

A couple of doors west is **Small City Bistro,** a proper bistro with a proper menu featuring specialties including beet and barley salad with pistachios ($7), polenta fries with chipotle aioli or roasted veggie sandwich ($7), and burgers ($8), all including soup or salad, and all in sumptuous portions.

Dinner may include tempura vegetables with soy wasabi aioli ($13), crispy southern-fried oysters ($15), caramelized fillet of salmon ($16), prawn and scallop mousse ravioli ($15), duck confit on roasted vegetable risotto ($17), and lamb ragout ($19). The patio in back is perfect in good weather months.

Small City Bistro, 1871 Oak Bay, (250) 598–2015. Hours: 11:30 A.M.–3:00 P.M. and 5:00–10:00 P.M. or midnight daily. Beer and wine. Wheelchair accessible. Credit cards: Visa, MasterCard.

Heading back eastward on Oak Bay you will find Country Clothing & Gifts; Past Time Antiques for the best in antiques, collectibles, and estate jewelry; Snugglepots children's store; the Bee Hive wool shop for knitting and crocheting supplies; Oak Bay Hardware; and the wonderful, small Village Patisserie, where you can get crème de menthe chocolate cheesecake, yam and squash salad with feta cheese and walnuts, and three-cheese pies topped with Brie!

Oak Bay Gallery shows interesting local-scene paintings and frames; China and Chintz offers its usual tempting home furnishings and accessories; Maresa Boutique offers women's clothing; and Oak Bay Village Wines, sister shop to Cook Street Village Wines, offers libations. Now you are back facing the

Blethering Place Tearoom & Restaurant, just in time to indulge yourself and try a light or afternoon tea. Enjoy!

In 2007 the stylish old lady, The Oak Bay Beach Hotel, was torn down to make way for a new hotel and condo complex. The Marina Restaurant, right at the Oak Bay Marina, offers excellent West Coast cuisine, a marvelous sushi bar, and sumptuous Sunday brunch, with a full and intriguing bar lounge, all with one of the most romantic views in greater Victoria. We'll come back to this restaurant again.

Where to Stay at University of Victoria

UVic Housing and Conference Services, Sinclair at Finnerly Road, $32–$65, May 1 to August 31 only, 999 units, shared baths, some kitchens, breakfast included, no pets; (250) 721–8396.

SIGNIFICANT OTHERS

Significant Others, in this case, refers to restaurants and other places of interest not located in the hard-core downtown mecca but that we highly recommend. They are worth the effort it might take to get there.

Brasserie L'Ecole may just be the best restaurant in Victoria. Unpretentiously Frenchish, L'Ecole owners chef Sean Brennan and sommelier Marc Morrison seem to be admitting that they are Canadian cooking French and manage to create a very French feeling within a Canadian space. Brennan was formerly chef at the Met Bistro and was chef and partner at Cafe Brio.

French posters decorate the walls of the narrow bistro, the downstairs of which was once a Chinese school, hence the L'Ecole reference. Every table is cozy, and we also enjoy dining at the bar, where the bartendress is delightful and knowledgeable of wines both French and otherwise. L'Ecole offers an excellent small selection of wines from the Rhone, Languedoc-Roussillon, Loire, and Bordeaux regions, as well as several from other countries.

The onion soup is terrific ($7), as are the mouthwatering butter-fried mussels in garlic, parsley, and wine; the endive salad is the curly scratchy kind, not Belgian endive; and the lamb shank and pan-fried skate wing are fabulous, with a side of Cobble Hill asparagus only $5 in season. Or try the roasted half Dungeness crab ($16) or hot smoked duck breast ($11). House specialties include duck confit, beer and goat cheese terrine, Sooke trout with sun chokes, fingerling potatoes, and anchovy butter ($19), red-wine-braised lamb shanks ($21), and beef short ribs, with sides at $5. A large bottle of Vittel is only $4, and the Bombay Safire gin martinis are huge and perfectly made. The cocktail list includes "Death in the Afternoon," a mixture of champagne and absinthe ($8). If a cheese course tempts, advise the server when you order your meal so the cheeses can warm to room temperature. Brasserie L'Ecole is a must.

Brasserie L'Ecole, 1715 Government Street, (250) 475–6260; Fax: (250) 475–6261; www.lecole.ca. Hours: 5:30–11:00 P.M. Tuesday–Saturday. Fully licensed. Wheelchair accessible. Credit cards: Visa, MasterCard.

Estevan Village is about ½ mile north of Oak Bay and is an even smaller community shopping area. Culinary highlights of the neighborhood are the Willow Tree Cafe; the local coffee, huge sandwich, and banana split hangout with sidewalk tables; and Paprika Bistro, the beloved baby of George and Linda Szasz.

Paprika Bistro looks very California, with two small, cozy rooms and warm mustard walls hung with Avis Rasmussen's appealing primary-color paintings and prints. George and Linda serve three generations' family recipes.

Specialty appetizers include beet and fennel salad ($8.50), West Coast Spot Prawn bisque ($9.95), and seared Digby scallops ($11.95). Dinner entrees delight with Nana Szasz's veal goulash ($19.95), slow braised Metchosin lamb shank ($26.95), Cowichan Bay Farm duck confit ($21.95), crispy pork belly ($24.95), and tiger prawn curry ($27.95).

Every day Paprika's kitchen makes terrines, pâtés, and variety meats and uses locally grown organic products. Worth finding, for sure.

Paprika Bistro, 2524 Estevan, (250) 592–7424; Fax: (250) 592–1316; www.paprika-bistro.com. Hours: from 5:00 P.M. Monday–Saturday. Beer and wine. Wheelchair accessible. Credit cards: Visa, MasterCard.

On the corner across the street from Paprika in tiny Estevan Village is a locals' favorite fish and chips joint, **Willows Galley,** which consists of an ordering counter and seven stools facing the windows. Most people get their fish and chips to go in newspaper cones (makes a great picnic at nearby Willows Beach), but we like to hang out here and listen to conversations and other people's fish preferences.

All fish meals include chips, coleslaw, and tartar sauce, so you can order varied sizes of halibut, cod, or shrimp, all deep fried. They also offer a Chiefs Plate with grilled halibut, chips, coleslaw, and chowder ($13.45), or the Treasure Chest, with the above fried with shrimp, scallops, oysters, and chowder (same price). The chowder is a meal in itself, and the coleslaw is worth the trip.

Carnivores will find plenty of burgers and subs, as well as seafood burgers and a Landlubber veggie burger ($4.75), soft ice cream, and frozen yogurt.

Willows Galley, Estevan "shopping center," (250) 598–2711. Hours: 11:00 A.M.–6:45 P.M. Wednesday–Sunday, hours may vary in summer. Not wheelchair accessible. Credit cards: Visa, MasterCard.

Many locals regard **Baan Thai** as the best Thai restaurant on Vancouver Island. Specialties include pla lard prik (pan-fried fish) at $12.95, swimming rama (beef with peanut sauce) at $10.95, veggie specials at $6.95, and excellent pad Thai (rice noodles with shrimp, tofu, and chicken if you wish) at $6.95. All dishes may have tofu substituted for meat. You also have your choice of hotness, and we recommend mild. Medium burns our lips, but if that sends you to heaven, go for it. Be sure to try this one!

Baan Thai, 1117 Blanshard, (250) 383–0050. Hours: noon–2:30 P.M. and from 5:00 P.M. on Monday–Friday, from noon on Sunday. Beer and wine. One low step to doorway. Credit cards: Visa, MasterCard, American Express, enRoute.

The **Canoe Club Brewhouse and Restaurant** is located at the foot of historic Chinatown (east of Fisgard, across Wharf) in a restored heritage 1894 powerhouse, right on the waterfront. Visit it just to experience the prize location.

At this Marina Restaurant Group outpost, enjoy house-made brews and a contemporary menu featuring local organics, seared Ahi tuna, mussels in dark ale broth with herbs and cream, lamb, and antipasto platters, plus handcrafted beers, ales, and lagers made in accordance with the Bavarian Purity Order of 1516.

Canoe Club Brewhouse and Restaurant, 450 Swift Street, (250) 361–1940; www.canoebrewpub.com. Hours: 11:00 A.M.–midnight Sunday–Thursday, 11:00 A.M.–1:00 A.M. Friday–Saturday. Beer and wine. Wheelchair accessible. Credit cards: Visa, MasterCard.

The **James Bay Tearoom and Restaurant** is a local and international favorite for British cuisine and afternoon tea. In a charming small building with flowers hanging outside, enjoy a breakfast of kippers and eggs; lunch of traditional sandwiches, soups, or meat pies; tempting sweets; and, of course, everything that goes with traditional, proper tea. Breakfast includes an omelet special on weekdays and eggs Benedict on weekends.

James Bay Tearoom and Restaurant, 332 Menzies at Superior, (250) 382–8282; www.thejamesbaytearoomandrestaurant.com. Hours: 7:00 A.M.–5:00 P.M. daily. Beer and wine. Wheelchair accessible. Credit cards: Visa, MasterCard.

Santiago's Cafe, an oasis of fun and hip Spanish ambience, serves an enormous selection of tapas, sangrias, umbrella drinks, and flan. Try it for someone's birthday. It's a hilarious experience.

Santiago's Cafe, 660 Oswego south of Belleville, (250) 388–7376. Hours: 11:00 A.M.–11:00 P.M. daily. Fully licensed. Restaurant is wheelchair accessible, restrooms are not. Credit cards: Visa, MasterCard, American Express.

Floyd's Diner is the new happening breakfast place in Victoria, founded by the guys who used to own Cup a Joe in James Bay, and replacing an old Chinese buffet restaurant at this highly trafficked corner.

All you have to do is barely step in the door or into the lineup outside and someone brings you a cup of coffee while you wait in this hubbub of nostalgia for Elvis, Einstein, Marilyn Monroe, and even Roy Rogers.

Breakfast is served "all day, baby," with excellent dishes called "The Elton," "Listen to Me When I'm Talkin' to Ya Son," "Huevos Incredibalos," and "Flapjack Cadillac." Loads of eggs Benedict choices such as "Eggs Ben-Hur" and "The Donald Trump-so good it'll make your hair (or whatever the heck you call that animal on his head) stand on end," while omelets include "The Marvin Gaye" and "Easy Rider."

Lunch brings fabulous sandwiches, burgers, and salads.

Floyd's Diner, 866 Yates Street, (250) 381–5114. Hours: 7:30 A.M.–4:00 P.M. Monday–Friday, 8:00 A.M.-4:00 P.M. Saturday–Sunday. Wheelchair accessible. Credit cards: Visa, MasterCard.

John's Place, owned by former Californian John Cantin, is generally recognized as the ultimate Victoria diner—or any diner for that matter. Images of Marilyn Monroe dominate the walls (along with several other 1950s and '60s favorites), vinyl benches dominate the booths, pies and cakes dominate your view at the door, and fantastic basic food dominates the menu. Enjoy the funk and junk with a crowd of cross-cultural, cross-generational, mellow with-its.

At breakfast you have to try the waffles or pancakes with or without fruit, or create your own omelet (our favorite is cooked fresh asparagus, mushrooms, and feta cheese), or eggs Benny with the best potatoes anywhere. Lunch and dinner go on until at least 9:00 P.M., with excellent Japanese noodle soups, authentic enchiladas, piled-high pastas, and crisp salads. John's banana bread melts in your mouth. One of our favorites.

John's Place now offers the very best in hard liquor, local brews, and specialty martinis from "The Porn Star" to "The Chocolate Fire."

> *John's Place, 723 Pandora Street, (250) 389–0711; www.johnsplace.ca. Hours: 8:00 A.M.–9:00 or 10:00 P.M. daily. Fully licensed. Wheelchair accessible. Credit cards: Visa, MasterCard.*

Ogden Point Cafe is a spectacular waterfront cafe at the breakwater where cruise ships dock.

A central gas fireplace highlights the restaurant upstairs from the Dive Centre with awesome views of the Pacific Ocean, and there's indoor and outdoor seating in good weather. Gail Patterson quit being a legal secretary and Bob Lumbley quit being a fisherman to create something for divers and the rest of us.

Locals out on their daily walks stop by and stay. Here are some of the reasons why: breakfasts of steamed eggs, waffles, fruit, yogurt, and muesli; excellent coffees and teas; Caesar, spinach, or Greek salads at about $5.50; daily soups and "the best clam chowder in Victoria" every day at about $4.50; sandwiches at $5.95 (with a side green salad, add $1.50); shepherd's pie; spinach and mushroom turnovers; and, best of all, desserts to die for, including choices for diabetics and those requiring lactose-free and fat-free sweets. No preservatives or salt added. One of Kathleen's favorites.

> *Ogden Point Cafe, 199 Dallas Road at Montreal Street and the Ogden Point Piers, (250) 386–8080. Hours: summer 7:00 A.M.–10:00 P.M. daily, winter 7:00 A.M.–7:00 P.M. daily. Wheelchair accessible by ramp from paved path to breakwater. Credit cards: Visa, MasterCard. Smoking on the sundeck.*

Finest at Sea (F.A.S.) Seafood Producers Ltd. is the lifelong love and project of angler Bob Fraumeni, who spent his youth fishing in Gonzales Bay in Victoria. He now has eight boats fishing sablefish (black cod), albacore tuna, wild B.C. salmon lingcod, halibut, and rockfish, and he employs more than one hundred B.C. anglers year-round.

F.A.S. fish have been in great demand in Asian markets for sushi because of their high quality and freshness. As the Japanese economy wavered, Fraumeni smartly opened his boutique fish store just a few hundred feet from Victoria's Fisherman's Wharf, where his boats dock.

Here visitors can eye live prawns, mussels, oysters, sea urchins, and Dungeness crabs, with generous tastes of hot or cold smoked salmon (the absolute best). Food fans must check this out!

F.A.S. Seafood Producers Ltd., *27 Erie Street, (250) 383–7764; www.fasseafood.com. Hours: 9:00 A.M.–6:00 P.M. Monday–Saturday, 9:00 A.M.–5:00 P.M. Sunday. Not wheelchair accessible. Credit cards: Visa, MasterCard.*

Victorians' favorite fish and chips place, **Barb's Place Floating Seafood Restaurant,** floats at Fisherman's Wharf. With only a couple of tables, this place does a huge business among local businesspeople who take a break and come down to the water, anglers, and visitors alike. The menu is short, to the point, and painted on the outside wall above the order windows, where you can get the biggest and best fish and chips in Victoria and even burgers. Come early and buy fish directly off the boats. Barb's was sold recently and is distinctly cleaned up and offers more tables and fewer bees. Ice cream, too. One of our favorites.

Barb's Place Floating Seafood Restaurant, 310 St. Lawrence, (250) 384–6515; www.barbsplace.ca. Hours: daily March–October 10:00 A.M.–dark. Not wheelchair accessible. Credit cards: none.

Be sure to get across Johnson Street Bridge (the blue bridge) to **Ocean Pointe Resort.** Cross the bridge (approach from Pandora or Wharf Streets as Johnson is one way east) and take the immediate right (west end) by foot (a ten-minute stroll from Wharf Street) or wheel, and the sidewalk/road will take you to Ocean Pointe for a few hours' minivacation.

Ocean Pointe's Boardwalk Restaurant and Terrace offer an exceptional Sunday brunch and view of the Inner Harbour, providing the ultimate taste and romance experiences for that time of day. Plan to stay a while so that you can sample the omelet station, the Chinese station, rows of salads from Thai to green and green Thai, the carving station with roasts galore, and the most orgiastic selection of desserts, including cheesecakes from Ely's in Chicago and Moevenpick ice cream. One of our favorites.

Ocean Pointe Resort, 45 Songhees Road, (250) 360–2999; www.opr hotel.com. Reservations required (250–360–5889). Hours: Two seatings:

Ocean Pointe Resort and a commuter seaplane, Inner Harbour

11:30 A.M. and 1:30 P.M. daily. Fully licensed. Wheelchair accessible by elevator. Credit cards: Visa, MasterCard, American Express, Diners.

If you are interested in buying B.C. wines to take home, try the **Ocean Pointe Resort Wine Shoppe.** Wine aficionados will enjoy this unusual collection of rare B.C. wines, including Lang, Cedar Creek, Gray Monk, Summerhill, Blue Mountain, Mission Hill's Library Releases, Calona, and St. Hubertus. The shop also offers wine seminars Sunday afternoons after brunch.

> ***Ocean Pointe Resort Wine Shoppe,*** *45 Songhees Road, (250) 360–5804. Hours: noon–8:00 P.M. Tuesday–Sunday. Wheelchair accessible by elevator. Credit cards: Visa, MasterCard, American Express, Diners.*

Marina Restaurant and Marina Cafe-Deli, both at 1327 Beach Street, are two of Victoria's best culinary rendezvous. **Marina Restaurant** properly boasts an exquisite view of the Oak Bay Marina and the lower mainland; it is almost a pleasant surprise that the food and service here are just as good. Extremely popular with its regulars, the Oak Bay Marine Group's Marina Restaurant specializes in local shellfish and fish, local pastas, salads, house-made breads and desserts (very local), with an interesting and imaginative local sushi bar, and elegant Sunday brunch ($28.95 adults, $23.95 seniors, $15.95 children under twelve). Monday is pasta special night ($6.95). Lunch includes Saltspring Island mussels, crab and halibut cheek cakes, spot prawn tarts, salads, sandwiches, burgers, Fanny Bay oysters, and chips ($7.95–$18.95), while dinner might include great clam chowder ($7.95), tempura fried calamari ($10.95), entrecote of beef with truffled garlic fries ($27.95), steak, scallops, lingcod, ahi tuna, and Cowichan Bay chicken breast "au vin" ($27.95–$35.95).

> ***Marina Restaurant***, *1327 Beach Street, (250) 598–8555; www.marina restaurant.com. Hours: lunch 11:30 A.M.–2:30 P.M. Monday–Saturday; dinner 5:00–10:00 P.M. Sunday–Thursday, 5:00–11:00 P.M. Friday and Saturday; Sunday brunch buffet 10:00 A.M.–2:30 P.M. Fully licensed. Mostly wheelchair accessible. Credit cards: Visa, MasterCard, American Express, Diners, enRoute. Reservations highly recommended.*

The **Marina Coffee House** is a hidden inexpensive spot with all-day full breakfasts and exotic salads and sandwiches. It's worth the wander to find this place, to say nothing of the view, equaled only by the Marina Restaurant upstairs. You

Marina Restaurant and Marina Coffee House at the Oak Bay Marina

walk down the stairs between the gift shop and the Marina Restaurant and follow the cafe flags around the deck to the water side of the building.

The panini sandwiches are great to share along with a salad. We chose the rice and garbanzo salad with apples, oranges, and light curry. The breakfasts ($2 to $7) are huge and hearty. Cafeteria style. One of our favorites.

Marina Coffee House, 1327 Beach Street, (250) 598–3890; www.marina restaurant.com. Hours: open daily, summer 7:00 A.M.–9:00 P.M. Beer and wine. Not wheelchair accessible. Credit cards: Visa, MasterCard, American Express, Diners, enRoute.

Formerly Ann Hathaway's Thatched Cottage & Olde England Inn, the revived and renamed **English Inn & Resort** is attracting lots of attention, primarily for its restaurant, the **Rosemeade Dining Room.**

Maria Hernandez, daughter of the owner of Pablo's Dining Lounge on Quebec Street and the Wharfside on Wharf Street, has preserved the best of the old architecture, while adding an extremely hip art deco decor that transports diners to another realm, all designed by talented Jeff Smith.

Chef Richard Luttman is a B.C. native who has cooked all his life, even when he had to fight his sisters for their toy stove. Luttman comes to Rosemeade via the great Four Seasons in Las Vegas and offers a unique dining experience, his Chef's Table, at which guests can dine in the kitchen and watch the chefs at work.

Chef Luttman's dining room dinner menu offers appetizers such as creamy tomato, clam, and smoked black cod chowder ($8); local Dungeness crab cakes, sun choke puree, and blood orange emulsion ($15); seared chopped scallop salad ($10); or sautéed sweetbreads ($8). Salads are interesting, as are main courses such as boneless slow braised beef short rib with red onion and goat cheese pierogies and beet root syrup ($24); Cowichan Valley duck breast with aged cheddar whipped potatoes ($26); beef tenderloin and marrow with flat parsley and celery root gnocchi ($29); herb brioche crusted venison loin with potato Gorgonzola strudel ($29); ahi tuna steak with black Beluga lentils, brussels sprouts, horseradish froth, and pinot noir reduction ($28); scallion marinated lingcod with prawn-cabbage and ham hock dumplings ($27); or a quartet of seasonally farmed local vegetables ($27).

All of this is set in a five-acre garden plunked into the Esquimalt neighborhood, with elegant rooms, a few of which still have a wee musty smell. (Room prices: $109–$199 off season, $199–$399 high season.) Great gazebo for weddings.

English Inn & Resort and Rosemeade Dining Room, 429 Lampson Street, (250) 388–4353 or (866) 388–4353; www.englishinnresort.com. Fully licensed. Wheelchair accessible. Credit cards: Visa, MasterCard, American Express.

Mount Royal Bagel Factory makes and supplies most of the better bagel-serving restaurants on Vancouver Island. The address is slightly misleading, because you actually find it by turning off Quadra Street onto Grant. It's a little joint on the left and well worth the effort.

Mount Royal Bagel Factory, 1115 North Park, (250) 380–3588. Hours: 7:00 A.M.–7:00 P.M. daily. Wheelchair accessible. Credit cards: none.

Charelli's Deli is one of our fondest finds. Mother Carmen and daughter Nicole took over an old Italian deli and, by responding to customers' requests, have assembled one of the finest cheese and import foods shops in Victoria. They specialize in Vancouver Island cheeses such as those from David Woods, Hillary's Cheeses, Moonstruck, Natural Pastures, and import cheeses and meats from the United Kingdom, Italy, Spain, Denmark, Belgium, France, Germany, the Netherlands, and even Quebec! Be sure to sample the Midnight Blue from Finland, St. Agur's from France, Dutch goat cheese, white Stilton, and the Chef de Paillot from Quebec. All cheese tastes are presented on individual gray marble slabs.

Meat fans will enjoy German bratwurst, Danish salami, and Spanish Serrano ham, as well as relatively inexpensive sandwiches made of all of these possibile ingredients. Be sure to check out all the imported delicacies in jars and tins around the walls of this hole-in-the-wall treasure trove, including oils, vinegars, truffles, foie gras, and caviar.

Charelli's Delicatessen, 2863 Foul Bay Road (on the way out to the University of Victoria), (250) 598–4794; www.charellis.com. Hours: 10:00 A.M.–6:00 P.M. Tuesday–Saturday, 11:00 A.M.–5:00 P.M. Sunday. Wheelchair accessible. Credit cards: Visa, MasterCard, American Express.

Right next door is **Robert Shaw Specialty Pies,** which has been in business since 1970 and apparently hasn't changed the prices or repainted the menu signs in all that time. Regulars gather at a couple of small tables inside and out for their coffee and tea, as well as ritual consumption of Shaw's divine traditional Scottish and English steak and kidney or chicken pies and sandwiches. You can indulge in owner Jack Galbraith's Lincolnshire pork pie ($2.35), fruit and other pies, or take home mini mince pies or cookies, sausage rolls, or their famous Melton Mowbray pies. A true Canadian British experience although this fine establishment was for sale at press time.

> *Robert Shaw Specialty Pies, 2865 Foul Bay Road, (250) 692–3314. Hours: 8:00 A.M.–6:00 P.M. Monday–Saturday. Wheelchair accessible. Credit cards: none.*

Wooden Shoe Dutch Groceries & Delicatessen, on Quadra Street near Hillside Avenue, features Dutch and other imported cheeses, Indonesian foods, Dutch meats, cookies, pickles, "bunwiches" to order, biscuits, cooking equipment, sixty varieties of licorice, Delft pottery and housewares, wooden and leather clogs, books, and tapes. Arie and Trudy Kuyvenhoven run an unusual deli that is worth the trip.

> *Wooden Shoe Dutch Groceries & Delicatessen, 2576 Quadra Street, (250) 382–9042; www.woodenshoedeli.com. Hours: 9:30 A.M.–5:30 P.M. Monday–Saturday, until 7:00 P.M. Friday. Wheelchair accessible. Credit cards: Visa, MasterCard.*

One of our absolute favorite out-of-the-way spots is the **Cook'n'Pan Polish Delikatessen.** As we walk in we smell the smells of our grandmothers' kitchens, and they weren't even Polish. Henryk and Josefa Kierebinski started the place with her family recipes, and you can view Henryk's military honors and appreciation certificates signed by Lech Walesa down the hallway wall.

Granddaughters Paulina and Janina Tokarski now offer a remarkable collection of "East European goods and cuisine," with traditional recipes used to make everything right here. Try the pierogies, cabbage rolls, slaska, bigos, unbelievable soups including flaki (tripe, chicken, and veggies), huge breakfasts, pâtés, pickles and sauerkraut, blood and many other sausages, Polish buns with cottage cheese or fruit, chalwa, sesame snaps, and a wide variety of combination sampler plates and sandwiches. Do not miss this deli or the jarred and canned imported goodies on the shelves!

> *Cook'n'Pan Polish Delikatessen, 1725 Cook Street, (250) 385–5509. Hours: 8:00 A.M.–7:00 P.M. Monday–Friday, 9:00 A.M.–5:00 P.M. Saturday. Wheelchair accessible. Credit cards: none.*

Our favorite place for pizza is the **San Remo Restaurant** on Quadra Street. The San Remo serves interesting Greek specialties with occasionally bland vegetables, but loads of people go there for the pizza and salads. The vegetarian specials are outstanding and filling for several people. The San Remo has added a gourmet import market next door.

San Remo Restaurant, 2709 Quadra Street, (250) 384–5255. Hours: lunch Monday–Saturday, dinner daily. Full bar. Wheelchair accessible from Quadra Street. Credit cards: Visa, MasterCard, American Express.

As winemakers in northern California's Sonoma Valley say, "It takes a lot of beer to make good wine." Here are two places where you can stoke up for whatever you have to do.

When you're over the blue bridge, you'll find **Spinnaker's Brewery Pub & Restaurant** on Catherine Street an excellent on-site microbrewery and restaurant. From downtown Victoria cross the Johnson Street (blue) Bridge and turn left onto Catherine Street.

While you wait for a table in the foyer, you can peer through the window and watch some brewing going on. Spinnaker's offers beers-of-the-day for drinking in the pub and restaurant including India Pale Ale, Hefeweizen, Tsarist Stout, Jamesons Scottish Ale, Honey Blonde Ale, and fruit beers. Breakfast is a real waker-upper with hearty foods to get your day going. At lunch or dinner try the fluffy fish and chips, Caesar salads, salmon salad ($15.95), smoked salmon and shrimp omelet ($11.00), Montreal smoked-beef sandwich ($9.95), pizzas, or huge burgers. Try the B.C. salmon cakes ($12), wild Pacific salmon, or B.C. halibut fish and chips ($12–$15), each served with Kennebec fries. Dinner may include a braised duck leg ($18), lamb shanks ($18), and a local seafood hot pot ($19). To get a view of the Inner Harbour, ask for a table near the window. Inquire about daily food and brew specials. Both are excellent and are local favorites. You might also try the Taproom Antipasti Bar, where you pay separately for each selection, and it offers fabulous malt vinegars, beers, and "aquifers" (waters from the earth). Innkeeper Paul Hadfield had added a "Paysan" dinner option of a four-course dinner served on large platters. Live music Sunday–Tuesday beginning at 8:30 P.M.

Spinnaker's Brewery Pub & Restaurant, 308 Catherine Street, (250) 386–2739; www.spinnakers.com. Hours: 11:00 A.M.–11:00 P.M. daily, bakery opens at 8:00 A.M. Wheelchair accessible. Credit cards: Visa, MasterCard, American Express, Diners.

Right in town, microbrew lovers should visit the **Vancouver Island Brewery,** one producer of "the Island's Own Beer!" This microbrewery makes Victoria Lager, Piper's Pale Ale, Hermann's Dark Lager, Wolf's Scottish Cream Ale, Victoria Island Lager, and Hermannator Ice Bock. Even better, you can take a tour of the state-of-the-art brewery during the summer at 11:30 A.M. and at 1:00 and 3:00 P.M., with tastes and a stop at a colorful, fun gift shop.

Vancouver Island Brewery, 2330 Government Street, (250) 361–0005; www.vanislandbrewery.com. Hours: 9:00 A.M.–6:00 P.M. Monday–Saturday. Wheelchair accessible. Credit cards: Visa, MasterCard.

THINGS YOU REALLY SHOULD SEE

There are a few more attractions not covered in any of our neighborhood tours that you really should visit.

The **Art Gallery of Greater Victoria** attracts exhibits of international renown and shows them in an almost homey, comfortable, friendly, and accessible atmosphere. It has the largest collection in British Columbia, holding 10,000 works.

Permanent exhibits include works by contemporary B.C. and other Canadian artists, such as Emily Carr, other North American and European works, and possibly Canada's finest collection of Japanese and Chinese art. Visit the only Shinto shrine in North America.

Once the temporary residence of B.C.'s lieutenant governor, the 1889 mansion was purchased by retailer David Spencer in 1903 and given to the Art Gallery of Greater Victoria in the 1950s.

Every August the gallery puts on an art festival on Moss Street, where you can watch artists, or do the painting yourself if you're so inclined, ending the day in a wonderful beer party in the museum parking lot. Lots of fun, lots of locals, low cost.

Art Gallery of Greater Victoria, 1040 Moss Street, (250) 384–4101; www.aggv.bc.ca. Hours: 10:00 A.M.–5:00 P.M. Monday–Saturday, until 9:00 P.M. Thursday, 1:00–5:00 P.M. Sunday. Admission: members free, adults $12, seniors and students $10, children ages six–seventeen $2, children five and younger free. Wheelchair accessible. (Buses 10 Haultain; 11, 14 UVic up Fort Street, get off at Moss.)

The **B.C. Aviation Museum,** heaven for aviation buffs, is basically a hangar where volunteers restore airplanes and construct engine displays as well as exhibit aircraft, from as early as 1911 to post–World War II.

> *B.C. Aviation Museum, 1910 Norseman Road, Victoria International Airport, Sidney, B.C.; (250) 655–3300; www.bcam.net. Hours: May 1–September 30: 10:00 A.M.–4:00 P.M. daily, October 1–April 30: 11:00 A.M.–3:00 P.M. daily. Admission: adults $7, seniors $5, children to age twelve free accompanied by an adult, group rates on request. Wheelchair accessible. Credit cards: none. Directions: Take Highway 17 (Pat Bay Highway), take Airport turnoff (McTavish Road), and turn right onto Canora Road to museum driveway.*

Beacon Hill Park, bound by Douglas Street, Dallas Road, Southgate Street, and Heywood, is one of the most relaxing places we know. The flowers are breathtaking year-round; there are lots of daytime-safe paths to walk; lots of activities for kids; the lakes are peaceful; and the birds, ducks, and squirrels talk to you. The park runs all the way to Dallas Road and the Strait of Juan de Fuca, facing Washington's Olympic Mountains.

For the kids there's an excellent Children's (petting) Farm with baby goats, peacocks, chickens, sheep, and potbelly pigs; just north of the restrooms and public telephone, there's a fun, colorful playground with a pretend train and lots of climbing equipment.

Watch cricket matches on the southeast side, Victoria Lawn Bowling Club matches on the east side, and soccer matches on the southwest side of the park. Or make use of a fine pitch-and-putt

World's tallest totem pole, Beacon Hill Park at Dallas Road

golf course. There's lots of parking along the park's roads, on side streets, or on Dallas Road.

In the Queen's Garden toward the southeast corner of the park, two plaques commemorate Queen Elizabeth's visits to the site, but the shrubs and trees seem to refuse to grow and look a bit forlorn.

Please pay attention to signs throughout Beacon Hill Park, which basically say please don't feed the animals.

Following the road southeast from the Children's Farm toward the totem and Dallas Road, notice the forty Japanese Sakura cherry blossom trees planted April 21, 1990, in hopes that "Friendship Will Bridge the Pacific Ocean."

The world's tallest totem pole is located at the southeast corner of Beacon Hill Park, adjoining the most natural part of the park. Carved by Mungo Martin, David Martin, and Henry Hunt, the totem is 127 feet, 7 inches tall. It was dedicated July 2, 1956. Lie on your back and experience the magnitude of this work and symbol, as Kathleen did for the photo.

Beacon Hill Park is bound by Douglas Street, Dallas Road, Southgate Street, and Heywood, beginning 1 block from Belleville (250–361–0364). Directions: Bus 5 or walk. All facilities are wheelchair accessible.

Most people want to see the **Butchart Gardens** (Benvenuto Avenue, Central Saanich). Beginning in 1904, Jenny and Robert Pim Butchart began to develop and beautify what used to be a worked-out quarry for their Portland Cement Company. Ever since the family has lived out its commitment to horticulture and beauty by cultivating hundreds of thousands of plants and flowers. Easy-to-walk paths take visitors through the exquisite sunken garden (once a limestone quarry); the ultimate rose garden, where each plant is labeled; the serene Japanese garden; and the classic Italian garden, which are all interspersed with sculptures.

Pick up leaflets in eighteen languages near the visitor center and the Benvenuto Seed and Gift Store and guide yourselves over the 130 acres. Visitor-center staff will answer all questions graciously about the plants grown here and the local area.

From June 15 to September 30, thousands of colored lights hidden among the flowers illuminate the entire gardens. Sing-alongs with the Butchart Gardeners happen Monday through Saturday nights from June 1 to September 30. A Lights Up! dance and variety show takes place weeknights from mid-June to early September, and spectacular fireworks light up the sky Saturday nights in

Butchart Gardens

July and August. The Christmas decorations are worth the trip. Take the bus to avoid traffic jams.

All Butchart Gardens dining facilities are excellent and range in price from economical to expensive. The Coffee Bar serves light snacks; the Blue Poppy Restaurant cafeteria serves terrific sandwiches, salads, hot dishes, and Afternoon Tea and High Tea at reasonable prices; and the Dining Room in the old Butchart residence ("Benvenuto") serves elegant lunches and dinners. A great espresso bar and ice-cream stand is at the top of the sunken garden.

The Benvenuto Seed and Gift Store sells gorgeous calendars, books, gardening implements, videos of the gardens, seeds of flowers growing there, gift cards, teapots and cups, and an abundance of other appropriate stuff. You can also get catalogues and plant identification help.

Butchart Gardens, Benvenuto Avenue, Central Saanich (866–652–4422 toll free; 250–652–5256 recorded; 250–652–4422 business; 250–652–8222 dining reservations; www.butchartgardens.com). Hours: open 9:00 A.M., gates close at different times all year, from early in winter to 10:00 P.M. in summer. Admission: summer adults $14.00–$25.00, juniors ages thirteen to seventeen $7.25–$12.50, children ages five to twelve $2.50. Beer and wine. Mostly wheelchair accessible. Credit cards: Visa,

MasterCard, American Express. In summer months, try to go early in the morning or late in the afternoon to avoid biggest crowds. Take B.C. Transit Bus 75 for a little more than $2 or Gray Line tours from the bus station behind the Fairmont Empress Hotel for $14–$49.

Victoria Butterfly Gardens is considered to be in Victoria but is technically in Brentwood Bay. The Butterfly Gardens includes an indoor tropical rain-forest replica with flowering plants, birds, waterfalls, and hundreds of exotic butterflies during warm months. Koi, carp, and goldfish swim in the "stream," and an excellent shop and good restaurant take care of your other needs. Gray Line runs a Shuttle Express to the Butterfly Gardens and the Butchart Gardens, which are fairly close. This is a great way to see both carefree.

Victoria Butterfly Gardens, 1461 Benvenuto Avenue, Brentwood Bay; (250) 652–3822 or (877) 722–0272; Fax: (250) 652–4683; www .butterflygardens.com. Hours: 9:30 A.M.–4:30 or 5:00 P.M. daily. March–October. Admission: adults $11.00, seniors and students $10.00, children ages five to twelve $5.75, children under age five free with paying adult. Wheelchair accessible. Credit cards: Visa, Master-Card.

Church & State Winery is right up the road from the Victoria Butterfly Gardens and well worth the visit to stimulate the palate. Opened in 2003, the original winery was the baby of British Columbia's best-known winemakers, Erik von Krosigk and Edd Moyes. Boasting an actual Viticulture Centre, the 21,000-square-foot facility on a twenty-five-acre former hay field is one of the most interestingly designed wineries in British Columbia.

Kim Pullen bought the closed facility in 2004.

Wines include Pinot Gris, Merlot, Chardonnay, Syrah, Petit Verdot, Pinot Noir, Pinot Noir Icewine, and Sauvignon Blanc.

Bill Dyer, once of Frogs' Leap Winery in Napa and Burrowing Owl in British Columbia's Okanagan Valley, serves as winemaker.

Church & State Winery, 1445 Benvenuto Avenue, Brentwood Bay; (250) 652–2671; Fax: (250) 652–2672; www.churchandstatewines .com. Hours: 10:00 A.M.–10:00 P.M. daily. Credit cards: Visa, Master-Card. Take B.C. Transit Bus 75 or a Gray Line tour from the Fairmont Empress Hotel.

Starling Lane Winery sits on a piece of land acquired by "Hanging" Judge Begbie from the British Crown in 1859, and it's currently called Heritage Farm Vineyard. John Wrinch serves as his own winemaker, while Jacqueline Wrinch manages the tasting room and agri-tourism events and sells the farm's products in the historic barn. Jacqueline's ornate white greenhouse is a local landmark that says you have reached Starling Lane.

Starling Lane produces internationally reviewed and much sought-after Ortega, Gewürztraminer, Pinot Blanc, Pinot Gris, Maréchal Foch, and Wild Blackberry Port. Call ahead or check the Web site because the winery sells out and does not open if they are out of wine.

> *Starling Lane Winery, 5271 Old West Saanich Road, (250) 881–7422; www.starlinglanewinery.com. Call for hours and to see if they have wine. Partly wheelchair accessible. Credit cards: Visa, MasterCard, American Express.*

Brentwood Bay Lodge, right in the neighborhood of Butchart Gardens, the Butterfly Gardens, and Victoria Estate Winery, is a sumptuous inn. A member of the exclusive Small Luxury Hotels of the World, it offers many "ocean" (Brentwood Bay) view rooms. Its quickly renowned Arbutus Grille is one of the area's leading restaurants. Sommelier Brian Storen, formerly of Sooke Harbour House and Malahat Mountain Inn, has won prizes for the best new wine list and Sommelier of the Year. Among his acquisitions is an 1888 Chateau Lafitte priced at, you guessed it, $1,888.

Executive chef Alain Leger oversees menus at both the Brentwood Seagrille and Pub, the latter a less expensive excellent venue within the complex where you can get classic burgers, sandwiches, and salads. Leger's background includes Diva at the Met, Pastis Restaurant in Vancouver, and as chef/menu developer for the Earl's fifty-two-unit restaurant chain. Arbutus Grille also holds a five-star rating from Canada Select.

Leger's menus might include seared sea scallops and Juan de Fuca spot prawns; flying squid and pickled lipstick radishes; local rock sole and Dungeness crab roulade; sockeye salmon; breast of Cowichan duckling; wood-grilled leg of wild caribou with fresh morel mushrooms; a nectarine tart with raspberry sorbet; and local cheeses.

The inn also boasts a spa, a fine-art gallery, the Fine Wine & Spirits Shop, executive conference facilities, and the Marina & Eco-Adventure Centre.

Brentwood Bay Lodge & Spa and Brentwood Seagrille & Pub, 849 Verdier Avenue, (250) 544–2079 or (888) 544–2079; www.brentwood baylodge.ca. Fully licensed. Wheelchair accessible. Room rates: $179– $699, depending on season and view. Credit cards: Visa, MasterCard, American Express.

Marley Farm Winery is one of the most fun winery visits for the whole family on the entire west coast of North America. Visitors will notice the red, green, and yellow color theme, and yes, there is a family relationship to singer Bob Marley and family, as well as an effort to help visitors relax into a Jamaican time pace. The Marleys' goal is to help others enjoy their little slice of Zion (heaven) here in the Mount Newton Valley.

Marley Farm Winery is the only fruit winery on Vancouver Island, but it also has one of Canada's best winemakers, Eric von Krosigk, as their grape wine winemaker.

While the vineyard occupies only five acres of the Marleys' forty-seven-acre property, the rest is fun farming for all. Children are welcome to visit the horses, chickens, turkeys, ducks, and pigeons. Sheep and geese do the weeding around here, and groups of seniors often come for tea.

The small gift shop is a trip into time and fun, with bright colors, tie-dye shirts, black and white sheep's wool yarn, and loads of fruit wines, grape wines, sherries, vinegars, and food tastes. The Marleys always suggest foods that go with their wines.

Grape wines produced here include Estate Pinot Noir, Novine Red (beef, sausages, grilled veggies); Novine White (trout, salmon, quiche, potatoes, and pasta); Pinot Grigio (flavored pork, poultry, seafood); and Pinot Noir (smoked salmon, pork, lamb, duck, and soft cheeses). Refreshing fruit wines include Loganberry (Italian flatbread, quiche, duck, turkey, and soft cheeses such as Camembert); Raspberry (chocolate, salads, coconut prawns or curry, and burgers); Blackberry and Blackberry Gold (biscotti or fruit salads); and Kiwi (spicy foods like Jamaican jerk).

Try the vinegars that come in bumble berry, kiwi, and peach flavors, as well as "Irie Mon" comic Rastafarian T-shirts.

Marley Farm Winery, 1831D Mount Newton Cross Road, Saanichton; (250) 652–8667; www.marleyfarm.ca. Hours: 11:00 A.M.–6:00 P.M. daily in summer, noon–4:00 P.M. Sunday October–December and March. Wheelchair accessible. Credit cards: Visa, MasterCard, American Express.

*Directions: Take the Mount Newton Cross Road west off Highway 17
(Pat Bay Highway) or east from West Saanich Road.*

Scottish immigrant Robert Dunsmuir built **Craigdarroch Castle** as a monument
to himself and the fortune he made in Vancouver Island coal, fulfilling the promise he made to his wife, Joan, before they left Scotland. *Craigdarroch* means "rocky
oak place" in Gaelic, which it was before he cut the trees down to build his status symbol.

Currently owned by the Craigdarroch Castle Historical Society, it seems
most attractive when the grass is green or at night in full moonlight. Built with
Vancouver Island sandstone and brick, the castle has four floors, thirty-nine
rooms, and eighteen fireplaces. In 1890 it cost $200,000 to build, including the
grounds.

The castle also served as the veterans hospital from 1919 to 1921 and as Victoria College, affiliated with McGill University of Montreal, from 1921 to 1946.
The gift shop sells charming English and Scottish trinkets, candies, biscuits,
cards, postcards, and interesting books.

*Craigdarroch Castle, 1050 Joan Crescent, (250) 592–5323; www.craig
darrochcastle.com. Hours: summer 9:00 A.M.–7:00 P.M. daily, winter*

Craigdarroch Castle

10:00 A.M.–4:30 P.M. daily. Admission: adults $11.75, seniors $10.75, students $7.75, children ages six to twelve $3.75, free for younger. Not wheelchair accessible. Credit cards: Visa, MasterCard, American Express. (Buses 11, 14 up Fort Street.)

Many locals take their daily walks through Beacon Hill Park and along **Dallas Road** (Bus 5 or walk), the latter for a particularly exhilarating view of the water and the Olympic Mountains. Many commemorative landmarks along the way note such sites or occurrences as Russian and Canadian boating accidents; Marilyn Bell's 1956 swim across the Juan de Fuca Strait from Port Angeles, Washington, to Victoria, British Columbia; Indian village sites; Horseshoe Bay; evidence of the retreat of the Third Ice Age; Japanese friendship; a water fountain for dogs; and Mile 0 of the Trans-Canada Highway.

Walking or driving along Dallas Road to the east of Beacon Hill Park is breathtaking. Sometimes the ocean climbs the breakwater, and often you can watch hang gliders imitating birds. A must.

Emily Carr House, located on Government Street, 4 blocks south of the Parliament buildings, memorializes the birthplace of Canada's most beloved painter and writer. Emily Carr rebelled against her strict English upbringing and followed her heart, roaming the British Columbia wilds, painting, writing, and taking in artists, writers, and other guests at the House of All Sorts around the corner on Simcoe Street (also the name of one of her most famous books). In her later years she wrote her best known work, *The Book of Small*. A lovely, privately operated (not by the Carr family) place to visit with a most interesting gift shop and pleasant and helpful docents. Signs in the "lit-

Emily Carr House, Government Street

erary garden" surrounding her house relate Carr's written work to plants in the family garden.

Emily Carr House, 207 Government Street, (250) 383–5843; www
.emilycarr.com or www.heritage.gov.bc.ca/emily_carr.htm. Hours: 11:00
A.M.–5:00 P.M. daily from mid-May to mid-October; call for an appoint-
ment the rest of the year. Admission: by donation, $5 suggested. Partly
wheelchair accessible. Credit cards: Visa, MasterCard.

Government House (1401 Rockland Avenue, 250–387–2080) is the official residence of the lieutenant governor, the Crown's ceremonial appointee who represents the queen and who occasionally steps in to communicate in a crisis. You can walk throughout the grounds, but you cannot tour the house. (Bus 1 Richardson and a walk.)

In good weather, hundreds of local brides and grooms have their wedding pictures taken in the gardens of Government House. Year-round, other locals protest the vast cost of maintaining the office and grounds of a somewhat political and powerless appointment.

The original Government House was purchased by the province from the heirs of George Cary, British Columbia's first (and unbalanced) attorney general. It burned down in 1899, as did its successor in 1977, after which the current mansion was built.

Glendale Gardens Greenspace and Pacific Horticulture College cultivates wonderful demonstration gardens that fascinate amateur and professional gardeners or the simply curious beauty fan. Browse through perennial flower displays, the Asiatic and Oriental lily collection, the rose garden with a hundred different varieties of miniature roses, and a rhododendron vale.

Glendale Gardens Greenspace and Pacific Horticulture College, 505
Quayle Road, (250) 479–6162; www.hcp.bc.ca. Hours: April 1–September
30 8:00 A.M.–8:00 P.M. Monday–Friday, 8:00 A.M.–6:00 P.M. Saturday–
Sunday; October 1–March 31 9:00 A.M.–4:00 P.M. daily. Mostly wheel-
chair accessible. Directions: Highway 17 (Pat Bay Highway), turn onto
Highway 17A, turn left off Beaver Lake Road, and the center will be on
your left. Admission: adults $7.50, seniors and students $5.25. (Bus 21
and a walk.)

The **Victoria Bug Zoo** is a budding biologist's heaven offering live weird little things called insects to look at while learning sustainable respect for tiny animals. All the insects, including scorpions, millipedes, tarantulas, African beetles, and Australian walkingsticks, are behind glass. An entomologist will answer your questions gently and knowledgeably. Delilah the yellow mantis keeps owner Carol Maier company at the front desk. You can also buy unique gifts such as fake tatoos, posters, books, jewelry, and specialty honeys here. You can have birthday parties in the Bug Zoo Party Room. One of our favorites.

Victoria Bug Zoo, 631 Courtney Street, (250) 384–2847; www.bug zoo.bc.ca. Hours: 9:30 A.M.–5:00 P.M. Monday–Saturday, 11:00 A.M.– 5:00 P.M. Sunday. Admission: adults $8, students $7, seniors $6, children three to sixteen $5, children two and under free. Annual pass $20. Wheelchair accessible. Credit cards: Visa, MasterCard, American Express.

WHERE TO STAY

All accommodations in Victoria appear in order of proximity to Victoria's Inner Harbour since it is the geographic focal point of most visitors' stays. Those listed first are closest to the Inner Harbour. Guest charges are in Canadian dollars

Chocolate-Covered Tarantulas

Carol Maier, president/owner/ entomologist, Victoria Bug Zoo

8 squares semisweet baker's chocolate
2 cups chow mein noodles
1 cup mini marshmallows
$\frac{1}{2}$ cup nuts, sliced or chopped
$\frac{1}{2}$ cup raisins
$\frac{1}{4}$ cup coconut, shredded

Carol Maier describes how to prepare her recipe: "Melt chocolate in a saucepan on the kitchen range or in an appropriate-size bowl in a microwave set on medium. Gentle heat is recommended. While the chocolate is melting, mix the other ingredients together. When the chocolate is thoroughly melted, pour it over the other stuff and stir gently to coat everything with chocolate.

"Spoon tarantula-size globs (for want of a better term) onto a cookie sheet or a sheet of wax paper. Lubricating the cookie sheet with a little cooking oil might help prevent sticking but isn't really necessary. The individual portions should be about the size of the body of a young adult *Brachypelma smithi*.

"In cool climates they can be left to cool at room temperature, but in warmer climates they should be placed in the refrigerator until hard."

and do not include sales taxes. Room rates vary and are shown to give the reader comparisons.

Downtown Victoria

Hotels

Splurge

Fairmont Empress Hotel, 721 Government Street (250–384–8111 or 800–441–1414; www.fairmont.com—click on Empress), $175–$599; 464 units; little dogs at $50 per stay; since 1909 world-famous symbol of Victoria; center of Inner Harbour; lounge, dining, high tea; special packages.

Abigail's Hotel, 906 McClure Street (250–388–5363; www.abigailhotel .com), $260–$400; 22 units, including 6 in coach house; gourmet breakfast; classic Tudor design; no pets.

Chateau Victoria Hotel, 740 Burdett Avenue (250–382–4221 or 800–663–5891; www.chateauvictoria.com), March–April $92–$215, May–June 15 $122–$282, June 16–September $119–$269, rest of year $85–$199; 177 units; roof-top restaurant; pool; bar; exercise room; dogs okay.

Queen Victoria Hotel and Suites, 655 Douglas Street (250–386–1312; www .queenvictoria inn.com), October 15–May 14 $115–$225 for two, including breakfast; May 15–October 14 $175–$400; AAA and senior discount; 146 units, all with balconies; indoor pool; many kitchens; no pets.

Marriott Victoria, 728 Humboldt Street (250–480–3800 or 800–792–2719; www.marriottvictoria.com), $229–$269 summer, off-season less; 236 rooms; opened in 2005; many views of Inner Harbour; Internet; pool; whirlpool; restaurant, lounge.

Royal Scott Inn, 425 Quebec Street (250–388–5463 or 800–663–7515; www.royalscot.com), summer $145–$230; 176 units; restaurant; indoor pool; near U.S. ferries; shuttle; no pets.

Hotel Grand Pacific, 463 Belleville Street (250–386–0450), $200–$410, $800 for suite; 308 units; harbor views on upper floors; $4^{1}/_{2}$ stars; no pets.

Victoria Regent Hotel, 1234 Wharf Street (250–386–2211 or 800–663–7472; www.regenthotel.victoria.bc.ca), June 15–October 15 $199–$399, remainder of year less; 41 units; by the water; restaurant; some fireplaces; packages; no pets.

Laurel Point Inn, 680 Montreal Street (250–386–8721 or 800–663–7667; www
.laurelpoint.com), $189–$389; 200 units, of which 135 have harbor views;
indoor pool; glass balconies; Japanese tubs; ocean views; lounge, dining; no
pets.

Delta Victoria Ocean Pointe Resort, 45 Songhees Road (250–360–2999 or
800–667–4477; www.oprhote.com), $195–$300; 250 units; looks back across
harbor; terrace; spa; bar; tennis; wine shop; no pets.

Best deals

Days Inn on the Harbour, 427 Belleville Street (250–386–3451 or 888–254–
0637; www.daysinnvictoria.com), May–June $135–$165, July–September
$173–$203, October–April $105–$125; 71 units; kitchens; near U.S. ferries;
great view of the Inner Harbour and the Fairmont Empress Hotel (ask for
the fourth floor facing the water); no pets.

Ramada Huntingdon Manor, 330 Quebec Street (250–381–3456 or
800–663–7556; www.bctravel.com/huntingdon), May–October $143–$239,
rest of year less; 116 units; Jacuzzi; lounge, restaurant; art gallery; near U.S.
ferries; no pets.

Harbour Towers Hotel, 345 Quebec Street (250–385–2405 or 800–663–5896;
www.harbourtowers.com), $107–$334; 185 units; restaurant; pool; sauna;
shuttle; harbor and water views; no pets.

Best Western Inner Harbour, 412 Quebec Street (250–384–5122 or 800–
528–5122; www.victoriahotels.com), $126–$219; 74 units; continental
breakfast; outdoor pool, sauna, Jacuzzi; no pets.

Clarion Hotel Grand Pacific, 450 Quebec Street (250–386–0450 or 800–663–
7550; www.hotelgrandpacific.com), $116–$224; 300 units; pool; restaurant;
fitness facility; spectacular views of the Inner Harbor; no pets.

Coast Harbourside Hotel & Marina, 146 Kingston Street (250–360–1211;
www.coasthotels.com), $140–$250; 132 units; pool; bar and grill; pets with
$20-per-day charge.

James Bay Inn, 270 Government Street (250–384–7151; www.jamesbayinn
.bc.ca), May–June $80–$150, July–September $106–$245, rest of year lower;
48 units; historic; lounge, restaurant; no pets.

Quality Inn Downtown, 850 Blanshard Street (250–385–6787 or 800–661–
4115), May–June 15 $99–$109, June 16–September $108–$201, rest of year
$79–$89; 56 units; Old Bailey Pub and Green Room Cafe; no pets.

Strathcona Hotel, 919 Douglas Street (250–383–7137 or 800–663–7476; www .strathcona.com), April–June 13 $79–$109, June 14–September $89–$119, October–March $59–$74; 85 units; pub was first in Victoria after prohibition; Big Band John's bar, Cuckoo's Nest sports lounge, Sticky Wicket restaurant, rooftop dining in spring and summer; no pets.

Swans Suite Hotel, 506 Pandora Street (250–361–3310 or 800–668–7926; www.swanshotel.com), $129–$259; 29 units; restored historic building; "2006 National Brewpub of the Year" downstairs.

Best Western Carlton Plaza, 642 Johnson Street (250–388–5513 or 800–663–7241; www.bestwestern.com), $80–$180; 103 units; expanded heritage hotel; restaurant, bar; no pets.

Bed-and-Breakfasts

There are dozens of nice bed-and-breakfasts in Victoria, and here is a list of those that are in designated heritage houses, or architectural or historic special places. For reservations or information on others, call (250) 479–1986, (250) 655–7173, (604) 733–2777, (604) 825–7416, (604) 738–7207, or (800) 561–3223.

Rosewood Inn, 595 Michigan, (250) 384–6644; 17 units; $125–$295

Birdcage Walk Guest House, 505 Government, (250) 389–0804; 5 units; $60–$105

Haterleigh, 243 Kingston Street, (250) 384–9995; 7 units; $135–$340

Beaconsfield Inn, 998 Humboldt, (250) 384–4044; 9 units; $150–$300

Ryan's, 224 Superior, (250) 389–0012; 7 units; $109–$239

Humboldt House, 867 Humboldt, (250) 383–0152; 6 units; $150–$325

Prior House, 600 St. Charles, (250) 592–8847; 6 units; $119–$299

Dreemskerry, 1509 Rockland, (250) 384–4014; 4 units; $110–$180

Postern Gate Inn, 145 Meares, (250) 744–8787; 4 units; $150, less off-season

4

Exploring Outside Victoria

T ry to squeeze out a little time to explore beyond Victoria proper. Within thirty minutes by car or bus, you can visit Elk Lake, stop in at fresh vegetable stands, walk in a rain forest, bask on a beach, or visit small towns along the way. Going up the west side of the island, visit Sooke, Otter Point, Point-No-Point, Jordan River, and Port Renfrew.

We have added several small farms that welcome visitors and add to your culinary and travel experience by letting you meet the farmers and learn about what they grow and how they do it.

VICTORIA TO SIDNEY

A day trip to Sidney is a fun and quick way to find out what life on Vancouver Island outside Victoria is like. Just thirty minutes away you can experience small-town Canada, with beautiful scenery to boot.

If you're driving, head north on Blanshard Street, which becomes Highway 17 (Patricia Bay Highway), which will take you to Sidney. If you prefer to have someone else do the driving, you can take Buses 70, 72, or 75.

You might want to stop along Highway 17 at **Michell Brothers Farm** and their store in the red barn east off the highway. Like many Van Isle growers, they are not officially certified organic because the bureaucracy is too great, but they grow only organic and sell from additional sources that might not be. Wares include fabulous jams and jellies, broccoli, six berry varieties, eggs, garlic, squash, tomatoes, and vegetable marrow.

Michell Brothers Farm, 2415 Island View Road, Saanichton; (250) 652–6770. Hours: 9:00 A.M.–6:00 P.M. daily. Wheelchair accessible.

West of Highway 17 via Brookleigh Road and right (north) on Oldfield Road to Walton Place or Bear Hill Road, you will find the fun **Dan's Farm and Country Market,** formerly Le Coteau Farms & Garden Centre at Oldfield and Bear Hill Road. Part of the Le Coteau family, Dan puts on a fabulous pumpkin festival and other events for the whole family, offers gazillions of apple and pear varieties, and has loads of information on planting vegetables and fruit trees.

Dan's Farm and Country Market, 304 Walton Place or 2030 Bear Hill Road, Saanichton; (250) 652–9100 or (250) 658–5888; www.dans farm.ca. Hours: 9:00 A.M.–5:00 P.M. daily. Partly wheelchair accessible.

Back on Highway 17, **Saanich Historical Artifacts Society** exhibits thousands of local artifacts; possibly the largest collection of working steam engines in Canada; an operational sawmill and a planer mill; a carpentry shop; a log cabin; an old schoolhouse; and a blacksmith's shop, where several trained blacksmiths produce souvenirs you can buy. You can also stroll on several miles of lush nature trails around the property and see Pioneer Chapel, a log cabin, and a nature pond. Catch the summer fair on Father's Day weekend, with demonstrations, hayrides, and country food. Or on the second weekend after Labor Day, see the fall threshing show. Lots of special events range from the Old English Car Fair & Swap Meet, to draught horse plowing, the Ford V-8 Picnic, and Christmas in the Village.

Saanich Historical Artifacts Society, 7321 Lochside Drive, Saanichton; (250) 652–5522; www.shas.com. Hours: 9:30 A.M.–noon daily, June– August 9:30 A.M.–4:00 P.M. daily. Wheelchair accessible.

Fairburn Farm is a complete culinary retreat on land first settled in 1886. A later owner, Mary Reid Jackson, named it Fairburn, which means "beautiful stream" in her father's native Gaelic.

Current owners the Archer family bought the property from foresters MacMillan-Bloedel, renewed the land, and formed the Vancouver Island Organic Cooperative. Fairburn Farm now houses the Archers' herd of water buffalo, and the family sells buffalo products, including milk, yogurt, and cheeses.

Mara Jernigan, co-leader of Slow Food Canada with Sinclair Philip of Sooke Harbour House, founded the Vancouver Island Feast of Fields in 1998 as a fund-raiser for the FarmFolk/CityFolk Society.

Jernigan now runs a cooking school at Fairburn Farm, houses paying guests at the farm for whom she will cook an interesting dinner from the farm's products, and serves an Italian Sunday lunch at 1:00 P.M. by reservation ($85).

Guesthouse guests also enjoy an organic breakfast of homemade granola, yogurt, juices, fruit, coffee, free-range eggs, and Cowichan Bay Farm pasture-raised chicken sausages.

For more information on cooking classes, which include lunch, visit www .fairburnfarm.bc.ca.

***Fairburn Farm**, 2210 Jackson Road, Duncan; (250) 746–4637; www .fairburnfarm.bc.ca. Partly wheelchair accessible.*

There are loads of other organic (many uncertified because of complicated paper-work in Canada) small farms scattered around southern Vancouver Island, especially within a short drive from Victoria. You can either just follow signs around the area or aim for the following highlights. For directions to individual farms, visit www.islandfarmfresh.com.

Babe's Honey Farm is a hugely popular natural honey producer based on wild mountain flowers since 1945. 334 Walton Place, Victoria; (250) 658–8319. Hours: 9:30 A.M.–4:30 P.M. Monday–Saturday, 11:00 A.M.–4:30 P.M. Sunday.

Heritage Farm & Vineyard is at Starling Lane Winery and offers raspber-ries, apples, hazelnuts, flowers, organic jams and jellies, fresh eggs, and lamb. Open noon to 5:00 p.m. Saturday and Sunday. 5271 Old West Saanich Road, (250) 479–4769; www.starlinglanewinery.com.

Hillside Farm grows organic produce, including lots of berries, beans, squashes, stone fruit, free-range chicken and goose eggs, and offers an art studio, farm tours, and art lessons. 1748 Mount Newton Cross Road, Saanichton; (250) 652–0650. Hours: Wednesday 9:00 A.M.–noon, Saturday 9:00 A.M.–5:00 P.M.

Meadowbrook Farm grows blueberries and makes all things blueberry. They use ladybugs for pest control. U-pick is offered during July and August. 205 Meadowbrook Road, Victoria; (250) 479–7166.

Mt. Newton Blueberries grows organic blueberries. You can pick or purchase the berries at a stand during July and August. 1438 Mt. Newton Cross Road, Saanichton; (250) 652–9035.

Oldfield Orchard & Bakery makes fabulous fruit pies from their berries and tree fruits. Their activities include an Octoberfest with a haunted house, a corn maze, and hayrides and pony rides. Hours: 9:30 A.M.–4:30 P.M. daily. 6286 Old-field Road, Saanichton; (250) 652–1579; www.oldfieldorchard.com.

Red Cedar Moon offers free-range eggs, organic produce, jams and jellies, kiwi, free-range chicken and turkey, artwork, art, and farm events. 7513 West Saanich Road, Saanichton; (250) 652–2088. Hours: Thursday–Saturday year-round.

Rosemeade Farms overlooks Lake Rosemeade with U-pick and We-pick berries, cherries, rhubarb, stone fruit, and loads of musical events. 1939 Meadowbank Road, Saanichton; (250) 652–1862. Open from 8:30 A.M. Monday–Saturday.

Saanichton Christmas Tree & Ostrich Farm gives touchy-feely tours and sells fruit, veggies, flowers, ostrich meat, chicks, and ducklings. 8231 East Saanich Road and 6999 West Saanich Road; (250) 652–3345; www.ostrichfarm.ca.

Silver Rill Corn is a longtime family farm and market selling corn and all sorts of veggies and berries. Hours: 9:00 A.M.–6:00 P.M. June–October. (250) 652–3854.

Sluggett Farms is family operated since 1876, with eight varieties of sweet corn and loads of other veggies. Hours: 10:00 A.M.–6:00 P.M. daily in summer. (250) 385–8688 or (250) 652–6396.

Smyth's Market Garden offers loganberries, figs, grapes, Asian pear-apples, seventy varieties of apples, and veggies. 966 Downey Road, North Saanich; (250) 656–1520. Hours: noon–dusk in season.

Sterling Farm offers jams and jellies, flowers, strawberries, and a Wild Flower Tea House. 6631 Oldfield Road, Saanichton; (250) 652–6506.

Sun Wing Greenhouses, Ltd. grow many varieties of tomatoes including heirloom, and other veggies, cherry tomato hanging baskets, and herbs. 6070 Oldfield Road, Victoria; (250) 652–5732; www.sunwingtomatoes.com. Hours: 9:00 A.M.–5:00 P.M. daily March–October.

One of our favorite stops for peace of mind along the way is **Beaver Lake/ Elk Lake Park,** about twenty minutes north of Victoria on Highway 17. First you will see the signs to Beaver Lake, and then the sign to Elk Lake comes up quickly with a short left-turn lane. Careful.

Elk Lake is a particularly popular sailboarding and rowing lake. More Canadian rowing medalists from the 1996 Olympics trained at Elk Lake than anywhere else in the world. Go Canada!

When you turn off to Sidney, you will find yourself on Beacon Avenue, the main street of Sidney, which looks on the surface like a midwestern U.S. town. Look further.

For fun transportation around Sidney on land, try **Celebration Carriage Services** (250–655–3672) for five scenic tours about town. They range from a ten-to-fifteen-minute minitour to the Grand Sidney Special through town to Tsehum Harbour, a former governor general's house. Just wait at the carriage stand outside Port Sidney Marina, late afternoon and early evening, Thursday–Sunday.

Around Sidney on water, try **Eco Cruising Tours** for tours around Sidney waterfront to Tsehum Harbour, Canoe Cove, Brentwood Bay, Swartz Bay, and to the "back door" of Butchart Gardens, which you enter (legally) with no lines or waiting. Cruise in solarium domed-glass-topped boats. $30–$50. (250) 655–5211; www.ecocruising.com. Cruises operate daily in summer and on weekends only in spring and fall. Forget it in winter.

The **Saanich Peninsula Visitor's Guide,** put out by the *Peninsula News Review,* is extremely helpful and available from them at (250) 656–1151 or from the Saanich Peninsula Chamber of Commerce, 9768 Third Street, Sidney, B.C. V8L 3S4; (250) 656–3616. You can get a **Heritage Walking Tour** guide from the Heritage Advisory Committee, 2440 Sidney Avenue, Sidney, B.C. V8L 1Y7; (250) 656–1184.

Now here's a quick walking tour of the most interesting part of **Beacon Avenue,** which has interesting shops, bookstores, and cafes, beginning with the south side and starting from the water end of the street:

The Sidney Bakery, 2507 Beacon, supplies locals with Nanaimo Bars (delectable layered squares of chocolate, coconut, chocolate, yellow icing, and chocolate!), scones, carrot cake, and doughnuts, with special senior discount days on Monday and Thursday. Temptations offers gourmet coffee, great soups, and sandwiches from $2.50 to $4.50, with soup and sandwich at only $4.75. Vintage clothing fans might enjoy the St. Vincent de Paul shop, and travelers should drop in at One Stop Travel Shop at 2495 Beacon. The Phoenix Restaurant serves Chinese food, among other cuisines, with a special menu and prices for seniors at lunch and dinner. At Beacon and Second Street, Serious Coffee offers light lunches, soups, and air-roasted coffees.

Baden-Baden, which also has a boutique on Fort Street in downtown Victoria, sells stylish European (primarily German) fashions for women and shares an entryway with Klee Wyck House, which specializes in popular-label shoes. Tivoli Gallery claims to be protected by angels (and probably is) and specializes in Italianate clothes and personal home accessories. Vegetarians and the health-interested can find a home at Sidney Natural Foods.

Starbucks fans can get their fixes at the corner of Beacon and Third Street and then move on to the Village Gallery up the street for local artists' paintings, art supplies, framing, and poster prints.

The pièce de résistance (or should it be nonresistance?) is famous **Lunn's Pastries Deli & Coffee Shop Ltd.** (2455 Beacon), which has won more confection awards than any other patisserie and chocolaterie on the west coast of North America. Awards include medals and trophies from England and France, including the International Bakers & Confectioners in London.

Besides enjoying a light lunch here, you can also indulge in frangipan tarts, griottes (cognac cherries in fondant), French candied orange peels, or Kirsch fondant kisses. The deli meat counter has a wide range of German and Hungarian salami sausages rarely seen on the West Coast. Save a few calories in your day for Lunn's.

Moving eastward on Beacon, you can visit Knightsbridge Gift Shops, Ltd. and Tunes & Tees for hip, with-it music and compatible T-shirts.

The Sidney Post Office, built in 1936, is interesting as a sample of local period architecture just east of Touch of Class Ladies Wear. It now houses J. Burke & Sons Tobacconists, Ltd. and JJ's Coffee, which offers soup and sandwiches ($7.50), Torrefazione Italia coffee, and Internet access.

Downstairs is the fabulous **Sidney Historical Museum,** which offers one of the best historic and human-scale displays of the region, the Saanich Peninsula, and the town of Sidney-by-the-Sea. You will enjoy great stories of early settlers such as the Brethour brothers and Roberts family, "Critchley's Store" and "The Kitchen," as well as history of the local Victoria Airport in World War II and of the B.C. Ferries.

The Saanich People lived here for thousands of years, primarily in winter, and in 1852 the Hudson's Bay Company "obtained" lots of the forest land from the Saanich People. Much of that land was purchased by William and Charles Reay, who first settled what is now the town of Sidney. Julius Brethour, first president of the Victoria and Sidney Railway, apparently first named the area Sidney in 1893.

The Marine Museum at the end of Beacon Avenue is closed while a huge hotel and condo complex is built, with the new Marine Museum supposedly to open in 2008.

> *Sidney Historical Museum, Beacon Avenue and Fourth Street, Sidney;*
> *(250) 655–6355; www.sidneymuseum.ca. Hours: 10:00 A.M.–4:00 P.M.*
> *daily May–October, 11:00 A.M.–3:00 P.M. November–April. Admission*
> *by donation. Wheelchair accessible via elevator.*

Also downstairs is Rogers' Chocolates.

The Olympia Restaurant at Beacon and Fifth is a local staple serving pizza, steaks, seafood, barbecue ribs, lasagna, Cuban lobster, and Alaskan crab. Monday is pasta night at $4.95.

Kathleen likes Muffet & Louisa for well-priced superb kitchen equipment such as Emile Henry and BIA porcelain and accessories for dining, bed, and bath. Local folks hang out at Alexander's Coffee Bar (set back from the street), where you can also get great bagel sandwiches. Scandia Restaurant features hearty breakfasts all day, liver and onions at $8.99, Wiener schnitzel at $13.95, Danish beef at $10.95, Danish bratwurst at $10.95, Danish Frikadeller meat cakes at $9.95, and a special senior menu.

At the eastern end of Beacon Avenue are several significant points of interest: the new **Cannery Building,** which houses a liquor store; the Sidney Bandstand; Sidney Fisherman's Market out on the pier; as well as two newish restaurants, the Beacon Landing Pub & Restaurant and the Pier Bistro & Marine Adventure Center, the latter of which is the terminal for the Sidney Spit Ferry, Gulf Island Cruises, and Wildlife and Eco Tours.

Beacon Landing Pub & Restaurant faces eastward above the rocks with spectacular views of the water and even the Lower Mainland. Owners Ritch and Soley Rothermel and Bill and Donna Phillips have long experience with beverage and food, as in Langford Liquor Board and the Six Mile Pub. The Phillips' son Steve serves as chef, after cooking his way around the United States.

At both lunch and dinner the thin-crust pizzas, pastas, burgers, clam chowder, beer-battered halibut, panini, cannelloni, and seafood are all good, as are the

Sidney Bandstand and Sidney Fisherman's Market, Beacon Avenue

"Share Platters" of antipasto, bruschetta, and cheese and fruit. More-hungry diners may enjoy steaks, osso buco, or seafood risotto. Specialties include Dungeness crab spring rolls, baked crab dip, calamari, and Dungeness crab and prawn cakes. Fully licensed.

The **Pier Bistro** hangs over the water and features gourmet burgers, deli sandwiches and wraps, great clam chowder, substantial salads, a special crab and shrimp cheese toast, breaded chicken Cordon Bleu, wild halibut or salmon, shepherd's pie, and steak and prawns. Organic sodas and organic Salt Spring coffee drinks.

Sidney calls itself the "Bookstore City," and you can cross Beacon at this point to visit a few of them. Beacon Books at 2372 Beacon majors in exceptional used books with a few China pieces, and you enter the Mystery Bookshop through Beacon Books for mystery and crime novels. Dollars Wild is a bargain store where everything costs $1.

Up Fifth Street you might want to check out Theo's Greek & Western Cuisine Restaurant, which serves just what it says.

Back on Beacon east of Fifth Street, Cornish's Book & Stationery sells great cards and a few books; Sweet Talk & Lace sells suggestively tempting feathers and lingerie and loungewear; Patricia's Yarn Shop fills knitting and needlework supplies; and Pottery Plus offers imported and local pottery.

As you look up Fourth Street, don't be alarmed at the Canadian Air Force PF 060 airplane apparently poised to take off from the Canadian military recruiting center. Don't worry, it's not going anywhere.

Be sure to visit Tanner's Books at the corner of Beacon and Fourth Street and its marvelous Children's Book Shop (this one deserves an award, if there were such things). You can't miss its red and white exterior and stairs. Tanner's is a marvelous, independent emporium with a great inventory of quiet things to do at home or in your hotel room, such as reading books and international newspapers, models of all kinds, greeting cards, candy, snacks, and stationery.

The Sidney Candy Man is jam-packed with Harlan's truffles, wrapped and fresh candy (some in jars you can reach into), and ice cream. There's a coffee bar in back.

We insist you go around the corner on Third Street to Galleon Books & Antiques for rare collections of children's book sets, North American native art and books, Canadiana, and lots of fun people. The Haunted Bookshop sells used and rare books, including a few mysteries. The Canadiana collection is exceptional.

Bistro Suisse replaced the Royal Polish Restaurant last year, introducing fine European cuisine cooked by Lucien Frauenfelder and co-owner Kim Perdigao; Frauenfelder's stepdaughter Tine is the restaurant's hostess.

Lunch includes soup, sandwiches, burgers, quiche, pasta, salads, bratwurst with sauerkraut (great aroma throughout restaurant), schnitzel with Caesar salad or fries, Reuben sandwich, and avocado and shrimp with brandy sauce ($5–$11). Dinner is slightly more adventurous, adding Swiss raclette, deep-fried Brie with blueberry sauce, Basler onion tart, rosemary-marinated lamb chops, filet of sole almandine, curry, scalloped veal Zurichoise, New York steak and garlic prawns, duck breast with apricots, scallops and prawns in Pernod sauce, beef stroganoff, vegetarian stir-fry, and cheese fondue Neuchateloise ($12–$24).

Bistro Suisse, 2470 Beacon Avenue, (250) 656–5353. Hours: 11:30 A.M.–2:30 P.M. and 5:00–8:30 P.M. daily, brunch 11:00 A.M.–2:00 P.M. Saturday–Sunday. Licensed. Wheelchair accessible. Credit cards: Visa, MasterCard, American Express.

At **Mineral World and Scratch Patch,** kids can look at rocks, participate in discovery and touching almost with abandon, and expend some high energy on the playground equipment in front while you scour the nearby shops adjoining the gorgeous marina.

Mineral World and Scratch Patch, 9891 Seaport Place, (250) 655–4367. Hours: 10:00 A.M.–5:00 P.M. daily, July–August 9:30 A.M.–5:00 P.M. Closed Christmas Day. Admission: by donation. Wheelchair accessible.

Back on Beacon, check out The Italian Bakery, which is worth a stop.

Deep Cove Chalet (11190 Chalet, 250–656–3541; www.deepcovechalet .com) is one of Victorians' favorite out-of-town restaurants and romantic dinner destinations, with a German and French menu emphasizing local seafood, lamb, and game. Sunday brunch is a reservations-only proposition at about $30, as is dinner. The **Blue Peter Pub & Restaurant** (2270 Harbour, 250–656–4551) is less expensive and intimate but has excellent fresh seafood, steaks, and pastas, as well as an outdoor patio overlooking the marina.

The **Spitfire Grill** is a terrific airport restaurant near but not in the Victoria International Airport, just around the bend to the left of the airport itself. The Spitfire caters primarily to airport folks, private airplane owners, and a collection of locals who know of its quiet reputation for really good, unfancy food.

It's good enough basic fare that we often make time for lunch here when we run last minute errands to the Fed Ex depot nearby. We love to sit at a window table and watch people taking helicopter or other flying lessons, get in their planes tentatively, take off, and land safely, with great sighs of exhaled anguish and needs for some solid food.

The shrimp Caesar salad with garlic toast ($10.95) is fabulously generous, or try the Spitfire Burger, a six-ounce beef burger with bacon, cheese, and mushrooms ($8.95). All sandwiches come with choice of soup, salad, or Spitfire fries. The seafood chowder is out of sight, and the vegetarian falafel is served with salad ($7.95). Other options include grilled foccacia sandwiches, wraps, a real turkey cranberry sandwich ($7.95), and more serious food such as a six-ounce sirloin steak sandwich with fried mushrooms ($9.95); liver and onions with bacon and veggies, mashed potatoes, or fries ($8.50); fish and chips ($7.95–$11.95); or chicken souvlaki ($7.95).

Spitfire Grill, 9681 Willingdon Road, Sidney; (250) 655–0122. Hours: 7:30 A.M.–9:00 P.M. daily. Fully licensed. Wheelchair accessible. Credit cards: Visa, MasterCard, American Express.

Where to Stay

Brentwood Bay

Brentwood Bay Lodge & Spa, 849 Verdier Avenue (800–454–6835); $193 and up; 33 suites, ocean views, fireplaces, cafe, wine bar, art gallery, Internet.

Best Value Motel, 1211 Verdier Avenue, corner Highway 17A (250–652–2012); $39–$59; 1 mile to Butchart Gardens.

Saanich

Cherry Bend Motel, 4879 Cherry Tree Bend (250–658–5611 or 800–881–7165); $75 and up; off-season $48 and up; some kitchens; no pets.

Saanichton

Quality Inn Waddling Dog, 2476 Mount Newton Cross Road (250–652–1146 or 800–567–8466); $99–$125; English-style inn; 30 units; pub, restaurant, beer and wine store, Internet.

Western 66 Motel, 2401 Mount Newton Cross Road (250–652–4464 or 800–463–4464; www.western66motel.com); $42–$80; restaurant, no pets.

Super 8 Motel, 2477 Mount Newton Cross Road (250–652–6888); $58 and up; 51 units; pets on approval.

Sidney

Dunsmuir Lodge, 1515 McTavish Road (250–656–3166); $99 and up, $45 large rooms; high on wooded slope, turn west from Highway 17, just south of airport, drive about 2 miles; licensed restaurant, lounge; open April–September; marvelous views, food, and service.

Victoria Airport Travelodge, 2280 Beacon Avenue (250–656–1176; www.airport lodge.com); $89–$165; poolside BBQ; licensed dining, pub; lounge, beer and wine store; closest to airport.

Latch Country Inn, 2328 Harbour Road (250–656–6622 or 866–810–6645); $95–$180; restored 1920 house overlooking harbor; adult oriented; art, antiques; licensed restaurant; no pets.

Best Western Emerald Isle Motor Inn, 2306 Beacon Avenue (250–656–4441 or 800–315–3377; www.bwemeraldisle.com); $99–$275; 63 units; sauna; pets for fee.

Cedarwood Inn and Suites, 9522 Lochside Drive (250–656–5551; www.the cedarwood.ca); $89–$160; 45 cottages, rooms, and suites; close to water; some Jacuzzis; small pets okay with fee.

VICTORIA TO PORT RENFREW

Going up the west side of the island, you can easily experience Vancouver Island's full range of beauty in a short day trip, or longer if you have time. Find your way to Royal Roads University, hike trails such as the Galloping Goose and those at Goldstream Provincial Park, and visit Sooke and its regional museum, all within forty minutes of Victoria. While Sooke has long been an independent community and is the home of the world-renowned Sooke Harbour House, it's nearly a suburb of Victoria, with sensible people commuting back and forth every day.

Farther afield, enjoy rain forests and beaches, visit Point-No-Point, and forage along the West Coast Trail and Port Renfrew tide pools within two hours of Victoria.

If you are driving to the west coast of the island, take Douglas Street north and follow the signs to Highway 1 toward Sooke. (You can also take 1A to Highway 14 for a more local route, but we have never done it without missing

If you are going to travel into the wilds of Vancouver Island, please be advised that deer, black bear, cougar, wolves, and many other species live in this area. They are wild animals and can be dangerous. Please do not attempt to approach them at any time. Enjoy, but do not disturb.

a turn.) When you reach Colwood, you'll take the exit from Highway 1 to Highway 14 (Island Highway). You're on your way.

If you wish to make the trip from Victoria to Sooke by public transportation, take Bus 50 (get a transfer), then Bus 61 from the Western Exchange (transfer) Centre at Colwood ($2.25 each way to Sooke). We enjoy it, but you may feel limited unless you like to walk a lot.

Anywhere along the interchange and parallel to Highway 14 runs the **Galloping Goose Trail and Park,** which begins in View Royal and continues for 42 kilometers (26 miles) along an old Canadian National Railway bed through the lush hills around Colwood, Langford, Metchosin, and Sooke. The trail is great for walking, mountain biking, and horseback riding. It begins at Atkins Avenue and Highway 1A, south of Highway 1. Never far from the highway, this trail helps you feel you're getting away while still being close to Victoria. In spring and summer you can see animals and flowers and enjoy great lookouts. Stay on the main trail. Once you get to Metchosin the trail will take you through several public parks. Dogs okay on leash.

Six Mile Pub at 494 Island Highway is a great place to stop for a beer, iced tea, lunch, dinner, snack, whatever. Open most the hours you need it. This newly restored pub building was built in 1855, making Six Mile the oldest pub in British Columbia and possibly in western Canada.

Six Mile Pub was originally built in 1855 and called Parson's Bridge Hotel after Bill Parson, who was not a parson but was the builder of the bridge giving access to the Sooke River area. As the hub of local activity, the hotel was always popular, especially with stagecoaches, whose drivers would stop to rest the horses, rest themselves, and, incidentally, drop off the mail.

In 1917 Prohibition closed all Canadian bars. Theoretically. Victoria remained dry until 1952, forcing fun-loving drinkers to go out of town (6 miles) to the Six Mile. Bootleggers unloaded barrels and barrels of liquor, leading to several decades of highly profitable business at the Six Mile Pub, British Columbia's rum-running headquarters.

The Six Mile's current owners, Bill and Donna Phillips, bought it in 1980 and restored its interior as accurately as possible. Their historic photo and memorabilia collections are must-sees.

From the outside it looks like a sedate Tudor establishment. On the inside it looks like many things: each room has a different personality to suit your mood—large banquet, small English with cozy booths, huge bar with small round tables and party atmosphere, an outdoor beer garden/waterfront patio, and herb and flower gardens.

The food is a bit eclectic, but everything is good. Roast beef, fish and chips, salads, penne pasta Alfredo, chicken teriyaki, beef or vegetarian lasagna, shepherd's pie, baked garlic prawns, dry pepper rib-bits, wraps, beef, halibut and salmon, paella, burgers on house-made buns, steaks, West Coast bouillabaisse, and maple cider salmon. One of our favorites.

Six Mile Pub, *494 Island Highway, (250) 478–3121; www.sixmilepub .com. Hours: pub 11:00 A.M.–11:00 P.M. Monday–Thursday, 11:00 A.M.– 1:00 A.M. Friday–Saturday, Sunday brunch 10:00 A.M.–2:30 P.M. Fully licensed. Wheelchair accessible. Credit cards: Visa, MasterCard.*

You will know **Colwood** by its used-car lots; Colwood Plaza, a small shopping center; and recognizable restaurants along the road. If you are driving, this is where you take the exit from Highway 1 onto Highway 14. If you are on the bus, you get off here at the Western Exchange Centre and get on Bus 61. There are no public phones or restrooms at the transfer station; there are a few rain shelters.

Fort Rodd Hill Historic Park, 603 Fort Rodd Hill Road off Ocean Boulevard, was named for an HMS *Fisgard* officer; the batteries and garrison were built from 1895 to 1900. The Fisgard lighthouse was built in 1860 and was the first permanent lighthouse on the Canadian Pacific coast. The band of the 5th (B.C.) Field Regiment, Royal Canadian Artillery, Victoria's oldest military unit, plays Sunday afternoons at 2:00 P.M. in summer.

Fort Rodd Hill Historic Park, *603 Fort Rodd Hill Road, (250) 363–4662; www.pc.gc.ca/lhn-nhs/bc/fortroddhill/. Hours: 10:00 A.M.– 5:30 P.M. daily. Admission: adults $3.95, seniors $3.45, youth $1.95, family/group $9.90. Annual passes available.*

After you pass through Colwood, you begin to see the true, deep beauty of the West Coast.

In **Metchosin,** originally called *Smetts-shosin* by natives (meaning "place of stinking fish"—those that washed up dead on the shore), Metchosin Road turns off Sooke Road (Highway 14) just past Colwood. You can visit Witty's Lagoon, Devonian Regional Parks, and Matheson Lake Regional Park for nature trails and right-on-top-of-it looks at West Coast plants and animals.

On the left side of Highway 14, the large, walled Tudor settlement has most recently been **Royal Roads University** (250–363–4569, tourist information; www.royalroads.ca/channels), originally a mansion built in 1908. The grounds and beautiful gardens are usually open 10:00 A.M.–6:00 P.M. From here it is 24 kilometers (14.4 miles) to Sooke.

Goldstream Provincial Park (www.goldstreampark.com) is accessible up Humpback Road from Highway 14. In November and December you can watch chum salmon run on the lower Goldstream River, just off Highway 1, 20 kilometers (12 miles) west of Victoria. Park naturalists explain the spawning scene. Do not bother the fish, throw anything into the water, or allow animals in the water. In the summer Goldstream is a great place to walk and picnic among the ancient cedar trees and big-leaf maples, as well as 600-year-old Douglas fir and arbutus trees, found only on Vancouver Island and southwestern British Columbia.

In **Langford,** the Glen Lake Family Restaurant is obviously the local hangout. If you climb Mount Finlayson in Mount Finlayson Provincial Park, you can experience unequaled views of the entire Victoria area. Finlayson Arm is a good place to start a hike along the Gowlland Range.

Now you just wend your way toward **Sooke,** marveling at the natural landscape.

Olde English Pub is thirty minutes out of Victoria on the right side going toward Sooke. The 17 Mile House pub is also popular with locals, but it may be difficult to get off the road in time for these unless you are alert beforehand.

Soon you start to see small bed-and-breakfasts, such as Hartmann House and Cooper's Guest House. Klee Wyk Antiques is on the left. So-called civilization indicators begin to pop up: a Shell gas/fuel station on the left, followed in another couple of kilometers by the campgrounds of Sunny Shores Resort, Grouches Lair on the Harbour, and Bed & Breakfast by the Sea on the left, then a native art gallery on the left and Nettie's Fruit Stand and a general store on the right.

Two kilometers from Grouches you cross the Sooke River and pass, unless you stop in, a Tudor-style pub on the left. Coming up on the right is Phillips Road, where you want to get off Bus 61 for the Sooke Region Museum and the Sooke Area Arena.

The **Sooke Region Museum and Tourism Information Centre** is one of the best small museums we have ever seen. Charmingly compact and historically accurate, its Moss Cottage (1870) is Sooke's oldest building and offers entertaining exhibits of local history and memorabilia and a complete history of the salmon and lumber industries in British Columbia. You can also visit the cabin of British captain James Edward Radcliffe's Chinese cook, the polemaker's shed, and the museum's fascinating gift shop, which features locally made First Nation jewelry; Coast Salish carvings by Herb Pelkey, Keith Willis, and Rita Willis of the Saanich

"Tsawout" Band; and Moss Cottage kitchen's organic jams. Also check out the museum's own *Guide to the Sooke Region* for deeply fascinating local history.

The staff of the tourism information center, inside and to the left, will answer questions, advise you on accommodations and restaurants, and even make some reservations.

Signs warn: VISITORS BEWARE. WITH THE INCREASING NUMBERS OF TRAV-ELERS VISITING OUR BEAUTIFUL WEST COAST BEACHES, IT IS UNFORTUNATE THAT SOME INDIVIDUALS ARE ALSO ATTRACTED WHO MAY AVAIL THEMSELVES OF VALUABLES LEFT IN LOCKED CARS. PLEASE DO NOT LEAVE VALUABLES IN UNATTENDED CARS.

The Sooke Region Museum puts on several annual events, including the Moss Cottage Christmas and tasty salmon barbecues.

Sooke Region Museum and Tourism Information Centre, 2070 Phillips Road (right off Sooke Road/Highway 14), (250) 642–6351; www.sooke regionmuseum.com. Hours: 9:00 A.M.–5:30 P.M. daily July–August, 9:00 A.M. to 5:00 P.M. Tuesday–Sunday September–June. Wheelchair accessible. Credit cards: Visa, MasterCard.

Up Phillips Road about ½ kilometer is the Sooke Area Arena, where the annual **Fine Arts Festival,** the largest juried art show in British Columbia, is held every August. The committee does an outstanding professional job of hanging this exhibit in what normally functions as the Sooke Minor Hockey Association and Sooke Figure Skating Club arena. The festival includes a cafe with excellent inexpensive sandwiches. The arena is wheelchair accessible; admission to the show is $5.

Sooke itself is forty minutes west of Victoria. Main attractions include salmon and halibut fishing, whale watching (loads of charters are available), hiking, and relaxing at nearby beaches and trails.

For centuries there was a Coast Salish settlement that thrived on abundant local fish, berries, clams, and wild birds. The aboriginal population in the area nearly killed each other off in tribal wars, leaving few natives when the Europeans arrived looking for gold and lumber in 1849. The Leech River gold rush in 1864 brought a swell in population to Sooke.

Annual events worth making the trip to Sooke include well-known All Sooke Day (third Saturday in July), featuring logger sports and a salmon barbecue; the Share the Spirit native festival; the King's Cup maritime festival; and the Sink or Swim Competition. In addition to the previously mentioned arts festival in August, there is a mountain-bike festival in a small, manageable environment.

Try the fish and chips trailer and Babe's honey and vegetable stand on the right going out. The fish, chips, and onion rings are divine, as is everything at Babe's.

Stone Pipe Grill is a great addition to Sooke, replacing the Sage Creek Trading Co. & Bistro. Owner Patrick Irwin brought the crew with whom he worked at a now-closed nearby restaurant and is doing everything right "my way." While appealing primarily to Sooke locals, visitors are treated equally well, all at reasonable prices.

Expect soups, salads, and appetizers such as Painted Desert, coconut prawns, seafood cakes, loads of burger choices, fish and chips, shrimp melt, Southwest chicken melt, pad Thai, steak sandwich, Greek chicken wrap, quesadillas, omelets, and shepherd's pie (all under $10).

Dinner adds jambalaya, blackened local red snapper, steaks, ginger-fried beef, Tuscan chicken, local pork roast, satays and curries, and pastas (all under $23). Check out desserts such as made-here cheesecake and apple-berry crumble, hedgehog mousse pie, and deep-fried ice cream and sundaes. Kids' menu includes chicken fingers or grilled cheese and fries, or Chef Boyardee mini beef ravioli with drink ($4).

Stone Pipe Grill, corner of Sooke Road and Otter Point Road, Sooke; (250) 642–0566; www.stonepipe.com. Hours: 11:00 A.M.–9:00 P.M. Sunday–Wednesday, 11:00 A.M.–10:00 P.M. Thursday–Saturday. Licensed. Wheelchair accessible. Credit cards: Visa, MasterCard, American Express.

A few steps away in the next little strip mall is **Otter Point Bakery & Tea Room,** which serves a small brunch buffet on Saturday ($12.95). Actually a bakery, Otter Point serves "tea" you can assemble from bakery items or their more formal Classic High Tea ($15.95) or Afternoon Tea ($4.99). The tearoom also prepares elegant picnics with twenty-four-hour advance notice that may include salmon pinwheels, crab quiche, chicken pâté, fresh fruit, blackberry rum trifles, scones, cheeses, Greek salad, and more.

Sometimes we go all the way to Sooke just to go to **Mom's Cafe.** American Tom Dee, a retired Boeing software engineer, bought Mom's years ago and has kept it as is. This is a logger- and fisher-friendly, funky joint where an occasional tourist fits in nicely with some of the best breakfasts anywhere. All-day breakfasts include the Logger's (three-egg omelets from $6.50 for two fillings) and the Canadian (lean back bacon and eggs Benedict at $5.95). Oyster and other burgers, bluenose seafood chowder in a bread basket ($5.95–$7.95), and salads compete at lunch. Dinner specials range from daily specials such as Stewsday shrimp fettuccine with garlic toast and Caesar salad at $9.95 to Jaeger schnitzel with salsa and cheddar ($10.95), liver and onions ($9.95), grilled oysters ($12.95), or a char-broiled steak platter ($11.95), garlic prawns, Bengal beef wraps, and pork pies.

Mom's Cafe, 2036 Shields Road, Sooke; (250) 642–3314; www.moms cafe.ca. Hours: "Opens at 6:58 A.M. for your convenience." Fully licensed. Wheelchair accessible. Credit cards: Visa, MasterCard.

Kids of all ages will enjoy the Scharf family's **Roche Cove Llamas Bed & Breakfast,** where you can take a picnic, go "llama hiking," visit the petting zoo, and see the fiber studio with llama yarn for sale, all in view of the ocean.

Roche Cove Llamas Bed & Breakfast, 1241/1245 Gillespie Road, Sooke; (250) 642–1795; www.rochecovellamas.com. Hours: noon–5:00 P.M. Sunday. Partly wheelchair accessible. Credit cards: Visa, MasterCard.

There are a number of parks and trails in the Sooke area. East Sooke Regional Park is a semiwilderness, 4,500-acre park ideal for both beginning and expert hikers, with beach, coastal and forest trails, petroglyphs, wildflowers, birds, and animals. At the beach you might see large California mussels (which provide natural protection for dog whelks), porcelain crabs, and sea worms. In low intertidal spots watch for purple sea urchins and giant green anemones. You can experience peace close to Victoria. Roche Cove Regional Park gives access to Sooke basin and Galloping Goose Trail. Sooke Potholes Provincial Park is a locally popular swimming and picnicking park on the Sooke River and is an ideal place to watch spawning salmon in the fall. Parking is limited. Whiffin Spit is a natural breakwater between Juan de Fuca Strait and Sooke Harbour. To get there, follow signs to the Sooke Harbour House, a destination restaurant and inn. A few feet past the inn and restaurant is a parking area at Quimper Park Regional Historic Site, and a twenty-minute walk takes you to the end of the spit with views of the harbor, the Olympic Mountains, seals, seabirds, and wildflowers. Viewable intertidal marine life includes a leaf-shaped crab (*Mimulus foliatus*), a small limpet (*Megate-bennus bimaculatus*), sea slugs, and a large red-headed anemone in the gravel. Wheelchair access is described as moderate.

Western Canada's finest inn and restaurant, **Sooke Harbour House,** at 1528 Whiffin Spit Road, is about forty minutes up the western side of Vancouver Island. As you head toward Sooke on the Island Highway, the sign for Sooke Harbour House is obvious. Wander through the residential neighborhood following the

Sole-Wrapped Lingcod

Chef Edward Tuson,
Sooke Harbour House, Sooke

6 sole fillets, minimum 6 inches long
6 3 oz. lingcod pieces, preferably from the head end
¼ cup chives, coarsely chopped
¼ cup unsalted butter
¼ cup breadcrumbs
½ tsp. salt
½ tsp. black pepper, finely ground
1 clove garlic, minced
3 leek greens, 8–10 inches long, blanched

Preheat oven to 400 degrees.

Cut leek greens in half lengthwise for tying. Season sole fillets with salt and pepper, wrap around lingcod, and tie bundle with leek strip. Place fish in the fridge.

Mix chives, butter, breadcrumbs, garlic, and salt and pepper in food processor for 4 to 5 minutes, or until smooth. Remove from food processor and place in a small bowl.

Remove sole lingcod roll and place 1½ tbsp. of chive crust on top of each fish roll. Place rolls on a well-oiled baking sheet and bake for 10 to 12 minutes or until the crust starts to brown on top.

Chef Tuson's notes: "Sole varieties that can be used are lemon Dover, petrale, and rock sole. This dish is delicious served with tomato or pesto sauce with a rose petal–Johnny Jump Up vinaigrette. Try it with a buckwheat noodle salad or roasted sweet peppers."

excellent signs until you find it (just a couple of minutes). You are in for a real treat. Reservations are a must.

Gourmet magazine has rated the inn among the top twenty-five around the world, and its restaurant as the top in the world in the category of authentic local cuisine, number two in the world in "elegant dining room," and number three in the world in "casual dining room" (and it's all the same dining room).

Sooke Harbour House also received the prestigious four-star rating from the Mobil travel guides. It is worth the entire trip if it fits in your budget. If it doesn't, you might consider a splurge. Gourmets, gourmands, chefs, restaurateurs, and food fans from all over the world enjoy the same food here as you do. The inn's decor and setting make you feel at home on the edge of the world. Charges include breakfast and lunch.

Its newest rooms offer understated elegance combined with a local unit's stained-glass shower, wood carvings, and exquisite views from bed. Check for Sooke Harbour House's art gallery, and co-owner Frederique Philip's book, *The Art of Sooke Harbour House,* is a must for art, food, and recipe lovers.

The whole menu changes daily, and each day there are separate seafood, meat, and vegetarian menus.

Guided by chef Edward Tuson, entrees might include wild Coho salmon, crisp Port Renfrew lingcod, Quadra Island Ebony mussels, a fresh whole Dungesess crab, kale and broccoli puree soup, mint lovage tofu flan, organically raised Rainbow Farm free-range chicken, and desserts and a wide range of artisan cheeses. All ingredients are organic ($70–$75). The wine list is superb.

Absolutely make sure to take the guided tour of Sooke Harbour House's edible landscaping, as well as their Seaweed Tour. Check out the fabulous downstairs Potlatch Room, completely decorated with the artwork of nearby First Nation artists.

Red Bandit Rockfish with Nasturtium Flower Butter

Chef Edward Tuson,
Sooke Harbour House, Sooke

6 5 oz. Red Bandit rockfish
  pieces (red snapper)
1 cup nasturtium flowers
1 cup Japanese bread crumbs
  (Panko)
$\frac{1}{2}$ cup unsalted butter at room
  temperature
1 tsp. minced ginger

Preheat oven to 400 degrees.

Place all ingredients except fish in a food processor and mix until a fine paste has formed (approximately three to four minutes). Place mixture between two pieces of parchment paper and roll $\frac{1}{4}$-inch thick, then refrigerate for 30 minutes.

Cut paste into shapes similar to the shapes of the fish pieces. Remove parchment paper from mixture and place the shapes on top of the fish. Bake for six to ten minutes depending on thickness of fish.

Serves six.

Sooke Harbour House, 1528 Whiffen Spit Road, Sooke; (250) 642–3421; Fax: (250) 642–6988; www.sookeharbourhouse.com. Hours: 5:30–9:00 P.M. daily, closed January 6–February 6. Fully licensed. Wheelchair accessible. Credit cards: Visa, MasterCard, American Express, Diners, enRoute.

As you travel west and north on Highway 14, in a few miles you must visit the delightful **Tugwell Creek Honey Farm & Meadery.** Co-owner Bob Liptrot has been keeping bees since he was seven, when he started to walk home from school by the home of a neighbor who had bees, and talked his way into painting bee boxes for him. Now with a master's degree in entomology, Liptrot works twelve acres with one hundred hives, each with 60,000 to 70,000 bees coming and going. Liptrot's wife and co-owner of the farm and meadery, Dana LeComte, served for several years as events and marketing coordinator at nearby Sooke Harbour House.

Licensed by British Columbia in 2003, Tugwell Creek is the first meadery in western Canada. It is unique in that it is "vertically integrated," meaning they breed their own bees, "house" them, extract the honey, and make wine, with all products as organic as possible (they cannot completely control where the bees nibble after Liptrot takes them into the mountains within 25 kilometers of the farm).

Lavender Honey Cheesecake

Tugwell Creek Honey Farm & Meadery,
Sooke

½ lb. shortbread cookies or graham crackers
5 tbsp. melted butter
3 tbsp. lavender petals, fresh or dried, tied in cheesecloth
6 oz. wildflower honey
8 oz. light cream cheese
1½ cups heavy cream
water

Place cookies or graham crackers in plastic bag and crush them until they are quite fine. Place crumbs in a bowl and combine them with the melted butter. Press this mixture into a 9-inch spring form pan and place in refrigerator for one hour.

To make the lavender infusion, pour 2½ tbsp. boiling water and 2 tsp. of honey into a small metal bowl and steep lavender in this for 15 minutes. Remove the lavender and let cool.

In a large bowl beat together the light cream cheese and honey until smooth, then gradually add lavender infusion until the mixture is smooth. Whip the cream until it forms soft peaks and then fold into the cheese mixture. Pour the filling over the crumb base and place in the refrigerator for 3–4 hours to set.

Sprinkle the top with lavender flowers to decorate before serving. Run a warm knife around the inside edge of the spring form pan. Slice to serve. Serves six to eight.

Tugwell Creek honeys are available in the on-site gift shop and tasting room as well as at Sooke Harbour House. Honeys include (and you can taste them all) Mountain Wildflower, Linden Tree, and Blackberry/Thistle. From these honeys they make barrel-aged Vintage Mead, Metheglin, Sack Mead, and Melomel honey wines. Do not miss!

Tugwell Creek Honey Farm & Meadery, 8750 West Coast Road, Sooke; (250) 642–1956; www.tugwellcreekfarm.com. Hours: noon–5:00 P.M. Wednesday–Sunday May–September, weekends only October–April. Wheelchair accessible. Credit cards: Visa, MasterCard.

As you continue on Highway 14, now called the West Coast Road, you will come to Gordon's Beach, a roadside beach named after the old Gordon fishtrap, with views of Juan de Fuca Strait and Sheringham Lighthouse.

Try the **Country Cupboard Cafe** ("Home Cooking with a Flair"), where Jennie Vivian and family serve terrific meals in their A-frame with a deck and patio among the Raggedy Anns, amusing collectibles, and dried flowers. Vegetables are grown along the path to the restaurant. Lunch specialties include huge lean beef or chicken burgers for less than $10.00, fabulous clam chowder ($5.95), fried Fanny Bay oysters ($8.95), and swimming scallops ($9.95). Dinner ranges from penne with sautéed vegetables ($15.95) to sautéed chicken and prawn linguine ($18.95), half-pound New York steaks ($19.95), baby back ribs ($19.95), and grilled wild salmon ($18.95) to their famous West Coast Seafood Bowl in a tomato fennel broth ($16.95). Jennie's desserts are famous. We dare you to leave without trying the white chocolate Irish Cream cheesecake.

Country Cupboard Cafe, 402 Sheringham Point Road at West Coast Road, Sooke; (250) 646–2323. Hours: noon–8:00 P.M. daily. Beer and wine. Not wheelchair accessible. Credit cards: Visa, MasterCard.

You pass through the unincorporated Shirley District and then arrive at **French Beach Provincial Park,** one of our favorites. About one hour from Victoria and 21½ kilometers (13 miles) from Sooke Centre, this popular sandy beach is good for investigating tide pools at the western end, and there's also a children's playground and campground. French Beach is a favorite feeding spot for migrating gray whales, and there are educational displays near the beach. There is lots of paid parking (price varies, up to $5—be sure to take coins and put the ticket on your dashboard), and there are almost one hundred campsites.

French Beach is completely wheelchair accessible, with paved paths (occasionally a little steep), and meshed nets to keep paths through the sand to the water.

Where to Stay in Sooke

Hotels, Motels, and Inns

Sooke Harbour House, 1528 Whiffen Spit Road (250–642–3421 or 800–889–9688; www.sookeharbourhouse.com); summer season $340–$600, November–April $300–$440, including breakfast; elegant dining; overlooks sea; charming garden terraces; antiques; Jacuzzis; fireplaces; small pets and children okay; wheelchair accessible.

Lakeside Hideaway, on Poirer Lake (250–642–2577; www.lakesidehideaway .net); $145–$155; lakefront cabins for doubles or families.

Point-No-Point, 1505 West Coast Road (250–646–2020; www.pointnopoint resort.com); west of Sooke; $130–$250; log cabins and suites; all meals; fireplaces, kitchens, some hot tubs; view of water, private beach; afternoon tea; fine restaurant.

Fossil Bay Resort, 1603 West Coast Road (250–646–2073; www.fossilbay.com); 15 miles west of Sooke; $230, $198 if two-day stay; cottages on cliff above waterline; sundecks, hot tubs, fireplaces; adult oriented; small pets okay with fee of $10.

Orveas Bay Resort, 2577 Sunnybrae Road (250–646–2304; www.orveasbay .com); 20 minutes west of Sooke via West Coast Road; $130–$275; sea views; hot tub; no pets.

Bed-and-Breakfasts

Hartman House, 5262 Sooke Road (250–642–3761; www.hartmanhouse.bc.ca); "Honeymoon" Suite, summer $250, winter $225; other $200–$220; 2 units; kitchenettes; full breakfast; English style; adult oriented; German spoken; no smoking, no pets.

Bed and Breakfast by the Sea, 6007 Sooke Road (250–642–5136; www.onthe seabnb.com); $120 with breakfast; private beach; no smoking, no pets; open April–December only.

House on the Bay, 7954 West Coast Road (250–642–6534); $110; 3 units; water view; hideaway; soaker tubs; smoking outside; no pets.

Whiffen Spit Lodge, 7031 West Coast Road (250–642–3041); $95–$165; 4 units; renovated 1920 country home; Jacuzzi; smoking outside; no pets.

Ocean Wilderness B&B, 109 West Coast Road (250–646–2116; www.ocean wildernessinn.com); $115–$170, winter $99–$150; 9 units; sea view; hot tub in gazebo; pets okay.

At the western end of French Beach is **Point-No-Point Resort, Restaurant & Tearoom,** an absolutely charming natural environment to rent a cabin, enjoy afternoon tea, or have an excellent West Coast cuisine lunch or dinner in the old house converted to a restaurant. Lunch offers chowders, salads, a daily frittata with salad ($8), chicken roll up ($11), grilled vegetable sandwich with Havarti cheese ($9), grilled wild salmon on a baguette with pesto mayonnaise ($12), or garlic prawns penne pasta ($13). At dinner, try grilled wild salmon ($25); beef tenderloin with tarragon anchovy sauce and spaetzle ($30); breast of chicken with sorrel, pancetta, French lentils, and roasted shallots ($26); or osso bucco ($28).

Point-No-Point also has twenty-five rustic yet updated 1950s cabins, all with kitchens, fireplaces, and stunning ocean views, and some with indoor or outdoor jetted bathtubs and double showers ($140–$250). One of Kathleen and Jerry's favorites.

> *Point-No-Point Resort, Restaurant & Tearoom, 1505 West Coast Road, River Jordan; (250) 646–2020; www.pointnopoint.com. Hours: 11:00 A.M.–4:00 P.M. daily, dinner served 5:30–8:30 P.M. Wednesday–Sunday. Tearoom open 11:30 A.M.–4:30 P.M. daily, with traditional English tea served 2:30–4:00 P.M. Beer and wine. Not wheelchair accessible. Credit cards: Visa, MasterCard.*

About 3 kilometers (2 miles) beyond Point-No-Point (about 65 kilometers from Victoria) is Sandcut Beach and Sandcut Creek Trail, for which you must park at the road and walk ten minutes down a beautiful rain-forest trail (and fifteen minutes back up) to the sand-and-pebble beach (mostly rocks) with romantic waterfalls and sandstone rock formations.

Another 3 kilometers (2 miles) brings you to the Jordan River, and River Jordan, a small logging community with an expansive view of the ocean where the Jordan River empties into the Pacific. This is an excellent spot for surfing, sailboarding, kayaking, and finding Purple Shore Crabs. It's a great picnic area with campsites for tents and vehicles right along the water, all made available by Western Forest Products Ltd., something of a conscience move after raping the forests.

Shakies Drive-In on the right is the local and surfer hangout for good fish and chips from $6.28 to $8.95, a shrimp basket at $7.75, and an oyster dinner at $7.75. You'll also find chicken, the Newfie Burger (cod), and Dairyland ice cream. Deal!

For a more formal meal with tables and chairs, try the **Breakers Cafe,** a cheerful white stucco place with bright flowers and international flags welcoming visitors from around the world. This is an excellent place to hang out and watch surfers and kayakers.

Three kilometers from the Breakers Cafe you reach the parking lot for **China Beach Provincial Park** and **Juan de Fuca Regional Park.** China Beach is obviously on the Pacific Ocean side of the road. You can park here and walk fifteen minutes down a pretty steep trail (don't forget you have to walk back up) through lush West Coast rain forest to a long, pristine sandy beach, of course rimmed with logs and California mussel beds. There's a hidden waterfall at the west end of the beach.

The **Juan de Fuca Trail** is 49 kilometers (30 miles) long and has two campsites between China Beach and Botanical Beach, intended for all levels of hiking ability (thank heavens); day use is encouraged.

From here on, notice clear-cutting residue, second-growth forests and other results of reforestation, as well as signs marking fires and replantings. You have to read them quickly, because they're small and cover lots of information.

West of China Beach the road becomes one lane (and rough at times) to Port Renfrew, with several one-lane bridges edged by huge logs, sharp curves, rock slides, wildflowers, clear-cut disasters, and replanted forests. You do not need a four-wheel-drive vehicle to make it to Port Renfrew. We do not mean to scare visitors away, but anyone who gets squeamish with curves or sharp drop-offs on the side of the road had better not go. But if you can make it, the trip is exhilarating and well worth it. We love it and can never wait to go back.

Mystic Beach and Mystic Beach Trail are a thirty-minute hike along a steep rain-forest trail to a romantic sandy beach surrounded by sandstone cliffs, shallow waves, and a waterfall. If you can, make it.

In another 2 or 3 kilometers along the West Coast Road you come to the entrance to a winding gravel road to Sombrio Beach, 90 kilometers (54 miles) or two hours from Victoria. This is a favorite of surfers because of the huge Pacific Ocean breakers. The beach is another ten-minute walk from the road. Sombrio Beach is one entry route to the Juan de Fuca Marine Trail, with parking, camping, toilets, and information at the east end of the beach. This is a fairly rugged part of the trail. There are two campgrounds 2 kilometers apart at Bear Beach, although the trail between the two is impassable at high tide.

Twenty kilometers (12 miles) from here, pay attention to the delicate wild-flowers on both sides of the road in late summer. The road climbs again, and then take caution—the repair work on a road washout may still be under construction. Thank heavens Vancouver Island lacks California's daily earthquakes! Six kilometers (3⁶/₁₀ miles) from this point is a great place to pull off the road and take photos. The Minute Creek clear-cutting project is one to remember. Three kilometers (2 miles) from Minute Creek we usually lose car radio contact, so if that happens, you know you're getting there.

PORT RENFREW

Arriving in Port Renfrew, you'll see on the left a supply store and the **West Coast Trail** Registration Centre, where you must register before embarking along the six-day hike on this remote and glorious trail from here to Bamfield. The authorities are not snooping into your life, but keeping a count of who leaves when to make sure everyone turns up safely eventually. Originally the trail was cut to transport shipwreck victims the 47 miles between Port Renfrew and Bamfield.

Recommended only for experienced hikers and back-packers, the West Coast Trail is part of the Pacific Rim National Park Reserve and is open May 1– September 30. The trail starts across the San Juan River from Port Renfrew. You get there by taking a ferry from the dock at the end of West Coast Road (Highway 14) at the Port Renfrew Hotel. The West Coast Trail is the only West Coast land connection between Highway 14 and Port Renfrew to Bamfield, Ucluelet, Tofino, and Clayoquot Sound. (The other way to get there is to drive from

West Coast Trail boat at the end of Highway 14, the West Coast Road, Port Renfrew

Victoria north on the Trans-Canada Highway and then west to Port Alberni and keep going.) Reservations are recommended, because only fifty-two park-use permits are issued each day. Registration and park-use permits are required.

> *West Coast Trail (800–435–5622, reservations or www.britishcolumbia .com/parks). Hours: 9:00 A.M.–5:00 P.M. daily May 1–September 30. Must be at trailhead by noon, or your reservation is forfeited with no refunds. Park fee: about $30.*

"Downtown" Port Renfrew is only 1 kilometer ($^6/_{10}$ mile) farther, identified by a gas station and the Galleon Cafe, which has extremely local seafood and ice cream, with a fish tank of neighborhood sea life right in the restaurant. Notice local Gary Pierson's painted mural on the wall showing the 130 shipwrecks off the Pacific Coast of Port Renfrew, which is known as "the graveyard of the Pacific." The public telephone and restrooms at the cafe are for customers only, so buy something.

At the next little rise you will see the twenty-two-room **West Coast Trail Motel** on the left, where Geneva Shen is a font of local lore. A few yards farther on is the $1.2 million **Lighthouse Pub and Restaurant** (250–647–5543).

Take a left turn; at the end of the road, and possibly the world, is the former site of the old Port Renfrew Hotel, which first burned on the kitchen side in 2003 and was torched in 2005 to make room for luxury cabins. The pub and cafe used to be habituated by true locals with time and stories to spare. Across the street are a public shower and Laundromat (separate) and two portable toilets that serve as public restrooms.

You may want to stop in at a pub when you get back from your forty-five-minute hike to **Botanical Beach Provincial Park** (www.portrenfrew.com/botbeach .htm), parking for which you reach by Cerantes Road, a narrow, bumpy gravel road. Drive as far as you can and then walk. Some vehicles can get to within a fifteen-minute walk. World-famous tide pools with lush brown and red algae, anemones, urchins, whelks, mussels, limpets, acorn and goose barnacles, purple sea stars, blood stars, and sea palms attract nature lovers and scientists from around the world. Best viewing when there's a low tide of 4 feet or less. Mill Bay, Botany Bay, and Shoreline trails offer hiking suitable for everyone, including young children and the elderly.

Dr. Josephine Tildon established Botanical Beach as the site of the University of Minnesota's marine station in 1900. She and her colleagues could only get to Botanical Beach's tide pools by steamship from Victoria to Port Renfrew. Such remoteness caused the station's closure in 1907. Fortunately the Nature Conservancy of Canada bought about three acres to preserve the original marine station site, and the area became a provincial park in 1989. Do not disturb or collect marine species!

Where to Stay in Port Renfrew

West Coast Trail Motel, Parkinson Road (250–647–5565 or 877–299–2200; www.westcoasttrailmotel.com); summer $69–$99, off-season $49–$69; 22 rooms. Lighthouse Pub and Restaurant next door.

Trail Head Resort, Parkinson Road (250–647–5468; www.trailhead-resort.com); $110–$225, off-season less; 4 kitchen units; small campground; sauna; dock, fishing charters; small store; several large cabins built in 2004.

Arbutus Beach Lodge, 5 Queesto Drive (250–647–5458); $59–$99; beachfront; adults; hot tub; no smoking, no pets; reservations recommended.

Beachview B&B, 11 Queesto Drive (250–647–5459 or 877–647–6499); $50–$70; beachfront.

Port Renfrew Recreational Retreat, corner of Parkinson and Baird Roads (250–647–0058; www.portrenfrew.com/portrenfrewnv/); 33 private RV sites on eleven acres, 8 campsites with fire pits, and a few cabins; fresh water; coin-operated showers, washers and dryers, toilets; propane, firewood, fishing tackle, bait, ice, and snacks in service building.

5

Up Island

I f you can plan to spend more than a few days on Vancouver Island, we hope you will make good use of your time to travel northward. Rare rain forests, rivers and streams, beaches, clean air, open spaces, mountains, fabulous resorts, native relics and art, and interesting local foods await you.

We guide you north from Victoria to Nanaimo on the Trans-Canada Highway (Highway 1) via Cobble Hill, Cowichan Bay, Duncan, Chemainus, and Ladysmith to Nanaimo. Then we describe trips to take farther north on Highway 19 to Campbell River, Port McNeill, and Port Hardy, and west from Nanaimo on Highway 4 to Coombs, Sproat Lake, Port Alberni, Tofino, and Ucluelet, including Pacific Rim National Park and its sultry rain forests.

VICTORIA TO NANAIMO

This blood pressure–lowering trip can take you from one and a half hours to all day, depending on how many stops you make to eat, drink, taste wine, bask, shop, or learn.

To leave the city, take Douglas Street north, which becomes Highway 1 North, also known as the Trans-Canada Highway. From here it is about 54 kilometers (32 miles) to Duncan. Mileage signs here show both kilometers and miles.

The Trans-Canada Highway, which of course begins at Mile 0 at Beacon Hill Park and Dallas Road in Victoria, turns right at Nanaimo and gets on the ferry to Vancouver so it can truly cross all of Canada.

Mile "0" of Trans-Canada Highway, Dallas Road and Douglas Street

Originally cut as a cattle trail over the Malahat pass in the mid-1880s, this western and island extension of the highway climbs from Goldstream Park over the summit of 356 meters (1,156 feet), enough to pop your ears, before it descends into Bamberton.

The entrance to Thetis Lake Park, a great place for picnics, will come up on the right. Just past Langford, you and the kids can take a break at the **All Fun Water Slides & Recreation Park.** Take the Millstream Road exit just 7 miles from downtown Victoria and enjoy a ¾-mile waterslide complex, two miniature golf courses, driving range, go-kart track, batting cages, bumper boats (these are fun), and more. The Western Speedway, "Canada's largest racing oval," has stock-car and late-model races plus demolition derbies. Vancouver Island's largest swap 'n' shop is held at the track every Sunday March–October (250–474–1275). There is also a family restaurant called the Yew Tree and an RV park with ninety-five sites, showers, Laundromat, lockers, sani-station, store, propane, and firewood;

RV park open year-round. (For reservations call 250–474–4546.) Voted "Victoria's Best Place for Family Fun."

> *All Fun Water Slides & Recreation Park, 2207 Millstream Road, Victoria; (250) 474–3184; www.allfun.bc.ca. Hours: 11:00 A.M.–7:00 P.M. daily mid-June–Labor Day. Admission: ages eleven and up $10 afternoon/$20 full day, ages four to ten $10/$15, under four free; special "spectator fee" includes hot tub and beach volleyball ($5/$6). Partly wheelchair accessible. Credit cards: Visa, MasterCard. No alcohol, no barbecues, no personal flotation devices. Free parking.*

Once you have turned north at exit 14 onto Millstream Road and passed the All Fun Recreation Park on your right (east) you will spot Bear Mountain Parkway on your left (be careful of on-coming traffic). Travel up the hill to gigantic **Bear Mountain** development, which has grown up since the last edition of this guide. At the heart of this gigantic landscape-changing and construction site are the **Bear Mountain Golf and Country Club** and the Westin **Bear Mountain Victoria Golf Resort & Spa.** The hotel and the golf course are reached by continuing on the Bear Market Parkway, which becomes Country Club Way. The Westin features 158 suites overlooking the fairways at $189–$229 and special rates. In that complex are five different dining establishments, meeting rooms, an auditorium and various facilities for conferences, and an athletic club. The golf course is described in the lists of golf courses in Victoria. Throughout the development are condominiums, townhouses, and homesites, which are available for rent, lease, or purchase.

Headquarters for both the golf course and the hotel are at 1999 Country Club Way, (250) 391–7160 or (888) 533–BEAR; www bearmountain.ca.

Goldstream Provincial Park (www.goldstreampark.com) is a favorite refuge for Victoria residents and visitors alike. It runs from Highway 1 here through to Highway 1 west of Victoria on the way to Sooke. Fabulous for summer picnicking (no camping), it offers tables under 450- to 500-year-old red cedars, reputed by some authorities to be the oldest trees in Canada, which when cut are used for canoes and totem poles.

From mid-October through November, thousands of chum, coho, and chinook salmon return up the Goldstream River (great to watch), which the Saanich people call "Selekta" to honor the role of the salmon, believed to be their elder brother who transformed people from a magical place under the sea. Traditionally men gaff the salmon with spears, and the women clean, fillet, and smoke the fish over alder fires, a right guaranteed to the Malahat people by treaty in 1850. Across from Goldstream Provincial Park are the reserves of the Malahat, Pauquachin, Tsawout, Tsartlip, and Tseycum bands. *Mostly wheelchair accessible, including restrooms.*

The trees are so lush here and the water so clear that you can take off your dark glasses in summer—in fact, you'd better, or it will seem like nighttime.

Just 1⁶/₁₀ kilometers (1 mile) past Goldstream you'll get your first spectacular look at Spectacle Lake, Victoria West KOA campground, the Ocean View Motel, and the **Malahat Restaurant and Malahat Mountain Inn,** a marvelous incarnation of the old Malahat Chalet, with up-to-date West Coast cuisine and a fabulous wooden deck facing the water from which you can watch migrating whales while you feast. Wild design mirrors line the walls surrounding burgundy booths and imaginative wrought-iron candelabra. At lunch chef Sean O'Connell offers seafood chowder ($8); warm tiger prawns and lobster salad ($15); "soup of the moment" ($6); chicken Parmesan or steak sandwich, halibut and chips ($13–$16); and frittatas ($11). Dinner includes stuffed chicken or Coho salmon ($22), Angus top sirloin ($22), 16 oz. king crab feast ($35), 12 oz. New York strip loin with grilled garlic prawns ($30), and salmon and prawns with Gorgonzola cream ($23).

If you want to spend the night, rooms at the inn range from $165 to $425. The latter includes dinner and champagne.

Malahat Restaurant, 260 Trans-Canada Highway, (250) 478–1979 or (800) 913–1944; www.malahatmountaininn.com. Full bar. Wheelchair accessible. Credit cards: Visa, MasterCard, American Express.

As you approach the Malahat summit, you will see a left turn to Shawnigan Lake (south end) and Shawnigan Lake Provincial Park, where you can hike, picnic, swim, or camp at Shawnigan Lake or Koksilah Provincial Park. Shawnigan Lake is the site of the historic "last spike" of the E&N (Esquimalt & Nanaimo) Railroad and an old restored church, now the Auld Kirk Gallery, and the Shawnigan Historical Museum.

Back on Highway 1, if heights don't bother you, stop at the summit rest area for a spectacular water view. If they do, don't stop here.

The **Aerie** resort in Malahat (thirty minutes from Victoria) is said by many to be the most romantic place in the world to have dinner or spend a night. This modern, luxurious inn overlooking Spectacle Lake was created by Austrian natives Maria and Leo Schuster to combine old-world Mediterranean elegance with the Pacific Northwest's natural grandeur. Leo had previously

The Aerie resort and restaurant

served as executive chef of Donald Trump's hotels, and Maria had owned a luxury resort.

Chef de Cuisine Christophe Letard blends classic French techniques with Pacific Rim creativity in either a la carte or tasting-menu formats. Tasting menu is $85, plus $60 for wine pairing and might include local venison and roasted sablefish and figs. The wine list ranks with some of the best.

Mushroom tour and hunt weekends are offered in October ($120), and every Sunday a local farmer leads tours of small Cowichan Valley farms ($99). The Aerie also offers a culinary experience package that includes three hours of chef instruction, a seven-course tasting menu, and a "chef for a day" orgy, or individual cooking classes ($450–$630 per couple).

The indoor swimming pool, helipad, private hiking trails, and superb restaurant make this a must-try if it fits your budget. If it doesn't, at least go see it. One of our favorites.

Aerie, 600 Ebedora Lane, Malahat; (250) 743–7115 or (800) 518–1933; www.aerie.bc.ca. Hours: dinner reservations 6:00–9:00 P.M. until last person leaves. Fully licensed. Wheelchair accessible. Credit cards: Visa, MasterCard, American Express, Diners. Directions: Drive Highway 1 toward Nanaimo for about thirty minutes, take the Spectacle Lake exit, and follow signs to the Aerie.

The Bamberton Park/Brentwood Ferry Road turnoff will take you along the water's edge to Mill Bay (5 kilometers) and loads of parks and outdoor recreation.

Along the highway you will come to the Deer Lodge Motel with great views, the Rose Bank Motel, and opportunities for floatplane tours. On the left comes the exit to the north end of Shawnigan Lake and Mill Bay Road. Notice the frequent blue provincial signs designating an artisan's working studio. Please visit and support local artists. Golfers can play at Arbutus Ridge, which you can reach by following Kilmalu Road along the coast north of Mill Bay past Arbutus ridge through Cowichan Bay, Maple Bay, Crofton, and Chemainus.

We suggest you leave the beaten path and visit a couple of excellent small wineries.

To get to **Cherry Point Vineyards,** just five minutes off Highway 1, take the Fisher Road exit south of Duncan, left for a minute on Telegraph, and then right onto Cherry Point Road. When you reach the huge wooden wine vat/sign, you've just passed the driveway. Fifty kilometers (30 miles) north of Victoria, Cherry Point Vineyards has thirty-four acres of gently rolling, comfortable, California-like vineyards and sheep ranch.

Wayne and Helena Ulrich sold the winery in April 2004 to the Quw'utsun' tribe's Khowutzun Development Corporation (KDC), which built the new 800-square-foot wine shop and tasting room with fabulous 20-foot ceilings made of exposed cedar, reminiscent of a Coast Salish longhouse. KDC, from whom the Ulriches used to buy blackberries for wine, now grow them around the vineyard to attract bugs away from the grapevines.

Cherry Point now focuses on Pinot Noir, Pinot Gris, Gewurztraminer, and Ortega varietals.

Check out their much-needed new bistro featuring local seafood.

Cherry Point Vineyards, 840 Cherry Point Road, RR #3, Cobble Hill; (250) 743–1272; www.cherrypointvineyards.com. Hours: 10:00 A.M.– 5:00 P.M. daily. Wheelchair accessible. Credit cards: Visa, MasterCard.

Cider alert!

Merridale Ciderworks *is Canada's only orchard dedicated solely to cider and wine apples. You can catch the orchard in splendiferous bloom in April or watch the fragrant press in October–November, and taste cider varieties of the moment if you go by.*

To get to Merridale, take the Trans-Canada Highway and turn west at the northern Shawnigan Lake exit. Go about 2 miles, turn right onto Cameron Taggart Road for 1²/₁₀ miles, and turn right onto Merridale Road to the end.

It's worth the trip to sample and purchase estate-grown, fermented English apple ciders such as Scrumpy, Cyser, Normandy Dry Cider, Merri Berri, Cidre Normandie, champagne-style Somerset, and Summer Berry Cider. You can take a self-guided tour through the cidery and apple orchard (watch for the apple-blossom fairies) and have lunch at La Pommeraie Bistro, where chef Dave Woolfall prepares large shared plates of mussels and oysters, onion and apple tarts, pizzas, quesadillas, crêpes, sandwiches, and cassoulet, all for under $20. Watch for jazz and art on Labor Day weekend in September and special cooking classes throughout the year.

Be prepared for a true country/dusty experience.

__Merridale Ciderworks__, 1230 Merridale Road, RR #1, Cobble Hill; (250) 743–4293 or (800) 998–9908; www.merridalecider .com. Hours: cidery: 10:30 A.M.–5:30 P.M. daily; bistro: 11:00 A.M.– 3:00 P.M. Monday–Saturday, 5:00–9:30 P.M. Friday–Saturday May long weekend–September.

Just west of the Trans-Canada Highway on Fisher Road, Gamboa Greenhouses (1360 Fisher Road, Cobble Hill; 250–743–9013; open March–November) grows interesting varieties of tomatoes, peppers, and hanging veggie baskets, all free of pesticides and using "biological control only."

Earthly Delights (3275 Shawnigan Lake Road, Cobble Hill; 250–743–3980) sells hanging and sitting pots, herbs, jams, jellies, pickles, beef, eggs, and baked goods, all of which you can sample in their coffee shop.

Glenterra Vineyards is a terrific and tiny winery not on winery association maps and worth the entertaining visit. John Kelly and Ruth Luxton create wines

Lamb Pot Roast

Merridale Ciderworks, Cobble Hill

2–3 lb. boneless lamb shoulder roast
1 tsp. dried thyme
salt and pepper to taste
3 slices bacon, chopped
4 carrots, sliced
3 onions, sliced
2 celery stalks, sliced
1 cup cider (fermented)
1 cup chicken stock
1 tbsp. tomato paste
2 cloves garlic, minced
2 bay leaves

Sprinkle lamb with salt, pepper, and half of the thyme. Roll meat up flat side out and tie tightly with a string.

In a large saucepan or Dutch oven, cook bacon over medium heat until crisp. Brown lamb on all sides in the fat remaining in saucepan. Remove lamb. Add carrots, onion, and celery. Cook over medium heat ten minutes. Stir in cider, stock, tomato paste, garlic, bay leaves, and remaining thyme. Place lamb on top. Cover and bake in 325°F oven for one and a half to two hours, stirring and basting occasionally.

Just before serving, discard bay leaves and add the reserved bacon. Serve with potatoes or rice and your favorite vegetables.

Serves six.

in a garagelike building across the gravel driveway turnaround from their home. Ruth is an accomplished chef and Culinary Institute of America graduate who has cooked with John Ash in Sonoma County, California.

To get to Glenterra, take Cobble Hill Road southwest from the Trans-Canada Highway and follow the signs.

John Kelly relies on files left to him by original owner John Harper, who started to grow grapes here after serving and sipping in Italy during World War II. Harper originally grew forty-two grape varieties in twenty rows on one little acre at this site. Now Kelly has four and a half acres planted of a total seventeen, and he farms with organic fertilizers and no pesticides or herbicides.

As a testament to the quality of Glenterra's limited estate-grown 500-case production, their wines are available at the best restaurants in British Columbia, including the Wickaninnish Inn, the Aerie, Sooke Harbour House on Vancouver Island, and at Bishop's in Vancouver.

Glenterra Vineyards, 3897 Cobble Hill Road, Cobble Hill; (250) 743–2330; E-mail: glenterravineyards@shaw.ca. Hours: 11:00 A.M.– 6:00 P.M. daily. Credit cards: Visa, MasterCard.

Venturi-Schulze Vineyards winery and vinegary, the smallest winery in the Cowichan Valley, is owned and lovingly nurtured by Giordano and Marilyn Schulze Venturi and their children. Their sparkling wine was served to Queen Elizabeth at Victoria's Fairmont Empress Hotel during the 1994 Commonwealth Games. Their wines include Angevine, Brandenburg No. 3, Brut Naturel, Chicks & Hens Brut, Harper's Row, Indigo, Madeleine Sylvaner, Millfiori, Mille Miglia, and occasionally Pinot Gris, Pinot Noir, Ortega, Fear of Flying, Micky's Dream, and a Brut Naturel Rosé. Venturi-Schulze wines often sell out before they hit the market, so check their Web site for restaurants where you may experience these exceptional wines. They are also the exclusive distributor for Leoni Gran Cheese, made with unpasteurized milk from Alberta cows.

You can try their fine wines, as well as their 100 percent pure balsamic vinegar, in their one-hundred-plus-year-old farmhouse surrounded by tall fir and maple trees. The family uses no pesticides or herbicides. As they value their privacy and time in the vineyards, and have several delicate ongoing research projects, it's recommended that you call ahead to visit.

Venturi-Schulze Vineyards, 4235 Trans-Canada Highway, RR #1, Cobble Hill; (250) 743–5630; www.venturischulze.com.

In the Cobble Hill area, you will find a fascinating collection of artisans and small, personal farms where you can buy superb products.

Engeler Farm (4255 Trans-Canada Highway, Cobble Hill; 250–743–4267; www.engelerfarm.com) offers Sunday Gourmet Farm Tours (with the Aerie resort), hands-on cooking classes, and guest-chef cooking classes in their farmhouse kitchen.

At Arbutus Ridge Farms (3295 Telegraph Road, Cobble Hill; 250–743–7599), Don and Debra McMurray raise brown free-range eggs and vegetables and make excellent salsa and pesto. *Hours: sunup to sundown daily.*

Jane Van Alderwegen Pottery (3380 Boyles Road, Cobble Hill; 250–743–5839) makes stoneware and porcelain stoneware, both functional and decorative. Phone first.

At Silverside Farms (3810 Cobble Hill Road, Cobble Hill; 250–743–9149), Jean and Bill Aten grow sweet raspberries and strawberries in July and August (order ahead) and sell homemade jams, jellies, berry vinegars, local honey and crafts, and fresh berry yogurt cones and Island Farm ice cream.

Thistledown Nursery (2790 Cameron Taggert Road, Cobble Hill; 250–743–2243) offers hanging baskets of flowers, planter boxes, and plants.

At Cobble Hill Pottery (3375 Boyles Road, RR #1, Cobble Hill; 250–743–2001), John Robertson and Harriet Hiemstra make unique, handcrafted, high-fired pottery. You can watch them work in their studio from 9:00 A.M. to 5:00 P.M. daily.

Cobble Hill Orchard (1310 Fairfield Road, Cobble Hill; 250–743–9361) grows fresh apples and juices and sells Glen and Wendy Robb's jams, jellies, apple butter, and pies, as well as dried and fresh flowers. Open Friday–Sunday in season, 10:00 A.M.–5:00 P.M. Call to make sure.

We recommend you stop for lunch at Cowichan Bay, which you can get to from Cherry Point Vineyards by turning left at the bottom of the driveway on Cherry Point Road. Follow the road farther than

Mushrooms and Cream

Giordano Venturi of Venturi-Schulze Vineyards, Cobble Hill

1 lb. small whole fresh mushrooms, well cleaned
$\frac{1}{2}$ cup whipping cream
$\frac{1}{2}$ cup aromatic white wine
2 oz. ($\frac{1}{4}$ cup) unsalted butter
2 tbsp. Venturi-Schulze balsamic vinegar
1 tbsp. all-purpose flour
salt and pepper to taste

Melt half the butter in a heavy skillet, and when it starts to foam, throw in the whole mushrooms. Keep simmering, shaking the pan, until the mushrooms are nicely browned. Add the salt, pepper, and wine, and simmer over low heat until the liquid has reduced to less than half.

Now sprinkle the flour on the mushrooms and stir quickly to prevent sticking. After a minute or so, add the cream and cook, stirring frequently for another couple of minutes. Turn heat off and stir in the rest of the butter, cut into small chunks. Stir in the balsamic vinegar and serve immediately.

Serve with meat main dishes or pour thickly over pasta with generous sprinklings of freshly grated Parmesan cheese. Serves four to six as a side dish.

Gingerbread Squares

Michelle Schulze of Venturi-Schulze Vineyards, Cobble Hill

²/₃ cup raisins

2 tbsp. Brandenburg No. 3 sweet wine or other sweet wine

Rind of 1 large orange, grated fine

2 cups + 2 tbsp. flour

1¹/₄ tsp. ground ginger

1 tsp. cinnamon

¹/₄ tsp. ground cloves

Pinch nutmeg

Pinch black pepper

1 tsp. baking soda

¹/₂ cup butter, softened

¹/₂ cup milk, luke-warm

1 cup molasses

Preheat oven to 350 degrees.

Put raisins in a small bowl and add orange rind and No. 3 (sweet) wine. Mix and let stand to soak.

Mix dry ingredients in another bowl.

Beat softened butter, milk, and molasses together in a bowl. Add the raisin mixture. Add dry ingredients and stir until combined. Do not overmix.

Pour batter into a greased 8 x 8 pan and bake for 35 minutes, or until toothpick comes out clean. Cool on wire rack. Cut into squares.

you think you should (it turns back inland), turn right onto Cowichan Bay (which is Cobble Hill Road on the west side of Highway 1), and follow it down to the water.

If you prefer to try another winery before lunch or dinner, don't miss **Blue Grouse Vineyards.** Going north on Highway 1, turn left onto Lakeside Road, and Blue Grouse will be on the left. Going south on Highway 1, turn right at the light at Koksilah Road, and turn left at Lakeside Road. Blue Grouse will be on the right. (Before you get to the winery, you may want to stop at Cali Farm, where the Daugenet family grows pesticide-, herbicide-, and synthetic fertilizer–free veggies, as well as free-range chickens and lamb. Call 250–746–6827.)

Hans Kiltz, a Berlin native with a doctorate in microbiology and a veterinarian specializing in tropical animals, spent twenty years doctoring large animals in Africa and Asia before coming to Canada in 1988 with his Philippine-born wife, Evangeline, to educate their children in a developed country. Salvaging many old vines on this property initially as a hobby, the Kiltzes have developed their project into a successful, sophisticated farmgate winery and thirty acres of vineyard.

Featured wines: Muller-Thurgau, Ortega, Bacchus, Pinot Gris, Pinot Noir, Siegerrebe, Gamay Noir, and Black Muscat. Son Richard serves as winemaker.

> *Blue Grouse Vineyards, 4365 Blue Grouse Road, Duncan; (250) 743–3834; www.bluegrousevineyards.com. Hours: 11:00 A.M.–5:00 P.M. Wednesday–Sunday April–September; Wednesday–Saturday October–March. Wheelchair accessible. Credit cards: Visa, MasterCard.*

Farther out Koksilah Road, Darrel and Anthea Archer's Fairburn Farm (13310 Jackson Road, Duncan; 250–746–4637; www.fairburnfarm.bc.ca) takes care of the Cowichan Community Land Trust, where they raise the only purebred herd of Bulgarian Murrah river water buffalo in North America. These dairy-producing water buffalo have no recorded cases of mad cow disease, and their milk can be made into cheese. The farm also produces and sells water-buffalo sausages, minced meat, roasts, and steaks. Afternoon tea and tours (by appointment), or stay in their cottage to really get to know the buffalo!

Head back to Cowichan Bay, conveniently located forty-five minutes north of Victoria, with its picturesque houses on pilings in the water. You might try Myron's By-the-Sea or the Bayshore Fish Market.

Our favorite is the **Rock Cod Cafe,** a center for believable funk humor and great informal dining with a deck hanging over the water adjoining boat and fishing docks and an indoor stage setting that makes you want to stay from one meal to the next. Among their "undersea adventures without getting wet" are the rock cod fish battered (not brutalized) with dill and flour, grilled (one of the two best fish and chips on Van Isle), and served with huge, tasty chips. You can also get a major chicken breast sandwich, plus salads, fish chowder, flash-fried crab cakes, shrimp or bacon sandwiches, burgers, and pastas. Tuesday night is bouillabaise night. Try the Sex in a Pan for dessert, an orgasmic combination of Oreos, chocolate cheesecake, and chocolate sauce.

Cowichan Bay

Rock Cod Cafe, 1759 Cowichan Bay, (250) 746–1550; www.rockcod cafe.com. Hours: open most of the time. Fully licensed. Wheelchair accessible. Credit cards: Visa, MasterCard.

Next door is the don't-miss Cowichan Bay Maritime Centre Museum and home of the Wooden Boat Society, which acquired and renovated the pier in 1988. Strolling through this roadside village, drop into Mixed Blessings consignment clothes; the Udder Guy's Ice Cream Parlour for old-fashioned, unadulterated, natural local ice cream; Pier 66 Take-out for oysters, fish and chips, or burgers; Timeless Co. for ethnic handcrafts and a clock with no hands; the Cowichan Bay Fish Market; and Tugboat Annie's Flea Market. We especially enjoy the Shellfish Emporium for books and charts. Watch boat-building and painting and attend workshops if you stick around a while. Take in the annual Cowichan Bay Boat Festival the first or second weekend in June. Contact: Cowichan Wooden Boat Society, P.O. Box 787, Duncan, V9L 3Y1; (250) 746–4955.

Old Farm Market, Duncan

Make a special visit to True Grain Bread and Hilary's Fine Cheeses for the finest in organic breads and delicate farm cheeses made nearby on Cherry Point Road. (Farm visits: 1282 Cherry Point Road, Cobble Hill; 250–715–0563 or e-mail hilarys@cowichan.com.)

Also visit the fascinating Marine Ecology Station, with views of minihabitats and aquaria of coastal marine life.

Be aware that you are experiencing the Cowichan Chemainus Ecomuseum, a 1,000-square-kilometer museum without walls funded by the British Columbia Heritage Trust and the Heritage Canada Foundation.

Check out local art galleries, which include works by residents of the native Coast Salish band. The first nonnative residents only arrived in 1862 on the HMS *Hecate* with governor James Douglas in tow. Stroll or wheel along the estuary and Hecate Park to enjoy shorebirds and wildlife.

You can now follow the road along the water or go back up to Highway 1 toward Duncan and Lake Cowichan.

The Old Farm Market and Moby Chix on the east side of the highway are musts. The market features fresh local vegetables, pastas, a deli counter with Coombs meat pies (fabulous), and terrific breads. Moby Chix makes and cuts the most interesting superb meats, sausages, and seafoods that we have ever seen. Our favorites.

Vignetti Zanatta Winery and Vinoteca Wine Bar is where winegrowing on Vancouver Island began four decades ago. Turn west (left) at the light at Allenby Road, then turn left onto Indian Road (which becomes Marshall Road when it crosses Glenora Road). Winery is on the left.

Loretta Zanatta makes wines simply in a solid, personal, old-world Italian method. So far the best are Ortega, a dry fruity white; Glenora Fantasia, a sparkling wine; Pinot Grigio; Fatima Brut; Allegria Brut Rosé; Auxerrois; Madeleine X Sylvaner; Taglio Rosso (brut); Damasco; and Pinot Nero. Plan to stop for lunch or dinner at the excellent seasonal Vinoteca, featuring many foods grown right here on the Zanattas' 120-acre farm.

Vinoteca Almond Torte

Jim Moody of Vinoteca/Vignetti
Zanatta Winery, Duncan

1¼ cups flour
1 tsp. baking powder
¾ cup sugar
¾ cup butter
1 package (7 oz.) soft almond paste
4 eggs
½ tsp. almond extract
raspberry sauce, for accompaniment

Preheat oven to 350°F. Line bottom of a 9-inch cake pan with a circle of parchment paper. Lightly grease and flour pan and paper. Sift flour and baking powder together and set aside.

In a large bowl, cream together sugar, butter, and almond paste until light and fluffy. Add eggs, one at a time, beating well after each addition. Stir in almond extract. Fold in flour mixture.

Pour batter into prepared cake pan. Bake until golden and until a wooden skewer (or toothpick) inserted into the center comes out clean (forty to fifty minutes). Cool ten minutes in pan, then remove from pan and cool on rack to room temperature.

Serve with raspberry sauce.

Chef Moody says, "This is a very moist cake that works well in winter with cooked fruit compotes. In the summer, accompany it with fresh fruit, especially raspberries, and of course a glass of Vignetti Zanatta wine."

At Vinoteca Restaurant chef Fatima de Silva makes crab cakes; filo wraps of fig, prosciutto, and goat cheese; salads; grilled veggies and cambozola on multigrain ciabatta; a veal scaloppini sandwich; tortellini; lemon risotto cakes with seafood; and crispy polenta at lunch. Dinner adds a seared portobello mushroom with cambozola cheese and balsamic vinegar, oven-roasted Cornish hen stuffed with figs and apples, duck breast with apricots, and seared beef with red wine and mushroom sauce.

Vignetti Zanatta Winery and Vinoteca Wine Bar, 5039 Marshall Road, RR #3, Duncan; (250) 748–2338; www.zanatta.ca. Hours: noon–5:00 P.M. Wednesday–Sunday, dinner Thursday–Saturday. Wineshop open March–December 1:00–4:00 P.M. Wednesday–Sunday or call ahead.

Godfrey-Brownell Vineyards is the product of two writers and publishers, Ellen Godfrey and Dave Brownell, who sold company after company and now live their dreams with a winery in what was once the home of some friends of ours, George and Norma Asp.

Ironically, the original 1856 land grant to this property was to another Brownell, a distant relation of Dave's, and since his purchase of the property, the rights of that original land grant have reverted to his family.

Erik von Krosigk (he's everywhere) serves as winemaster, and Dave as winemaker, combining efforts to create organic Chardonnay, Pinot Noir, Pinot Grigio, and a blackberry bubbly, using French oak barrels from the Napa Valley. With sixty acres to plant eventually, Godfrey-Brownell is reaching for quality before quantity.

Godfrey-Brownell has planted "weeds" and olives, keeps compost piles, and has saved twenty-five acres for conservation as a perpetual harvest woodlot.

Godfrey-Brownell now hosts gourmet Cowichan Valley cycling tours and mushroom hunts. The tours include a bakery, a cheese company, and a picnic back at Godfrey-Brownell Vineyards.

Enjoy Chardonnay, Scarlatti Sisters blend, Beau Geste Gamay Noir, and William Maltman Double Red (Foch and Gamay).

Godfrey-Brownell Vineyards, 4911 Marshall Road, Duncan; (250) 715–0504; www.gbvineyards.com. Hours: 10:00 A.M.–5:00 P.M. daily, later if gate is open.

Those of you unaccustomed to aggressive billboard advertising will be startled by the roadside gallery approaching Duncan, the commercial hub of the Cowichan region and an absolute must-stop for native history and totem sightings.

For the Freshwater Eco-Centre at the Vancouver Island Trout Hatchery (1080 Wharncliffe Road, Duncan; 250–746–6722; 10:00 A.M.–3:30 P.M. daily), turn east onto Trunk Road, angle to the right onto Marchmont Road, and then turn right onto Lakes Road to Wharncliffe. Turn right, and you'll find the hatchery, slide shows, and discovery games, as well as learn about native fishing techniques, Japanese fish printing, and fish anatomy.

Where to Stay at Malahat

Malahat Mountain Inn, 260 Trans-Canada Highway (250–478–1979); www.malahatmountaininn.com. Wheelchair accessible. $165–$425; The latter includes dinner at the fabulous restaurant and champagne.

Malahat Ocean View Motel, 231 Trans-Canada Highway (250–478–9231); $65–$125; ocean view, fireplaces, decks; grocery and post office; pets okay.

Where to Stay at Cowichan Bay

Oceanfront Grand Resort & Marina, 1681 Cowichan Bay Road (800–370–9416); $145 and up; 55 rooms; restaurant; indoor pool; spa; Internet.

Wessex Inn, 1846 Cowichan Bay Road (250–748–4214); $40–$65; Tudor-style on waterfront with sea views, balconies; no pets.

Heading toward **Duncan,** one sign instructs you to turn left for totems, which is very hard to do because of traffic. Wait for the signal and turn left onto Cowichan Way to the **Quw'utsun' Cultural and Conference Centre,** 200 Cowichan Way. An elegant and tastefully designed tribute to First Peoples, the center affords employment and skills-learning opportunities for natives and learning and pleasure experiences for visitors. As you take guided tours or follow a map yourself, watch native totem carvers and demonstrations of Cowichan knitting, Salish weaving, and decorative beading; enjoy inexpensive delicious native cuisine (such as rabbit, venison, buffalo ribs, halibut, and local oysters) in the Riverwalk Café for Tluhwtluhw (local oysters), Thuqi cakes (wild Pacific salmon and spring onions), Ma'uqw (roasted duck), fiddlehead and blackberry shortcake (and take home native berry preserves); or experience a traditional lunch of salmon hot off the fire at the Bighouse Restaurant (you'll see native

Hand-carved canoe at Quw'utsun' Cultural and Conference Centre, Duncan

dancers, too!). You can purchase authentic, majestic original native art in the Native Art Gallery or prints and souvenirs in the gift shop.

The Mid-Day Salmon BBQ ($17–$29) and Cultural Tour includes native dancing and a welcome at the traditional NanNum Circle. The menu includes native scow bread, local spring greens with blackberry vinaigrette made every September, barbequed wild salmon, local baby potatoes, vegetable kabobs, and blackberry-apple pie.

> ***Quw'utsun' Cultural and Conference Centre***, *200 Cowichan Way, Duncan; (250) 746–8119; www.quwutsun.ca. Hours: summer 9:30 A.M.–5:00 P.M. daily, winter 10:00 A.M.–4:00 P.M. daily with reduced prices and programming. Admission: adults $13, seniors and students $11, children $2, craft activities $1–$2 extra, families $30. Midday salmon barbecue show Tuesday–Saturday at noon July–September, adults $35, including admission, seniors and students $33, children $24. Wheelchair accessible. Credit cards: Visa, MasterCard.*

Once you get to **downtown Duncan** a couple of blocks north, follow the yellow footprints on the sidewalks to take your own tour of the City of Totems, originally named Alderlea, the name of W. C. Duncan's farm once located here. Begun in 1985, the Duncan Totem Poles Project aimed to promote Duncan as a tourist attraction and more than accomplished its goal. On the city side of the 1912 train station, several totems decorate the lawns. Be sure to visit the Cowichan Valley Museum in the 1912 Duncan Train Station next to the highway. The museum shows life here from the 1880s.

Just up Station Street a few doors from the train station visit **Judy Hill Gallery & Gifts** (22 Station Street; 250–746–6663; www.judyhillgallery.com) for the best collection of native carvings, masks, jewelry, authentic Cowichan sweaters, books, baskets, and the work of more than a hundred B.C. artists. Hospitable, well-informed staff make browsing or shopping here a pleasure. For superb and affordable fresh food, try Asta Pasta at the corner.

One of the most exciting recent developments in Duncan is the 731-seat Cowichan Theatre (2687 James Street, Duncan; 250–748–7529; www.cowichan theatre.bc.ca), a performance venue for local groups and traveling professional artists, including the Victoria Symphony Orchestra, Atlantic Ballet of Canada, and the Cowichan Aboriginal Film Festival.

For a local culinary experience, try the **Arbutus Cafe** (195 Kenneth Street, 250–746–5443) for breakfast, lunch, or dinner of huge hamburgers; a cod, shrimp, and cheese burger; stir-frys; and wraps—all for less than $8.

The best dinner spot downtown for health-conscious food is **Gossips**, at 161 Kenneth Street (250–746–6466). Open Tuesday–Saturday. Also check out **Volume One** bookstore (149 Kenneth Street, 250–748–1533) down the street.

There's a downtown farmers' market on weekends behind the chamber of commerce in the Blockbuster Video/Overwaitea parking lot off Highway 1.

One of our most pleasant discoveries is **Alderlea Vineyards Ltd.,** northeast of Duncan. Roger and Nancy Dosman sold their "collision repair business" in Vancouver a few years ago and switched "from crushed cars to crushed grapes," their true passion.

To visit Alderlea, take Highway 1 north of Duncan a couple of minutes to Herd Road. Turn right (east) at the light onto Herd Road, right (south) onto Lakes Road, and left onto Stamps Road. Alderlea will be on your left. It's five to ten minutes from the highway.

Alderlea, the original name of Duncan, welcomes you to bring a picnic and is one of only two wineries on Vancouver Island (Venturi-Schulze is the other) that makes its wine solely from grapes grown on its own property—right here. We highly recommend a visit. You can enjoy their Clarinet, Bacchus, Pinot Gris, Hearth (port-style dessert wine), Heritage Hearth, Auxerrois, Chardonnay, Pinot Noir, and Pinot Auxerrois. A beautiful site.

The Dosmans ask visitors to call ahead, because sometimes they sell out of wine as soon as it is released and close for the summer.

Alderlea Vineyards Ltd., 1751 Stamps Road, RR1, Duncan; phone and fax: (250) 746–7122.

Just north of Duncan, take Highway 18 west to Lake Cowichan. Follow the road through the Cowichan Valley through Demonstration Forest. The Lake Cowichan area claims title as the "Fly-Fishing Capital of Canada," and for good reason. A fishing path wanders for 31 kilometers (19 miles) along the Cowichan River from Robertson Road clubhouse to Cowichan Lake. Enjoy Lake Cowichan village and Kaatza Station Museum in Saywell Park in the old E&N railway station. There are loads of places to hike, golf, camp, picnic, water-ski, swim, boat, sailboard, and fish along the river and lake. The B.C. Forest Research Station at Mesachie, Gordon Bay Provincial Park at Honeymoon Bay, and the Sutton Creek Wildflower Ecological Preserve are all worth visiting.

Off the Island Highway (Highway 1) to the east are the small coastal communities of Maple Bay and Crofton, which along with Chemainus and tiny Genoa Bay make up the municipality of North Cowichan.

The picturesque village of **Maple Bay,** with a whopping population of 1,848, give or take a few, is 8 kilometers (5 miles) east of Duncan, about halfway up the Sansum Narrows, which separates Vancouver Island from Salt Spring Island. This protected cove is heaven for rowers, kayakers, canoers, water-skiers, and divers. Sansum Narrows is a mecca for fishers of salmon, lingcod, and sea bass. Hiking trails on Maple Mountain and the local museum are both interesting.

Crofton's 2,500 residents switched jobs to pulp and paper milling in 1957 when the community's economy moved from mining to forestry. Take a mill tour in the summer, or just visit the shops and waterfront in the village for a peaceful stroll. You can take a B.C. ferry between Crofton and Vesuvius on Salt Spring Island as part of a triangle trip with Victoria.

Don't miss the **B.C. Forest Discovery Centre,** also in Duncan, a fabulous learning and nature experience for the whole family that focuses on forestry practices and preservation. There's an exhibit of the history of logging, a miniature town, a logging camp, and a ranger station, plus twenty-minute rides on a full-size steam train, picnic areas, sawmill, playground, totem poles, and logging truck display. An affiliate of the Royal British Columbia Museum, the Forest Museum has a cozy gift shop and ice-cream and snack bars. Do not approach or feed the wild mink.

B.C. Forest Discovery Centre, 2892 Drinkwater, Duncan; (250) 746–1251, (250) 746–0377, or (866) 715–1113; www.discoveryforest.com. Hours: 9:30 A.M.–6:00 P.M. daily May–September. Steam train runs Victoria Day (Monday before May 24)–Labor Day. Admission: adults $7, seniors and students $6, children ages five to twelve $4, under age five free, families $25. Mostly wheelchair accessible. Credit cards: Visa, MasterCard.

As you make your way northward, the North Cowichan Municipal Hall will be on the east side of the highway. Jerry's Diner, which always seems to be full of locals, is great for good, solid meals at good prices. For a more elegant dining experience featuring German cuisine, try the Inglenook Restaurant, 7621 Trans-Canada Highway, Duncan (250–746–4031); open after 5:00 P.M.

Where to Stay in Duncan

Best Western Cowichan Valley Inn, 6474 Trans-Canada Highway (250–748–2722); June 27–September 5 $110–$116, off-season less; 42 units; pool; dining, pub; meeting facilities; liquor store; near B.C. Forest Discovery Centre; pets at manager's discretion.

Silver Bridge Inn, 140 Trans-Canada Highway (250–748–4311 or 888–858–2200; www.travelodgeduncan.com); $55–$75; 34 units; by Cowichan Native Village; small pets okay.

Chemainus

Continue north on Island Highway or take Crofton Road, which becomes Chemainus Road, along the water to charming **Chemainus,** one of the oldest European settlements on Vancouver Island. Immigrants moved here to farm in the 1850s. After logging operations decreased and the highway bypassed the town, someone had the bright idea of creating a city of murals and dubbed the place "The Little Town That Could." Now the town has thirty-six murals and thirteen sculptures that decorate the exteriors of the town's quaint buildings. Named for Tsa-meeun-is (Broken Chest), a legendary shaman and prophet, Chemainus now boasts the professional Chemainus Theatre, loads of boutiques, antiques malls, and restaurants, many of which offer light fare. The Willow Street Cafe offers muffins and scones, espresso drinks, quesadillas, wraps, soups, and sandwiches, as does the Muffin Mill. Mandolinos Restaurant has pasta, pizza, seafood, and steaks. Saltair is a quaint rural English pub, and the Water-

Chemainus's Heritage Square mural

ford Inn & Restaurant, in an old Victorian, serves fine cuisine at lunch and dinner (full bar).

As you take yourself on a tour of the murals, check out the Chemainus Valley Museum in Waterwheel Park, at what was the train station, and the Information Centre (9758 Chemainus Road at Mill Street, 250–246–3944) in an old railroad car (good public restrooms and telephone here). Across the way is Heritage Square, with its exquisite First Peoples mural, antiques shops, teahouses, small shops, and galleries. Horse-drawn tours start from the park down by the water.

From Chemainus you can take a ferry to Thetis and Kuper Islands to fish, relax, sample wine, and cruise (on boats, that is). As you leave town going north, we suggest you follow the natural beauty of Old Chemainus Road along the water until it brings you back to Highway 1.

Ladysmith

Once back on Highway 1, you'll know you're in **Ladysmith** by the startling number of fast-food places. It is actually a charming town once you get into it.

Ladysmith is located smack-dab on the forty-ninth parallel, the line across North America that separates Canada from the United States—except on Vancouver Island. It would have been the border if the United States had its way in the 1846 treaty negotiations. The town, first called Oyster Harbour, was named after the site of a British victory in the Boer War by James Dunsmuir, and many of its streets are named for British generals in that war.

The older, spruced-up part of Ladysmith, First Avenue up the hill a block west of the highway, has many antiques shops and boutiques for a fun browsers' diversion and is occasionally used as a movie set. Scarra RV Park is convenient if you need it. Buckingham's Browsorium offers eclectic antiques along the highway (when they're open). We enjoy the Printingdon Beanery for great coffee and snacks, and Fraser and Naylor Booksellers. Hemer Provincial Park on Cedar Road has picnic facilities and forest trails along the shore for day hikes and horseback riding, fishing, waterskiing, kayaking, and canoeing. A $2^{7}/_{10}$-mile hike on the Holland Creek Trail System takes you through lush rain forest with streams, bridges, and waterfalls. Stzuminus Park, 5 miles north of Ladysmith, offers camping and hiking trails. You can swim in the warm water of Ladysmith Harbour.

Ladysmith claims that the surrounding waters are "a world center for oyster production." Local restaurants serving the bivalve mollusks include the Page Point Inn Restaurant, Phoenix Inn Restaurant, and Mahle House Restaurant. If you're in town the weekend of Mother's Day, don't miss the annual Oyster Feast held at the Frank Jameson Recreation Centre, at which area restaurants concoct their best oyster dishes. Past masterpieces have included pan-fried oysters, oysters in vodka sauce, and oyster chowder.

Traveling north from Ladysmith, notice the lavender wildflowers along the road. Signs advertise accommodations and restaurants in Nanaimo, and then you come to the Nanaimo Airport, from which you can get flights to mainland Canada and Washington state. On the west side of the road across from Nanaimo Airport, be sure to stop (maybe on the way back so you don't get killed twice turning left across the highway) at Johnson's Smart Market, a wonderful locally run emporium of fresh unsprayed vegetables, locally caught wild Pacific seafood (including Dungeness crabs for $7, sockeye lox, and lingcod), tasteful dried flower arrangements, breads, and condiments. Submarine sandwiches are only $3.95. One of our favorites.

You pass, unless you want to stop, Mountainaire RV Park and Campsite. Check out the Nanaimo River Fish Hatchery for an astounding learning experience.

Even if you don't dare try it, get off the highway and follow the can't-miss signs to the **Bungy Zone Adrenaline Centre,** on the Nanaimo River. Just an hour north of Victoria, it's only a couple of minutes off the road and thrilling just to watch. This is the "only Legal Bridge Bungy Jump Site in North America." Bungy Zone claims that "48 percent of women jumped naked." (They also host an annual Naked Weekend in mid-February. Brrr!) Signs all around you warn against jumping if you have any physical problems. You can also watch this from the E&N train, or buy stuff at the shop to pretend you dared.

Check Bungy Zone's Web site for cautions and information on how to prepare for various jumps

A Bungy Zone takeoff. Aaaaaaahhhh!

> **Bungy Zone Adrenaline Centre** *(250–753–5867 or 800–668–7771; www.bungyzone.com). Hours: 10:00 A.M.–6:00 P.M. Friday–Monday March–June 21 and Labor Day– October 31; daily June 22–Labor Day. Admission: jumps $60–$100. Not wheelchair accessible. Credit cards: Visa, MasterCard. Free daily shuttle from Victoria or take the Greyhound bus from Victoria, a B.C. Ferry, or the Harbour Lynx Ferry to Nanaimo, with free shuttle to Bungy Zone ($125 round-trip package).*

If you have time, follow the signs to Petroglyph Provincial Park, which is not on many maps but has a unique and ancient display of huge prehistoric rock carvings and mythological sea creatures. Wheelchair accessible.

Nanaimo

Nanaimo (Nuh-nigh-mo), known as the Harbour City, is Vancouver Island's second-largest city, with 71,000 people and twenty-four parks. It has a beautiful waterfront, though you have to look around the high-rise apartment buildings and hotels to see it. The wharf, walkways, shops, and cafes at the marina and north of town can't be beat (see map later this chapter).

The discovery of coal in 1851 brought hopeful settlers to the area, which was originally the site of five separate native villages (called *snenymo*). Incorporated in 1874, Nanaimo is the third-oldest city in British Columbia, and confusing to drive in. Streets go at angles and change names along the way. To drive through town, just follow the signs to Highway 1.

Head down toward the **Bastion,** built in 1852 by the Hudson's Bay Company as protection from native Haida raids. It's the only remaining

Nanaimo's Bastion

such structure in North America. During the summer be sure to catch the Bastion Guards. Held daily at 11:45 A.M., their performances re-create the firing of the noon cannon to eerie bagpipes. Read the wall map near the Bastion for the Nanaimo Heritage Walk and get tourist information from the young, costumed information mavens in the Bastion from 10:00 A.M. to 4:00 P.M. Pioneer Waterfront Plaza is just below the Bastion.

The Waterfront Walkway begins to the north of the Bastion and will take you to Georgia Park, Swy-A-Lana Tidal Lagoon, and Maffeo-Sutton Park. Georgia Park pays permanent tribute to original native inhabitants with canoe and totem poles. Swy-A-Lana is the only man-made tidal pool in Canada—great summer swimming and picnicking. From Maffeo–Sutton Park you can take a short ferry ride to Newcastle Island, and from the B.C. Ferries dock you can take a twenty-minute ferry ride to gorgeous Gabriola Island.

B.C. Ferries to Victoria and Vancouver leave from the north end of Nanaimo at the foot of Brechin, on which you turn east from the Island Highway.

The E&N Railroad stops way up the hill.

Pioneer Waterfront Plaza is both a resting place (for your feet and bum) and a downstairs waterfront development of cafes, galleries, and small shops, with plenty of metered parking.

A visitor's first challenge is to reach the **Nanaimo District Museum,** 100 Cameron Road, atop a rocky knoll in Piper's Park overlooking the waterfront, a

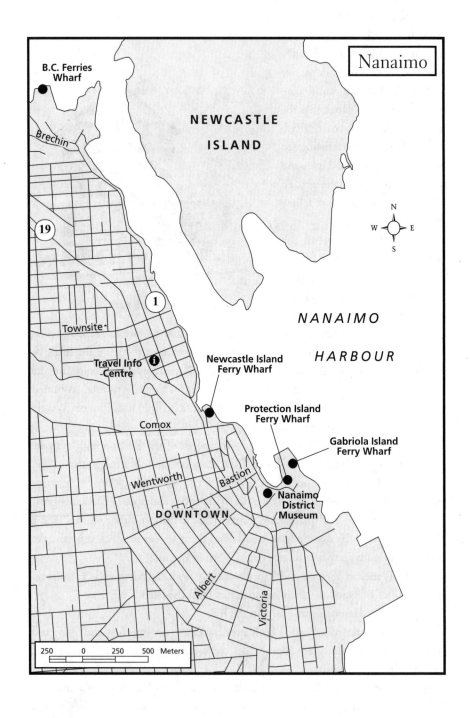

B.C. Ferries
Wharf

NEWCASTLE

ISLAND

Brechin

19

1

N
W + E
S

Townsite

NANAIMO

Travel Info
Centre

Newcastle Island
Ferry Wharf

HARBOUR

Comox

Protection Island
Ferry Wharf

Gabriola Island
Ferry Wharf

Wentworth

Bastion

Nanaimo
District
Museum

DOWNTOWN

Albert

Victoria

Nanaimo

250   0   250   500 Meters

block south of the Bastion. Climb two steep flights of stairs from Front Street or drive around the west side of the knoll on Cameron Road and turn up the curving driveway to the top.

This compact museum is worth the effort and includes re-creations of a Salish village, a mine, and early Nanaimo. Petroglyphs (ancient native designs etched in rock) can be copied by rubbing on paper with pencil. We were particularly fascinated by the history of the charlatan Brother XII and his witchlike mistress, Zee, who formed a cult at nearby Cedar Point and took both dignity and fortunes from their followers between 1927 and 1933 before disappearing.

Nanaimo District Museum, 100 Cameron Road, Nanaimo; (250) 753–1821; www.nanaimomuseum.ca. Hours: summer 10:00 A.M.–5:00 P.M. daily; winter 10:00 A.M.–5:00 P.M. Tuesday–Saturday. Not wheelchair accessible. Admission: adults $2.00, students and seniors $1.75, children 6–12 75 cents, children under 6 free.

Check out **Old City Quarter** by going up the hill on Bastion from the waterfront, which becomes Fitzwilliam above the highway. Visit the small shops in Fitzwilliam Gate near the top of the hill. The Nanaimo Art Gallery (900 Fifth Street, 250–755–8790) at Malaspina University–College campus hosts important exhibitions from across Canada and is dedicated to involving the community in art and art appreciation. The Festival of Banners brings community artists of all ages and their work to the local and visiting publics by hanging entries from lightposts around Nanaimo.

Serious hiking and canoeing are available at Nanaimo Lakes, Green Mountain, on the Nanaimo River, and at Overton Lakes. Long Lake affords boating, waterskiing, swimming, or fishing. Morrell Nature Sanctuary, behind the army base on Nanaimo Lakes Road, and Piper's Lagoon Park, off Hammond Bay, are bird-watchers' paradises.

Sportfishing for salmon, cod, or red snapper and shellfish is superb by fishing charter. California and Steller's sea lions come to feed on spawning herring from November to April, and seagulls, cormorants, and bald eagles scavenge for the scraps.

Don't miss the hilarious Bathtub Race on the fourth Sunday in July, the Nanaimo Festival all summer, the Nanaimo Country Fair the third week in August, and the Vancouver Island Exhibition in mid-August.

From a culinary viewpoint Nanaimo has become increasingly attractive. Artistic fine foods, diners, cafes, dock-fresh seafood and chowders, comfort foods, and fast foods are all plentiful. Stewart Street, along the water, has several good restaurants and cafes, most of which feature local seafood.

Wesley Street Restaurant, across from St. Andrew's Church, was rescued in 2001 by Gaeton Brousseau, a native of Quebec City, and Linda Allen. Brousseau cooked for ten years in France and several years in England and Arizona before he and his wife moved to Gabriola Island, just off the coast from Nanaimo, where he managed a large marina. Since reopening Wesley Street, Brousseau has expanded the wine list to seventy-five vintages, the best list in Nanaimo.

Chef Daniel Caron's menu features local products such as organic vegetables from nearby growers, practically from hook or net to table seafood, and Alberta organic beef. Dinner entrees start at $21.95 for pan-seared B.C. wild salmon. Dinner might also include bouilliabaise ($24.95), Cowichan Valley Farm duck confit with white bean ragout ($20.95), grilled venison ($25.95), or a chicken breast stuffed with wild mushrooms and goat cheese. Caron also offers a $39 four-course tasting menu Friday–Saturday.

Wesley Street Restaurant, #1-321 Wesley Street, Nanaimo; (250) 753–6057; www.wesleycafe.com. Hours: from 5:30 P.M. Monday–Saturday. Wine and beer. Wheelchair accessible. Credit cards: Visa, MasterCard.

Also try the Mahle House, 2104 Hemer Road at Cedar, in an orange house with fabulous local seafood specialties (250–722–3621; Fax: 250–722–3302; www .island.net/~mahle/).

Here's a list of **Nanaimo restaurants,** from which you can gather some feeling of what else is available:

Beefeater's Chop House and Grill, 1840 Stewart Avenue, (250) 753–2333.
Cafe Casablanca, Dorchester Hotel, 70 Church Street, (250) 754–6835.
Delicado's, 358 Wesley Street, (250) 753–6524; popular, great wraps; lunch and dinner.
Earl's Restaurant, 2980 Island Highway North, (250) 756–4100; umbrella drinks.
Gateway To India, 202 Fourth Street, (250) 755–4037; lunch and dinner.
Gina's Mexican Cafe, 47 Skinner Street, (250) 753–5411; lunch and dinner.
Katerina's Place, 15 Front Street, (250) 754–1351; Greek; view.
Lighthouse Bistro and Pub, 50 Anchor Way at Seaplane Terminal, (250) 754–3212.

Moxie's, #102 at 6750 Island Highway North, (250) 390–1079; lunch, dinner, Sunday brunch.

Seoul Garden, 75 Front Street #1, (250) 753–5044.

Zougla Restaurant, 2021 Estevan Road, (250) 716–3233.

Where to Stay in Nanaimo

Coast Bastion Inn, 11 Bastion Street (250–753–6601; www.coasthotels.com); $99–$189; 117 rooms; on inner harbor; water views; restaurant, lounge, pub; sauna, whirlpool, exercise room, hair salon; shuttle; wheelchair accessible.

Best Western Dorchester Hotel, 70 Church Street (250–754–6835; www .dorchesternanaimo.com); $95–$180; center of harbor, right above water; restaurant, lounge; shuttle; wheelchair accessible; no pets.

Best Western Northgate Inn, 6450 Metral Drive (250–390–2222; www.best westernnorthgate.com); $89–$129 summer, $69–$119 rest of year; 72 units recently renovated; restaurant, pub; Jacuzzi, sauna; wheelchair accessible; pets okay with $20 fee.

Buccaneer Inn, 1577 Stewart Avenue (250–753–1246; www.buccaneerinn .com); summer $70–$190, rest of year $70–$150; 11 suites, 2 studios; some fireplaces; close to harbor and ferries; water views; recently renovated; nonsmoking; no pets.

Days Inn Nanaimo Harbourview, 809 Island Highway South (800–329–7466); $99–$175, off-season less; 79 rooms; pool; wheelchair access; pets okay.

The Inn on Long Lake, 4700 North Island Highway (250–758–1144; www .innonlonglake.nanaimo.com); $120 and up; 62 rooms; Internet kiosk; scenic; pets okay.

NANAIMO TO PORT HARDY

From Nanaimo the Trans-Canada Highway (Highway 1) takes you to the B.C. Ferries so you can cross the Strait of Georgia to the lower mainland of British Columbia. To drive northward on Vancouver Island, take Terminal Avenue in downtown Nanaimo and head north. It becomes Highway 19 and takes you to Campbell River, Port McNeill, and Port Hardy.

Just north of Nanaimo, first-time visitors and some locals are shocked at the strip-mall developments and Wal-Mart, Costco, and the biggest mall on Vancouver

Island. To many they seem grossly out of place, but to others they bring urban convenience and consumer goods to the country.

Rhododendron Lake, which you reach by following signs off Highway 19, $7^2/_{10}$ kilometers (4 miles) south of Parksville along a forestry road, is a sense-blowing reserve of wild rhododendrons that date from before the last ice age.

Parksville

Parksville, a popular sportfishing headquarters, is a city of 9,000 residents 23 miles north of Nanaimo on Highway 19, at the junction of Highway 4 to the West Coast. It's the beginning of Beach Country, where life centers around the waterfront. Artsy shops and galleries and a plethora of cafes, pubs, and restaurants make this a great place to stop, for an hour or a lifetime. (Several resorts are the town's main features. See "Where to Stay.") When the tide is out, the sand and warm water make beachcombing and swimming ideal for the whole family. At the International Sandcastle Competition, builders of all ages race to create between tides.

Freshwater streams west of Parksville offer trout and steelhead fishing, and salmon, halibut, and cod fishing and diving abound offshore. Golfers can choose among four eighteen-hole golf courses. The Brant Festival every April celebrates the arrival of thousands of migrating Brant geese with arts and food all weekend. Check out the History Museum, heritage buildings, and the petroglyphs along Englishman River.

Parksville and Qualicum Beach artists abound (www.oceansideartscouncil .com). Follow blue artisan signs to studios in downtown Parksville, at the Train Station Gallery on Alberni Highway 4A, in Columbia Beach, Coombs, Qualicum Beach, and north on Highway 19A around Horne Lake Road.

Where to Stay in Parksville

Rathtrevor Resort, 1035 East Island Highway (250–248–2622); $130–$157; condos on Rathtrevor Beach; honeymoon suite; kitchens; fireplaces; hot tub; tennis, volleyball, badminton, two pools, playground; family oriented; no pets.

Beach Acres Resort, 1015 East Island Highway (250–248–3424; www.beach acresresort.com); $230–$330; 50 beachfront and forest cottages and town houses on twenty-three acres at Rathtrevor Beach; kitchens, fireplaces;

indoor pool, sauna; restaurant, patio; tennis courts, volleyball, badminton, basketball; no pets.

Tigh-Na-Mara Resort Hotel, 1095 East Island Highway (250–248–2072; www.tigh-na-mara.com); $179–$309; 142 units, log cottages and oceanview condos on Rathtrevor Beach; fireplaces; kitchens; Jacuzzis, indoor pool, spa; tennis; restaurant, lounge; playground, summer children's program; pets in off-season only.

Gray Crest Seaside Resort, 1115 East Island Highway (250–248–6513); $89–$159; on Rathtrevor Beach; kitchens; honeymoon suite; pool, whirlpool, sauna; playground; no pets.

Holiday Inn Express Parksville, 424 West Island Highway (250–248–2232); $69–$104; 87 units; indoor pool, Jacuzzi; meeting rooms; continental breakfast buffet included; pets okay.

Sandcastle Inn, 374 West Island Highway (250–248–2334 or 800–335–7263; www.sandcastleinn.net); $69–$139; kitchenettes; continental breakfast; under 12 free.

Qualicum Beach

Qualicum Beach feels like a modest version of an English or French beach community, with inns and restaurants along the water and expansive beaches with formal walkways and beachcombing (not exactly aerobic). But you can also find swimming, nature hikes, golf, tennis, lawn bowling, and spelunking. Explore the Old Power House Museum and local artists' studios at the Old School House Gallery, Sir Douglas Gallery, Qualicum Bay Seaside Gallery, and Murray's Signs.

A favorite stopping place here is the **Beach House Cafe,** where Keiko and Hans Kaltenbach produce delightful solid meals with a German twist, such as an excellent traditional Caesar salad at only $4.95; a house-made spaetzle with wild mushrooms at $8.95; a succulent oyster sandwich with fries, slaw, or Caesar salad for just $7.95; and steak and mushroom pie for $8.50.

Beach House Cafe, 2775 West Island Highway, Qualicum Beach; (250) 752–9626. Hours: 11:00 A.M.–10:00 P.M. daily. Fully licensed. Partly wheelchair accessible. Credit cards: Visa, MasterCard.

The Kaltenbachs serve Warsteiner beer and are right next door to the Captain's Inn Motel and Sand Pebbles Inn and Restaurant—in case you make the best decision and stay.

Caesar Salad Easy Blender Dressing for Ten

Keiko and Hans Kaltenbach of the Beach House Cafe, Qualicum Beach

3 egg yolks
5 large garlic cloves
5 strips of anchovy fillets
$\frac{1}{2}$ tsp. black ground pepper
pinch of salt
pinch of chicken soup–base powder
few drops of Tabasco sauce
few drops of Lea & Perrins Worcestershire sauce
3 cups vegetable oil or olive oil
$\frac{3}{4}$ cup red wine vinegar

Put everything except oil and vinegar in a blender, mix well, and then slowly add oil and vinegar to get a creamy consistency. Pour over your favorite greens and sprinkle generously with Parmesan cheese.

As you wander northward you will pass lots of places you might want to try: the Shady Post Oceanside Pub, the Ben Bow Inn, the Hard Rock Brown Egg Farm, and the Big Qualicum Fish Hatchery and Indian Reserve.

Also be sure to check out the Cola Diner/Horst G. Loewel Gallery (6060 West Island Highway, Qualicum Beach; 250–757–2029), a classic part of the old Coca-Cola restaurant/gas station chain. There's tons of Coke memorabilia, as well as greasy specialties ($5.95–$9.95) to match the period. Don't miss the Marilyn Monroe mural!

Where to Stay in Qualicum Bay and Qualicum Beach

Qualicum Bay

Bed-and-breakfast reservation service (250–335–0506); free; year-round.
Qualicum Bay Resort, 5970 West Island Highway (250–757–2003); $50–$65; pets okay.

Qualicum Beach

Qualicum Heritage Inn, 427 College Road (250–752–9262 or 800–663–7306); $79–$109; historic Tudor hotel overlooking ocean; some fireplaces; indoor pool, Jacuzzi; licensed restaurant, pub; pets okay.

Old Dutch Inn, 2690 West Island Highway (250–752–6914 or 800–661–0199); July–September $100–$119, remainder of year $70–$100; 43 rooms; across highway from beach; licensed dining, lounge; indoor pool, sauna; gift shop; pets okay.

Sand Pebbles Inn, 2767 West Island Highway (250–752–6974 or 877–556–2326); $70–$120; 21 units; on beach; some kitchens; restaurant; small pets okay.

Casa Grande Inn, 3080 West Island Highway (250–752–4400; www.casagrande inn.com); summer $150 and up, rest of year, $85 and up; 17 units; Jacuzzi; some wheelchair accessible.

Bowser

Gardeners may want to visit the Island Sun Greenhouses at Arbutus Bay.

From here on you see many more gorgeous trees than you see people. Most locals like to stop at the **Fanny Bay Inn,** known affectionately as the "FBI," once a hotel and important landmark pub. Owners Dave and Betty Hopkins restored the old lady to its original 1930s look with dark beams, lighter walls, and genuine English pub decor. Visitors and locals mingle like family, with local workers, Harley-Davidson riders, and government workers from Victoria all enjoying big pub food, a roaring fire, dartboards, and the island's largest cribbage board. One of David's favorites.

Where to Stay in Bowser

Seacroft Resort, 85 Coburn Road (250–757–8474); $65–$85; cottages and lodge rooms on oceanfront; fireplaces; deck; lounge; boat launch, fishing tackle, boat rentals and charters; no pets.

Comox Valley

At **Courtenay** the traveler is now in the heart of the **Comox Valley,** which was the coal-mining center that fueled much of Vancouver Island between the last half of the nineteenth century and the early years of the twentieth. While Courtenay is a classic small town that rolls up the rugs early and never unrolls them on Sunday, you may want to check out Kitty Coleman Woodland Gardens (6183 Whitaker Road), the Courtenay and District Museum and Paleontology Centre (207 Fourth Street), or the Comox Valley Art Gallery (367 Fourth Street).

Besides Courtenay, historic towns in the valley include **Cumberland** to the west of the main highway and **Comox** on the bay east of Courtenay via Comox Road.

North of the center of Comox at 1250 Knight Road is the expanded terminal of the Comox Valley Airport (250–897–3123), with flights to Vancouver, Calgary, and Edmonton. Little River Road leads to the Little River Ferry, which goes to Powell River on the mainland.

In Comox you can check out the Cumberland Museum and Archives (2680 Dunsmuir Avenue), Comox Archives & Museum Society (1729 Comox Avenue), and the Comox Air Force Museum (Canadian Forces Base, 19 Wing). If you're in the area at the end of July, you can enjoy the three-day Comox Nautical Days festival at the Comox marina, or the Filberg Festival, held during the same time, which features arts, crafts, and entertainment at Filberg Park (61 Filberg Road).

There are plentiful **restaurants in the Comox Valley,** mainly of the fast-food variety. For full meals, the following offer quality and variety:

Atlas Cafe, 250 Sixth Street, Courtenay; (250) 338–9838; breakfast, lunch, and dinner daily.

Kingfisher Oceanside Restaurant, 4330 Island Highway South, Courtenay; (250) 338–1323; open daily all day.

Old House Restaurant, 1760 Riverside Lane, Courtenay; (250) 338–5406.

Rickey's All Day Grille, 1-795 Ryan Road, Courtenay; (250) 334–9638.

Tita's Mexican Restaurant, 536 Sixth Street, Courtenay; (250) 703–0602.

Village Restaurant, 2104 Cliffe Avenue, Courtenay; (250) 334–3812; Thai dinners Tuesday–Sunday.

Yamato Japanese Restaurant, 597 Cliffe Avenue, Courtenay; (250) 334–2025; dinner daily, lunch Tuesday–Friday.

Edgewater Marine Pub & Bistro, on the harbor at 1805 Beaufort Avenue, Comox; (250) 339–6151.

Where to Stay in the Comox Valley

Courtenay

Kingfisher Oceanside Resort and Spa, 4330 South Island Highway (250–338–1323 or 800–663–7929; www.kingfisherspa.com); $95 and up; 64 units; has four-star rating; oceanview rooms with balconies, kitchenettes; pool, whirlpool; restaurant, lounge; shuttle to airport and train; small pets okay.

Coast Westerly Hotel, 1590 Cliffe Avenue (250–338–7741); $111–$154, a few suites at higher rates; downtown; 108 units, some rooms overlook Courtenay River; saunas, exercise room, indoor pool; restaurant, pub; beer and wine store; pets okay with fee; nonsmoking.

Comox

Port Augusta Motel, 1950 Comox Avenue (250–339–2277); $95–$170; 43 rooms; near Comox Harbour; pool; restaurant, lounge.

Kye Bay Guest Lodge & Cottages, 590 Winslow Road (250–339–6112 or 866–658–6131; www.kyebay.com); $900–$1,350 weekly; waterfront views of Georgia Strait; beach; cottages; barbecue; play area; no pets; April 5–October 15 only.

Jasper's Seaside Resort, 5730 Coral Road (250–334–4141 or 888–813–3533; www.jasperseasideresort.com); $105–$175, weekly and monthly rates available; beachfront condos; ten minutes to airport; no pets.

Alders Beach Resort, 179 Williams Road, Merille (250–337–5322 or 877–425–3373); $690–$1,540 weekly; oceanfront cottages; beach; volleyball; no pets.

Campbell River

From Courtenay north along Highway 19, the scenery just becomes more beautiful, rugged, and exciting, as does the road. Thirty miles north of Courtenay and 167 miles from Victoria, **Campbell River** is the last major town going north on Highway 19 toward Port Hardy. It is one of Vancouver Island's self-proclaimed "salmon capitals," since record numbers are caught here where the Campbell River flows into Discovery Passage. Once "the end of the road," it is now a distribution center for the northern end of the island. Only five people lived here in 1900, and now vacationers flock here to hike, camp, and fish for sixty- to seventy-pound chinook salmon and take guided fishing tours in search of Tyee (chinook more than thirty pounds). Don't miss the annual Salmon Festival in July for water sports, street dancing, a fishing derby, war canoe races, and salmon galore.

Absolutely worth a stop is the **Museum at Campbell River,** across from the Ceremonial Torii Gate at Sequoia Park, with a spectacular view of Discovery Passage. It contains a fascinating collection of artifacts and collectibles from Campbell River's early history as well as local First Nations history, including carvings, paintings, prints, and jewelry. The museum's Archives Research Centre chronicles ethnography, settlement, and industrial history of northern Vancouver Island. Experience coastal history through interactive exhibits and vintage-film viewing, and walk paths through marked indigenous plants.

> *Museum at Campbell River, 470 Island Highway, Campbell River; (250) 287–3103; www.crmuseum.com. Hours: summer 10:00 A.M.– 4:00 P.M. Monday–Saturday, noon–4:00 P.M. Sunday; winter noon– 4:00 P.M. Tuesday–Saturday. Admission: $5, $12 per family. Wheelchair accessible.*

In Campbell River you can take the TimberWest Timber Tour, the Westmin Resources Mine Tour, and a tour of the Quinsam Salmon Hatchery. Nearby trails include Beach Trail, Ripple Rock Trail, Willow Creek Nature Trail and Conservation Area, Canyon View Trail, and the Mitlenatch Island and Bird Sanctuary (250–337–2400).

Where to Stay in Campbell River

In selecting where to stay, note that on Island Highway, even numbers are across the highway from the ocean, while odd numbers are on the water.

Painter's Lodge & Fishing Resort, 1625 MacDonald Road (250–286–1102; www.painterslodge.com); June 15–August $219–$355, September–October 9 $175–$239, rest of year lower; many tour packages; on oceanfront; pool, hot tubs; lounge, pub, gourmet seafood dining with sea view; two tennis courts, fitness center; boats; airport shuttle; no pets.

Salmon Point Resort, 2176 Salmon Point Road (250–923–6605; www.salmon point.com); May–August $90–$175, rest of year $65–$120; oceanside cottages; 155 RV hookups; playground; pub, restaurant; boat launch, fishing charters.

Coast Discovery Inn, 975 Shoppers Row (250–287–7155); $135–$170; 88 units; near marina and mall; Jacuzzis, sauna; pub, restaurant; beer and wine store; health club; meeting rooms; packages; pets okay.

Best Western Austrian Chalet Village, 462 South Island Highway (250–923–4231); $105–$159; 59 units; ocean views, lofts; indoor pool, sauna; pub, restaurant; putting green, Ping-Pong; pets okay.

Bachmair Hotel, 492 South Island Highway (250–923–2848); $99–$180; 23 units; balconies overlook water; kitchens, Bavarian furnishings; fishing charters; pets okay.

Campbell River Lodge and Fishing Resort, 1760 Island Highway (250–287–7446; www.campbellriverlodge.com); rates vary by season; 28 units; parklike setting on Campbell River; whirlpool; dining room, pub; variety of fishing and adventure packages; pets okay with fee.

Anchor Inn, 261 Island Highway (250–286–1131); $99–$129; 77 rooms; oceanfront; balconies, some kitchenettes; licensed dining room, lounge; patio; sushi bar; hot tub; meeting rooms; fishing charters; pets okay.

Haida Harbourside Inn, 1342 Island Highway (250–287–7402 or 800–215–2167); $75 and up; 70 units; downtown; ocean views; breakfast included; coffee shop, lounge, pub; live entertainment; beer and wine store; fishing charters; no pets.

Strathcona Provincial Park

Highway 28, which runs west from Campbell River, is your best route to enormous **Strathcona Provincial Park,** the oldest provincial park in British Columbia. It is named for Donald Alexander Smith, First Baron Strathcona, a Canadian pioneer and one of the big guys in construction of the Canadian Pacific Railway. Lord Strathcona drove the last iron spike into the twin steel rails that finally united Atlantic and Pacific Canada on November 7, 1885.

Strathcona Park has animals and birds not living in other parts of Canada, as well as Della Falls, the highest waterfall in Canada, which falls from Della Lake to Drinkwater Creek; Forbidden Plateau; Golden Hinde Summit, the highest point on Vancouver Island; and Buttle Lake. Look from a distance for deer, Roosevelt elk, wolf, the occasional cougar, chestnut-backed chickadee, red-breasted nuthatch, winter wren and kinglet, gray jay, Steller's jay, band-tailed pigeon, blue grouse, and the unique Vancouver Island white-tailed ptarmigan. Nature walks, short trails, and real hiking trails attract devoted nature lovers from all over the world.

Strathcona Provincial Park (250) 286–3122; www.strathcona.bc.ca; Strathcona Park Lodge, P.O. Box 2160, Campbell River, B.C. V9W 5C9; lodge, elderhostel, alpine chalet, cabins; education center. Reservations a must.

Sayward

Forty-three miles north of the "big city" of Campbell River, you come to the old farming and forestry community of **Sayward,** the southern border of the North Island region. Here Island Highway (Highway 19) turns inland for approximately 120 miles.

Sayward was established at the mouth of the Salmon River in the late 1890s and now stretches to Kelsey Bay. Sayward has the world's largest cypress (yellow cedar) tree. Visit the North Island Forestry Centre one and a half hours north.

Charter bear-watching tours, hike, kayak, cycle, fish, or shop in antiques and craft shops.

Now you pass through an area of uninhabited panoramic beauty, snowcapped mountains, and tree-bordered lakes. This is heaven on Earth for naturalists and photographers. Gravel roads lead to Schoen Lake Park, where there is winter skiing, and Nimpkish Lake, where there is boating.

Port McNeill

Then the highway swings back to the east coast of the island at **Port McNeill,** 124 miles north of Campbell River and about 300 miles by road from Victoria. Port McNeill has a foot of airstrip for every resident (2,500) and is paradise for recreational anglers. Ferries connect from here to Sointula on Malcolm Island and with Alert Bay on Cormorant Island. Cruise ships pass by Broughton Strait, and you can enjoy whale watching, bird-watching, hiking, logging sports, sailboarding, sportfishing, heli-fishing, caving, kayaking, and scuba diving. Art galleries, native crafts, and the Port McNeill Heritage Museum (250–956–9898; www.portmcneill.net/museum.htm) dot downtown.

Port Alice (gateway to the Pacific by way of Neroutsos Inlet) is 19 kilometers down a scenic winding road. Another side trip is Telegraph Cove, 12 kilometers from Port McNeill, located on a road about where Highway 19 hits the east coast of Vancouver Island before it turns north toward Port McNeill. Once a busy lumber community, it was also the northern end of a telegraph line that dangled from tree to tree from Campbell River. In the summer the small (population: twenty), quaint town is overrun by wilderness lovers, water-sports fans, and whale watchers. (There are lots of orca-oriented cafes, as well as an all-whale radio station.)

Where to Stay in Port McNeill

Haida-Way, 1817 Campbell Way (250–956–3373 or 800–956–3373); $91–$129, $71–$105 off-season; 62 units; near downtown; coffee shop, licensed dining, pub; fishing and whale-watching charters; no pets.

Black Bear Resort, 1812 Campbell Way (250–956–4900 or 866–956–4900); summer $138–$165, suites $205 and up, off-season $125–$145, suites $190; new; 40 rooms; free DSL Internet in every room; kitchenettes; ocean views; cable TV; continental breakfast; facials; nonsmoking; wheelchair accessible; no pets.

Dalewood Inn, 1703 Broughton Boulevard (250–956–3304 or 877–956–3304; www.dalewoodinn.com); $135–$165, suites $205 and up, off-season $125–$145, suites $190; near wharf; licensed dining; continental breakfast; fishing charters; pets okay.

Port Hardy

Another 28 kilometers (17 miles) up the Island Highway, you come finally to **Port Hardy,** the end of the line on Vancouver Island. The largest community in the region, with 5,000 people, Port Hardy was named for Vadm. Thomas Masterman Hardy, in whose arms Admiral Nelson died in the famous Battle of Trafalgar. The first people arrived here 8,000 years ago, and the first white settlers came after 1900. In the years since, it has followed the usual island pattern: coal, lumbering, fishing, sportfishing, and tourism. Now you can enjoy water sports, wildlife and whale watching, beach hiking, shops, galleries, a wildlife and bird sanctuary, and the Port Hardy Museum & Archives.

Many visitors come here to take B.C. Ferries' northern route to Prince Rupert, a fifteen-hour daylight trip (in summer) on the Inside Passage to the Queen Charlotte Islands and on to Alaska.

Where to Stay in Port Hardy

Almost every home in Port Hardy has become a bed-and-breakfast, but we give you a few of the better inns:

Entrance to Port Hardy (Photo courtesy of Bob Carver)

Thunderbird Inn, 7050 Rupert Street (250–949–7767 or 877–682–0222; www .thunderbirdinn.com); $65–$99; 48 units; center of town; coffee shop, dining, pub; entertainment; beer and wine store; fishing charters; no pets.

Airport Inn, 4030 Byng Road (250–949–9434; www.airportinn-porthardy.com); $65–$95; 45 units; near airport; coffee shop, licensed dining and lounge; beer and wine store; fishing and hunting packages; small pets okay.

Pioneer Inn, 4965 Byng Road (250–949–7271 or 800–663–8744); $95–$105 in summer, less in off-season; 38 units; near Quatse River; coffee shop, licensed dining room; pets okay; 20 RV sites also.

Glen Lyon Inn, 6435 Hardy Bay Road (250–949–7115 or 877–949–7115; www .glenlyoninn.com); $95–$115 in summer, off-season $65–$85, larger suites up to $165; 44 units, all with harbor views; at mouth of Glen Lyon River, see salmon run and eagles feeding in August and September; licensed restaurant, lounge; boat launch, moorage, fishing charters; pets okay.

Quarterdeck Inn and Marina, 6555 Hardy Bay Road (250–902–0455 or 877–902–0459; www.quarterdeckresort.net); May–September $125–$145, rest of year $89–$99; 40 units; all ocean views; whirlpools; pub; tours and charters; some fireplaces and hot tubs; continental breakfast.

NANAIMO TO TOFINO

While the trip from Nanaimo over the mountains to U about four hours, it is one of unequaled beauty. Wind throug Sproat and Kennedy Lakes, explore French Beach and the Pacific Rim National Park's rain forests, and learn about native cultures and environmental activities in Tofino, Clayoquot Sound, and Ucluelet. Newly built and older resorts and restaurants offer once-in-a-lifetime taste experiences, maximizing the use of local seafood, sometimes caught within sight of the dining room.

This trip west from Nanaimo to Tofino includes stops at Port Alberni, Ucluelet, and Pacific Rim National Park, and a possible final stop in Bamfield. Start by taking Highway 19 toward Parksville. Five kilometers north of the Petro Canada station on Highway 19 is a left turn to Highway 4A, which takes you to Highway 4 (Pacific Rim Highway).

Alert: You need to know the following: The trip from Nanaimo to Tofino will take about four hours, give or take a few stops. Leave Nanaimo in the morning to avoid afternoon sun in your eyes (and then return in the afternoon so the sun is behind you in the west). Be sure to get gasoline in Nanaimo if you plan to drive straight through to Tofino. Except for campgrounds, there are really no accommodations between Parksville and Port Alberni, a distance of 50 kilometers (31 miles). Some of the roadway between Port Alberni and Pacific Rim National Park is narrow, straight down-or-up slopes, winding, and occasionally partly washed out. *Do not* drive this part of Highway 4 for the first time at night.

Highway 4 is a two-laner and the only way to get to Tofino. Drive cautiously due to surprise curves, mud, and narrow lanes.

The Road House Inn, 8 kilometers from the interchange, is a potential beer or snack stop. Five kilometers from the Road House Inn, you are in **Coombs,** an old-fashioned farming community with latter-day country crafts boutiques.

As you approach town from the east, after the Homestead Restaurant, a driving range and petting farm, a tattoo studio, and more, you finally come to the famous **Old Country Market,** with goats on the roof.

Old Country Market produces breads and pastas that strikingly resemble those at the Old Farm Market south of Duncan. There's a good cafeteria/cafe here with sandwiches you order ingredient by ingredient, fish and chips, oyster sandwiches, daily specials, and espresso. An outdoor window vends ice-cream and frozen-yogurt cones to die for, and sometimes you almost do on a hot day. The produce is inexpensive and fresh; much is even organic and locally grown. There's

...o an intriguing gift-for-yourself emporium with teapots, marmalades, imported clothes, and baskets.

Several small local craft shops are up the driveway. Check them out.

In another few kilometers you pass the Coombs Rodeo Grounds and Island Butterfly World at Winchester Road. Two kilometers (1²/₁₀ miles) on the right is Hillier's Sausage Company (worth a stop for excellent German and Polish sausages) and Hillier's Water Garden. Another 2 kilometers brings you to a local hangout, the Midway Cafe & Gas—a good pit stop on the left, followed by a fruit stand and Seafood Cafe.

Now you start to enter heaven, just fifteen minutes (sans stops) from Parksville. **Little Qualicum Falls Provincial Park** is a great site for family camping, picnicking, and inhaling, with waterfalls crashing in the Little Qualicum River gorge. You can swim in natural pools or at nearby Cameron Lake, where there is also boating, waterskiing, fishing, and the Mount Arrowsmith Trail. From the highway you can see Cameron's gorgeous setting in the straight-up mountains. Along the road here, rock cliffs actually hang out over the roadway at times. Don't look and drive. If you have a picnic along, try the Beaufort Picnic Site on the lake.

Just west, you must stop at world-renowned Cathedral Grove in **MacMillan Provincial Park.** Donated by H. L. MacMillan of the giant lumber company MacMillan-Bloedel, Cathedral Grove is one of the few remaining primeval uncut stands of timber accessible to the public. Thousand-year-old growth includes Douglas fir, western hemlock, grand fir, and western red cedar. Signs warn: 300,000 VISIT HERE ANNUALLY AND EVERY TOUCH HURTS. IF WIND BLOWS, DO NOT GO ON PATH SINCE OLD-GROWTH TREES CAN FALL WITHOUT WARNING.

In another 10 kilometers you reach the 1,272-foot summit of the roadway and railway of the Beaufort Range. Almost in a blink are Mount Arrowsmith Ski Area to the left and Mount Arrowsmith Park, alpine terrain with T-bars and rope tows for skiers of all levels. A little hard to get to, there is a day lodge, cafeteria, and rental shop. Summer hiking and views are fantastic, with visibility to Van Isle's east coast and even across the Strait of Georgia to the mainland.

Port Alberni

Port Alberni, with a population of 20,000, is 31 miles west of Parksville. Even though it appears on maps to be inland, it is actually at the head of the Alberni Inlet from the Pacific Ocean. Its primary industries are lumber and fishing and all the businesses that support workers in both. It suffered tsunami damage in 1964.

You know you're arriving when you see the Port Alberni City Museum and Information Centre on the left, slightly uphill from the rest of town. Enjoy the extensive collection of Nuu-chah-nulth art and artifacts here. The site of British Columbia's first industrial sawmill in 1862, Port Alberni hosts an annual Forest Week celebration in May, complete with a decked-out heavy-equipment parade.

This is a great place to buy fishing and other outdoor equipment and camping supplies you may have forgotten. Local stores and even Kmart fill those needs. Try the Sports Fishing & Outdoor Centre or Northport Plaza. The Clam-bucket Seafood Restaurant serves fresh local seafood (surprise), and check out Curious Coho Books. Don't miss the Port Alberni Salmon Festival on Labor Day weekend, with a $25,000 first prize.

If you prefer to continue your trip to Tofino and Bamfield by boat, Port Alberni is where you can get the MV *Lady Rose* and the MV *Frances Barkley* to those destinations, as well as to Bamfield, Ucluelet, and the Broken Group Islands. Barkley Sound Service is at 5425 Argyle Street (250–723–8313).

You might want to explore the wharves and marina, where there are lots of artists' studios and small boutiques in a beautiful setting along Alberni Harbour Quay, Port Alberni's park and marketplace on the harbor, at 5440 Argyle Street (250–723–2181). Marinas where you can dock your boat include Clutesi Haven Marina (250–724–6837), China Creek Marina (250–723–9812), and Fish Harbour (250–723–2533).

When the highway comes to a T at the end of the inlet, you head right toward Tofino and cross the inlet on a small bridge. The Rainforest Tree House will be on the right. Try the Clintas Indian Crafts store at Tses-Haht Reserve for convenience foods, hot coffee, and any other emergencies and gasoline. *Local tip:* This is your last chance for fuel before the rugged drive to Ucluelet or Tofino.

After you pass the Arrowvale Campground, aviation fans might want to stop at the Home of the Mars Water Bombers, the largest water bombing plane fleet in the world, headquartered at gorgeous, warm (in summer) Sproat Lake. To your left, Sproat Lake, which is 17 miles long and 1 mile wide, has forty campsites and 146 picnic tables with terrific swimming, boating, and fishing for cutthroat and rainbow trout from April to November, not to mention the pristine air year-round. You can also walk on trails to see prehistoric petroglyphs at Sproat Lake Provincial Park at the north end of the lake near Port Alberni. Both are named for Malcolm Sproat, founder of Port Alberni sawmills and later B.C. agent general in London and Indian land agent until 1880.

Where to Stay in Port Alberni

Best Western Barclay Hotel, 4277 Stamp Avenue (250–724–7171 or 800–563–6590; www.bestwesternbarclay.com); $129–$199, off-season $99–$179; 86 rooms; the only true hotel in town; 10 blocks to harbor marina; dining; pool, sauna, tennis; boat launch, fishing charters; no pets.
Coast Hospitality Inn, 2835 Redford Street (250–723–8111 or 877–733–8111; www.hospitalityinnportalberni.com); $115–$135, off-season $99–$119; restaurant, pub; beer and wine store; fishing charters; pets okay.
Bluebird Motel, 3755 Third Avenue (250–723–1153 or 888–591–3888; www.bluebirdmotel.net); $46–$69; 14 units; closest to harbor; Lady Rose tour boat; Alberni Forest Information Centre; no pets.
Timberlodge, Highway 4 (250–723–9415); $75–$95; 22 units; dining (except November–March), lounge; sauna, indoor pool; pets okay; also 24 RV sites.
Somass Motel, 5279 River Road/Highway 4 (250–724–3236; www.somass-motel.ca); $60–$125; 14 units; across from Somass River; pool; boat parking, 1 block to boat launch; pets okay; also 6 RV sites.
Hospitality Inn, 3825 Redford Street; (250–723–3111); $119–$139; cabins, apartments, suites, Tudor style; dining; lounge; pool; Internet; newly renovated.

Where to Stay at Sproat Lake

Maples Resort Motel, 9624 Lakeshore Road (250–723–7533 or 877–855–1200; www.maplesresort,com); $140 $170, less off-season; cabins, apartments, suites; beach; moorage, boat rentals; waterskiing; no pets; some RV locations.
Westbay Hotel, 10695 Lakeshore Road (250–723–2811); average $70; 15 units; lakeside licensed dining, beer and wine store; moorage, boat rentals; no pets.

We find the trip from Sproat Lake to Tofino to be one of the most beautiful and exhilarating drives in the world. It is well worth overcoming fears, if possible, just to experience these natural wonders. You can also take Pacific Coast Line (PCL) tour buses from Victoria's downtown bus station or Nanaimo if you prefer not to drive. If you're driving, pray that a bus or semi-truck doesn't sit on your tail going down the hill.

Taylor Arm Provincial Park, along the north shore of Sproat Lake, has group camping sites by reservation only and an undeveloped beach. The Taylor River offers good cutthroat trout fishing in spring. The devastation of a 1964 forest fire left gray tree ghosts that are finally mingled with some new growth. Near a turnoff to a rest area on the right, stop at a wide curve and look back at the tall, thin, pink wildflowers in the foreground and the sad burnt tree stumps in the distance.

At Sproat Lake you can tour the base of the fire-fighting air bombers.

You can also see snow on some peaks to the west, even in summer, and begin to feel ocean winds from the west. Soon the Kennedy River will run along the road for 18 miles with you. There is a pull-off here to allow others to pass. Please use it if you're holding up traffic.

You may lose radio reception along here. Notice the signs marking which forest stands were cut, burned, and/or replanted and when. There's another pull-off, and 2 kilometers later the road becomes four lanes at the bottom of a grade, but don't get excited—it's only for a brief spell.

The road, now called the Pacific Rim Highway, was blasted out of rock above Kennedy Lake, Vancouver Island's largest at 24 square miles. There's good trout fishing wherever creeks flow into the lake. Four kilometers later is a beach with boat launching, and another for swimming and picnics down a short road.

Pacific Rim National Park

Soon the highway turns north, at **Pacific Rim National Park.** Turn right 21 miles (34 kilometers) to Tofino and left 5 miles (8 kilometers) to Ucluelet. The Park Information Centre is $1^2/_{10}$ miles (2 kilometers) to the right of this junction, with informative staff offering advice, maps, and brochures on the park.

Ucluelet and **Tofino,** two former fishing villages, are now major tourist destinations since they are on the ocean and are excellent for camping, fishing, surfing, whale watching, kayaking, and walking on the beach. Between the two towns lies Long Beach, one of the finest beaches on the island, with a provincially maintained rain forest and access to the beach for wheelchairs, as well as easy parking near the beach. Both towns are launching points for boat tours, charters, and various explorations; have good dining, scenic vistas, and interesting shops; and in Tofino the best exhibit of modern native art.

Fine points: *Official Guide to Pacific Rim Park Reserve,* an outstanding collection of local history and information on beaches, intertidal zones, tide pools, rain forest, recreation, and trails, is an excellent book for lovers of nature, beaches, wildlife, and rain forests. Written by J. M. MacFarlane, H. J. Quan, K. K. Uyeda, and K. D. Wong, and published by Blackbird Naturegraphics, Calgary, Alberta, it's available in bookstores on Vancouver Island.

You are driving through the **Long Beach Unit** of Pacific Rim National Park, extending from Ucluelet on Barkeley Sound on the south to Tofino on Clayoquot Sound on the north. Long Beach itself rolls on through the broad curve of Wickaninnish Bay for 10 kilometers (6 miles). It was hard to get to until the paved highway was completed in 1970, but Long Beach now receives more than 450,000 tourists annually, 80 percent between May and October. Sea lions, starfish, and respectful people mingle delicately along this romantic stretch.

Ten kilometers (6 miles) north of the junction going toward Tofino you reach **Wickaninnish Beach,** a part of sandy Long Beach named for one of the Clayoquot chiefs at the time Europeans arrived in the 1770s. Surfing and sailboarding (wet suits required— for your sake) and strolling or wheeling are popular activities

Rain forest of Pacific Rim National Park

here. Long Beach is completely wheelchair accessible, has good restrooms and outdoor shower, public telephones, $2 parking for one hour, and $5 day pass usable at all Pacific Rim beaches. There's also a reminder: PLEASE REFRAIN FROM COLLECTING ANYTHING WHILE IN A NATIONAL PARK; and a caution about Long Beach's severe riptide: NOVICE SURFERS/BODY BOARDERS SHOULD STAY 200 METERS FROM SMALL ROCK. Check out the Wickaninnish Bay and Interpretive Centre at the end of Wickaninnish Road. If you are lucky, you may see some of the estimated 26,000 whales that pass by here on their annual migration to the warmth of Mexico—just like human Canadians!

Within another 4 kilometers (2⁴/₁₀ miles) you can enter the rain forest, an experience that will send you rhapsodic. Combers Beach, 1 kilometer (⁶/₁₀ mile) north of here, is actually a continuation of Long Beach. Green Point Campground in 2 kilometers (1²/₁₀ miles) is the only major campground within the park. Teeming tide pools form here from seawater flowing into cracks of bedrock. Schooner Cove is a bay with a long white-sand beach to which you have to hike from the parking lot between Portland Point and Box Island, where harbor seals hang out on the rocks occasionally. Hikers can get here at low tide.

Long Beach Golf Course is on the right.

Radar Hill was used by the Royal Canadian Air Force during World War II, and you can see why: spectacular views of the edge of the world—including Meares Island, Tofino Inlet, and the Gowlland rocks.

After you officially leave the park, you will come to Pacific Rim Ranch, with trail rides available at Pacific Rim Resort, and Pacific Sands Beach Resort on the left (oceanside), Orca Lodge on the right, and then Wickaninnish Inn.

The **Wickaninnish Inn** is an elegant and environmentally sensitive restaurant and inn that's right on the edge of the world, 3 miles south of Tofino at Chesterman Beach, the longest beach on the west coast of Vancouver Island outside Pacific Rim National Park. Recycled old-growth lumber removed from St. Anne's Academy in Victoria gives its interior a heavy, cedar-beamed, warm, solid wood appearance. Giant windows in every room overlook the Pacific Ocean all the way to Japan, with waves crashing under the dining room during storm season. Try the Ancient Cedar Spa for a very special, romantic, full spa experience.

In the On-the-Rocks Lounge you can sample single-malt Scotches and then move on to the Pointe Restaurant for breakfast, lunch, or dinner prepared under the guidance of restaurant manager Yvonne Ouwerkerk and Chef de Cuisine Andrew Springett.

The restaurant features seafood caught within a stone's throw; chanterelles, boletus, angel wings, and pine mushrooms are brought in from neighboring forests; gooseneck barnacles come off the rocks on the beach; organic greens; rabbit and venison; Oyster Jim's shellfish; and Indian Candy made from salmon marinated for six days and smoked comes from Tofino.

Breakfast includes house-made granola, free-range eggs, local sausage and bacon, or a smoked black cod, pancetta, and Qualicum cheese frittata. Lunch emphasizes elegant, imaginative sandwiches such as the wild salmon BLT, and

Wickaninnish Inn, at the end of Chesterman Beach

dinner includes a salmon tasting, local Dungeness crab, grilled beef tenderloin and braised short rib, and loads of local seafood.

> **Wickaninnish Inn,** *Osprey Lane at Chesterman Beach, Tofino; (250) 725–3100; www.wickinn.com. November–February $220–$1,000, March–May $240–$1,000, June–September $400–$1,500, October $280–$1,000; ocean views; full-service spa; two-person soaker tubs, Jacuzzis; fireplaces; balconies; fine restaurant; exercise room; pets okay; about 3 miles south of Tofino. Wheelchair accessible. Credit cards: Visa, MasterCard, American Express, Diners.*

One of the most beautiful and natural fine-resort settings along this coast is the native-run **Best Western Tin Wis Resort and Conference Centre** (www.tinwis .com; $119–$345), on traditional land of the Tla-O-Qui-Aht First Nations people, with all rooms overlooking MacKenzie Beach. If you can't stay there, at least park and walk to the beach. A paved path helps with wheelchairs. Outdoor dining is superb in any weather short of rain. The woodwork alone is worth the trip.

From here on you will see lots of motels and lodges. It is imperative to make reservations during the summer.

Tofino

Tofino, or "Tough City," is small and easy to get around, and it boasts the best mean temperature in Canada. Highway 4 becomes Campbell Street in Tofino, which is basically 5 blocks long and 3 blocks wide, although some development is happening as more people try to escape "civilization." The Spanish named the town for Don Vincent Tofino, a famous Spanish hydrographer with a reputation for native fights and wild living. But don't let the nickname scare you. Much of that has been cleaned up with aggressive social and self-help programs.

Several restaurants serve good food, including the **West Coast Crab Bar** (601 Campbell, 250–725–3733), where you order your half or whole crab hot or cold. Try the crab chowder, Caesar salads, and garlic toast, and enjoy the decent house wines and cheerful, upbeat atmosphere. A happening place where many locals stop. Book reservations.

Locals also frequent the **Schooner Restaurant and Motel** (331 Campbell, 250–725–3444) for its great basic food with a flair at reasonable prices in an amusing shipwreck atmosphere. At breakfast, Eggs a Paire is $4.95 with perfect potatoes and toast; the Kitchen Sink includes almost all of it, from spicy sausage to mushrooms, in an omelet at $7.50; and Kathleen's favorite, the Eye Opener, contains fresh oysters, mushrooms, and green onions.

Crab Chowder

Jacques Forgues of the West Coast Crab Bar, Tofino

28 oz. clam nectar
28 oz. milk
5 large potatoes
½ cup flour
¼ tsp. garlic powder
¼ tsp. paprika
1 tsp. lemon pepper
1½ tbsp. chicken soup base
16 oz. fresh crabmeat

Cut potatoes into medium cubes and steam twelve minutes. Mix clam nectar, milk, spices, chicken broth, and flour; stir well. Add potatoes and crabmeat. Simmer for three hours. If too thick, add more milk. Serves six.

Lunch and dinner are memorable, and the house ghost is included. Sole Clayoquot in a delicate lemon caper sauce is excellent at $16.95, or you might try the seafood hot pot of curried yummies at $17.95. Local oysters are a must. The Schooner has historical maps and paintings and a public phone outside, and it's a member of Cuisine Canada and the Canadian Culinary Alliance.

Across the street, the **Loft** (346 Campbell, 250–725–4241) serves a local seafood clubhouse sandwich with smoked salmon and shrimp for $8.50, corned

Roy Vickers's Eagle Aerie Gallery, Tofino

beef hash and poached eggs at $6.95, or the required half crab at lunch for $9.95 and $13.95 at dinner.

Ready for dessert? **Chocolate Tofino** offers chocolatier Gordon Austin's hand-crafted chocolates, homemade ice cream, sorbets, sundaes, and gelato. There are also loads of mostly organic cafes around town.

If you stay out too late and don't want to walk home, call Tofino Taxi, (250) 725–3333.

Tofino has several galleries with local arts and crafts, and you can find them easily on your own. If you only have time for one, stop in at Roy Vickers's **Eagle Aerie Gallery** at 350 Campbell (250–725–3235). As the only native artist with his own gallery, Vickers and his work inspire and dominate. He also shows work of other First Peoples artists, such as that of his brother Art Vickers as well as Ed Hill. Each picture has a legend with it, so you can learn just by reading. All woodwork within the gallery was carved by native artists, including the rails, canoes, and eagles.

Roy Vickers is a recovering drug and alcohol addict and is proud of it. A percentage of sales of certain works is given to First Peoples recovery programs. The entire gallery feels like a life-revering chapel. Vickers also has another gallery in Sidney.

A block north and down the hill are some stops well worth the short walk along Main Street, which is just above the Wharf and Meares Landing.

Wildside Booksellers carries the best selection of regional travel and adventure books we have seen, and it also sells excellent coffee and wind toys, runs the bed-and-breakfast next door, and books kayaking lessons and trips.

The Rainforest Interpretive Centre is a place adults and kids absolutely must experience. Friendly staff and educational exhibits mix in one room with clusters of local children drawing, weaving, listening, learning about nature, and telling stories. You can enjoy a panoramic view of Tofino and Clayoquot Sound from the back deck. Pacific Rim Whale Festival (250–726–4447) goes on from mid-March to early April. There's a Sea Fest Labor Day Weekend, and the Pacific Rim Summer Festival for two weeks in mid-July.

Fine points: You'll find pay phones at First and Main Streets.

At **Meares Wharf** you can get boats to see Clayoquot Sound—both its beauty and its devastation due to clear-cutting. Loads of fishing charters are available, and almost anyone in town can set you up and make a booking for you. Chinook Charters, at 450 Campbell Street (250–725–3431 or 800–665–3646), will take

Kayak lesson before takeoff into Clayoquot Sound, Tofino

you fishing, whale watching, or on a tour of Clayoquot Sound. Reservations recommended. Other tours take you birding, bear watching, and on Tla-ook Cultural adventures conoe tours.

Annual events include the Western Ho Down, Tofino Art Festival, and the Tofino Film Festival—all in September.

It is mandatory to make reservations ahead to stay in Tofino.

Where to Stay on the Beach

Wickaninnish Inn, see text page 233.

Best Western Tin Wis Resort, 1119 Pacific Rim Highway (250–725–4445; www.tinwis.com); January–March $125–$265, April–June $165–$305, July–September $220–375, October–December $145–$285; 85 units; on the beach; licensed restaurant, lounge; pets okay with fee; 2 miles south of Tofino.

Pacific Sands Beach Resort, 1421 Pacific Rim Highway (250–725–3322; www .pacificsands.com); $160–$535; 65 units; condos and cabins on 1-mile-long beach; decks or patios; no pets; 4 miles south of Tofino.

Orca Lodge, Pacific Rim Highway (250–725–2323; www.clayoquot-orca.com); June–October $169–$269, off-season $69 and up; 40 units; dining, licensed lounge; continental breakfast; pets okay; some rooms have wheelchair access; 2–3 miles south of Tofino.

Crystal Cove Beach Resort, MacKenzie Beach (250–725–4213; www.crystalcove beachresort.com); July–September $200–$340, rest of year $105–$235; 30 units; oceanfront log cottages with kitchens, fireplaces, hot tubs; eighty RV sites; 2 miles south of Tofino.

Ocean Village Beach Resort, 555 Helleson Drive (250–725–3755); high season $135–$175, March–June 20 $105–$135, October 13–February $90–$120, cottages on beach; kitchens; indoor pool, whirlpool; no pets; 2 miles south of Tofino.

Long Beach Lodge Resort, 1441 Pacific Highway (877–844–7873; www.long beachlodgeresort.com); $289–$569, less off-season; 60 units; ocean views; dining; balconies; pets okay; 4 miles south of Tofino.

Where to Stay in Downtown Tofino

Days Inn, 634 Campbell Street (250–725–3277); summer $139–$219, off-season $108 and up; variety of 63 units; harbor views; some decks and fireplaces; marine pub, restaurant; moorage, fishing charters; no pets.

Cable Cove Inn, 201 Main Street (250–725–4236; www.cablecoveinn.com); $125–$195, off-season less; adults; waterfront; decks, fireplaces, hot tubs, Jacuzzis, four posters; continental breakfast; no smoking, no pets; view of Clayoquot Sound.

Schooner Motel, 311 Campbell Street (250–725–3478; www.schoonermotel .com); $49–$135; 16 units; town center, overlooks harbor; kitchens; no pets.

Maquinna Lodge, 120 First Street (250–725–3261); summer $120–$170, off-season $50–$100; 32 units; pub; beer and wine store; no pets.

Ucluelet

From Long Beach, instead of turning left to go back toward Port Alberni and Nanaimo, continue straight toward **Ucluelet,** self-proclaimed "Whale Watching Capital" of the world. Ucluelet, an old fishing port first settled in prehistoric times, is somewhat protected from Pacific storms and close to the channels where migrating salmon feed. The name comes from *yu-clutl-ahts,* which means "the people with a good landing place for canoes."

In 1959 Ucluelet became connected by road with Port Alberni, ending a century of reliance on boat transportation. Unofficial motto: "On the Edge."

An obvious fun place to drink and dine in Ucluelet is the Canadian Princess Hotel, a docked ship you can't miss on the left (water side) coming in to town on Peninsula Road, the main street in town. The food is generous and good. There are several motels.

Try Crow's Nest Books, which also has public telephones, and the chamber of commerce on Main Street for more information. Main runs down to Government Wharf. Blueberries Bakery Cafe & Cappuccino Bar on Peninsula Drive is a must-stop for locals. We like it, too. On the way down to the water you'll find the Tourist Information Centre and Roman's Galley Restaurant, an obviously locally popular restaurant with bar and Italian food.

A final culinary note: Smiley's Family Restaurant is the local people's hangout for good breakfasts, burgers, fish and chips, and bottomless coffee cups.

The gas station at the north side of Ucluelet is the last chance for fuel, water, restrooms, and telephones before the climb over the summit back to Port Alberni. Visit Bamfield, if you wish, or head back to Nanaimo and Victoria.

Nearby you can enjoy more of the Pacific Rim National Park Reserve and its Gold Mine Trail, Florencia Bay, Wickaninnish Bay & Interpretive Center, Bog Trail on Wickaninnish Beach Road, Green Point Campground, Long Beach, Schooner Trail, and Radar Hill.

Where to Stay in Ucluelet

Canadian Princess Resort, Peninsula Road (250–726–7771); $90–$200; a permanently moored 235-foot-long historic coast steamship with 76 staterooms; fishing excursions, nature cruises; fully licensed restaurant; no pets; not wheelchair accessible.

Terrace Beach Resort, 1002 Peninsula Road (250–726–2901; www.terracebeach resort.ca); $99–$369; cabins and suites; unique ocean and natural views; children under 12 free; Jacuzzis; pets okay with fee.

A Snug Harbour Inn, 460 Marine Drive (250–726–2686 or 888–936–5222; Fax: 250–726–2686; www.awesomeview.com); 4 individualized rooms overlooking water, $175–$325; hot tub; private beach; breakfast; large community room; unique romantic setting.

West Coast Motel, 247 Hemlock Street (250–726–7732; www.westcoastmotel .com); March 14–September 21 $79–$289; most of 20 rooms overlook harbor; indoor pool, sauna, exercise room, squash; dining in season; no pets.

Island West Fishing Resort, 160 Hemlock Street (250–726–4624); $59–$99 depending on season; overlooking harbor; private marina; pub-restaurant; guided fishing and whale watching; pets okay; 39 RV sites adjacent.

Thornton Motel, 1861 Peninsula Road (250–726–7725; www.thorntonmotel .com); summer $119–$215, off-season $79–$185; 19 units, some with kitchens and one two-bedroom suite; near marina; no pets.

Pacific Rim Motel, 1755 Peninsula Road (250–726–7728 or 800–810–0031; www.pacificrimmotel.com); $85–$150, off-season less; 55 units overlooking harbor.

Bamfield

Bamfield is a 300-person fishing village and sea rescue station that is the northern terminus of the West Coast Trail from Port Renfrew on the southeast side of Barkley Sound, and that was the departure point for the Pacific cable to Australia from 1902 to 1959. Bamfield was named for retired ships carpenter William Eddy Banfield, the first settler in 1849, but when the post office was established the name was misspelled as "Bamfield," and it stuck.

An oddity: Bamfield is reputed to have the highest per capita education of any town in Canada. The reason is that most of the populace are marine biologists and highly educated scientists in the field.

Bamfield can be reached by turning left onto Third Avenue off Highway 4 in

Port Alberni and continuing for 62 miles. Or you can take the trip by ferry (Barkley Sound Service, 5425 Argyle at Port Alberni marina). It has become a popular destination for hikers, whale watchers, anglers, kayakers, scuba divers, canoeists, and tourists. From the boardwalk you can watch boats float by. Visit the Bamfield Marine Station (250–728–3301; tours 1:00–3:00 P.M. Saturday–Sunday May–August), located near the mouth of the Bamfield Inlet, and see its lobby area (open to the public year-round) to view historical and scientific displays.

Where to Stay in Bamfield

Bamfield Trails Motel, Frigape Road (250–728–3231); $129–$169; 31 units, including 19 kitchenettes that sleep as many as 6; overlooks inlet; pub, boat and plane tours; pets okay.

Bamfield Inn, Customs House Lane (250–728–3354); $80–$120; historic lodge overlooking harbor; dining, lounge; hot tub; fishing charters; no pets.

Seabeam Fishing Resort & Campground (250–728–3286); overlooking Grappler Inlet; boat rentals and charters; also 8-unit lodge with shared baths, use own bedding ($15–$40).

6

The Other Islands

A long the eastern shore of Vancouver Island in the Strait of Georgia lie the Gulf Islands: Salt Spring, Pender, Saturna, Mayne, Galiano, Thetis, Valdes, Gabriola, Lasqueti, Denman, and Hornby. Farther north, in the narrow passage between the Lower Mainland and Vancouver Island, are the Discovery Islands, which include Quadra, Cortes, and Sonora. Cormorant and Malcolm Islands dot the northern exit from the Johnstone Strait in the open sea. All offer excellent fishing, whale watching, native arts, and dining. Enjoy with respect.

GULF ISLANDS

Salt Spring Island

Salt Spring lies along the east coast of Vancouver Island from just north of Swartz Bay to a point opposite Chemainus and has sixteen public parks, eleven clear lakes, three villages, and two golf courses, as well as small organic farms, cheese makers, and wineries.

Take your choice of three B.C. Ferry routes: from Swartz Bay landing at Fulford Harbour, from Crofton to Vesuvius Bay, or from Vancouver (Tsawwassen) to Long Harbour. All take about thirty-five minutes. Seaplanes also bring passengers from both Vancouver and Victoria.

Salt Spring was the first Gulf Island settled, in 1858, and by black Americans. From 1859 the island was called Admiral Island, with locals holding out for Salt Spring after the briny pools, and it was officially renamed Salt Spring by the Geographic Board of Canada in 1905. Salt

Spring is now a "commuter island" to Victoria, full of 1960s American draft evaders and artisan food producers.

Your best bet is to take an automobile on the ferry, giving you the freedom to explore Salt Spring, from its rambling roads to several very swimmable lakes, and to get a spectacular view of the channel from Mount Maxwell's peak. If you land at Fulford, drive over the hill from Fulford to the principal community of Ganges, home of Art-Spring, a 265-seat theater and gallery. Mahon Hall downtown hosts ArtCraft, an all-summer exhibition featuring 200 Gulf Island artists and artisans. Art-Craft hours are 10:00 A.M.–5:00 P.M. daily from mid-May to mid-September.

Salt Spring's substantial artists' colony has more than thirty-five galleries and studios, plus bookstores and shops. Enjoy a variety of restaurants and pubs close to Fulford Harbour and Ganges, including Vesuvius Oceanfront Bar & Grill, Anise Family Restaurant & Inn, and the Artist's Bistro, Shipstones English Pub, La Cucina Italian Grill, the Oystercatcher, and many cafes in Ganges.

Fulford village is charming and low-key, with an outdoor flea market, pub, collectibles shops, and excellent coffee. There's also the Vesuvius Inn, a historic church, and a friendly atmosphere. For camping try St. Mary Lake inland, or shore facilities at Ruckle Provincial Park and Mouat Provincial Park.

The Salt Spring Festival of the Arts peps up Ganges for four weeks starting the first full weekend in July. Catch the irreverent performances of the Hysterical Society (250–537–4167).

Tarte aux Pommes au Fromage Blanc

Susan and Julia Grace of Moonstruck Organic Cheeses, Salt Spring Island

large pastry round (crust)
4 large apples, sliced
butter
cinnamon, nutmeg, and brown
**   sugar for tossing and**
**   sprinkling**
Moonstruck Fromage Blanc
**   (Brie or Camembert)**

Preheat oven to 400°F. Make a larger than usual round of pastry and lay in pie plate so that the edges fold over the sides. Fill with sliced apples and dot with butter. If you wish, you may toss the apples in cinnamon, nutmeg, and a little brown sugar. Fold over the pastry, leaving about a 6-inch round in the center. Spread the exposed apples liberally with Moonstruck Fromage Blanc and then coat the cheese with brown sugar. Bake for ten minutes at 400°, then reduce the temperature to 350°. The pie is done when the pastry is lightly browned and you can hear the apples bubbling (about another thirty minutes). This tart never lasts a meal, so if you want leftovers, make two.

Other events include Sea Capers in mid-June, ArtSpring Home Tour in mid-July, Fulford Day in mid-August, and the Fall Fair the third weekend in September.

Food lovers absolutely must make a trip to **Moonstruck Organic Cheese— Makers of Fine Organic Cheeses.** To get there from Fulford Harbour, where the ferry brings you, follow Fulford-Ganges Road north to Cusheon Lake Road and turn right. When Cusheon Lake Road ends at Beddis Road, turn right onto Beddis. Moonstruck is less than a mile on the left.

Julia and Susan Grace offer farm and cheese-making tours on Thursday from 1:30 to 3:00 P.M. and are open for farm sales June 1–September 30 or by appointment in winter.

Julia converted from raising veggies for sale and cooking for fans to making cheese after Susan yearned to have a cow and finally bought one. Now Susan manages the "herd" of sixteen super-clean jerseys, and Julia makes highly unusual and divine, as well as certified organic, cheese. Kathleen is totally addicted to Blossom's Blue and Blue Moon. Other cheeses include Savoury Moon, Beddis Blue, White Moon, White Grace, Baby Blue, and Ash-Ripened Camembert.

Moonstruck Organic Cheese—Makers of Fine Organic Cheeses, 1306 Beddis Road, Salt Spring Island; (250) 537–4987; www.moonstruck cheese.com. Call to visit.

Salt Spring Island has two wineries, and we encourage you to visit them soon.

Salt Spring Vineyards beat its neighbor, Garry Oaks Winery, by one-half hour in September 2002 to get the first winery license on Salt Spring Island. Located on top of Lee Hill, where cyclists stop to exclaim they made it, Salt Spring Vineyards also offers bed-and-breakfast accommodations consisting of two pleasant rooms with lots of wood, Jacuzzis, and a shared hot tub and shower in the vineyard.

Stressing romance at this shingled, barnlike winery, Salt Spring offers Gewurztraminer, Blanc de Noir, Pinot Gris, Chardonnay, Leon Millot/Foch, Pinot Blanc, Merlot, Ortega, and Pinot Noir.

Salt Spring Vineyards, 151 Lee Road at the 1700 block of Fulford-Ganges Road, Salt Spring Island; (250) 653–9463; www.salt springvineyards.com. Hours: noon–5:00 P.M. Saturday September–May, noon–5:00 P.M. daily late May–mid-September, other times if you call ahead. Wheelchair accessible. Credit cards: Visa, MasterCard.

Garry Oaks Winery is the pride and joy of Marcel Mercier and Elaine Kozak, who left careers in land and resource management systems development and public policy and trade work, respectively. When visitors ask the couple if they have ever done this before, their pat answer is "Which part, exactly?"

Marcel first made fruit wines with his grandmother in Alberta, and he and Elaine are joined by renowned winemaker Ross Mirko and Sid Kozak, who enjoyed a long career in the film industry and holds down the wine-store fort. Ross shares undergraduate degrees in psychology with Elaine, which makes their interests and wines blend even better. Mirko also has his own label, Calliope Vintners. Watch for the "two-dog bird squad," Talus (the Terrible), a Norwegian Elkhound; and her cousin Casper (the Gentle Giant).

The name Garry Oaks derives from the Garry oak (Oregon white oak or *Quercus Garryana*), named for Nicholas Garry, deputy governor of the Hudson's Bay Company in the early nineteenth century. Garry oaks are used to craft wine barrels, producing flavor deemed to be the most like French oak of any North American wood. Try their wines, all the results of sustainable farming, including Pinot Gris, Blanc de Noir, Zeta, Fetish, Gewurztraminer, Pinot Noir, and Labyrinth, as well as their sense of humor!

Garry Oaks Winery, 1880 Fulford-Ganges Road, Salt Spring Island; (250) 653–4687; http://garryoakswine.com. Hours: noon–5:00 P.M. Wednesday–Sunday May–October.

The annual Salt Springs Apple Festival is held on the first Sunday each October to celebrate more than a century of apple growing on the island. A tour beginning at an extensive exhibit at Fulford Hall covers fifteen farms and more than 200 apple varieties and has several luncheons, art, talks, tastings, and demonstrations. For information call (250) 653–2007.

Drop by the Gulf Islands Brewery, 270 Furness Road (250–653–2383), and sample Salt Spring Golden Ale, Mayne Sail Ail, Pender Island Porter, and Sturna Island Extra Stout while watching an operating brewery at work.

Where to Stay

For more information on vacancies and accommodations on the island, call Salt Spring Island Visitor Information Centre, (250) 537–5252.

Hastings House, 160 Upper Ganges Road, Ganges (250–537–2362 or 800–661–9255; www.hastingshouse.com); $525–$910; 18 rooms; historic; listed in *1000 Places to See Before You Die;* spa; dining; wheelchair accessible.

Salty Springs Spa Resort, 1460 North Beach Road (250–537–4111; www.salt springsspa.com); $109–$299; kitchens, decks; no phones; no pets.

Cusheon Lake Resort, 171 Natalie Lane (250–537–9629; www.cusheonlake .com); May 16–October 14 $135–$202, rest of year $105–$165; log and A-frame chalets; beach, fishing, boats; no pets.

Harbour House Hotel, 121 Ganges Road (250–537–5571 or 888–799–5571); $74–$89; 35 units; overlooks harbor; restaurant, pub; beer and wine store; no pets.

Pender Islands

Just east of Salt Spring Island in the Strait of Georgia are the two Pender Islands (North and South), linked by a short bridge. You will find balmy summer weather, coves, and well-kept beaches for boating and.swimming; arts and crafts studios; a nine-hole golf course; and great scenic hikes. The big events of the year are the Pender Island Summer Solstice Festival in June and an all-summer farmers' market.

Mortimer Spit offers kayaking, swimming, and small-boat launching. Beaumont Park includes a white shell beach and loads of hiking and walking, as do Brooks Point, Medicine Beach, and even the Pender Island Golf & Country Club.

Take B.C. Ferries from Swartz Bay on Vancouver Island and Tsawwassen on the mainland. Schedule is varied. Hanna's Air flies in to the Penders from Salt Spring Island.

Where to Stay

Arcadia-by-the-Sea, 1329 MacKinnon Road, North Pender Island (250–629–3221); $108–$186; three cottages; decks, pool, tennis, croquet, some fireplaces; no pets; May–September.

Inn on Pender Island, 4709 Canal Road, North Pender Island (250–629–3353 or 800–550–0172; www.innonpender.com); $79–$149; cabins; lodge; hot tub; licensed restaurant; small pets okay.

Winter Vegetable Lasagna

Chef Hubertus Surm of Saturna Island Lodge and Bistro, Saturna Island

FOR THE LASAGNA

9 egg lasagna noodles
2 lb. butternut squash
2 medium-size eggplants
2 medium-size zucchinis

FOR THE SAUCE

2 cups crushed tomatoes
1 green bell pepper, diced small
$\frac{1}{2}$ red bell pepper, diced small
2 cups onion, diced small
2 tbsp. garlic, crushed
1 tbsp. cumin
1$\frac{1}{2}$ tsp. black pepper
2 tbsp. paprika

dash cinnamon
dash Tabasco
1 tbsp. fresh lemon juice
olive oil to sauté
salt to taste
2 cups ricotta cheese
1 cup Parmesan cheese, freshly grated
1 cup Monterey Jack cheese, grated

Preparing the lasagna

Cook lasagna noodles for eight to ten minutes and let cool. Peel and cut butternut squash into $\frac{1}{4}$-inch-thick slices and steam for five minutes.

Slice one eggplant lengthwise into $\frac{1}{2}$-inch slices and the other into $\frac{1}{2}$-inch cubes. Steam for five to seven minutes. Grill and season with salt, fresh pepper, and a little fresh lemon juice.

Cut zucchini into $\frac{1}{4}$-inch slices and grill and season as above.

Preparing the sauce

Sauté onion, garlic, spices, Tabasco in olive oil for five to seven minutes. Add red and green peppers, tomatoes, cubed eggplant, and lemon juice. Cook until mushy and remove from heat. Cool.

Assembling the lasagna

Oil bottom of an 8-by-12-inch pan. Place a layer of noodles on the bottom, and then continue to layer with eggplant slices, half the sauce, a third of the Parmesan and ricotta, and more noodles; the butternut squash (sprinkled with nutmeg), another third of the Parmesan and ricotta, the remaining noodles, zucchini, the second half of the sauce, and then the remaining third of the Parmesan and ricotta. Top with Monterey Jack. Bake at 350°F for twenty minutes. Serves eight.

Saturna Island

Saturna Island (31 square kilometers) lies just east of the Penders and south of Mayne and is the most southerly and least populated of the Gulf Islands. The Community Center at Lyall Harbour, where the ferry docks, is where things happen. Still fairly primitive, Saturna is ideal for hiking, boating, and not disturbing wildlife, which includes peregrine falcons, bald eagles, and wild goats.

Enjoy nature's marvels at Veruna Bay, Winter Cove Marine Park, Thomson Park, East Point Regional Park, Lyall Harbour Beach, and Narvaez Bay. Most of Saturna Island's land is now part of the Gulf Islands National Park Reserve.

Reach Saturna by B.C. Ferries from Swartz Bay on Vancouver Island and Tsawwassen on the mainland, as well as by flight on Harbour Air (604–278–3478) or Sea Air (604–273–8900). Boaters dock at Winter Cove Marine Park.

An added benefit to traveling to Saturna Island is **Saturna Island Vineyards** and its bistro. Saturna Island has lassoed one of British Columbia's finest winemakers, Eric Von Krosigk, a graduate of the Beverage Engineering program at the University of Geisenheim in Germany. Eric is making fine Chardonnay, Pinot Gris, Riesling Simalkameen, Golden Mile Franc, Riesling Brut, Gamay, Pinot Noir, and Merlot.

To get to the winery from the ferry, follow East Point Road to the General Store, turn right onto Harris Road (next to the recycling center), and follow Harris all the way up and over the mountain. When you reach the bottom (of the mountain and the road), turn left, and you are at the winery. The signs help.

And, most conveniently, you may want to book reservations at the winery-related Saturna Island Lodge and Bistro, whose fine chef, Hubertus Surm, creates meals that will tantalize your senses. To get directly to the lodge from the ferry, take the first right onto Boot Cove Road. At the stop sign, turn right onto Payne Road, go to the next stop sign, and the lodge is the first driveway on the right.

Saturna Island Vineyards, 130 Payne Road, Saturna Island; (250) 539–5139 or (877) 918–3388; www.saturnavineyards.com. Winery hours: 11:30 A.M.–4:30 P.M. Wednesday–Sunday May–September, 11:30 A.M.–2:30 P.M. March 1–May 1. Wheelchair accessible. Credit cards: Visa, MasterCard.

The most exciting public event on Saturna is the annual Canada Day Lamb Barbecue, held July 1 at Winter Cove Marine Park. The Saturday Afternoon Market in July and August is a local gathering event, and the Studio Tour held during the August long weekend is a must for art fans.

Where to Stay

East Point Resort, East Point Road (250–539–2975 or 877–762–2073; www .eastpointresort.com); summer weekly $850–$1,250, spring and fall $140– $150, winter $90–$130; beach, launch, boat rentals.

Breezy Bay B&B, 131 Payne Road (250–539–2937; www.saturnacan.net); $60–$95; 1890s heritage house; beach, views, kayaking; no pets.

Mayne Island

Although smallest of the Gulf Islands, Mayne Island has a long history as an active community, dating from the 1860s when it was a stopping point for miners crossing the Georgia Strait to and from the Fraser goldfields on the mainland. Lying just north of Pender and east of Salt Spring, Mayne is the first island on your left when taking the ferry from Tsawwassen to Swartz Bay. The First People lived here 5,000 years ago.

Mayne is well covered by forest and a network of roads to several sheltered bays, including Village Bay, Miners Bay, and Horton Bay, all with docking facilities. Reach Mayne by B.C. Ferries from Swartz Bay on Vancouver Island and Tsawwassen on the mainland. Mayne has art galleries and studios, buildings dating from the nineteenth century, a museum (once a jail), lovely resorts and beaches, and the 1885 Georgina Point Lighthouse.

Oceanwood Country Inn enjoys international fame for its lodging with water views from all rooms and for its cuisine. Jonathan Chilvers's English country home features crackling fireplaces, full bookshelves, and a wonderful kitchen overlooking Navy Channel. Ride bikes, listen to Mozart, walk, kayak, play tennis or chess, or drink champagne in the bathtub in front of the fire. Breakfast and tea included. Rates range from $139 to $349 for two people, depending on room and season, with breakfast and afternoon tea included. Oceanwood's restaurant overlooks the water, with the five-course prix fixe dinner available for $48.

Oceanwood Country Inn, 630 Dinner Bay Road, Mayne Island; (250) 539–5074; www.oceanwood.com. Hours: dinner from 6:00 P.M. Fully licensed. Dining room wheelchair accessible with help; restroom is not. Credit cards: Visa, MasterCard.

Quick Coffee Cake

Oceanwood Country Inn, Mayne Island

FOR THE CAKE BATTER

$^{1}/_{2}$ cup unsalted butter, cut into bits and softened

1 cup sugar

2 eggs

2 cups all-purpose flour

1 tsp. baking soda

1 tsp. baking powder

$^{1}/_{2}$ tsp. salt

1 cup buttermilk

1 tsp. vanilla

FOR THE TOPPING

$^{1}/_{3}$ cup firmly packed brown sugar

$^{1}/_{4}$ cup granulated sugar

1 tsp. cinnamon

$^{1}/_{2}$ cup chopped walnuts

Preheat oven to 350°F and lightly butter a 9-by-13-inch baking dish.

In a large bowl, beat all the cake batter ingredients together until smooth and fluffy with an electric mixer. In another bowl, stir together all the topping ingredients.

Pour half the batter into the baking dish and sprinkle half the topping mix evenly over it. Repeat with the rest of the batter and topping mix.

Bake in the middle of the oven until a tester comes out clean, about thirty minutes. Let cool in the pan.

Variations: You can add $^{1}/_{4}$ cup of sun-dried cranberries, dried blueberries, dried apricots, raisins, or currants to the mix.

Where to Stay

Blue Vista Resort, 563 Arbutus Drive (250–539–2463); $50–$95, off-season less; 8 cottages; decks; beach; pets okay with fee.

Mayne Inn Hotel, 494 Arbutus Drive (250–539–3122; www.mayneinn.com); $89–$119; 8 rooms; water views; licensed dining room, lounge; no pets.

Fernhill Lodge, 610 Fernhill Road (250–539–2544); $74–$139; sauna; licensed, dinner by reservation; no pets.

Galiano Island

Long, narrow Galiano Island stretches from its southern tip just across a narrow passage from Mayne Island northerly to a point east of Ladysmith on the forty-ninth parallel.

Take B.C. Ferries from Swartz Bay on Vancouver Island or from Tsawwassen to Sturdies Bay, or fly in via Hanna's Air or Harbour Air. Boaters dock at Montague Harbour.

Geared to natural recreation, Galiano (named for Spanish explorer Dionisio Galiano, who named the island for himself in 1792) features hiking, camping, and bird-watching in three scenic provincial parks; fishing; boating; moped touring; kayaking; and white shell beaches. Accommodations, eateries, and stores are concentrated in four settlements: Sturdies Bay ("downtown"), Georgeson Bay, Montague Harbour, and Spotlight Cove. Resourceful Hummingbird Pub runs its own bus from the Montague Park Marina to the pub mid-May–October. For a dining treat try La Berengerie (250–539–5392) at Montague Harbour, where ex-Parisian Huguette Benger prepares fabulous meals from vegetarian to venison, praised by *Northwest Best Places*.

Annual events include the North Galiano Jamboree on Canada Day, July 1; Lion's Club Fiesta the first Saturday in August; and Galiano Island Wine Festival in the middle of August.

Galiano Island Books (250–539–3340) has an exceptional selection of local authors' work, regional interest and history, and books for all ages and interests, all right near the ferry dock.

Call Galiano's visitor information line: (250) 539–2233.

Where to Stay

Galiano Inn and Spa, 134 Madrona Drive (250–539–3388 or 877–530–3939; www.galianoinn.com); $249–$299; 10 oceanfront suites; built in 2000 with luxuries, gardens, fireplaces; breakfast included.

La Berengerie, Montague Harbour Road (250–539–5392); $50–$75; 3 rooms; hot tub; licensed restaurant and vegetarian cafe; complimentary ferry pickup; no pets.

Woodstone Country Inn, Georgeson Bay Road (250–539–5544); $90–$145; licensed dining; no smoking, no pets.

Driftwood Village Resort, 205 Bluff Road East (250–539–5457); $65–$159; cottages; decks; fireplaces; hot tub; pets okay with fee.

Cliff Pagoda B&B, 2851 Montague Harbour Road (250–539–2260); $50–$70; Japanese-style country inn; harbor views; complimentary ferry pickup; canoes and mountain bikes; no pets.

Little tourism activity exists on Thetis and Valdes Islands, so we move on to Gabriola Island via ferry from downtown Nanaimo.

Gabriola Island

Gabriola (gay-bree-OH-la) Island is an underdiscovered paradise only twenty minutes from Nanaimo by B.C. Ferries that run seventeen times daily. Don't miss the petroglyphs near Degnen Bay, historical farm and community buildings, the huge caves in the sandstone cliffs called the Malaspina Galleries, and First Nations burial grounds.

Kayak, play tennis, ride horses, sail, hike, and beachcomb, all within walking distance of everything. Enjoy the environment and wildlife, including otters, seals, eagles, and deer (whose ancestors swam from Vancouver Island) at three waterfront provincial parks: Twin Beaches, Brumburg, and Sandwell. Moor your boat at Silva and Degnen Bays. Call (250) 247–8807 or log on to www.silverbluecharters.com for Silver Blue Charters for fishing and sightseeing.

Artisans' and artists' galleries and studios are open to the public. Check out Malaspina Galleries, which is actually a collection of caves in sandstone carved by ocean

Arbutus tree on Gabriola Island

waves over the years. Golfers get their fix at the Gabriola Island Golf and Country Club.

This is pub country, where you can meet locals at Silva Bay Pub, White Hart Pub, Windecker's Restaurant, Latitudes at the Sterling Resort, and the Sunset Lounge at the Surf Lodge, with a splendid view of the strait.

For more information call the Gabriola Chamber of Commerce (250–247–8455 telephone and fax) or the Visitor Information Centre (250–247–9332; www.gabriolaisland.org) at the Folklore Village Centre.

Where to Stay

Surf Lodge, 885 Berry Point Road (250–247–9231); $55–$70; restaurant, lounge, pub; seven minutes from ferry.

Silva Bay Inn, 3415 South Road (250–247–9351); $79, off-season $69.

The Haven Resort Seminar and Conference Centre, 240 Davis Road (250–247–9211 or 877–247–9238); $70–$228; 45 suites, rooms, and cabins; hot tubs, pool, waterfront views; auditorium; ideal for conferences; meals served year-round; promote personal and professional development.

Arbutus Bluff B&B, 1425 Coats Drive East (250–247–9170; www.arbutusbluff .ca); $80–$135; breakfasts; fireplaces.

Newcastle Island

For a quick nature outing from Nanaimo, take the ferry from Matteo Park on Nanaimo's waterfront (250–391–2300) to Newcastle Island Provincial Marine Park for camping, historic sites, and trails. No vehicles. Pets must be on leash. Check out the Pavilion for cultural and natural history. Lots of swimming, paddling, waterskiing, and fishing. At low tide you can actually walk (wear boots or old shoes) to the Dinghy Dock Pub near the Protection islands.

Lasqueti Island

For a real getaway you can take a people-only water taxi from French Creek (north of Parksville on Highway 19) for a forty-five-minute trip to Lasqueti Island. Hike from the village of Lasqueti to Spring Bay to observe eagle nests, turkey vultures, river otters, sea lions, and whales and explore caves. False Bay is considered "downtown." Call (250) 248–8912 at the French Creek Marina & Store for more information. Call the only hotel for transportation information:

Lasqueti Island Hotel & Resort, Weldon Road, (250–333–8846); $90; licensed restaurant; no pets; no TV, no phones.

Denman Island

Opposite Fanny Bay lie Denman Island, a mile away, and Hornby Island, two of the most popular beach vacation sites in British Columbia.

Catch the B.C. Ferry at Buckley Bay, 75 kilometers (46 miles) north of Nanaimo on the Island Highway, for a 1¹/₂-kilometer (1-mile) ride to Denman Village on the island. Be sure to visit artisans' and artists' studios and the co-op craft outlet. Camp at eighty-acre Fillongley Provincial Park and hike or bike over trails around the island, the flattest of the Gulf Islands. Rent a canoe or kayak and paddle over to nearby Sandy Island Provincial Marine Park or visit Boyle Point Provincial Park. Check out the Denman Seniors & Museum Society Activity Centre (1111 Northwest Road at Seniors Community Hall, 250–335–0880) for local lace and artwork, native artifacts, settlement collections, and local cultural and natural history.

For Denman and Hornby information, call (250) 335–1636 or log on to www.denmanis.bc.ca.

Where to Stay

Fillongley Provincial Park (250–954–4600); April–October; on east side of island; vehicle rate $17.00 per night; winter $9.00, seniors $8.50; 10 campsites; 3 kilometers from ferry.

Hawthorne B&B, 3375 Kirk Road (250–335–0905; www.hawthornehouse.ca); $105; 4 units in renovated 1904 house; water view; wheelchair accessible; no smoking.

Hornby Island

Cross Denman Island on Denman Road (fifteen minutes) and catch the Hornby ferry at Gravely Bay, for another 1¹/₂-kilometer trip to Hornby, the northernmost sighting location of both the deep-sea six-gill shark and opossums.

Hornby Island may be the best spot in British Columbia to camp, hike, bike, and loll on the beach. Tribune Bay has some of the warmest ocean water in British Columbia. We also recommend visiting the Hornby Island Co-op for loads of what you may or may not need.

For a change of pace, you can bird-watch at Helliwell Bay Provincial Park, which also boasts a 5-kilometer hike through an old-growth forest of huge weather-beaten firs, pines, and oaks. Please stay on the paths and keep dogs under control to preserve the habitat and cormorants. In spring you can see sea lions over at nearby Flora Islets.

Where to Stay

Sea Breeze Lodge, Fowler Road (250–335–2321 or 888–516–2321); June 15–
September 15 $1,680 weekly for couple, children ages two to six $304, ages
seven to twelve $387, ages thirteen to seventeen $525; off-season $90–$120
for cabins; 12 oceanside cottages; hot tub; fishing, boat rentals; American
plan meals during summer; petroglyphs; no pets.
Ford's Cove Marina, Ford's Cove (250–235–2169); $525–$550 per week; cottages on water; fishing supplies and boat fuel; no pets.
Tribune Bay Campsite, Saltspray Road (250–335–2359; www.tribunebay.com);
120 sites; large sandy beach; toilets, showers; April–October; $28 minimum,
with power $30, without vehicle $22.

DISCOVERY ISLANDS

Quadra Island

Just 3 kilometers (2 miles) east of Campbell River lies Quadra Island, which is
ideal for sportfishing and finding First People pottery and other art. It also has
two internationally praised lodges.

Take a ten-minute B.C. Ferry ride from downtown Campbell River. Attractions include Kwagiulth (Kwakwaka'wakw) Museum and Cultural Centre
(250–285–3733) on Wei Wai Road at Cape Mudge Village, with its displays of
costumes and masks from potlatches and other ceremonies. Nearby are the petroglyphs at We-Wai-Kai Beach and the native-built Tsa-Kwa-Luten Lodge,
which includes a big house and First People cultural activities. Hiking, fishing,
boating, and scuba diving (oh, so cold) round out the possibilities, not to mention eating and loafing.

Quadra Island is the home of April Point Lodge & Fishing Resort, part of
the Oak Bay Marina restaurant and resort group. *Condé Nast Traveler* magazine
once chose this full-service resort as "one of the best places to stay in the world"
(see "Where to Stay"). April Point has also been featured in *Gourmet* magazine
and *Northwest Best Places.*

Where to Stay

April Point Lodge & Fishing Resort, April Point Road (250–285–2222;
www.aprilpoint.com); suites, cabins, houses, and 49 rooms $165–$340, guest

houses $175–$375; hot tubs, fireplaces; licensed dining, lounge; fishing; heli-pad, seaplane connections.

Tsa-Kwa-Luten Lodge, Lighthouse Road (250–285–2042); $130–$380, off-season $70–$180; West Coast native theme featuring elegant woods and design; ocean views; beach; dining; sauna; guided fishing; no pets.

Whiskeypoint Resort, 725 Quathiaski Road, Quathiaski (250–285–2201; www.whiskeypoint.com); $89–$149, off-season $69–$104; harbor views; kitchenettes; pets okay with fee.

Cortes Island

Reached by Quadra Island B.C. Ferry from Campbell Bay, little Cortes, at the entrance to Desolution Sound, offers miles of white sandy beaches, an old whaling station at Whaletown, a historic church, and trails that span this most beautiful of the Discovery Islands and its lakes. The Hollyhock holistic healing center (800–933–6339) is on Cortes Road.

Also visit Smelt Bay Provincial Park, known for smelt sprawning, beach walks, paddling, hiking, and occasional swimming. Just north of Smelt Bay is Manson's Landing Provincial Marine Park, as well as Hague Lake Regional Park and Von Donop Provincial Marine Park, a preservation joint effort between B.C. Parks and the Klahoose First Nation.

Where to Stay

Cortes Island Motel, Manson's Landing (250–935–6363 or 888–935–6363; www.cortesislandmotel.com); $89–$99, off-season $79–$89; 10 units; only motel on island; some kitchens; family suites; near beach; pets okay; 9 miles from ferry.

Smelt Bay Provincial Park (250–954–4600); June–September; 25 kilometers (13 miles) south of ferry terminal.

Sonora Island

Just north of Quadra Island is sprawling Sonora Island, which can be reached only by private boat or plane. It is home to upscale fishing resort **Sonora Resort and Conference Centre** (250–287–2869), which starts at more than $2,000 for a minimum of two days as part of a flying package from Vancouver and guided fishing trip. Amenities include tennis, lap pool, hot tub, billiard room, gourmet dining, and licensed lounge. By boat it is 48 kilometers (30 miles) from Campbell River.

Cormorant and Malcolm Islands

Far to the north in the open water of Labouchere Passage (also called the Queen Charlotte Strait) and east of the town of Port McNeill lie Cormorant and Malcolm Islands. You can reach both by auto ferry from Port McNeill. The trip is twenty-five minutes to Malcolm and forty-five minutes to Cormorant.

Cormorant Island. Little Cormorant Island is a cornucopia of native artifacts. These include the potlatch collection at U'Mista Cultural Centre on Front Street (250–974–5501 or 250–974–2626), the second tallest totem pole in the world (constructed in 1973 by carver Jimmy Dick and skilled aides), and traditional native dances at the Big House. Members of the Kwakiutl (Kwakwaka'wakw) Nation, famed for their art, own half the island.

Alert Bay, the only town, has a long history as a trading post, fishing and cannery center, and stopover for Klondike gold rushers. The town has the ferry terminal; information center; Nimpkish Burial Ground, studded with totem poles; and the Alert Bay Museum (250–974–5024; www.village.alertbay.bc.ca). Slightly inland is Gator Gardens, a cedar forest ideal for bird sighting.

Check out the 'Namgis Burial Grounds to the right of the ferry dock, marked by carved poles (do not touch), the Alert Bay Ecological Park, and the Alert Bay Library and Museum.

Two taxi companies transport visitors and locals. For whale watching or fishing, try Seasmoke Tours (250–974–5225) in downtown Alert Bay or Cannery Row Lodge (250–974–5213).

Where to Stay

Orca Inn, 291 Fir Street (250–974–5322); $39–$65; overlooks strait; licensed restaurant; no pets.

Ocean View Cabins, 390 Poplar Street (250–974–5457); $50–$80; 14 cabins; 1 mile from ferry; overlooks bay; pets okay.

Malcolm Island. Malcolm Island was the site of a turn-of-the-twentieth-century Finnish utopian farming colony, *Sointula*, which means "harmony" in Finnish. The original cooperative general store, Hole in the Wall Art Gallery, and the Sointula Finnish Museum (to the left of the ferry dock; 250–973–6353 or 250–973–6764) provide a taste of the founding community. Bere Point Regional Park offers sportfishing and whale watching.

Take a ferry from Port McNeill or from nearby Cormorant Island.

Where to Stay

Malcolm Island Inn, 210 First Street (250–973–6366); $44–$51; beachfront; licensed restaurant; store, bank; fishing and whale watching tours; pets okay.

There are also three small bed-and-breakfasts: **Ocean Bliss** (250–973–6121), **Sea 4 Miles** (250–973–6486), and **Rogue Retreat** (250–973–6222).

7

Outdoor Things to Do

This is our outdoor chapter. Not everyone wants to spend all their time shopping. In fact, some people come to Vancouver Island to experience unusually fine natural wonders. Or a combination of urban and wild. This covers most of what you can do to get closer to nature and to your spirit while exercising your body.

BIKING

Vancouver Island is ideal for casual or organized biking. Most highways have bike lanes. The trip over the mountains to Tofino and Ucluelet on Highway 4 can be harrowing because the road is narrow in places to start with, and in a few places the shoulder and pavement edge have washed out. Check with bike shops for latest information. (See chapter 2 for a list of bike shops.)

Cycletreks, 450 Swift Street (250–386–2277 or 877–733–6722; www.cycletreks.com), the most extensive bicycle-tour operation in Victoria, is connected to Great Pacific Adventures whale watching. They offer self-guided tours, as well as guided one- to seven-day tours with accommodations (rates from $69 a day to $1,800 for seven days; be sure to call ahead).

DIVING

Cousteau Society and National Geographic leaders agree that "the emerald sea" along British Columbia's shorelines offers some of the best diving in the world. Vancouver Island's bays and inlets, along with currents from the Pacific and between islands, attract abundant and varied marine plant and animal communities, almost as diverse as the divers who come to visit them.

The water is colder than what you may encounter off Monterey, California, for example (brr), but warmer than many inland lakes. The temperatures require use of 6 millimeter (³/₄-inch) wet suits or dry suits. With these heavier suits, be sure to pay attention to buoyancy control.

Because of Vancouver Island's moderate climate, you can dive year-round. Visibility is best in winter, often exceeding 20 meters (66 feet). In summer, seasonal plankton bloom and can go down 10–20 meters (33–66 feet), below which visibility is good.

You can find some good diving from shore, but the best is to be had off boats. Contact professional dive shops for daylong or several-day charters and excursions. Charter operators do not allow hunting or collection of specimens under a "look but don't take" policy. There is a strong commitment to conservation and preservation in B.C. waters.

Southern Vancouver Island. Currents coming from different directions support a very exciting and diverse marine life here. Good shore diving is found at Ogden Point (Dallas Road) breakwater overlooking the Juan de Fuca Strait and Washington's Olympic Mountains or at Ten Mile Point.

At Race Rocks, which is accessible only by boat, swift currents support multihued invertebrates such as giant barnacles, basket stars, brooding anemones, and pink hydrocoral. In the fall, hundreds of California and Steller's sea lions hover on these same rocks, often performing for their diving audience.

Near Sidney there's a special attraction for trained wreck divers: the HMCS *MacKenzie,* a project of the Artificial Reef Society of British Columbia. The society has made the 100-meter (330-foot) destroyer safe for exploration by properly trained divers.

Nanaimo and north. Halfway between Qualicum Beach and Courtenay you can take a ferry to Denman and Hornby Islands. In the summer, if you're lucky, you might see the rare six-gill sharks that can grow to more than 6 meters (20 feet). Look for them around Flora Islets, which are part of Helliwell Provincial Park off the southeastern corner of Hornby Island.

Using professional charters is highly recommended.

Giant Stride Diving, 60 Kenneth Street, Duncan (250–748–8864; Fax: 250–748–8962).

Hornby Island Diving, Ford Cove, Hornby Island (250–335–2807; www.hornby islanddiving.com).

Ocean Explorers Diving, 1690 Stewart, Nanaimo (250–753–2055 or 800–233–4145; Fax 250–753–2004; www.oceanexplorersdiving.com).

Seafun Divers Ltd., 300 Terminal Avenue, Nanaimo (250–754–4813; Fax: 250–754–5383).

Sundown Diving, 22 Esplanade Street, Nanaimo (250–753–1880; Fax: 250–753–6445; www.sundowndiving.com).

Blue Meridian Dive Center, 1956 Zorkin Road, Nanaimo (250–753–2055).

Campbell River. Campbell River is a town about halfway up Vancouver Island that overlooks Discovery Pass, which is a sort of bottleneck at the northern end of Georgia Strait. The swirling waters create eddies and currents that sustain profuse marine life. At "Row and Be Damned" on Quadra Island, you might see strawberry anemones on the rocky bottom, kel greenlings, lingcod, octopus, rockfish, sculpins, and occasionally meter-long feather-duster worms, sponges, and wolf-eels.

Abyssal Diving, Quadra Island (250–285–2420 or 800–499–2297); charters and lodge; underwater photography; $165 per diver, per day.

Beaver Aquatics Ltd., 760 Island Highway, Campbell River (250–287–7652; Fax: 250–287–8652); classes, equipment; since 1985.

Pacific Northwest Diving Adventures, P.O. Box 58, Manson's Landing, Cortes Island V0P 1K0 (604–935–6711, phone and fax).

Port Hardy and Queen Charlotte Strait. Sighting killer whales here on the water's surface is fairly commonplace, but seeing one underwater is not. You might, though, spot schools of dolphins and porpoises, or—more likely—the Pacific white-sided dolphins will spot and circle you.

The coast of northern Vancouver Island is diver heaven. You can see dense gatherings of pink soft coral, sponges, giant barnacles and anemones, basket star, rockfish, lingcod, wolf-eels, warbonnets, and sculpins.

Caution: Some of the swiftest tidal minglings in the world occur here, occasionally resulting in tidal currents that are more than twenty knots.

The plus side of these exchanges is the radiant collection of marine life you can see at slack tide, including gooseneck barnacles and brooding anemones. Liveaboard dive vessels are recommended.

North Island Dive and Charter, Market and Hastings, Port Hardy (250–949–8006; www.northislanddiver.com); charter; equipment; instruction.

Stubbs Island Charters, 24 Boardwalk, Box 7, Telegraph Cove (250–928–3185, 205–928–3117, or 800–665–3066; Fax: 250–928–3102).

Sun Fun Divers, 1630 McNeill Road, Port McNeill (250–956–2243; www.sun fundivers.com); charters; instruction.

West Coast of Vancouver Island. Barkley Sound, on which Ucluelet is the principal metropolis, is the main dive interest in the area to the south of Pacific Rim National Park.

Among the broken group of islands scattered through the sound you will encounter shallow reefs and profuse marine life, such as wolf-eels, octopus, rockfish (including china and vermilion rockfish), lingcod, purple-ringed top snails, tube worms, finger sponges, large fish-eating anemones, and nudibranchs. Barkley Sound is also known as Vancouver Island's other place to spot six-gill sharks.

Foggy weather has contributed to more than a hundred ships wrecking in the area over the centuries, resulting in unusual collections of marine life living within dead boat shells.

From here you can also take charters to Clayoquot Sound, Nootka Sound, Kyuquot, and Cape Scott and watch gray whales migrate south almost anywhere along the west coast of Van Isle.

Pacific Spirit Charters, 4924 Argyle Street, Port Alberni (604–723–1291 or 800–547–1291; Fax: 250–723–6817).

Subtidal Adventures, P.O. Box 78, 1950 Peninsula Road, Ucluelet V0R 3A0 (250–726–7336 or 877–444–1134).

FISHING

It seems as if there are almost as many fishing guides and charters as there are people needing guidance in fishing waters. All the fishing professionals here treat novices as well as old-timers, the latter of whom probably don't need much help.

Fishing resorts and fishing tours for freshwater and ocean are great experiences of Van Isle. In both cases, you usually don't need to bring your own equipment unless you want to. You can arrive in Victoria, see a brochure and decide this looks like fun, make a call and a reservation, and off you go to heaven, hoping never to have to return home.

Freshwater lakes, rivers, and streams have wild rainbow and cutthroat trout, Dolly Varden char, kokanee salmon, and hatchery-grown introduced species. There are more than one hundred steelhead rivers and creeks on Vancouver Island, most accessible by car. Most lucrative fishing rivers include the Cowichan, Campbell/Quinmsam, Keogh, Cluxewe, and Nimpkish Rivers on the island's east coast, and the Stam/Somass and Gold Rivers on the west coast. Cowichan Lake is known as the fly fishing capital of Canada.

Freshwater Fishing

Nimmo Bay Resort Ltd., Box 696, Port McNeill V0N 2R0 (250–956–4000; Fax: 250–956–2000; www.sharphooks.com); Craig Murray uses helicopters for "helifishing" to various choice locations; also rafting and caving; 9 chalets.

Hidden Cove Lodge, Box 258, Port NcNeill V0N 2R0 (250–956–3916; Fax: 250–956–3213); Dan and Sandra Kirby. Whale and bear watching tours May–October; 3 cottages; dining room; diving charters.

Salmon Run in Goldstream Provincial Park, north of Victoria, off Highway 1; November; call (250) 387–4363 for timing.

For local lake fishing try Elk Lake and Beaver Lake (they run together) off Patricia Bay Highway (17).

Ocean Sportfishing

Ocean sportfishing is extremely popular all over Vancouver Island. Almost every outdoors shop, hotel, motel, bed-and-breakfast, or cafe server in Victoria or anywhere else on the island can set you up with a fishing charter, guide, tour, or equipment.

Since listing the larger companies would mean the smaller ones never get larger, we suggest you make your accommodations reservation for where you want to be or go and book fishing through your hosts. Most charters supply all equipment.

Adam's Fishing Charters, 19 Lotus Street, Victoria (250–370–2326 or 250–727–5575; www.adamsfishingcharters.com); veteran charter operator Adam Heffelfinger departs from Inner Harbour. Call ahead. Rate: $85 per hour.

Canadian Princess Resort, 1948 Peninsula Road, Ucluelet (250–726–7771); seven-hour trip for chinook, sockeye, coho, and pink salmon (leaves 6:00 A.M.) or four-hour trip bottom fishing for halibut, lingcod, red snapper (leaves 2:30 P.M.); also whale watching and nature cruises; 43- and 52-foot deep-sea cruisers.

Oak Bay Charters Ltd., 2141 Newton Street, Victoria (250–598–1061 or 800–413–1061; www.oakbaycharters.com); year-round salmon fishing, sightseeing, cruises; at Oak Bay Marina.

Reel Action Fishing Charters, 961 Haslam Avenue, Victoria (250–478–1977 or 250–644–6536); salmon, halibut, and bottom fish around Victoria and Sooke.

Reel Obsession Sports Fishing, 3139 Carran Road, Victoria (888–855–7335; www.reelobsession.ca).

Weigh West Marine Resort, 634 Campbell Street, Tofino (250–725–3277 or 800–665–8922; www.weighwest.com); five boats for charter fishing with guides. Rates: charter, $75 per hour per boat (four people plus guide); whale watching $29 each person.

GOLF

Golf is only a minor obsession with Vancouver Islanders, which they come by naturally given their Scottish-British heritage. Nearly every town and many neighborhoods have golf courses. Greater Victoria alone has fifteen and is Canada's number one golf city, attracting major golf aficionados from around the world.

Victorians believe that you can play golf 365 days a year here (except, of course, for that one snowy week in early 1997). As is true in most of the Pacific Northwest, golf devotees play with umbrellas, slickers, covered carts, and rain hats year-round.

Golf Courses in Greater Victoria

Ardmore Golf Course, 930 Ardmore Drive, North Saanich (250–656–4621); nine holes, 2,821 yards, par 34.

Bear Mountain Golf and Country Club, 2020 Country Club Way (250–744–2327 or 888–533–2327; www.bearmountaingolf.com); designed by Jack

Nicklaus; opened 2003; in Bear Mountain Resort; eighteen holes, 7,212 yards, par 72.

Cedar Hills Municipal Golf Course, 1400 Derby Road, Victoria (250–595–3103); eighteen holes; men: 5,008 yards, par 67; women: 4,975 yards, par 68.

Cordova Bay Golf Course, 5333 Cordova Bay Road, Saanich (250–658–4444); eighteen holes, 6,500 yards, par 72.

Glen Meadows Golf and Country Club, 1050 McTavish Road, North Saanich (250–656–3921); eighteen holes, 6,850 yards, par 72.

Gorge Vale Golf Club, 1005 Craigflower Road, Victoria (250–386–3401); eighteen holes, 6,382 yards, par 72; book one day in advance, or Thursday for weekends.

Mount Douglas Golf Course, 4225 Blenkinsop Road, Victoria (250–477–8314); nine holes, 1,500 yards, par 30.

Olympic View Golf Club, 643 Labora Road, Victoria (250–474–3671); park-like setting; elegant; eighteen holes, 5,562 yards.

Prospect Lake Golf Course, 4633 Prospect Lake Road, Saanich (250–479–2688); nine holes, 2,121 yards, par 32 (with tricky sixth-hole water).

Royal Oak Golf Course, 40 Marsett Place, Saanich (250–478–9591); nine holes, 2,031 yards, par 32.

Uplands Golf Club, 3300 Cadboro Bay Road, Victoria (250–592–1818); eighteen holes, 6,315 yards, par 70.

Victoria Golf Club, 1110 Beach Drive, Oak Bay (250–598–4322); eighteen holes, 6,015 yards, par 70; along the water.

Outside Victoria

Arbutus Ridge Golf Club, 3515 Telegraph Road, Cobble Hill (250–743–5000).

Broome Hill Golf & Country Club, Sooke (250–624–6344).

Comox Golf Club, 1718 Balmoral Avenue, Comox (250–399–4444).

Cowichan Golf & Country Club, 4955 Trans-Canada Highway, Duncan (250–746–5333).

Crown Isle, Clubhouse Drive, Courtenay (250–338–6811).

Duncan Lakes, 6507 North Road, Duncan (250–746–6789).

Eaglecrest Golf Club, 2035 Island Highway West, Qualicum Beach (250–752–6311).

Fairwinds Golf Course Ltd., 3730 Fairwinds Drive, Nanoose Bay (250–468–7666).

Fiddler's Green Golf Centre Inc., 1601 Thatcher Road, Nanaimo (250–754–1325).

Galiano Golf & Country Club, 24 St. Andrews Street, Galiano Island (250–539–5533).

Glengarry Golf Links, 1025 Qualicum Road, Qualicum Beach (250–752–8786).

Gold River Golf & Country Club, Box 819, Gold River V0T 1G0 (250–283–7335).

Ladysmith Golf Club, 380 Davis, Ladysmith (250–245–7313).

Long Beach Golf Course, Tofino (250–725–3332).

Longlands Par 3 Golf Course, Comox (250–339–6363).

March Meadows Golf & Country Club, 10298 South Shore Road, Honeymoon Bay (250–749–6241).

Morningstar International Golfcourse, 525 Lowrys Road, Parksville (250–754–8232).

Mount Brenton Golf Club, 2816 Henry Road, Chemainus (250–246–9322).

Mulligans Executive Par 3, 4985 Cotton Road, Courtenay (250–338–2440).

Nanaimo Golf & Country Club, 2800 Highland Boulevard, Nanaimo (250–758–5221).

Pacific Playground Golf Course, Saratoga Beach, Campbell River (250–337–8212).

Pender Island Golf & Country Club, 2305 Otter Bay Road, Pender Island (250–629–6659).

Pleasant Valley Golf Course, Highway 4, Port Alberni (250–724–5333).

Port Alberni Golf Club, 6449 Cherry Creek Road, Port Alberni (250–723–5422).

Port Alice Golf & Country Club, Box 460, Port Alice (250–284–3213).

Pryde Vista Golf Course, 155 Pryde Avenue, Nanaimo (250–753–6188).

Qualicum Beach Memorial Golf Club, 115 Crescent Road, Qualicum Beach (250–752–6312).

Salt Spring Island Golf & Country Club, Ganges (250–537–2121).

Sequoia Springs Golf Club, 700 Petersen Road, Campbell River (250–287–4970).

Seven Hills Golf Course, Port Alice Highway, Port Hardy (250–949–9818).

Storey Creek Golf Club, McGimpsey Road, Campbell River (250–923–3673).

Sunnydale Golf Society, 5291 Island Highway, Courtenay (250–334–3342).

Courses offering golf vacation packages include Crown Isle Golf Club (praised by *Golf Digest*, near Courtenay, 250–338–6811); Fairwinds Golf & Country Club (Nanoose Bay, twenty-five minutes north of Nanaimo, 250– 468–7666); Glengarry Golf Links (near Qualicum Beach, 250–752–8786); Eaglecrest Golf Club (Qualicum Beach, 250–752–6311); and Morningstar International (between Parksville and Qualicum Beach, 250–754–8232).

HIKING

Vancouver Island offers extremely satisfying novice or expert hiking, either on well-cared-for paths or on land few people have experienced.

We mention hiking along trails throughout our itineraries, but here are a few highlights:

Pacific Rim National Park on the island's west coast is a newer park with excellent trails and abundant wildlife and rain forests, six hours from Victoria. Western Wilderness Excursions (250–727–2356) gives rain-forest tours, which we guarantee will hook you.

Goldstream Provincial Park offers day hiking and a few tent campsites with grand forests, rushing water, and amazing wildlife, all just forty minutes from Victoria. Freedom Adventure Tours (250–592–2487) leads hikes in the Sooke area.

West Coast Trail, which you reach from Port Renfrew, is a six-day hike for experienced hikers. Either drive there or take the West Coast Trail Express shuttle, (250) 280–0580.

KAYAKING AND CANOEING

Kayaking and canoeing in Canada are often lumped together as "paddling," in the sense of propelling oneself through water in a skinny boat with a paddle or oar. Every hotel, motel, bed-and-breakfast manager, and jitney driver knows someone who can arrange kayaking or canoeing for you. Most outdoors outfitter stores sell or rent kayaks and either give lessons or connect you with someone who does.

It is important that you do all the safety things and wear all the safety stuff they tell you to. We highly recommend lessons, particularly if you've never paddled this seriously before.

On Vancouver Island you can paddle out from Victoria's Inner Harbour, where the water can be pleasantly calm or pleasantly rough and challenging. Paddling within the Inner Harbour and the Gorge on calm days is like paddling on a still, glassy lake.

More experienced paddlers might try waters between Oak Bay and Gonzales Bay, McNeill Bay, Cattle Point, the Trial Islands ecological reserve, or the Discovery Islands and their marine recreation area and campgrounds. On Van Isle's west coast, try Albert Head to Witty's Lagoon, Weir's Beach by William Head to Pedder Bay, and (for experienced kayakers) from Pedder Bay through Eemdyk Pass to Becher Bay, and then an even tougher route from Becher or Pedder to Race Rocks. Even more risky but doable is the East Sooke Park shoreline toward Whiffin Spit near Sooke Harbour. What a way to arrive at Sooke Harbour House!

For more information consult May Ann Snowden's *Island Paddling: A Paddler's Guide to the Gulf Islands and Barkley Sound.*

We also recommend you try one of the great outdoors shops in Victoria. **Ocean River Sports** (1824 Store Street, 250–381–4233) has everything you need, rents kayaks and canoes (with paddles), and gives lessons and tours for kids and adults. It also has a great mailing list, so you can plan trips around its tours. The personnel gladly dispense enthusiasm and confidence for free.

Here are some others to try:

Jeune Brothers & Peetz Great Outdoors Store Ltd., 570 Johnson Street, Victoria (250–386–8778).

Mayne Island Eco Camping, Tours, and Charters, 359 Maple, Mayne Island (250–539–2667; www.mayneisle.com/camp).

Ocean Explorations, 602 Broughton Street, Victoria (250–383–6722 or 888–442–ORCA; www.oceanexplorations.com).

Salt Spring Kayaking Ltd., 2935 Fulford, Ganges, Salt Spring Island (250–653–4222; www.saltspringkayaking.com).

Sea Otter Kayaking, Ltd., 149 Lower Ganges Road, Salt Spring Island (250–537–5678; www.seaotterkayaking.com).

Sports Rent, #3, 1950 Government, Victoria (250–385–7368; www.sportsrentbc.com).

Victoria Canoe & Kayak Club, 355 Gorge West, Victoria (250–361–4238; www.vckc.ca); ask for newsletter.

KID STUFF

Beacon Hill Park, off Douglas Street and Dallas Road (250–381–3253), is an ideal place for kids and adults to work off energy and relax. There's a full, climbable playground; washrooms and telephone right next door; lots of walking and beautiful flowers; music on Sunday afternoons; a wading pool at the Douglas Street entrance; and the fabulous Children's Zoo. No food is sold here, but just outside the Douglas Street entrance is Beacon Drive In, home of Victoria's best soft ice-cream cones and greasy foods. Watch for Kids Fest in early September.

Greater Victoria Public Library, Broughton Street between Douglas and Blanshard, has a kid-friendly kids and teens department just to the right of the door as you go in. Washrooms are right next to this area.

Other fun places for kids, discussed elsewhere in this book, include Victoria Bug Zoo (631 Courtney Street, 250–384–BUGS); Victoria Butterfly Gardens (West Saanich and Keating Cross Roads near Butchart Gardens, 250–652–3822); Miniature World (649 Humboldt Street, 250–385–9731); Crystal Garden (713 Douglas Street, 250–381–1213); All Fun Water Slides & Recreation Park (2207 Millstream Road, 250–474–3184); Royal London Wax Museum (470 Belleville Street, 250–388–4461; some kids might get scared); and Royal British Columbia Museum (675 Belleville Street, 250–356–7226 or 250–387–3014).

And watch for Children's Day at Sooke Regional Museum in August. Call (250) 642–6351 for timing.

SKIING

Despite its fabulously varied terrain, Vancouver Island really has only two ski areas: Mount Washington Ski Resort and Forbidden Plateau.

Mount Washington Ski Resort is the island's largest ski area and British Columbia's third largest, with twenty groomed runs, sixty marked, four chair lifts, and a beginners' tow and bunny hill. Nineteen miles of trails can take you to Strathcona Provincial Park. Be sure to stay on the trails. You can rent equipment at the resort; book ahead for resort accommodations. Mailing address: P.O. Box 3069, Courtenay V9J 1L0 (250–338–1386; 250–338–1515 for snow report). Full-day rates are about $30 for adults.

To get there you can take Gray Line of Victoria's Mount Washington Ski Express (700 Douglas Street, 250–388–5248) or you can drive (about five hours). Take Douglas Street north, follow Highway 1 (Trans-Canada Highway) past

Nanaimo, and then go north on Highway 19 toward Courtenay. Follow signs to Mount Washington.

Forbidden Plateau is an ideal ski area for beginners, families, timid skiers, and less-than-perfect skiers. That's a lot of us. The vertical drop is 1,150 feet, and with twelve groomed runs there is one chair lift, three T-bars, and a rope tow. They have heavenly uncrowded bunny hills with little hotshotting going on. At 2050 Cliffe Avenue, Courtenay (250–338–2919); about $25 for adults. Rent equipment there.

SWIMMING

Crystal Pool and Fitness Centre is Victoria's primary swimming place. Indoors it has a 50-meter racing and swimming pool, diving pool, and children's pool. It also has other health facilities, including whirlpool, steam, weight, and aerobics rooms.

> *Crystal Pool and Fitness Centre, 2275 Quadra Street, (250) 361–0704, (250) 361–0732 for schedule. Hours: 7:00 A.M.–11:30 P.M. Admission: adults $4, children ages six to twelve $2, family (must have someone older than sixteen within arm's reach in pools) $8. Wheelchair accessible. Fifty-meter pool and tots' pools. Buses 23, 26.*

Elk Lake and Beaver Lake, 8 miles north of Victoria on Highway 17 (Patricia Bay Highway on Saanich Peninsula), are good spots for swimming. The lakes have lifeguards and pleasant picnic areas, plus sailboarding, boating, kayaking, and canoeing. Other places include Recreation Oak Bay (1975 Bee Street, Oak Bay; 250–595–7946) for swimming and indoor court sports; and the Saanich Commonwealth Place (4636 Elk Lake Road, 250–727–5300), a state-of-the-art family swim center with Olympic-size pools, diving, slides, and ozonated water.

WALKING (AND OTHER) TOURS

Tours of all sorts are available almost anywhere from almost anyone and are a most convenient way to get oriented in a new place, see exactly what you want to see, or find out what you might want to see more of. Since this chapter focuses on the outdoors, that's what we emphasize here. (See chapter 2 for more tours.)

Victoria is a walker's best friend. Many locals walk through Beacon Hill Park and along Dallas Road daily, often stopping for refreshments at the Beacon Drive In on Douglas Street or the Ogden Pointe Cafe & Dive Centre.

Architectural Walking Tours (203–245 Bastion Square, Victoria; 800–667–0753) of the Inner Harbour and Old Town are conducted by the Vancouver Island Chapter of the Architectural Institute of British Columbia. July–Labor Day. Tours leave at 1:30 P.M. Admission: free.

Craigdarroch Castle Society (250–592–5323) makes tours of the historic neighborhoods of James Bay, Rockland, and western Victoria.

Lantern Tours in the Old Burying Ground (250–598–8870). The Old Cemeteries Society of Victoria hosts tours of Victoria history through its cemeteries July–August, 8:30 P.M. nightly from the steps of Christ Church Cathedral, corner of Quadra and Rockland.

North Island Forest Tours (250–956–3844) leave from Beaver Cove, Port McNeill, Port Alice, Port Hardy, Cleagh Creek, Holberg, and Woss for five-hour tours and nature walks through working forest heritage.

Royal Blue Line picks up at the Black Ball Ferry terminal on Belleville and runs city tours and bus trips to the Butchart Gardens.

WHALE WATCHING

Vancouver Island affords high-percentage whale watching because three pods of orca killer whales live here and have favorite feeding spots along its coasts. Just like fisher guides, every inn, hotel, motel, and bed-and-breakfast manager or jitney driver knows someone who takes people whale watching. Local tip: Gray whales feed in Tofino from March through October. Try to go with legitimate, established tour guides:

Chinook Charters, 450 Campbell Street, Tofino (250–725–3431 or 800–665–3646); cruises through Clayoquot Sound.

Cypre Prince Whale Tours & Fishing Charters, 430 Campbell Street, Tofino (250–725–2202 or 800–787–2202).

Great Pacific Adventures, 811 Wharf Street, Victoria (250–386–2277); $79–$89 adults, $55 children. Tours not recommended for pregnant women or persons with neck or back problems.

Jamie's Whale Station, 606 Campbell Street, Tofino (250–725–3919 or 800–667–9913); bed-and-breakfast accommodations available.

Ocean Explorations, 602 Broughton Street, Victoria (250–383–6722 or 888–442–ORCA; www.oceanexplorations.com); $85 adults, $64 students, $59 children; three 12-passenger boats.

Sea Trek Tours & Expeditions Ltd., 441B Campbell Street, Tofino (250–725–4412 or 800–811–9155); to Meares Island rain forest, Meares Island.

SeaQuest Adventures, 591 Braemar Avenue, R.R. 2, Sidney (250–656–7599); from Port Sidney Marina.

Springtide Whale Tours, 1207 Wharf Street, Victoria (250–384–4444 or 800–470–3474); $89 adults, $59 children; 61-foot boat.

Subtidal Adventures, 1950 Peninsula Road, Ucluelet (250–726–7336); Ucluelet's oldest charter boat company for gray whale adventures.

Whaling Canoe Adventures, Blackfish Wilderness Adventures, Victoria (250–216–2389); very extensive.

8

History of Victoria and Vancouver Island

Vancouver Island was one of the last places in the world Europeans discovered. The Spanish were in California, the American colonies declared their independence from Great Britain, and Quebec city and Montreal were well established before caucasians found the island.

First Peoples reached Vancouver Island more than 7,000 years ago. When the Europeans arrived, they found three related language groups: The Kwakiutl had the northeast corner, the Coast Salish occupied the territory from Victoria past Nanaimo, and the so-called Nootka lived on the west coast.

The natives were and are among the most artistic in the Western Hemisphere, with particular skills in carving. Unlike most people of the new world, they valued acquisition and display of private property, including slaves taken in raids upon their neighbors. Their social structure was in three layers: nobles, common people, and slaves, whose lives existed at the whim of their owners. One charming practice was to bury a slave alive in the hole before a new totem pole was inserted.

The natives lived primarily on a fish-oriented economy, starting with herring in the late winter caught in nets or scooped in with giant rakes, followed later by halibut and then salmon. The Nootkas went whale harpooning in packs of a half dozen canoes. Berries, roots, and meat from otters, seals, deer, and bears supplemented their diet.

Giant cedar trunks were carved into sleek and speedy 60-foot canoes. Cedar also provided bark, which could be shredded into a sort of thread to weave blankets, clothing, and baskets. Natives lived in longhouses, structures with permanent wooden frames that were divided into family cubicles. In late spring the wood siding was carried to the coast to build a temporary village for the season.

The desire to display wealth led to the potlatch (from *patshatl*, which meant "giving"), a celebration for almost any cause in which visiting tribes were given lavish gifts and were expected to reciprocate. Often, valuable possessions were broken or canoes burned to show that the owner was too rich to care. As the ultimate conspicuous consumption, occasionally a valuable slave would be ceremoniously clubbed to death during such a festive event.

It was a male-dominated society in which marriages were arranged by uncles and chiefs and women had little to say—except for the women who were shamans. They were respected and thought to possess mystical powers.

In circa A.D. 499 five Chinese Buddhist monks, led by Hui Shen, sailed to Vancouver Island (they called it Fusang) and returned to China. Their story triggered Russian interest in North America 1,200 years later.

The Spanish made forays north in 1774. On August 8 of that year, in bad weather, Capt. Juan Perez Hernandez anchored the *Santiago* off the western shore of Vancouver Island but did not land.

On July 12, 1776, Capt. James Cook set out for his third exploration of the Pacific Ocean, armed with the highly accurate chronometer invented by John Harrison, England's preeminent clock innovator. It made east to west navigation possible no matter how rough the sea or erratic the humidity. Unlike the Spanish explorers, who did not have a similar device, Cook would know exactly where he was and be able to return to a given place. His two ships were the 420-foot old tub *Resolution* and the smaller but more maneuverable *Discovery*. On board was nineteen-year-old junior officer George Vancouver, who had sailed with Cook since he was fifteen.

COOK DISCOVERS NOOTKA SOUND

After navigating around South America and crossing the Pacific and discovering the Hawaiian islands, Cook headed northeast and reached the Oregon coast in March 1778 before being forced offshore by a storm. He sailed northward, desperate to find a safe landing to repair a mast and take on fresh water.

On the morning of March 28, the weather front lifted enough to reveal the mountains of Vancouver Island, and by afternoon the search for an anchorage was rewarded with the view of an inlet that promised shelter—amazingly, the same spot where Spanish captain Perez had anchored briefly four years earlier. Leading the way into the inlet was the *Resolution*, with Capt. William Bligh at the helm—the same Captain Bligh who would gain infamy as the tyrannical master of the mutinous *Bounty*.

They were soon surrounded by more than thirty canoes filled with natives led by the tall Maquinna, chief of one of two dozen tribes on the island's west coast. For a month Cook's ships berthed at what is now Bligh Island, while they cut a tree for a new mast, caulked the ship, and began trading for furs, particularly otter, which native nobles liked to wear as cloaks and hats.

The Europeans had a poor ear for local names and worse for definitions. Thus, Cook mistook the local words *nu-tka* (noot-tick-ka), which meant "go around," for the name of the place or its people, which he thought was "Nootka." However, the natives in the inlet called themselves the Mowachaht, and their villages were Tahsis, Kopti, and Yuquot. Today, scholars refer to the language group of the twenty-four west coast tribes as the Nootka people after Cook's mistake. The anchorage soon became universally called Nootka Sound.

Captain Cook met his death in Hawaii during a fight with natives over a stolen boat. His ships continued on to China, where the men sold otter pelts, causing a fashion sensation.

When Cook's ships made it back to England, the publication of his journals stimulated British interest in the west coast of the island, still thought to be part of the mainland. First on the scene was the *Harmon,* skippered by James Hanna, who reached Nootka Sound in August 1785. However, as a joke Hanna's crew exploded gunpowder under Maquinna's chair, causing a fight in which twenty natives were killed.

The East India Company sent four ships to Nootka Sound in 1785 and 1786 but lost interest in the long haul and expense. However, they left behind a young physician, John Mackay, who was too ill to travel.

Charles William Barkley steered his *Imperial Eagle* into Nootka Sound in June 1787. With him was his seventeen-year-old red-haired bride, Frances, the first white woman to set foot on Vancouver Island, who wrote literate journals for her husband. Dr. Mackay informed Barkley that this land was probably an island. Barkley headed south of Nootka and found Clayoquot Sound and then the broad entryway to Alberni Inlet, which he modestly named Barkley Sound.

Swinging around the southern cape of the island, he was startled to find his ship in a wide strait. He exclaimed, "This is Juan de Fuca's Strait," and the name remains. Almost 200 years earlier, a Greek captain, Apostolos Valerianos, had been employed by the Spanish to explore the west coast. The Greek gave himself the Spanish name Juan de Fuca.

Other explorers doubted de Fuca because he often embellished his reports with fantastic discoveries in order to justify his employment. Among his claims was that in 1592 on the North American coast he had sailed into a wide strait and beyond that a broader sea at latitude 47 and 48 degrees (but no longitude), identifiable by a high rock pillar on the southern shore of the entrance. Such a formation exists near Cape Flattery and is called Fuca's Pillar.

Capt. John Meares survived after being caught in ice in Alaska and made it to Nootka Sound in 1788 with two ships of his own. Meares brought materials to build a schooner for trading up and down the coast and bought a parcel of land from Maquinna to establish a permanent settlement.

The first American ships to arrive were the *Lady Washington* and the *Columbia,* the latter captained by Robert Gray and the first U.S. ship to sail around the world. In 1792 Gray returned to the northwest and discovered the Columbia River, which he named for his sturdy ship.

Two Spanish ships landed at Nootka in March 1789, commanded by Estaban Jose Martinez, who completed a fort on an island. Martinez seized four ships sent by Meares, sending two to Mexico and holding their commander. British sailors were packed off to China on an American ship that happened to show up.

THE BRINK OF WAR

Meares sailed from China to England and presented to the government an exaggerated demand for British action against Spain for his claimed losses and mistreatment of his crews. He stormed against the "insult to the British flag" while hiding the fact that his ships carried Portuguese papers. Prime Minister William Pitt put fourteen naval ships on readiness for action and obtained promises of support and warships from Holland and Prussia. The "Nootka incident" had brought the two greatest sea powers—Britain and Spain—to the brink of war.

The French Revolution had made Spain's alliance with France worthless, and the Spanish had to deal. A negotiated settlement called the Nootka Sound Convention was reached on October 28, 1790, in which Spain lost ground for the first time since 1493, when the Pope—no great cartographer—divided the new world at a longitudinal line between Spain and Portugal. Meares got a hefty financial settlement, his buildings and possessions were restored, and, more significantly, it was agreed that Spain's dominion was limited to lands in its actual possession or approved by treaties.

Meanwhile, the Spaniards sent a barque to reconnoiter the coast of present-day Sooke and Royal Roads. At each landing its captain, Manuel Quimper, formally "took possession" of the land for Spain.

In 1792 the Spanish commander at Nootka, Francisco Eliza, sailed up the east coast of the island beyond Nanaimo, proving conclusively that this land mass was an island. A thorough exploration was conducted along the east coast of the island by Alejandro Malaspina, an excellent Italian navigator sailing for Spain. After he completed his trip around the globe, Malaspina found that his sponsoring admiral had been sacked. Malaspina was clapped in jail and eventually banned from Spain, leaving his detailed charts moldering in storage.

VANCOUVER EXPLORES THE COAST

The British government sent out the sloop *Discovery* and the armed tender *Chatham,* both under the command of George Vancouver, Captain Cook's one-time midshipman. From the Spanish he was to receive ships and goods seized from Meares and then make a thorough survey of the northwest coast. Vancouver was equipped with several chronometers for accurate mapmaking and navigating, and a naval surgeon, Archibald Menzies, to collect botanical specimens.

Starting April 29, 1792, Vancouver and the master of the *Chatham,* William Broughton, began a meticulous survey of the shorelines of the Strait of Juan de Fuca, which Vancouver claimed for King George. Proceeding up the east coast of the island, they encountered two Spanish ships. Together the English and Spanish explored the coastlines for three weeks until Vancouver and Broughton left on their own to thread the passage to the northern cape of the island and then south to Nootka to settle matters with the Spanish.

Waiting for Vancouver was the Spanish naval commander for the west coast, Juan Francisco de la Bodega y Quadra. The two men struck up an instant friendship but were unable to reach a settlement on anything more than returning Meares's property. After agreeing to refer the issues to their governments, as a final gesture of friendship Vancouver proposed that the island be named Quadra and Vancouver Island. This name lasted until the 1840s, but Quadra died in 1793.

Vancouver mapped the mainland coast, left for England, and died in 1798, never returning to North America.

Into the western picture slogged Alexander Mackenzie, a partner in the North West Company, a fur-trapping outfit that had established a trading post on Lake Athabasca in the northeast corner of what is now Alberta Province. On May 9, 1793, accompanied by an assistant, six husky *voyageurs,* and two Indians, he headed toward the Rocky Mountains in a 25-foot canoe. Battling turbulent currents and managing a portage up steep cliffs, they crossed the Continental Divide in five weeks and found a tributary to the Fraser River.

After canoeing 400 miles down the treacherous Fraser, Mackenzie struck out overland toward the ocean. Mackenzie reached Elcho Harbor near Bella Coola, the first man ever to cross the continent. On a large rock he painted the words: ALEXANDER MACKENZIE FROM CANADA BY LAND 22 JULY 1793. It would be another dozen years before Americans Meriwether Lewis and William Clark reached the Pacific and even longer before there were further overland explorations by the British.

SPAIN BACKS OFF

British and Spanish officials met at Nootka on March 23, 1795, raised the British flag, and began the dismantling of the Spanish fort. Spain was through in the northwest, never again to venture north of San Francisco Bay. The race for the fur business and settlement of the land was now between the British and the Americans.

The North West Fur Company sent Simon Fraser over the Great Divide in 1808, and on the west side he canoed down the Fraser River into what he called New Caledonia—a poetic name for Scotland. In 1811 the source of the Columbia was found by another North West explorer, David Thompson.

The fate of the British-American rivalry in the northwest was going to be settled a continent away. On June 19, 1812, the United States declared war on Great Britain on the complaint that the British warships were impressing American merchant seamen and trying to restrict American trade. For many of the war hawks, the real American aim was to annex part of eastern Canada. In the spring of 1813, the British dispatched two warships to back up the claims of the North West Company against those of American John Jacob Astor's company at Astoria (now Oregon). Before the British arrived on the Pacific Coast, the isolated Astorians sold their outpost to the Northwesters at a distress price.

BRITISH-U.S. STALEMATE

The War of 1812 ended in a draw. In 1818 the United States and Great Britain agreed that they would put off for ten years the issue of authority over what was called Oregon Country by the Americans and the Columbia Department by the

The Beaver *in the Inner Harbour in 1874*

British—today's British Columbia, Oregon, Washington, Idaho, and a corner of Montana. Meanwhile, settlement and commercial use by citizens of both countries would be permitted. In 1827 the United States and Britain decided on ten more years of joint occupation.

In 1821 the Hudson's Bay Company and the North West Company merged under the name Hudson's Bay Company, saving money and gaining a total monopoly of the fur trade in Canada. In 1825 HBC factor (a title for the company's frontier bosses) Dr. John McLoughlin established Fort Vancouver on the north shore of the Columbia as the western headquarters for the HBC.

In 1835 "Napoleon" George Simpson, HBC's chief in Canada, ordered the *Beaver,* the first steamship to appear on the west coast of the new world, to explore the coast and rivers, supply company outposts, and pick up furs in order to make remote permanent posts unnecessary.

Simpson had met James Douglas in 1828, at age twenty-five the second in command at Fort Vancouver. Douglas was born in Guiana, the illegitimate son of a Scotch merchant and his Creole mistress from Barbados. He was educated in Scotland, where he had to gain respect with his fists, and joined the North West Company as a clerk when he was sixteen. At twenty-two he was named assistant to factor William Connolly at Fort St. James in the northern area of

New Caledonia. Three years later he married Connolly's sixteen-year-old daughter Amelia, who was half Cree Indian, "by the custom of the country" (an Indian ceremony), often repudiated or ignored by traders when they wished to desert their native wives. Amelia insisted that—unlike her mother—she would not be abandoned, and in 1837 the Douglases were married by the HBC chaplain at Fort Vancouver.

Skipper William H. McNeill of the *Beaver* explored Vancouver Island's coast in 1837 and reported favorably on the harbor at its southern tip known as "Camosun" or "Camosack" (mispronunciations of "Cammossung," which was native language for "the gorge"). Although HBC factor McLoughlin did not want to move his center of operations, Simpson ordered him to send Douglas to sail up on the *Cadboro* in 1842 for a final evaluation of the site as a new western headquarters for HBC.

FOUNDING FORT VICTORIA

Douglas's report was enthusiastic, stating that "the place itself appears a perfect 'Eden' in the midst of the dreary wilderness of the north west coast" and adding that "there is no other seaport north of the Columbia where so many advantages will be found combined." He also reported that the inlets at Sooke and Esquimalt had potential, but their rocky entrances required substantial improvements to be safe for shipping.

On March 13, 1843, Douglas returned on the *Beaver* to select the exact site for the post. He and fifteen of his men embarked the next morning at Clover Point, walked to Beacon Hill, and then turned back to the inner harbor where Douglas decided to build the fort. The HBC ruling council had intended to name its newest outpost Fort Adelaide for the Queen's baby girl, or Fort Albert for the Queen's husband. However, the council diplomatically changed its collective mind and sent word that the name would be Fort Victoria, to honor the mother rather than the child or consort.

Several thousand Coast Salish natives lived in the area's numerous villages, each occupied by a particular clan or subgroup. These included the Songhees (a corruption of the name Stsanges), made up of six different groups living around what is now Victoria. One group was the Is-Whoy-malth, which has come down to us as Esquimalt (pronounced ess-kwy-malt). Two tribes, both apparently called Saanich, lived on the peninsula of that name. There were also the Sooke, who inhabited the area from Sooke to Point-No-Point, and beyond them, two tribes of Clallams who had migrated across the strait from the Olympics. At Cadboro Bay there was a substantial village of the so-called Songhees. This settlement had existed for at least 2,500 years, with a fort to protect them against coastal raiders like the Haida. Northerly up the east coast of the island and inland was a large band, the Cowichan.

The Songhees across the gorge agreed to supply pickets for a fence for the fort at the rate of forty pickets for one blanket. Leaving a melancholy Charles Ross in charge, with twenty-five-year-old Roderick Finlayson as Ross's assistant, Douglas went to the mainland to inspect other HBC trading posts.

Sited above the natural wharf of steep shoreline, the HBC crew of workmen built an 18-foot stockade fence, 330 feet by 300 feet. Using only axes, handsaws, and chisels, they constructed a three-story bastion armed with a nine-pound cannon and pocked with portholes from which to fire at enemies.

By the time Douglas returned in October, there were two finished log dwellings, and a main hall and quarters for the "officers" of the HBC were under way. A Christmas party with a rocket display from the *Cadboro* was held in the main building. The *Beaver* brought horses, cattle, equipment, and wheat seed, which was planted in December. The dyspeptic Ross died of an intestinal ailment in June 1844, having been ill most of the year, and Finlayson was put in day-to-day charge of Victoria.

Trouble arose when some of the imported oxen were killed and roasted by the Songhees. Finlayson demanded payment, and the chief of the village became very angry. Soon Cowichan reinforcements appeared on the scene, and the fort was peppered with rifle shots from the growing crowd of war-whooping natives. The fifty HBC men in the fort were outnumbered at least fifty to one.

Finlayson ordered the cannon fired at an empty Songhee lodge, and with one shot it was blasted into a pile of boards and splinters. He told the native leaders that he would do the same to the rest of the village just north of the fort. The power of the cannon convinced them to pay for the oxen. Finlayson then demanded that the Songhees remove their village, which they refused to do. As a face-saving settlement he offered to have his men perform the labor of dismantling the lodges and transporting the village across the gorge.

DRAWING THE BORDER

During the next round of British-U.S. negotiations on the future of "Oregon," which took place in Washington, D.C., the British offered to make the dividing line the forty-ninth parallel from the Rocky Mountains to the Columbia River and then down that river to the coast (thus retaining the western two-thirds of present-day Washington state for the English), with Victoria and any other port below the forty-ninth to be "free" to the United States. The offer was rejected in one day.

President James K. Polk countered with a proposal that Oregon be divided at the forty-ninth parallel—including across Vancouver Island—with no British navigation rights on the Columbia below the border, but offered to make an American Victoria a free port for the English. This proposal was promptly dismissed by the British.

In his State of the Union message of December 2, 1845, Polk claimed that all of Oregon should belong to the United States. The British made a new compromise offer: The border would be the forty-ninth parallel, except that the southern portion of Vancouver Island would remain British, and they would have certain trade rights south of the border. Polk said no.

American sentiment for taking the entire Oregon territory grew rapidly, with the slogan "Fifty-four-forty or fight" trumpeted in the press. That demand would have stretched U.S. territory clear to Russian Alaska, cut off the Pacific Ocean coastline from any British use, and incorporated large areas in which there were almost no Americans.

On May 13, 1846, the United States declared war on Mexico, aimed at acquiring California, Arizona, New Mexico, and the rest of Mexican territory north of the Rio Grande. Eight days later, on May 21, President Polk gave notice to Great Britain that the joint occupation agreement would be terminated in one year. The British navy began preparing for a sea war with the United States, basically over who would get the southern tip of Vancouver Island. Even a limited war with England, or British naval interference, would jeopardize the entire Mexican enterprise, so the Senate approved the British compromise offer.

Three days later, on June 15, 1846, British negotiator Richard Packenham and U.S. Secretary of State James Buchanan signed the convention: All of Vancouver Island would be British, while the forty-ninth parallel would divide the rest of what was then called Oregon. Left undecided was the fate of the islands between Vancouver Island and the Washington coast; joint authority over them would continue until resolved by arbitration.

DOUGLAS TAKES OVER

Western HBC supervisor McLoughlin retired on January 1, 1846, and moved south to lead the formation of the American state of Oregon. James Douglas was named in his place.

Farming began to provide sustenance (particularly potatoes) for the fifty men in the fort and for British sailors on ships sent into the Esquimalt harbor during the threat of war with the United States. A sawmill was built on a stream flowing to Esquimalt, but after 1848 its principal customers were San Franciscans who needed lumber to build houses and commercial establishments for the influx from the California gold rush.

British navy ships *Fisgard, Pandora,* and *Constance* surveyed the harbors at Victoria, Esquimalt, and Sooke in 1846 and produced a detailed map in 1849.

The HBC began hiring people in England to fulfill particular job descriptions and sent them to the new colony. Among the first were the Reverend John Staines and his wife, Emma, to serve as chaplain and jointly as school-teachers to the children of the HBC employees. Staines was instantly annoyed that neither schoolhouse nor church had been provided, so he had to operate out of log cabins. Emma—the only totally white woman in Victoria—did not hide her attitude of superiority toward the half-breed wives of the HBC men.

A bankrupt former army officer, Capt. Walter Grant, was sent to be chief surveyor and to start colonizing by bringing eight men to plant farms. There were two problems with Grant: He knew nothing about surveying, and he knew nothing about farming.

Governor James Douglas

He brought his cricket bats and balls, a library, and two small ornamental brass cannons, but no transit or level.

After several slow and inaccurate surveys, the charming, hard-drinking Grant resigned as surveyor in early March 1850. He did succeed in building a small lumber mill in Sooke that year, but its output was meager. Before leaving in 1853 to rejoin the army, Grant sold his property in Sooke to John Muir, his stalwart wife, Annie, and other members of the Muir family.

The Muirs were a tough breed of Scots who had come in 1849 as coal miners for HBC's Fort Rupert diggings at the northern tip of the island. Their first two years were disasters. Meat on board the HBC ship went bad, and the coal at Fort Rupert was of poor quality. The HBC man in charge jailed two of the Muirs for sedition after they complained about conditions. The Muirs chose to quit mining and buy Grant's land at Sooke and soon had the island's first steam-powered lumber mill producing. Also getting into the lumber business in Metchosin, between Victoria and Sooke, was an HBC ship captain, James Cooper, financed by partner Thomas Blinkhorn. Soon they had a lumber ship running from Victoria to San Francisco on a regular basis.

The worst impediments to settlement in Victoria were the policies of the HBC. The company had reserved a 20-mile radius from Victoria for its own officers to purchase. The price was set at a pound (more than $5) an acre for a minimum plot of one hundred acres, a fairly steep charge intended to attract only gentlemen farmers. Below the border, the American government was virtually giving away land.

The HBC had formed the Puget Sound Agricultural Company, which needed to sell its land south of the border in order to transfer the operation to Vancouver Island, where four large farms were laid out. The theory was that the farms would be operated by squires who brought in families of farmworkers from the British isles. But what the colony needed was hands-on settlers, like HBC retiree John Work, who planted a farm he called Hillside.

THE COLONY OF VANCOUVER ISLAND

With the border question settled, the British government decided to make Vancouver Island a crown colony and leave the mainland under the Colonial Office. Recognizing the control of the island by the Hudson's Bay Company, the government leased the entire island to the HBC at the nominal rate of seven shillings a year (less than $25) for five years with the proviso that the company had to successfully encourage colonization or lose its lease. Constituting the island a British colony also marked the dropping of the name Quadra from its dual label.

Secretary of State for Colonies Earl Grey did not want James Douglas as governor. Officially Grey expressed concern that Douglas was too much the company man, and he would have a conflict of interest as official leader as well as chief factor for the HBC. Unofficially there was also the matter of class prejudice because Douglas was not upper crust—not even close—but a bastard, partially black, Scottish not English, married to a half-breed. A thirty-one-year-old barrister with social connections named Richard Blanshard wanted an appointment that would launch his governmental career. Thus, young Blanshard was appointed the first governor of Vancouver Island Colony on July 9, 1849, and started the long trip around the Horn in September.

Governor Blanshard stepped off the ship *Driver* on March 9, 1850, to read to a handful of sailors and HBC officials the proclamation of formation of the crown colony and his own appointment. The ground underfoot was deep mud, and a light snow flecked his soft mutton-chop whiskers.

Poor Blanshard. By experience and temperament he was ill-suited to the frontier, and much of the time he suffered from the aftereffects of malaria. The real power lay with Douglas since almost everyone worked for the company, and the island was leased by the HBC. After six months as a figurehead, Blanshard sent in his resignation on November 18, 1850, but it took ten months for his request and its acceptance to travel to London and back.

In August 1851, Blanshard appointed a legislative council made up of Douglas as chairman; John Tod, a frontier-tough HBC veteran turned farmer (whose farmhouse in Oak Bay is the oldest building in western Canada still standing); and Captain Cooper. Finally in September 1851, the acceptance of Blanshard's resignation came, and with it the appointment of James Douglas as governor of the Colony of Vancouver Island. The Colonial Office made Blanshard pay his own way home.

Gradually new settlers arrived, some under the misapprehension that this was a land where hard work was not necessary, others as servants, workmen, miners, disappointed California gold rushers, navy men, and those sent by the HBC. A small colony of Hawaiians (called Kanakas), recruited as laborers and household servants, were housed in cabins outside the fort.

Of the four large farms laid out by the Puget Sound Agricultural Society, only two were successful: Constance Cove on the southwest bank of the gorge operated by Thomas Skinner, and the Craigflower sheep-raising station at the head of the gorge set up by PSAS director Kenneth McKenzie. Viewfield Farm, at the western side of the entrance to the inner harbor, was a flop.

Capt. Edward Langford, an ex-officer in charge of the farm at Colwood, built a small mansion on the way to Sooke and was a charming host, especially to naval officers interested in Langford's five pretty daughters, who could play the colony's only piano. Even Douglas sent his daughter Agnes to study at a Langford daughter's academy for young ladies. But as a farmer he never got his hands dirty. Langford is credited with giving Victoria its first flavor of English manners, and he displayed upper-class habits by running up huge bills (seventy gallons of liquor in one year) on credit with the HBC before departing for England in 1861.

More prosperous were the Cadboro Bay Farm (Uplands), run directly by the HBC; the Beckley Farm, cleared south of James Bay; the Ross Farm, east of Beacon Hill Park and developed by the son of the late Charles Ross; and the spreads of Work and Tod.

The James Bay area got its kick start as the neighborhood for homes of the socially prominent when in 1851 Governor Douglas built a two-story house, the first with plastered interior walls, located just behind where the provincial archives building now stands.

DOUGLAS AS GOVERNOR/DICTATOR

Governor Douglas was a virtual dictator who expected the legislative council to rubber stamp his decisions. He faced several challenges besides stimulating immigration. He wanted to build up trade in lumber, coal, and farm products to replace furs as a long-term basis for the island's economy. Vancouver Island needed roads, harbor improvements, and schools for the increasing number of children.

Douglas was unhappy with Reverend Staines, both as God's representative and as an educator, and the antipathy was mutual. Mrs. Douglas was a particular target of the superior airs of the Staineses and a handful of other English snobs. Never mind that Amelia Douglas was attractive, a strict mother, and performed many quiet charities, including serving as midwife to young women, like Mrs. Yates, wife of an HBC ship's carpenter. Mrs. Douglas was also tough, having talked a Carrier Indian band into freeing her husband when she was still in her teens.

Young Dr. John Sebastian Helmcken was not one of the snobs. Two days after Christmas in 1852, he married pretty seventeen-year-old Cecilia Douglas.

Governor Douglas gave them an acre for a house next door to his own property. The Helmcken house still stands by the Royal British Columbia Museum.

James Yates, the former HBC carpenter who owned a popular tavern, objected to paying an annual license fee of 120 pounds. One night his friend Captain Cooper left Yates's place shouting against "taxation without representation" before tumbling facedown in the muddy street. Newcomers shared the sentiment, resenting the assumed power of the HBC to raise revenue, sell property at an inflated price, and rule their lives. Particularly objectionable to entrepreneurs like Cooper was the iron-clad rule against trading with the natives on the mainland.

Amelia Douglas

On February 4, 1854, a public meeting stirred up by Staines, Cooper, Yates, Langford, and Skinner voted to send the Reverend Staines to the Colonial Office in London with a laundry list of grievances, including Douglas's alleged "gross partiality, acrimony, malice, and indecorum." Staines did not get far. The ship *Duchess of San Lorenzo*, on which he sailed, was battered by a storm off Cape Flattery, turned on its side, and foundered. Staines was found a few days later clinging to the wreckage, dead of exposure. The anti-Douglas movement also foundered.

FIRST PEOPLES IN A NEW WHITE WORLD

Douglas managed to keep relations with the natives on a relatively even keel by a mixture of diplomacy, force, justice, and trade and by using friendly native leaders as go-betweens.

In 1850 and 1852 Douglas negotiated treaties with Indian bands to obtain title to much of the land from Sooke to Fort Victoria and beyond. In 1851 he began "buying" land from the First Nations, starting with Saanich, northeast of the fort.

Ownership of specific plots of land was a foreign concept to most Indians, but they eventually were willing to sell the right to "use" much of the land so long as the agreement guaranteed that the existing tribal villages would be exempted and that open land would be available to them for hunting and fishing. In return the tribes received money, blankets, and tools. These were easy terms for the HBC because they were vague and in the long run not strictly honored, since white settlers were allowed to overrun much of the open land.

The basic problem for the First Nations was the breakdown of native society. The rhythm of the seasonal taking of fish, gathering, hunting, and preserving, as well as the making of baskets and carvings, had been interrupted forever. Social classes had been muddled, the role of chiefs and women, for better or worse, confused, and the ancient litanies and ceremonies corrupted. The lure of money offered by sex-starved male settlers and sailors sometimes led the men of a family to force wives, daughters, sisters, and slaves into prostitution. Money, unknown two generations earlier, replaced barter and work.

And there was the disease of hard liquor, unknown on the island until the white man's arrival. Although the official policy of the HBC prohibited sales of liquor to the Indians, it was poorly enforced. Whiskey became the symbol and reality of loss of dignity and self-respect. In this they followed the example of many of the settlers, who all too often had become drunkards. Faced with the end of civilization as they had known it, some natives simply gave up. Nevertheless there survived a strong vein of pride, respect for talent, and eventually revival of First Nations's culture.

One of the first acts of Douglas as governor was to have streets laid out in Victoria in 1851 by thirty-year-old Joseph Despard Pemberton, a trained engineer from Dublin sent by the HBC to replace Grant as chief surveyor. However, the streets were dusty lanes in summer and muddy messes in winter. Within two years there was a total of seventy-nine homes in and around the fort. The nonnative population of the Victoria area was 300 men, women, and children. Another 150 settlers lived elsewhere on the island, including a handful in Sooke and Fort Rupert, and 125 at the new community of Nanaimo (Joseph Pemberton's corruption of the native word *Syn-ny-mo*, which meant "the great and mighty people").

CHIEF COAL'S REWARD

The coal at Fort Rupert was scant and of poor quality. HBC officials let it be known that there would be rewards to anyone, white or Indian, who found new veins. An Indian named Che-wech-i-kan had seen imported coal used in the forge in Victoria, but it took him a year to return to a vein of coal he knew about, load up his canoe, and paddle down to Victoria. HBC trader Joseph

Inside the stockade at Fort Victoria

McKay was sent back with the intrepid native, who took him to Nanaimo Bay, and what became known as the Douglas vein, near the present-day Malaspina Hotel. It was so rich in quality that it was mined for twenty-eight years. For his efforts the Indian received a bottle of whiskey, and McKay gave him the official title of *Tyee Coal* (Chief Coal) for life.

Douglas promptly bought 6,000 acres at Nanaimo for the HBC and rehired John Muir to start up the mine with full authority over its operation. Muir brought his relatives up and within six days sent 4,380 barrels of coal by ship to Fort Victoria. He erected a house, a company store, several other buildings, and the bastion armed with two cannons. Nanaimo produced coal for almost a century, and the sturdy bastion still can be visited. Douglas hoped the coal sales would provide needed revenue, but the market had been overestimated, and nine years later, in 1862, the HBC sold its mining claim to a British corporation, the Vancouver Mining and Land Company.

Three schools, including the still surviving Craigflower School, were built by 1855; they required a nominal fee of $5 or so per year. There were soon other schools, private and parochial (Catholic and Anglican), but the first free schools were built

The Fort Victoria Bastion

in the 1860s and 1870s. Construction of a road between Victoria and Sooke began in 1854. In 1856 colonization was encouraged when the HBC Board in London adopted a plan of installment purchases of land on the island.

Increasingly, warships put in at Esquimalt, and in 1865 it became the Pacific headquarters of the Royal Navy, replacing leased facilities in Valparaiso, Chile. The young naval officers and sailors became a popular addition to the social life of the colony, giving it a distinct English flavor.

THE GOLD MINERS' INVASION

The event that changed Victoria forever was the report of the discovery of gold on the mainland along the Thompson and Fraser Rivers. White settlers in the interior had observed Indians scooping gold from the creek beds, and by 1857 the possibility of wealth from gold was an open "secret" in Victoria.

On April 25, 1858, the first shipload of 450 American gold seekers clambered down from the *Commodore*, paid $5 for a mining "license," loaded up with supplies, and then were ferried to the mainland. Within four months 16,000 hopeful miners poured through Victoria. In response to this American invasion, Douglas decreed, entirely without legal authority, that no American boat could enter the Fraser River carrying liquor or arms without a license issued by the HBC. Then he sent a British gunboat to enforce this ban.

Compared to California's bonanza, the Fraser River gold rush never amounted to much in actual metal taken from the ground, but the influx of people changed the near wilderness to a land of opportunity. Among the immigrants to Victoria in 1858 was a Nova Scotian who had been a California '49er, whose birth name was William Smith. Smith had petitioned the California legislature to change his name to Amor DeCosmos ("lover of the world").

DeCosmos founded a newspaper, the *British Colonist*. The first 150-copy issue was printed in December 1858 and sold for 25 cents. In 1860 the *Colonist* became a daily, making it the oldest daily newspaper on the west coast of North and South America.

Victoria leaped in population from 500 to 5,000 and then slipped back to 1,500 permanent residents by the end of 1859. Stores, the Victoria Hotel (the first hostelry of brick, still standing at 901 Government Street), cafes, and the first theater (1857) had been built. Douglas released lands reserved by the HBC and urged his friends and associates to buy the prime acreage, advice that made several men wealthy.

British Colonial Secretary Bulwer Lytton proposed that the HBC give up its lease of Vancouver Island, which would remain a colony, and a new crown colony would be formed on the mainland called New Caledonia. Queen Victoria rejected New Caledonia as a name and suggested British Columbia instead to make it clear it was British and to avoid confusion with the French island of New Caledonia in the South Pacific.

Lytton agreed to retain Douglas as governor of Vancouver Island and also appoint him governor of British Columbia on condition that Douglas terminate all of his connections with the HBC, including stock, position, and salary.

Thus on August 2, 1858, the bill creating British Columbia was approved; Douglas received his commission as its governor on November 19, 1858. In December he became Sir James Douglas when the Queen conferred on him the Order of the Bath. Replacing Douglas as HBC chief for the west was his son-in-law Alexander Dallas.

A small army of bureaucrats was dispatched by the Colonial Office, including alcoholic George H. Cary as attorney general for Vancouver Island, who would go insane and then die within a half dozen years, and Douglas's implacable political enemy, Capt. James Cooper, as harbor master.

LAW, ORDER, AND JUDGE BEGBIE

With increased population came rowdiness and crime. In 1858 Douglas named farmer August Pemberton, the uncle of surveyor Joseph Pemberton, commissioner of police and magistrate of the police court, to catch and then try drunks, thieves, and hoodlums. At the same time the British government sent Royal Irish Constabulary veteran Chartres Brew to handle law enforcement on the mainland. Pemberton would later marry Brew's sister.

Judge Matthew Begbie, 1859

The legislative council adopted what may have been the first gun control ordinance in the new world, a ban on "belt guns," which the Victoria police enforced against the Americans who arrived with revolvers on their hips. When a band of San Francisco criminals known as "the forty thieves" landed, police commissioner Pemberton and his handful of constables rounded them up and threw them onto the first ship back to California.

Douglas began his dual administration by appointing magistrates of his new domain to handle lesser civil cases and criminal matters. In those areas that were primarily native territory, Douglas named natives to these positions, an unusual show of faith in the First Nations. However, a judicial system designed and administered by someone with legal knowledge was a necessity.

The most notable appointment from England was Matthew Baillie Begbie, as chief judge for the new colony of British Columbia, who was instructed to bring law and order to the mining country. A thirty-nine-year-old civil lawyer who had never seen the inside of a criminal courtroom, Begbie was a strongly built 6 feet, 4 inch man with a well-kept beard and piercing eyes. Although considered inconsistent by legal purists, Judge Begbie brought respect for the law and fear to those who did not show respect. For several years he rode circuit, often accompanied by police inspector Brew, holding court wherever the crime was charged.

Begbie could be a terror in the courtroom. When a jury voted to bring in a verdict of manslaughter instead of murder against an American shooter, Judge Begbie called the jurors a pack of horse thieves who deserved to hang. To a prisoner acquitted after being charged with killing a man in a barroom brawl: "Go, and sandbag some of the jurymen! They deserve it!" Once a drunken miner tried to pick a fight with the judge in a frontier tavern. Begbie knocked him cold with one punch.

Judge Begbie stayed on the bench until 1894, becoming chief justice of the combined colonies of British Columbia and Vancouver Island and of the province when the colony became part of Canada. During the thirteen years he personally conducted trials, he sent twenty-seven men to the gallows, twenty-two of whom were Indians. Nine of the hangings were performed publicly in front of the Victoria police station.

In 1875 he was knighted, and in 1877 he built a large house in the Fairfield area with three tennis courts, a sport he vigorously promoted and played. He never married. He was a founder of both the Victoria Philharmonic Society (1859) and the Union Club (1879). His funeral in 1894 was one of the largest in Victoria's history. The law school at University of Victoria is named for him.

Peter O'Reilly, a tall former official of the Irish Revenue Police, showed up in Victoria in 1859 with nothing but a letter of recommendation from the British secretary of state. Douglas promptly sent young O'Reilly deep into the mainland as a magistrate and assistant gold commissioner. Upon his arrival in Kootenay Valley, magistrate O'Reilly announced to the assembled populace, "Now, boys, there must be no shooting, for if there is shooting there will surely be hanging."

Young John Carmichael Haynes, a former constable for Brew, was appointed justice of the peace. He promptly made his reputation by riding into a mining town and single-handedly stopping a 1,000-man lynch mob bent on hanging a man who turned out to be innocent. Henry Crease served more than a decade as attorney general for the colony, and in 1870 joined Begbie on the Supreme Court. In both positions he was tough on miscreants.

"Never in the pacification and settlement of any section of America have there been so few disturbances, so few crimes against law and order," wrote H. H. Bancroft, the great on-the-scene western historian, about Victoria and British Columbia during their frontier days.

English civil engineer Joseph Trutch and his American wife, Julia, landed in Victoria in May 1859. Douglas gave Trutch lucrative contracts as surveyor of the lower Fraser River, for construction of the Cariboo Road and a bridge over the Fraser with part-payment being the right to collect tolls for seven years.

Benjamin Pearse purchased 300 acres northeast of the fort before he turned thirty and in 1860 built the first mansion outside of the James Bay neighborhood, which he called Fernwood, at the corner of Fort and Fernwood. Beacon Hill Park was set aside for public recreation, and soon there were a cricket field, a horse race-track, and a seven-hole golf course on its grounds.

THE BIRDCAGES, THE PIG WAR, AND PREJUDICE

To house the government of Victoria Island, five buildings were erected on the south side of the Inner Harbour in 1859, using the colonial design commonly employed in the Orient. Painted in deep red with white trim and ornamented with filigree and pagoda-like roofs, they were promptly nicknamed "the Bird-cages." A bridge across the east end of James Bay was constructed the same year to extend Government Street between downtown and the new buildings.

In June 1859, an American settler on San Juan Island shot an HBC-owned pig. The HBC demanded that the American be fined and forced to pay for the pig, but the shooter claimed that there was no fine under American law. At stake

The Birdcages (old Parliament buildings)

was whether English or American law governed, and the two squads of soldiers—British camped at one end of the island and American at the other—were ready to enforce the law as they saw it. American reinforcements were sent from Oregon, and their captain declared this was "United States territory." The British countered with two navy steamers anchored off San Juan Island. What became known as the Pig War was settled before it escalated further when Gen. Winfield Scott, chief of staff of the U.S. Army, arrived in November to negotiate with Governor Douglas. The joint authority over the San Juans continued.

The American Fugitive Slave Act and the Dred Scott decision of the Supreme Court placed blacks in free states in constant jeopardy of being awarded to owners from slave states. This prompted a letter to Governor Douglas from a group of blacks in San Francisco asking if they would be welcome on Vancouver Island. The answer was yes. Thus thirty-five black Americans booked passage to Victoria on the first ship of gold seekers from California. In thanks for this hospitality, at the time of the Pig War forty-three black Americans created the Victoria Pioneer Rifle Company, commonly called the African Rifles. They trained in natty uniforms from England.

Many of the black immigrants became pillars of the community. Peter Lester and Mifflin Gibbs established Lester & Gibbs, which quickly matched the HBC store as a retail market in the city. Wellington Moses and his wife hosted a boardinghouse on Fort Street that catered to English women who demanded quality. Escaped slave Sam Ringo owned Ringo's, a popular restaurant on Yates Street.

Gibbs was elected three times to the city council. Like many of the other Americans, a majority of the black community returned to the United States by the end of the 1860s, including Gibbs. Within three years of his return he was elected the first black judge in the United States. Unlike the Hawaiians who lived in cabins along Humboldt Street and the Chinese community centered on Fisgard Street, the blacks lived wherever they wanted, including a group that settled on Salt Spring Island.

Despite the fact that many of the Chinese merchants were very successful and Chinese servants were managing Caucasian households, the Chinese were subjects of discrimination. Later the city of Victoria adopted a policy that no Chinese could be hired by the city, and a provincial $50 head tax on each Chinese immigrant was imposed in 1885. It eventually escalated to $500.

A smallpox epidemic in 1862 killed a third of the Indian population of the island. It started at their annual summer gathering at the Songhee settlement on

Wharf Street from Fort Street, 1860s

the west side of the Gorge and spread to native villages in the north. Europeans and Americans who contracted smallpox usually recovered with damaged complexions, but it was often fatal for natives.

That same year, two bride ships sponsored by the Anglican Church arrived, carrying women from England and Australia via San Francisco, most of whom were seeking husbands among the successful miners, and some of whom came to ply an ancient profession. Both groups were generally successful.

VICTORIA IN TRANSITION

San Francisco businesses flooded in, including Wells Fargo stagecoaches and the Union Iron Works, manufacturer of locomotives, girders, and railroad tracks. Victoria's first cast-iron piers were used in construction of the building at 1127 Wharf Street and 15 Bastion Square. The piers are stamped "P. Donahue," president of Union Iron Works.

Brick buildings on Wharf Street replaced the wooden structures that had been used in the 1850s. The hastily raised tents of 1858 and 1859 were no more.

Government Street from the corner of Fort Street, 1866

City streets were improved, but oil and gravel would await the turn of the twentieth century. A bridge spanning the Gorge for a road to Sooke and beyond was built at Point Ellice.

The city of Victoria was incorporated and the first municipal election held on August 16, 1862. By a show of hands a gathering of some 400 voters elected as mayor Thomas Harris, a sports-loving butcher who weighed 300 pounds. At the first council meeting, when Harris sat down his chair collapsed under his weight. Despite this inauspicious start, the city council attacked a series of problems, such as pollution. The location of privies and the hours for transportation of what was euphemistically called night soil were limited, slaughterhouses and tanneries were outlawed within city limits, and downtown buildings were restricted to one story.

Natural gas from the Victoria Gas Company lit its first store in September 1862, and a short time later it began installing streetlights. In 1863 the Albion Iron Works was founded. The Spring Ridge Water Company prepared plans in 1864 to deliver water into the city from a nearby spring through pipes made of hollowed logs. That same year, telegraph lines from the east reached the west coast, delivering messages and news in minutes instead of months. A connecting Atlantic cable followed in 1866.

On the mainland, the gold in the Fraser River and Cariboo area had pretty much played out by 1864, and the miners headed back to the United States, causing an economic depression in Victoria. There was a brief flurry of gold fever when an exploration party found some of the metal west of Sooke that same year. This Leechtown strike petered out in a single season.

Adding to the town's economic woes was the collapse of Macdonald's Bank and a loss of $100,000 to its depositors. Originally an HBC employee, the charming and young Alexander Macdonald had founded the bank and built a mansion on Michigan Street. While he was conveniently on the mainland, a burglary of the bank was apparently staged by Macdonald in collusion with an employee to cover up the bank's insolvency. Macdonald soon skipped town in the middle of the night on a departing ship.

On the positive economic side were discoveries of additional rich veins of coal near Nanaimo and the construction of a lumber mill at Alberni Inlet. Starting in 1859, Governor Douglas issued several proclamations that made land available to settlers at reasonable prices. Potential farmers colonized the Saanich Peninsula as early as 1858, and by 1862 they began settling the Cowichan Valley over the hills from Victoria, the Comox Valley north of Nanaimo, and Salt Spring and Gabriola Islands. Coal mines attracted men to Courtenay and other small communities that sprang up along the east coast of the island.

March 1864 marked the end of an era as Sir James Douglas's terms as governor of the two colonies expired. He retired with almost universal praise and a gala civic banquet. To replace Douglas, the British Colonial Office chose two career colonial officials: courtly Arthur Kennedy for Vancouver Island and bumptious Frederick Seymour for British Columbia. Kennedy shepherded the Common School Act for free education through the Vancouver Island Assembly. The British Parliament adopted an act merging the two colonies as British Columbia, officially proclaimed on November 19, 1866. London chose Seymour as the governor of the unified colony.

VICTORIA WINS OUT

Seymour had the power to declare New Westminster, on the mainland, the colony's capital, but he tossed the ball to the combined legislative council, with the recommendation that New Westminster be chosen. For Victoria it was do or die. To avoid the economic dustbin, the city needed the spending that government offices would bring and the prestige as the chief city of the colony.

Dr. John Sebastian Helmcken

Dr. Helmcken introduced a resolution in the council proposing Victoria as the capital, and after a daylong debate, Victoria won by a vote of thirteen to eight. Governor Seymour maneuvered a new vote of the council, for which advocates of New Westminster had been lobbying. William Franklyn from Nanaimo was to give a prepared speech favoring New Westminster, calling Victoria "Nanaimo's cruel stepmother." This break in the ranks of Vancouver Islanders could sway two more uncertain votes and spell disaster for Victoria. Dr. Helmcken made sure Franklyn had a few drinks, and his seatmate, William Cox, first shuffled the pages of Franklyn's speech and then picked up Franklyn's eyeglasses and surreptitiously removed the lenses. Half-drunk and unable to read, Franklyn stumbled to a halt after a few sentences. A bemused council again voted for Victoria.

The same week Victoria became the provincial capital, the British Parliament passed the British North American Act, creating the Dominion of Canada, composed of Lower Canada (Quebec), Upper Canada (Ontario), New Brunswick, and Nova Scotia, effective July 1, 1867. The same day the North American Act was adopted, American Secretary of State William Seward signed a treaty with Russia for the purchase of Alaska, which put British Columbia in a pincers between American territories.

Governor Seymour sank into chronic alcoholism. He fell ill of dysentery, died on June 10, 1869, and was buried at the naval base in Esquimalt. Seymour was replaced by Anthony Musgrave, governor of Newfoundland, who was instructed to promote the entry of British Columbia into Canada.

In Victoria, Amor DeCosmos was an outspoken proponent of joining the Dominion—at first in his *Colonist* (which he had sold) and later in the pages of his new paper, the *Standard;* as a

Amor DeCosmos

member of the legislative council; and as an organizer of the Confederation League. On the other side, forty-four Americans petitioned President Ulysses S. Grant to propose the annexation of British Columbia by the United States. In the meantime, with the admission of Manitoba as a province, the western border of Canada moved closer.

Governor Musgrave sent a message to the legislative council at the Birdcages on February 16, 1870, asking for union with Canada provided the national government assumed the colony's debt, guaranteed some internal improvements, and "if a railway could be promised." After three days of debate the opponents were satisfied, and on March 12 the proposal passed unanimously.

During the debate Dr. Helmcken predicted that "the United States will probably ultimately absorb both this Colony and the Dominion of Canada." Nevertheless, Musgrave appointed Helmcken, together with B.C. lands and works commissioner Joseph Trutch and Dr. Robert Carrall from the Cariboo, to negotiate with the Canadian government about conditions of joinder. Helmcken became more enthusiastic about a Canadian rail line as they rode the train across the American prairie.

They fared much better than anticipated. If British Columbia would join Canada, the colony's debt would be paid, Esquimalt would be the naval base with a new dry dock, the B.C. legislative council would become a more popularly elected body, and the province's population for subsidies and parliamentary representation would be initially counted almost double (60,000 instead of 36,000) by including Indians and Chinese. And best of all, the government agreed to finance a railroad to the west to begin in two years and be completed in ten. The railroad promise was made even though there were no surveys of potential routes, no known usable passes over the Rockies, no organization to design or build the rail line, and no decision as to the location of the western terminal.

BRITISH COLUMBIA JOINS CANADA

The Canadian Act incorporating British Columbia into Canada passed in March 1871 was confirmed in May by the Queen, with July 20, 1871, set as the incorporation day. At midnight of July 19 in Victoria bells were rung, Roman candles and other fireworks shot off, and crowds cheered themselves hoarse. The *Colonist* called it "the Birth of Liberty." One side effect of confederation was that the national government took over administration of Indian affairs and promptly prohibited the natives from commercial fishing.

Joseph Trutch was appointed lieutenant governor for British Columbia (under the governor general for Canada), the Crown's representative on the scene. Voting franchise was granted to all males, and an election of twenty-five members of the legislative assembly was conducted. However, the right of native Indians and Chinese to vote was canceled by legislation in 1874. After immigration began from Japan and India, the vote was denied to those of Japanese ancestry (1895) and to East Indians (1907).

Canada's first prime minister, John A. Macdonald, and Trutch both wanted Helmcken as premier of the new province, but the doctor, a widower with three children to raise, declined. Instead Trutch chose lawyer John Foster McCreight, who proved ill-suited due to his bad temper and meager knowledge of politics. For thirty years there were no political parties in British Columbia, and on national issues the voters leaned toward whatever helped the province.

The Reverend Edward Cridge was sent from London in 1854 to replace the unfortunate Staines as minister for the Church of England. By 1856 he had built the mother church for both colonies. Dean Cridge was never one to avoid controversy in support of what he believed. He welcomed the American blacks who arrived in 1858 and resisted the efforts of some of his flock who wanted them seated in segregated pews. Later he stormed out of a new church built for his congregation when he disagreed with the liturgical philosophy of the minister sent by the bishop to give the inaugural sermon. The result was an unseemly dispute with Anglican bishop George Hills, who had Cridge locked out. In 1876 Cridge founded the Reformed Episcopal Anglican Church, built on property donated by Douglas.

The Catholics, first on the scene in 1843, built a church in Esquimalt in 1847, followed by a small church in Victoria (a shack plastered by the priest himself) in 1853. That year, Father Modeste Demers became bishop for Vancouver Island and arrived by canoe from the American shore of Puget Sound. Demers erected the first St. Andrew's in 1858. Father Augustin Brabant lived with the Nootka people for many years, and Father Peter Rondeault canoed to Cowichan Bay, where he constructed a stone church with the help of Indian laborers in 1864. The United Church of Canada, the Presbyterians, the Baptists, and the Methodists were all established in Victoria by 1863.

In 1862 the Jewish community, which had grown through immigration from San Francisco, built Temple Emanuel. Today it is the oldest synagogue in continuous service in North America and the second-oldest congregation in the west (San Francisco's Temple Emanu-El is the oldest). Most of the residents of Victoria attended the cornerstone-laying ceremony in a show of ecumenical goodwill.

Husky Methodist missionary Thomas Crosby, with the voice of a prophet, toured the island tirelessly in a crusade against alcohol and the whiskey dealers who sold to the Indians. His other targets were the continued practice of slavery by some Indian tribes and the sale of their teenage daughters to the lonely miners, millworkers, and farmers—often at an age that would make it a crime in most societies.

While often this form of concubinage would end with the unfortunate girl abandoned when the weather turned warm or the "husband" wanted to move on, in some cases the relationships blossomed and became permanent marriages—how many, no one knows. As the old Northwesters had learned, Indian women more often than not were hardworking, agreeable companions.

FARMING, LUMBERING, MINING

Settlers, some of them squatters on unoccupied land, began various forms of agriculture. Dairies, cattle and sheep ranches, vegetable gardens, and potato and hay fields sprinkled the countryside from Victoria, through the Saanich Peninsula, Cowichan Valley, Chemainus, Nanaimo, and north to Comox Valley. Roads were actually just trails over hills and through forests, so farm products usually came to Victoria by boat.

Serious lumbering began to take hold, starting with clearing the forests for farms and communities, building sawmills and then selling lumber to builders in Victoria and the towns, and finally shipping wood products for foreign purchase.

The first large mill was constructed at Alberni (now Port Alberni) at the head of Alberni Inlet, with seventy workers under the direction of manager Gilbert Malcolm Sproat (for whom Sproat Lake is named). It was ideal because ships could sail all the way into the heart of the forest up the inlet from the west coast. However, within a few years the hills around the mill had been denuded of timber, and without transportation farther into the woods there were no more trees for the mill, and it closed down.

That became the pattern for the early lumber business. A site by the coast or a convenient harbor would become a lumber bonanza and then be clear-cut before being abandoned for a new available forest. There seemed to be an unlimited supply of cedar, Douglas fir (named for botanist David Douglas, who explored the island around 1830), pine, oak, and other valuable timber. More than a half dozen towns flourished until the timber was gone, and then the lumber company would move on to a new forest, leaving a rotting ghost town in its wake. Chemainus proved to be an exception, where a mill operated from 1862 to 1983.

The biggest industry was coal mining, reaching a million tons a year before the end of the nineteenth century. And the biggest man in coal was Robert Dunsmuir. Promising his wife a castle if she would accompany him, Dunsmuir came from Scotland in 1851 as an HBC mine manager at Fort Rupert. He stayed on to supervise operations for the British company that bought the HBC mines in Nanaimo. In 1869 he discovered the Wellington coal field, established an instant coal empire, and became a robber baron in the mold of Americans like John D. Rockefeller and Andrew Carnegie. Dunsmuir built company towns, got elected to the provincial legislature against a candidate backed by his employees, hired cheap Chinese labor, and was more concerned with profit than mining safety.

Explosions, cave-ins, and accidents occurred in the mines with depressing regularity, but promised improvements were not forthcoming. A strike of miners in 1877 for a 20 percent raise in wages was put down with the help of government troops who evicted miners from their homes. When the miners returned to work, their pay was slashed. On May 3, 1887, 150 out of 157 men on the afternoon shift were killed in an explosion at Number One mine at Nanaimo. The flag on the Nanaimo bastion is still flown at half-mast every May 3. The Japanese government sent a consul to investigate the conditions at the mines of R. Dunsmuir & Sons in 1891 and recommended that the 500 young Japanese miners leave. Some 373 men were killed in the mines between 1884 and 1912.

WADDY'S DREAM

All of British Columbia wanted the promised transcontinental railroad, but Victorians felt passionately that the western terminal had to be at Victoria in order to retain its status as Canada's western port. The dream of a western terminus in Victoria—or more accurately, across the gorge at Esquimalt—had sprung full-blown from the mind of Alfred Waddington, an inveterate crusader, who came north from San Francisco after making a small fortune in the gold rush. "Waddy" was a character, second only to DeCosmos, who fought for government reform with a flood of pamphlets. Once the province was unified, he was elected to the Assembly.

In 1864 he struck on the novel idea of a railroad hopping across the islands from Bute Inlet on the mainland to a point on Vancouver Island near Campbell River and then south to Esquimalt. Obsessed with his scheme, over the next eight years he spent much of his fortune on his own survey crews and cutting a path just

Alfred Waddington, crusader

east of his chosen inlet, combined with trips to Ottawa and London to sell his idea. No matter that his cuts collapsed and nineteen of his survey crew were massacred in revenge for raping several Indian women.

Within days after Prime Minister Macdonald promised to start building a transcontinental railroad in two years, the national government authorized twenty-one survey parties to search out a right-of-way west from Winnipeg and a practical pass over the Rocky Mountains. Over the next few years the leaders of the various surveying teams argued for their favorite routes. There were tales of heroism and endurance high in the mountains, but no decision. Remarkably, the most suitable and southerly opening in the mountains—Kicking Horse Pass—had been discovered by geologist Dr. James Hector as early as 1857, but it was ignored because Dr. Hector had been badly hurt by a landslide at the site (he was so seriously injured that Indian workers started to bury him), and it was an English and not Canadian expedition.

Never mind the details or the hazards, Victoria had fallen in love with Waddington's plan as an alternative to terminating the railroad on the mainland.

Prime Minister Macdonald was challenged in the next election by the Liberal Party, led by Scottish-born stonemason Alexander Mackenzie (no relation to the explorer), in 1872, and he needed the support of Victoria parliamentary seats—which he got. In a cynical payoff, exactly two years after admission of British Columbia, Macdonald's government again declared that Esquimalt would be the terminus and arranged for an official celebration there of the "first turn of sod" for the terminal, delighting Victorians. The dignitaries then went home and waited.

Macdonald was voted out, and Mackenzie, who said the railroad promise to British Columbia was "insanity," was chosen prime minister in January 1874. The result was that only segments of the railroad would be built in the east. Victorians and British Columbians in general felt betrayed. Emotions ran high, particularly since the nation was suffering from an economic depression. Waddington died of smallpox in 1872, but his scheme lived on.

That same year, German Kaiser Wilhelm, acting as independent arbiter, ruled that the border between the state of Washington and British Columbia (the decision of which had been put on hold since 1846) would run through the channel just 10 miles south of Saanich, instead of the midpoint in the Strait of Juan de Fuca, thereby awarding the San Juan Islands to the United States. The Americans had won the Pig War at the arbitration table.

RAILROAD POLITICS

Amor DeCosmos, his beard and hair tinted with black dye, replaced the testy John Foster McCreight—who had punched out a legislator—as B.C. premier in December 1872. When Mackenzie and the Liberals took power, DeCosmos decided to become pragmatic for once in his career. Figuring the railroad to British Columbia would be delayed for the foreseeable future, he negotiated a tentative deal with the national government: If it would build a dry dock at Esquimalt to increase naval business, then DeCosmos would relent on holding the national government to the "terms of union" and waive the guarantee of a ten-year completion date for the railroad.

The "Lover of the World" had badly miscalculated hometown sentiment. When he presented his proposal to the Assembly on February 7, 1874, 800 Victorians gathered downtown to denounce it. Led by Dr. Helmcken and Senator William MacDonald from Victoria, the mob poured across the James Bay Bridge and invaded the Birdcages. The Assembly Speaker and DeCosmos fled to the Speaker's office, where they were locked in. Taking over the Assembly, the

The Inner Harbour, 1870s

protesters formed the Terms of Union Preservation League on the spot. DeCosmos promptly resigned. His successor as premier, George A. Walkem, although from the mainland, backed the Esquimalt terminus and called DeCosmos a man who had "all the eccentricities of a comet without any of its brilliance."

Governor General Lord Frederick Dufferin decided an official tour by the Queen's representative might be helpful, and he and his wife arrived at the Esquimalt harbor on August 16, 1876. Socially their visit was a success, with ten days of parties, Indian canoe races, a tour of the island, and driving the first piling for the promised dry dock. But politically Lord Dufferin found the hearts of Victoria hardened.

The week after Lord Dufferin left, the B.C. legislature voted nineteen to nine in favor of a resolution to secede from Canada. When the resolution reached London, it was shelved. Annexation to the United States was openly discussed. Nevertheless, on July 22, 1878, Prime Minister Mackenzie chose the mainland Burrard Inlet (near present-day Vancouver) as terminus for the railroad.

Waddington's scheme was a dead duck.

While the hope of a city died, so did its founder, on August 3, 1877. Sir James Douglas was laid to rest after a funeral at Dean Cridge's new church, with hundreds lining the route of the procession. The *Colonist* editorialized: "Today a whole province is in tears."

Victoria built a new city hall in 1878 when Roderick Finlayson was mayor. Six years later the city almost lost the building to a man owed $25,000 by the municipal government. Victoria officials had carelessly allowed the creditor to obtain a default judgment from the court, and in December 1884 a public sheriff's sale of the building was held. As the bidding opened, Joseph Spratt, head of Albion Iron Works, jumped up and announced that he would pay the judgment provided that no one else bid up the price. Spratt, representing a group of thirteen citizens, stared around, daring anyone to challenge his offer. No one did, and the city hall was saved.

VICTORIA COMES OF AGE

The 1880s became a decade of modernization for Victoria. The city acquired Beacon Hill Park from the province and began a century of planting, lake creation, and laying paths to augment the existing greenery and playing fields. A telephone system with one hundred subscribers opened (1880), water from dammed-up Elk Lake reached Victoria (1881), electricity to businesses became available (1882), electric streetlighting began replacing gas lights (1883), a new wooden bridge for wagon traffic was built across the Gorge at Point Ellice (1885), firemen began to be paid (1886), a provincial museum was set up in the Birdcages (1886), the first public lavatory was built—men only—at Bastion Square (1888), home mail delivery was initiated (1888), construction commenced on the Jubilee Hospital (1889), and installation of a city sewer system was begun to replace privies and septic tanks (1890). A second newspaper, the *Daily Times,* appeared in 1884.

Victoria's first renowned artist was Phoebe Pemberton (daughter of surveyor general Joe Pemberton), who studied in London and was the first woman to be awarded a gold medal in Paris. Some of her classic works can be viewed at the Art Gallery of Greater Victoria. In the last half of the nineteenth century, Victoria's leading photographer was a woman, Hannah Maynard, who specialized in portraits, street scenes, Indians, and news events.

The First Nations's traditional potlatch was declared illegal by the Canadian national government in 1884, on the grounds that these celebrations led to wastefulness and wanton revelry. Provincial Chief Justice Begbie ruled against strict enforcement of the ban, but the Canadian parliament passed an amended statute to thwart his judicial interference.

Canadian Pacific Railroad workmen (including more than 6,000 Chinese), directed by American engineer Andrew Onderdonk, scraped, dug, and blasted their way through the British Columbia mountains and down the Fraser River Canyon to complete the linkup with the national railroad, which had crept across the plains from Winnipeg. The last spike was driven on November 7, 1885, and the first train from Montreal pulled into Fort Moody, a few miles east of the water's edge, on July 4, 1886.

DUNSMUIR BUILDS AN EMPIRE

Construction of the promised Esquimalt and Nanaimo Railway was held up by lack of federal will, lack of financing, and inability to find a company willing to tackle the job. Finally, in 1884, coal king Robert Dunsmuir put together a syndicate, including San Franciscan Charles Crocker, and haggled his way with the national government into a contract with a $750,000 subsidy *and* two million acres of Vancouver Island land. Farms, mills, mines, and formerly isolated communities were now connected with Victoria. The coming of the E & N spawned the town of Duncan in the Cowichan Valley.

Joan Dunsmuir got the castle promised by her husband, for in 1887 he ordered the construction of a baronial monument to his success on a commanding hill in the Rockland neighborhood, which he called Craigdarroch Castle. Dunsmuir died in 1889 just before the castle's completion, leaving behind a nasty legal fight between Joan and son James over ownership. Their other son, Alexander, was in California representing company interests, founding the town of Dunsmuir, building a mansion in Oakland, and drinking himself to death.

In addition to King Coal, Vancouver Island's economy received a boost by the growth of the fish-canning industry in the 1880s, using Indian women and Chinese at starvation wages. The industry produced more than a million cans a year at its peak. By 1920 it became evident that the salmon catch was dropping due to overfishing in spawning rivers such as the Fraser. Large stands of timber were opened up to lumber-company blades by the building of new roads, the development of such coastal ports as Port Renfrew, and the installation of short-line railroads from the forest to the coast beginning in Chemainus in 1900, followed by a railway to Port Alberni.

SNUGGLING AND SMUGGLING

There were other businesses operating in Victoria. Prostitution had first begun in the Victoria area with Indian female slaves. Soon there was an infusion of women from California, several of whom became madams operating houses and strings of girls. A third wave consisted of Chinese women, the virtual slaves of Chinese men who had country girls shipped in. White-slave rings of kidnapped or misled women from Europe added to the mix.

The legislature decided to license the houses as dance halls rather than shut them down. A report by the Victoria chief of police to the city council in 1886 listed fourteen known brothels on Broad, Broughton, and Wharf Streets with at least fifty-two prostitutes. Reputedly a tunnel ran from the exclusive Union Club to one of the houses. In addition, there were more than one hundred Chinese courtesans on Fisgard, some Indians, and freelancers. Bawdy houses operated openly in Port Alberni and Nanaimo.

Polite society chose to turn a blind eye. Many of the women managed to marry their way out of the profession and take a proper place in the community, so no one wished to look too closely into personal histories. Eventually the prostitutes were forced into a red-light district rivaling San Francisco's Barbary Coast—with one-dollar girls on Chatham Street and three-dollar girls on Herald Street. In 1907 a fire swept the area, only temporarily shutting down business. In 1910 there was an official abatement of the district, which scattered rather than stopped prostitution.

Some things never change. In February 1998 the Victoria police reported in the *Times-Colonist* that its principal concerns in regard to prostitution were protecting streetwalkers from assault and making sure that runaways of the ages "twelve, thirteen, and fourteen" were not involved in the "sex trade."

Avoidance of American import duties led to smuggling of everything from lumber to liquor from coves around Victoria to Washington state. After the United States adopted Asian exclusion policies, Chinese men wishing to get into the United States were carried across the sound in fishing boats but might be tossed overboard if an American cutter approached. These smugglers were a rough bunch who did not hesitate to beat or kill anyone crossing them. Author Jack London patterned the title character of *The Sea Wolf* after Capt. Alex McLean, one of the most vicious.

Opium was a major smuggled commodity since it could be produced legally in Victoria in fourteen factories (some in Fan Tan Alley) and sent to the United States, where the drug was illegal. Women's bustles were a favorite place to transport the opium, since hardly anyone would search a woman. In 1908 opium production was outlawed in Canada, and the open factories closed.

In 1890 the first electric streetcar lines were laid up Government and Douglas Streets from Fort Street to Hillside, and out to the new Jubilee Hospital at Richmond and Cadboro Bay Roads as well as to the Willows Hotel, fairground, sports fields, and exhibition hall nearby. Within a year the rails were extended beyond the hills to Oak Bay, and over the bridge across the Gorge at Point Ellice to Esquimalt. During the following dozen years, a web of streetcar lines linked all of Victoria. The easy transportation stimulated the growth of posh developments along Rockland Avenue and in Oak Bay. Victoria's official population swelled to 21,735 by 1891. Victoria's streets became macadamized in stages beginning in the late 1890s.

The Victoria and Sidney railroad up the Saanich Peninsula was inaugurated in 1896, but it closed down when an electric interurban line opened in 1913. It lasted only a decade, but a Canadian National Railways line ran between Victoria and Sidney from 1917 to 1935. They were both victims of the popularity of the automobile and improved roads. However, they made movement to these suburbs practical and popular.

The Victoria Theatre (later the Royal) opened in 1885; 1893 saw the founding of the Victoria Yacht Club and the Victoria Golf Club. The first primitive

Government Street at Fort Street, 1890s

movie theater, the Searchlight, opened its doors in 1897. At the turn of the twentieth century, Klondike gold instant millionaire Alex Pantages started the Pantages, the first of his famous chain of vaudeville houses and theaters across the United States and Canada.

A four-day celebration of Queen Victoria's birthday was winding up on May 26, 1896, with a regatta and mock battle staged on the far side of the Gorge. Streetcar Number 16, crowded with 140 sightseers—double its seating capacity—made its swaying way to the Point Ellice Bridge. Conductor George Farr joked, "If we get over the bridge, we'll be lucky." A few seconds later the center span of the bridge collapsed, catapulting Number 16 into the water. Fifty-five passengers (including Farr) died in the wreck, despite heroic efforts of holiday boaters. The Point Ellice disaster holds the dubious distinction of being the worst streetcar accident in the history of North America.

In 1906 some 243 property owners in the Oak Bay area petitioned the city of Victoria to be annexed, but they were turned down. Thus Oak Bay incorporated as a city in July of that year, made up of the Uplands farm (which was developed into 523 lots with paved roads, underground utilities, and strict landscaping requirements) and lands of families of pioneers Tod, Pemberton,

Point Ellice streetcar disaster, May 26, 1896

McNeill, and Ross. Edwardian-style homes were built there for several decades, starting in the 1880s.

Saanich was also incorporated as a city that same year, and Esquimalt followed in 1912.

THE GARDEN CITY

Twenty-five-year-old architect Francis Mawson Rattenbury stepped ashore at Victoria with a satchel full of drawings from his uncle's London firm and a head full of dreams of big designs. A month later the provincial government announced a competition for the design of a large Parliament building to replace the Birdcages. Remarkably, Rattenbury won the competition over fifty-eight entries from other architects, all of them older and more experienced, with a design that made it obvious that he had a clear understanding of what made a building monumental.

He soon became a favorite of the Canadian Pacific Railroad, which employed his talents for thirty years. He also designed major additions to Parliament between 1911 and 1916.

Victoria made a conscious decision at the turn of the twentieth century to play to its strength: tourism. Herbert Cuthbert founded the Tourist Development Association in 1901, which he ran for fifteen years with the support of city businesses.

Francis Rattenbury

Victorians lived up to their self-created legend. In April 1903, the Tally Ho horse-drawn tourist carriages clopped around the city streets for the first time. The cluster streetlights made their appearance in 1911. In 1937 the city council began providing and funding the now traditional hanging flower baskets. English-style double-decker buses, rickshaws, and boats for water tours became part of the Victoria scene.

The Canadian Pacific expanded into all phases of travel, beginning with the purchase of coastal passenger ships with *Princess* names as well as three sleek liners to cross the Pacific. In 1891 the CPR's *Empress of India* landed at Victoria to great fanfare after crossing the Pacific from Yokohama, Japan, in just ten days. The CPR also purchased the E & N Railroad in 1905 and began planning a hotel with more than 500 rooms on James Bay, to be named the Empress.

Buying the marshland east of the bridge, the CPR filled it in, drove wooden pilings down to bedrock, and then convinced the city to build a causeway to replace the bridge, thus completing the site for the hotel. Francis Rattenbury was the obvious choice as the architect. The Empress immediately became a symbol of the city's English elegance ("high tea at the Empress"). Since it opened in 1908 it has played hostess to King George VI, Queen Elizabeth, Winston Churchill, Franklin D. Roosevelt, Princess Margaret, the King of Siam, and thousands of other notables.

Jenny Butchart wanted to beautify the land-scarring pit left from the limestone quarry that her husband, Robert—a cement baron—had pioneered on their large estate overlooking Tod Inlet. When the excavation was exhausted in 1904, the Butcharts began carting in soil and planting flowers, trees, shrubs, and lawns until the Butchart Gardens became a forty-acre expanse of floral beauty open to the public.

Nature did not always cooperate with Victoria. There were major fires in the city in 1883, 1904, and 1907, mostly destroying old wooden structures. During the night of October 26–27, 1910, several square blocks of downtown along Government and Broad Streets between Trounce Alley and Fort Street burned down. The snowstorm of the century that fell in February 1916 clogged the streets, knocked streetcars off their tracks, and paralyzed the city. In the winter of 1996–97, another fluke snowstorm stopped almost everything in Victoria for several days because its snowplows had been sold in 1990.

"The Graveyard of the Pacific" is an apt name for the seas north and south of the entrance of the Strait of Juan de Fuca, because at least 130 ships were sunk or shipwrecked along the Vancouver Island coast and the Strait. The worst sinking was the *Pacific*, an American side-wheeler, which went down in a collision in 1870 with a loss of 275 lives and only two survivors.

In 1906 the *Valencia*, a steamship from San Francisco, missed the Strait and crashed onto the rocks at Shelter Bight on the western shore of the island. It took two days for the ship to break up and sink, with no help from the uninhabited 60-foot cliffs above. Since there were no means to reach them in time, 136 passengers drowned. The shock of this tragedy prompted the province to carve out the 47-mile-long West Coast Trail from Port Renfrew in the south to the fishing hamlet of Bamfield at Alberni Inlet. Although a rugged hiking trail, it was passable to bring help and for wreck victims to find shelter beneath the towering cliffs.

RICHES, RESOURCES, AND DISCONTENT

West coast Canada's first successful pulp mill for paper manufacture opened at Swanson Bay on Vancouver Island in 1909. Provincial chief forester H. L. MacMillan set up a B.C. lumber marketing program in 1912. After World War I, he left the government to join with American J. H. Bloedel in developing a vertically integrated lumber company that owned forestlands, mills, and ships, eventually becoming the giant MacMillan-Bloedel Company.

The provincial government gladly encouraged such developments by granting twenty-one-year leases of timberlands to companies willing to build and operate a mill. A branch line of the railroad reached Port Alberni to rejuvenate lumbering there. The fur business was a shadow of the HBC days, but seals were still killed for their skins until the Canadian government outlawed sealing on the west coast in 1911.

Victoria acquired a site for industrial development in 1911 when it paid the surviving Songhees $434,000 for their Indian reserve on the west side of the Gorge and relocated them in Esquimalt.

The commencement of construction of the Panama Canal, which would make travel and trade from Europe and the east coast much shorter and safer, set off a euphoric escalation of public optimism and real-estate values in Victoria. Between 1908 and 1912 lot prices multiplied as much as eight times. Fortunes were made, particularly by many of the more than one hundred real-estate firms, while Victorians dreamed of spectacular growth. In 1913 the real-estate bubble burst, causing a general recession, losses of fortunes, and a tidal wave of bankruptcies. The Bank of Montreal foreclosed on the new owner of Dunsmuir's castle and sold it to the city for $35,000. Only wartime ship construction and other military manufacturers restored the economy.

In Cumberland, near Nanaimo, coal miners went on strike in 1913 for better working conditions and safety, and a May Day sympathy general strike across the island followed. The premier called out troops, supposedly to protect property from strikers' vandalism and restore order, but in reality to help the owner, James Dunsmuir, bring in strikebreakers. The army occupied the Nanaimo–Cumberland–Ladysmith area until the start of the world war a year later.

POLITICS, PATRIOTISM, AND PROHIBITION

Provincial government was conducted without political parties for its first thirty years. This meant that, to be elected, each premier had to put together a personal coalition, without long-term responsibility for developing and maintaining a specific program. Thus, there were fourteen premiers between 1871 and 1903, usually lasting only for a year or two. The system changed when thirty-two-year-old Richard McBride took office in June 1903 as a Conservative who required his supporters in the Assembly to follow policies of the party.

McBride's most audacious act as premier occurred the week England went to war with Germany in August 1914. Rumors of an impending attack on Esquimalt Naval Station by German cruisers were rife, and with no British ships on hand, Victoria and Vancouver were virtually defenseless. Over in Seattle lay two new submarines built for the navy of Chile, but the Chilean government had defaulted on payment. So McBride secretly sent a provincial check of $1,150,000 to the shipbuilding company, and the next morning the subs sailed into Esquimalt Naval Base, where nervous gunners almost fired on them. Eventually the subs proved leaky and never saw action.

The fear of naval attack turned to rage in May 1915, when a German submarine in the Atlantic sank the passenger ship *Lusitania*, in which more than a

The army comes to Nanaimo to put down strike, 1913

dozen Victorians died, including Lt. James Dunsmuir Jr. In Victoria a well-liquored mob of about 500 (cheered on by a thousand more) trashed a German beer garden, the German Club, the Kaiserhof Hotel, and a brewery with a German name (which was British owned) and began looting stores. When the crowd marched on the mansion of Lieutenant Governor Frank Barnard to ridicule his wife, who was of German heritage, Premier McBride sent out the militia to put a stop to the rioting. However, he succumbed to public demand by interning German aliens in camps until the end of the war.

Victoria's special contribution to the war effort was Arthur Currie. A real-estate broker who was on the brink of bankruptcy after the 1913 real-estate collapse, Currie was colonel of a reserve unit with no military experience. When he was asked to command a new Victoria battalion headed for France, Currie was so poor he could barely afford a new uniform.

Promoted to commander of the First Canadian Division, he was outspoken in rejecting the bullheaded British and French strategy of sending waves of troops into the face of enemy fire. He demanded precision, planning, careful reconnaissance of the battleground, and use of a variety of tactics. After leading Canadian troops to victory at the Battle of Vilmy, where the Germans were stopped cold, Major General Currie replaced an English general as commander of the entire Canadian Corps in 1917. His leadership made his troops effective and proud to be Canadians and not just cannon fodder. After the war he did not return to Victoria but became head of McGill University.

An anti-alcohol campaign had gone hand in hand with the women's drive for the vote. On October 1, 1917, as a wartime measure British Columbia adopted a prohibition against liquor production and sales. Within a few months, eighty saloons and hotels that had relied on pub business closed their doors in greater Victoria. Smuggling liquor from the United States and running illegal stills became profitable industries. In 1919 the United States adopted the prohibition amendment to its constitution, and in 1921, British Columbia repealed its prohibition act, so the flow of smuggled liquor was reversed to run south from British Columbia into the United States.

The provincial repeal of prohibition gave each municipality the right of local option to choose prohibition for its jurisdiction. To the surprise of many, in a referendum the people of Victoria voted not to allow sales of liquor by the glass. If anyone in Victoria wanted a drink, he had to have it at home or drive out of town for it. Restaurants, tourist hotels, and private clubs might find a way to provide a drink—Winston Churchill was served whiskey in a silver goblet at the Empress—but alcoholic drinks could not be sold legally within the city limits.

Remarkably, for a city relying on tourist trade, the ban was continued by public vote in 1931. Finally it was lifted in 1954, with the first cocktail lounge opening in the Strathcona Hotel. In 1925 a surprising hockey team, the Victoria Cougars, as the top western Canadian club, won the national championship and the Stanley Cup. Shortly thereafter on the founding of the National Hockey League, the Cougars moved to Detroit as the Red Wings.

A BIT OF ENGLAND AND EMILY CARR

Architect Francis Rattenbury and his wife, Florrie, were no longer speaking to each other when he began his affair in 1923 with the enticingly beautiful twenty-six-year-old Alma Pakenham. He and his partner, Percy James, were designing his last two great projects: the Canadian Pacific Steamship Terminal on the Inner Harbour (now the Royal London Wax Museum) with its stately precast concrete columns, and the Crystal Gardens, originally an ambitious multiuse amusement center.

Francis and Alma harassed Florrie unmercifully until she granted Rattenbury a divorce in 1925. Appalled by his conduct, Victoria society ostracized Rattenbury and his young bride, while his clients cut him off. In 1930 the couple moved to England, where Rattenbury took up serious drinking. In a few years Alma took up with their eighteen-year-old chauffeur. Under Alma's influence, her young lover beat the famed architect to death on March 24, 1935. When the youthful killer was sentenced to hang, Alma stabbed herself

Emily Carr

several times in a messy suicide. Her lover's death sentence was commuted.

In 1927, Victoria's chief of publicity, George Warren, a former San Franciscan who had never been to England, coined a new slogan for the city: "a little bit of old England." (It replaced his earlier invention, "follow the birds to Victoria.") While this sobriquet referred to a style of conduct—polite, genteel, restrained—it was also reflected in the private as well as public gardens, and the Tudor-style homes (more than fifty designed by Samuel Maclure) built in the Rockland section and Oak Bay during the first quarter of the twentieth century.

Victoria was not quite ready for Emily Carr. Growing up in the James Bay cluster, Emily was forever in rebellion against the memory of her English-born father, who had ruled the family with an "unbendable iron will" (her words) until his death in 1888 when she was sixteen. She studied art beginning at age seventeen, first in San Francisco and later in London and Paris; drew native women at Ucluelet; cartooned for a left-wing newspaper; lived in the woods to get a feel for the forests; and ran a boardinghouse, which she called the "House of All Sorts," for anyone who needed shelter. But most of all she painted Vancouver Island in a rich, impressionistic style, catching the mood of the countryside. Although praised by the leading Canadian artists of the east, her art was sneered at by westerners, who expected graphic representations and who, as Emily put it, "couldn't see the forest for the trees."

Lauren Harris, the director of the Canadian National Gallery of Art, began a campaign to introduce Emily to the greater world of art in Ottawa and New York. Suddenly in 1927 she became a national celebrity. Victoria and Vancouver reluctantly embraced Emily Carr.

The Malahat Road in the early 1920s (Courtesy of Canadian National Railways)

Her unconventional way of life was barely tolerated by Victoria's society, and rumors that she was a lesbian were whispered about. She left the mystery unresolved in her *Growing Pains: An Autobiography* when she said, "I gave my love where it was not wanted; almost simultaneously an immense love was offered to me which I could neither accept nor return." Some event, or somebody, deeply wounded this passionate woman, who had been a Victorian prude unwilling to paint nudes.

By her late sixties, arthritis curbed her painting and teaching, but the reading of one of her old manuscripts on CBC radio was immensely popular. There followed publication of *Klee Wyck* ("the smiling one"), which won the Governor's Prize. In the half dozen years left to her, she wrote five more books, which were all instant best-sellers, including *The Book of Small* and *The Heart of a Peacock*.

DEPRESSION, WAR, AND CULTURAL REVIVAL

Faced with the Great Depression, Dr. Simon Fraser Tolmie, a veterinarian, and his Conservative administration (1928–33) were paralyzed. In greater Victoria 12,000 people were out of work, and in Saanich 380 families went on relief. In Victoria, many homes purchased for inflated prices in the 1920s were lost to foreclosure for failure to pay taxes or mortgages. The Victoria city government hired the unemployed for a great cleanup campaign, which allowed it to claim it was "the cleanest city in North America."

Canada followed Great Britain into World War II in 1939. Once again, military expenditures stimulated the economy and revived the shipyards. On June 20, 1942, a Japanese submarine lobbed a volley of shells at the Point Estevan lighthouse on the west coast north of Nootka Sound, the first attack on Canadian soil since the War of 1812.

When the Japanese bombed Pearl Harbor on December 7, 1941, and overran Hong Kong and much of the South Pacific, panic gripped the island. Japanese immigration to Vancouver Island dated from the 1870s, and a majority were Canadian citizens. There was no evidence of disloyalty or sabotage by any of them. Nevertheless, in early 1942 Canada followed the lead of the United States, and all 10,000 people of Japanese descent on Vancouver Island were transported to internment camps in such towns as New Denver in the Kootenays. This left their property, farms, fishing boats, and businesses for sale at dirt-cheap prices. A majority never returned. Years later the government of Canada, embarrassed by this obviously racist and illegal act, paid partial reparations to the survivors.

Voting rights were restored to people of Chinese and East Indian ancestry in 1947, and to native Indians and those of Japanese descent in 1949.

Victoria's streetcar system was dismantled in 1948 to be replaced by fleets of buses. The last streetcar to run was draped in black crepe.

Starting in the 1890s, when Cowichan women began knitting sweaters with ancient native designs, the revival of Indian art grew. Using modern steel knives, young natives with artistic talent found they could carve even better than their ancestors. Totem poles were raised by a new generation of carvers, encouraged by the work of artists such as Chief Wilks James, who carved a splendid pole on the Nanaimo waterfront in 1922. Crops of poles rose in downtown Duncan, in Thunderbird Park in Victoria, and at the Cowichan Native Village in Duncan. Native art appeared in galleries from downtown Victoria to Tofino on the west coast. A carving industry developed, both from master carvers and mass-produced copies. Modern artists with roots in the ancient designs added new dimensions to the renaissance in native art.

When the ferries between Vancouver City and Vancouver Island went on strike in 1958, Premier W. A. C. "Wacky" Bennett seized the ferries and kept them for the province, built new terminals, and created the government-run B.C. Ferry Corporation. In 2003 the ferry system was privatized by sale to a nongovernment corporation.

The University of Victoria was founded in 1963, with a campus built on the green rolling bluffs above Cadboro Bay northeast of the city. UVic soon took its place as one of the leading Canadian universities and the dominant national collegiate basketball power for both men's and women's teams. Its law school has been rated best in Canada.

Victoria's newspaper rivals the *Colonist* and the *Daily Times* merged in 1980 into the *Times-Colonist*. Alternative, entertainment, and neighborhood newspapers like *News* and *Monday* (which comes out on Thursday) have sprung up in the years since.

The history of Victoria and Vancouver Island can be summed up in a roll call:

The First Peoples lived in harmony with its natural wonders.
Capt. James Cook found it.
George Vancouver explored it.
James Douglas came to find furs and created a colony.
Roderick Finlayson built a fort.
Joseph Pemberton laid out a city.
John Tod and John Work cultivated the land.
John Muir founded two towns, a mill, and a mine.
Amor DeCosmos and Alfred Waddington dreamed its dreams.
John Helmcken and Joseph Trutch gave it stability.
Matthew Baillie Begbie brought law and order.
Robert Dunsmuir and H. R. MacMillan exploited its resources.
The woodsmen, the miners, and the fishermen boosted the economy.
The Chinese and a dozen other nationalities provided their labor.
Francis Rattenbury designed its monumental buildings.
Jenny and Robert Butchart turned a crater into a garden.
Emily Carr painted its beauty and described its life.
The Canadian Pacific brought the visitors.
Its religious leaders gave it moral tone.
Its shops, restaurants, and hostelries provided excitement.
Native carvers, weavers, knitters, and artists revived the culture.
And the people gave it the charm.

9

List of Lists

Here are lists that you can use to quickly find places to visit and events to attend.

ANTIQUES SHOPS

Victoria

Note: Listing is according to walking pattern, from downtown and then walking east on Fort Street.

1800 Shop Antiques, #3, 1113 Langley Street near Fort Street (behind Murchie's), (250) 384–3215.

Penny Black Antiques, Stamps & Coins, #1, 1113 Langley Street (behind Murchie's), (250) 389–2210.

Liberty Victoria Antiques & Art, 618 Broughton Street, (250) 385–6733.

TJ's Decorative Art, 716 View Street, (250) 480–4930.

JR Antiques, 706 Fort Street, (250) 380–6624.

Recollections Antique and Collectible Mall, 817A Fort Street, (250) 385–1902; www.recollectionsantiques.com.

Classic Silverware, 826 Fort Street, (250) 383–6860.

Pacific Antiques, 829 Fort Street, (250) 388–5311.

Romanoff & Co. Antiques, 837 Fort Street, (250) 480–1543.

Old 'n' Gold, 1011 Fort Street, (250) 361–1892; www.oldngold.com.

David Robinson Antiques, 1023 Fort Street, (250) 384–6425.

Antiek Dolls, 2625 Shakespeare Street, (250) 382–3203.

Faith Grant The Connoisseur Shop Ltd., 1156 Fort Street, (250) 383–0121.

J. & J. Jewellery & Gifts, 1044 Fort Street, (250) 361–4480.

Vanity Fair Antique & Collectibles Mall, 1044 Fort Street, (250) 380–7274; www.vanityfairantiques.com.

Charles Baird Antiques, 1044A Fort Street, (250) 384–8809.

Domus Antica Galleries, 1038–1040 Fort Street, (250) 385–5443.

The Glass Menagerie, 1036 Fort Street, (250) 475–2228; www.glassmenagerie .com.

Old Vogue Shop, 1034 Fort Street, (250) 380–7751.

Applewood Antiques, #1, 1028 Fort Street, (250) 360–1889.

Jean Hutton Custom Framing Prints Old & New, 1016 Fort Street, (250) 382–4493.

Kay's Korner, 337 Cook Street, (250) 386–5978.

White Ram Antiques, 2669 Bridge, (250) 383–5581.

Voss Art & Antiques, 102 Monterey Mews, 2250 Oak Bay Avenue, (250) 386–1850.

South-Central Vancouver Island

Post Office Mail, 340 Esplanade, Island Highway, Ladysmith; (250) 245–7984.

Downstairs Collectibles & Antiques, 466 St. Julian Street, Duncan; (250) 748–2270.

Ma's Collectibles, 9766 Willow Street, Chemainus; (250) 246–9583.

Mr. Wumbley's Curios & Collectibles, 9748-G Willow Street, Chemainus; (250) 416–0009.

Willow Antique Mall, 9756 Willow Street, Chemainus; (250) 246–4333.

BOOKSTORES

We include major downtown Victoria and Sidney bookstores you can get to easily, as well as secondhand and antiquarian bookstores. (Unless otherwise noted, the following are located in Victoria.)

New Books (and some used)

Atman Bookstore, 4492G Happy Valley in Metchosin; metaphysical, spiritual, meditation tapes; (250) 474–4622.

Blue Moon, 148 Fulford-Ganges, Salt Spring Island; (250) 538–1889.

Bolen Books, 78, 1644 Hillside Avenue in Hillside Shopping Center, (250) 595–4232; a huge multi-interest local, modern bookstore with everything imaginable and excellent service.

Cadboro Bay Book Ca., 3840B Cadboro Bay, (250) 477–1421; a lovely neighborhood bookstore with large selections of children's and gardening books, as well as art and literature.

Chapters, 1212 Douglas Street, (250) 380–9009; the mother of all Canadian chain bookstores.

Coles—The Book People, Mayfair Shopping Center, 3147 Douglas Street, (250) 388–3199; general Canadian chain bookstore with some discounts on interesting remaindered books.

Dark Horse Books, 623 Johnson Street, (250) 386–8736.

Fairfield Book Shop, 247 Cook Street, (250) 386–9095; large selection of current paperbacks, including science fiction, new and used.

Ivy's Bookshop, 2184 Oak Bay Avenue, Oak Bay Village, (250) 598–2713; general books for adults and children in a cozy atmosphere.

Miners Bay Books, 478 Village Bay Road, Mayne Island, (250) 539–3112.

Munro's Books, 1108 Government Street, (250) 382–2464; full range of new books on every topic, great discount tables, large children's selection, personal care, thought by many to be Canada's finest bookstore.

Russell Books, 734 Fort Street, (250) 361–4447; new and old books, run by fascinating family.

Smithbooks, The Bay Centre Mall, (250) 384–3077; general chain bookstore with good travel and Canadiana sections, discounted remainders.

Triple Spiral Books, 3 Fan Tan Alley, (250) 380–7212; metaphysical supplies and services, excellent book collection, spiritual readings, classes in natural magic, elegant artwork by owner.

Bookstores in Sidney

In a nice bit of self-promotion, in 1996 Sidney's literary merchants adopted the unofficial name of Book Town. Nowadays Sidney lives up to its name with charming bookstores clustered in 3 blocks of Beacon Avenue, and in the first blocks of Third, Fourth, and Fifth Streets around the corner from Beacon. Suiting every taste, try these:

Beacon Books & Collectibles, 2372 Beacon Avenue, (250) 655–4447.

The Book Cellar, 2423 Beacon Avenue, (250) 653–3969; military history, maps, in old post office basement.

The Children's Bookshop, 2442 Beacon Avenue, (250) 656–4440.

Compass Rose Nautical Books, 9785 Fourth Street, (250) 656–4674.

Galleon Books & Antiques, 9803 Third Street, (250) 655–0700.

The Haunted Bookshop, 9807 Third Street, (250) 656–6805.

Press Gang Books, 2448-B Beacon Avenue, (250) 656–5641.

Tanner's Books, 2436 Beacon Avenue, (250) 656–2345; large stock, maps.

Time Enough for Books, 2424 Beacon Avenue, (250) 655–1964.

Secondhand and Antiquarian Bookstores

A-AA-ABA Books, 1600 Quadra Street, (250) 389–0777.

Archie's, 145 Menzies, (250) 385–4519.

Beacon Books, 145 2372 Beacon, Sidney; (250) 655–4447.

Fairfield Book Shop, 247 Cook Street, (250) 386–9095.

Haultain Books, 1500 Haultain, (250) 592–1555.

Oak Bay Books, 1964 Oak Bay, (250) 592–2933.

Renaissance Books, 579 Johnson Street (upstairs), (250) 381–6469.

Russell Books, 734 Fort Street, (250) 361–4447; our favorite for used books.

Sabine's, 3104-115 Fulford-Ganges, Salt Spring Island; (250) 538–0025.

Smart Book Shop, Royal Oak Shopping Center, 4430 West Saanich Road, (250) 721–4200.

Snowden's Books, 619 Johnson Street, (250) 383–8131.

Tell Me A Story Family Bookshop, 1848 Oak Bay Avenue, (250) 598–8833.

Timeless Books, 676 Granderson Road, (250) 474–3324.

GALLERIES

(The following are located in Victoria.)

Alcheringa Gallery, 665 Fort Street, (250) 383–8224.

Art Gallery of Greater Victoria, 1040 Moss Street, (250) 384–4101.

Caswell Lawrence Fine Art Gallery, 1014 Broad Street, (250) 388–9500.

Community Arts Council of Greater Victoria, 6G, 1001 Douglas Street; (250) 381–2787.

Emily Carr House, 207 Government Street, (250) 383–5843.

Fran Willis Gallery, #200, 1619 Store Street, (250) 381–3422.

Martin Batchelder Gallery, 712 Comorant Street, (250) 385–7919.

Open Space, 510 Fort Street, (250) 383–8833.

West End Gallery, 1203 Broad Street, (250) 388–0009.

Winchester Galleries, 1010 Broad Street, (250) 386–2773; 1545 Fort Street, (250) 595–2777.

LAUNDROMATS

There are two downtown Victoria Laundromats, both within walking distance of the Inner Harbour.

One nameless Laundromat hides under the Tourism Victoria Centre at the Inner Harbour, next to Milestone's cafe. There are also showers, restrooms, and public telephones here.

Another, Prestine Drycleaners & Laundromat, 255 Menzies, is about 4 blocks from Belleville, next to the James Bay Coffee Company, a great place to sip away your laundry time.

NIGHTLIFE/MUSIC

(The following are located in Victoria.)

Bartholomew's Bar & Grill, 777 Douglas Street, (250) 388–5111; cozy, noisy pub with good local bands almost nightly at 8:30 P.M.; good food, too.

Big Bad John's, Strathcona Hotel, 919 Douglas Street, (250) 383–7137; a dark bar with all the peanuts you can eat.

Blethering Place, 2250 Oak Bay Avenue, (250) 598–1413; teahouse turns into music place Friday–Sunday evenings.

Boom Boom Room, 1208 Wharf Street, (250) 381–2331; theme nights, DJs, big dance floor.

Bowman's Rib House, 825 Burdett Avenue (Cherry Bank Hotel), (250) 385–5380; sing-along Wednesday through Sunday nights.

Cambie, 856 Esquimalt, (250) 382–7161.

Charles Dickens Pub, 633 Humboldt Street (in Fairmont Empress Hotel), (250) 361–2600; music some weekends, usually no cover.

Cuckoo's Nest, 919 Douglas Street, (250) 383–7137; sports bar and grill in Strathcona Hotel; karaoke or DJ music most nights.

D'Arcy McGee's, 1127 Wharf Street, (250) 380–1322; friendly Irish pub on Victoria scene with open mike and Celtic music nights.

Diego's, 3386 Douglas Street, (250) 475–7575; live music Friday and Saturday nights, sports lounge.

Due West, 741 Goldstream Avenue at Highway 1A, Westwind Plaza Hotel, (250) 478–8334; dance to Top 40 Wednesday–Saturday evenings; Friday buffet dinner show.

Evolution, 502 Discovery, (250) 388–3000; alternative music.

Fat Tuesday's, 123 Gorge Road, (250) 383–7545; live R&B music some nights.

The Foxtail Lounge, 1450 Douglas Street, (250) 383–4157.

George & Dragon, 1302 Gladstone Avenue, (250) 388–4458; hot live music, improv comedy, acoustic open stage.

Hermann's Jazz Club, 753 View Street, (250) 388–9166; every day the best in live jazz; sometimes a minimum charge of $4.

Hugo's Lounge, 625 Courtney Street, (250) 920–4844; pub with microbeers, good menu.

Irish Times, 200 Government Street, (250) 383–7775; live music nightly.

James Bay Inn, 270 Government Street, (250) 384–7151; music Friday and Saturday evenings or afternoons.

Legends, 919 Douglas Street, (250) 383–7137; large dance floor, 1980s and '90s music, some live, some DJ, some special concerts, every night; a fixture for more that three decades.

Luckey Bar, 517 Yates Street, (250) 382–LUCK.

McMorran's Beach House, 5109 Cordova Bay Road, (250) 658–5527; various live performances.

Moka House, 345 Cook Street, (250) 388–7377; popular coffeehouse has live music, often on weekend nights; no cover.

Monty's Showroom Pub, 1400 Government Street, (250) 386–3631; exotic dancers.

Pagliacci's, 1011 Broad Street, (250) 386–1662; oh-so-popular restaurant features top local musical groups Sunday through Wednesday evenings.

Prism Lounge, 642 Johnson Street, (250) 388–0505; alternative lifestyles.

Rathskeller Restaurant & Schnitzel House, 1205 Quadra Street, (250) 386–9348; German oompah music Friday and Saturday.

Soundgarden, 1630 Store Street, (250) 380–2733.

Starbucks on Cook, 320 Cook Street, (250) 380–7606; live music on Friday evening.

Steamers Pub, 570 Yates Street, (250) 381–4340; local brews; hip music with special shows by hot new musicians (lots of Celtic); no cover.

Sticky Wicket Pub & Restaurant, 919 Douglas Street (Strathcona Hotel), (250) 383–7137; English atmosphere, excellent brews, rooftop dining in summer.

Sugar Night Club, 860 Yates Street, (250) 920–9950; dancing, music.

Swan's, 506 Pandora Street, (250) 361–3310; house-made ales and beers at this popular gathering spot; varied live music Sunday–Thursday; no cover.

Sweetwaters Niteclub, 27–560 Johnson Street in Market Square, (250) 383–7844; dancing to hits from the 1970s, '80s, '90s; dress code and cover charge Friday and Saturday.

Tally-Ho Motor Lounge, 3020 Douglas Street, (250) 389–9411; comedy Tuesday and Saturday; dancing Wednesday–Saturday.

PHARMACIES

We list the pharmacies most convenient to downtown Victoria, with the additions of some that are open late.

London Drugs, 201–911 Yates Street, (250) 381–1113. Hours: 9:00 A.M.–10:00 P.M. daily, 10:00 A.M.–8:00 P.M. Sunday.

McGill & Orme, 649 Fort Street, (250) 384–1195. Hours: 9:00 A.M.–6:00 P.M. daily.

Pharmasave, 230 Menzies Street, (250) 383–7196. Hours: 9:00 A.M.– 6:00 P.M. daily.

Shoppers Drug Mart, 3575 Douglas Street (Town & Country Shopping Centre), (250) 475–7572. Hours: 9:00 A.M.–midnight daily.

POPULAR BUS DESTINATIONS

Here are some popular attractions and the Victoria Regional Transit buses to take to them from downtown Victoria. You can catch most buses on the east side of Douglas Street across from the Bay Centre and Coast Capital Savings and at other stops along the street. Signs over the bus stops list which buses stop at which corner. (Unless otherwise noted, these attractions are located in Victoria.)

Antique Row, 700–1000 blocks of Fort Street and more; Buses 5, 10, 11, 14.

Art Gallery of Greater Victoria, 1040 Moss Street; Buses 10 Haultain, 11, 14 UVic.

Beacon Hill Park, Douglas Street at Superior (Southgate) through to Dallas Road; Bus 5.

Butchart Gardens, 800 Benvenuto Avenue, Brentwood Bay; Bus 75.

Canadian Forces Base, Esquimalt; Buses 23, 24, 25, 26.

Canwest Shopping Centre, 2945 Jacklin Road; Buses 50, 51.

Craigdarroch Castle, 1050 Joan Crescent; Buses 11, 14.

Craigflower Manor, 110 Island Highway; Bus 14 Craigflower.

Crystal Pool (swimming), 2275 Quadra Street; Bus 6.

Elk Lake and Beaver Lake Regional Park, Haliburton Road at Sayward Road; Buses 70, 75.

Emily Carr House, 207 Government Street; Bus 5.

Fisherman's Wharf, St. Lawrence and Erie Streets; Bus 30/31 James Bay.

Fort Rodd Hill National Historic Site, 603 Fort Rodd Hill Road; Bus 50 (plus a scenic walk).

Goldstream Park, Bus 50, then Bus 57 and a short walk.

Gonzales Hill Regional Park, off Denison Road; Bus 2 Gonzales (and an uphill hike).

Government House, 1401 Rockland Avenue; Bus 1 Richardson.

Gyro Park, off Sinclair Road with beach and playground; Bus 11.

Hillside Shopping Centre, 1644 Hillside Avenue; Buses 4, 10, 27, 28.

Horticulture Centre of the Pacific, 505 Quayle Road; Bus 21 and walk.

Juan de Fuca Recreation Centre, 1767 Island Highway; Buses 50, 51, 52, 61.

Kinsmen Gorge Park, Tillicum Road and Gorge Bridge; Buses 10 Gorge, 26, or 14 Craigflower and a walk.

Mattick's Farm, 5325 Cordova Bay Road; Bus 30 or 31, then 32.

Mayfair Shopping Centre, 3147 Douglas Street; Buses 30, 31.

Mount Douglas Park, off Ash Road with hiking trails to viewpoint; Bus 28.

Mount Tolmie Park, off Mayfair Drive; Bus 14 UVic (and uphill hike to viewpoint).

Oak Bay Recreation Centre, 1975 Bee Street; Buses 7, 11.

Oak Bay Village, Oak Bay Avenue at Hampshire Road; Bus 1 Willows and Bus 2 Oak Bay.

Panorama Leisure Centre, 1885 Forest Park Drive, Sidney; Bus 70.

Peninsula Trail Rides, 8129 Derrinberg Road; Bus 70.

Point Ellice House, 2616 Pleasant Street off Bay Street; Bus 14 Craigflower.

Royal Roads University (Hatley Castle), Sooke Road; Bus 50, then Bus 61 or Bus 52.

Saanich Centre, Quadra Street at McKenzie Avenue; Buses 6, 26.

Saanich Commonwealth Place, Elk Lake Drive; Buses 6, 30, 31 and a short walk, or 70, 75.

Saanich Historical Artifacts Society, 7321 Lochside Drive; Bus 75 (and a long walk).

Saanich Plaza, Blanshard Street at Ravine Way; Buses 30, 31, 26.

Sandown Harness Raceway, 1810 Glamorgan Road; Buses 70, 72, walk.

Saxe Point Park, off Fraser Street; Buses 24, 25.

Sidney Fisherman's Market, Beacon Avenue at the water, Sidney; Buses 70, 72, 75.

Sidney Museum, 2538 Beacon Avenue, Sidney; Buses 70, 72, 75.

Sooke Pot Holes, Sooke Road at Sooke River Road; Bus 50, then 61.

Sooke Regional Museum, Sooke Road at 2070 Phillips; Bus 50, then 61.

Swan Lake Nature Sanctuary, Swan Lake Road; Buses 70, 75, 26 or 51 and walk.

University of Victoria (UVic), Finnerty Road; Buses 4, 11, 14, 26, 39 UVic, 51.

Uplands Park/Cattle Point, Dorset Road and Beach Drive; Bus 11 or 1 Willows and a short walk.

Victoria Butterfly Gardens, 1461 Benvenuto Avenue; Bus 75.

Water Slides (All Fun Recreation Park), 2207 Millstream Road; Bus 50, then 57 and a walk.

Willows Beach, Beach Drive and Dalhousie Road; Bus 1 Willows.

Witty's Lagoon, 4021 Metchosin Road; Bus 50, then 54 and a long hike (Monday–Saturday only).

RESTROOMS

We all know that often the hardest thing to find in a new place is a clean, usable, functioning washroom or restroom. In addition to those in restaurants and fast-food places, here are a few in Victoria available without purchase, no questions asked if you conduct yourself properly.

Parliament buildings, Government and Belleville; to the left as you go in front door, up or down a half flight. *Not wheelchair accessible.*

Royal British Columbia Museum, Government and Belleville; to the left as you enter main door, down hallway. *Wheelchair accessible.*

Causeway, north end to left of Milestone's deck; also showers and Laundromat here. *Not wheelchair accessible.*

Sam's Deli, 805 Government across from Tourism Victoria; to left of front door at back wall. *Wheelchair accessible, barely.*

Bay Centre Mall, Fort and Government; ground floor about halfway back on north side and fourth floor to the right in the food area. *Wheelchair accessible.*

Murchie's Tea & Coffee Ltd., 1110 Government Street, next to Munro's Books and across from the Bay Centre; downstairs in back. *Wheelchair accessible from Langley Street.*

Greater Victoria Public Library, Broughton and Blanshard above Douglas; turn right inside front door, way over to right wall, down short hallway. *Wheelchair accessible.*

THEATERS

(All of the following are located in Victoria.)

Belfry, 1291 Gladstone, (250) 385–6815; prestigious and highly praised theater company produces several plays a year in the intimacy of a converted church.

Langham Court Theatre, 805 Langham Court, (250) 384–2142; performances by the Victoria Theatre Guild.

McPherson Playhouse, 3 Centennial Square, Pandora and Government Streets, (250) 386–6121; Victoria's Pacific Opera, September–May; Victoria Symphony, August–May; British comedy in summer; light opera and musicals by the Victoria Operatic Society; other major entertainers in concert.

Newcombe Theatre, 675 Belleville, (250) 356–0726; Royal British Columbia Museum Theatre; slide shows and documentaries.

Phoenix Theatre, University of Victoria, (250) 721–8000; high-quality student productions.

Royal Theatre, 805 Broughton at Blanshard, (250) 361–0820 or (250) 386–6121; touring plays, concerts, and dance.

In summer there is also the **Fringe Theatre** (250–383–2663), which puts on street comedy and other acts at various locations during the On the Fringe Festival, and the Shakespeare Festival, in which two Shakespearean troupes alternate nightly in a large tent next to the Inner Harbour for several weeks. Advance purchases of tickets (from $10) at the tent are strongly recommended.

10
Annual Events and Festivals

GREATER VICTORIA, SOOKE, DUNCAN, COWICHAN VALLEY

January

Polar Bear Swim, January 1, Elk Lake.

Pacific Cup Hockey Tournament, Victoria; a three-day tournament of old-time hockey players, Memorial Arena and other venues; (250) 361–0537.

February

Pacific Northwest Wine Festival, dates and sites vary; tastings, banquet of wineries of British Columbia, Washington, Oregon, Idaho; call any local wineshop.

Fine Arts Festival, University of Victoria, Department of Fine Arts; (250) 721–7755.

Flower Count, Victoria's annual weeklong count of displayed flowers, sponsored by Greater Victoria Chamber of Commerce; (250) 383–7191.

March

Victoria French Festival, first half of March; many events; (250) 388–7350.

Be A Tourist In Your Own Hometown, Victoria; second weekend; cheap ticket packages.

Victoria Rock and Gem Show, third full weekend; 195 Bay Street; www.island net.com/-v/ms.

Victoria Sewing & Crafts Show, third full weekend; Victoria Conference Centre; (250) 479–7316.

April

Terrivic Dixieland Jazz Party, Victoria; five-day international festival, last five days of month; (250) 953–2011; www.islandnet.com/-bbs/jazz.html.

Spring Art Show, second weekend through middle of month; Cowichan Native Village, 200 Cowichan Way, off Highway 1, Duncan; (250) 746–1633.

Brentwood Rowing Regatta, Mill Bay; fourth weekend; Brentwood School.

Greater Victoria Performing Arts Festival, first full weekend in April through middle of May; one ticket ($15) covers all shows at twelve venues—dance, music, singing; (250) 386–9223.

May

Cinco De Mayo Celebration, Victoria; three-day Mexican fiesta, weekend closest to May 5; Market Square; sponsored by Victoria Immigrant and Refugee Centre; (250) 361–1909.

National Forestry Week, Duncan; first full week; special displays and programs at B.C. Forest Museum, on Highway 1 just north of Duncan.

Government Street Market, on 1600 block, every Sunday through September.

Shawnigan Rowing Regatta, second weekend; Shawnigan Lake School.

Literary Arts Festival, third Thursday–Sunday; (250) 381–6722; E-mail: literary@ write.com.

Heritage Days, Village of Lake Cowichan; third full weekend; (250) 749–6681.

Victoria Day Parade, Victoria; a provincial holiday, Monday before May 24, honoring Queen Victoria's birthday, featuring 142 entries from British Columbia and loads of American high-school bands down Douglas Street from Mayfair Mall to the Convention Centre behind the Fairmont Empress Hotel; (250) 382–3111.

Luxton Pro Rodeo, weekend of Victoria Day; Luxton Rodeo Grounds, Sooke and Luxton Roads; (250) 478–4250; E-mail: sandywest@home.com.

Mill Bay Country Music Week, last week; line dancing for three days at Cowichan Community Center; country music for four days, Keey Park Arena.

Esquimalt Lantern Festival, last Saturday evening; Spinnaker's to West Bay Marina; (250) 383–8557.

June

Buccaneer Days Craft Sale, second Saturday and Sunday; Archie Browning Curling Rink, Esquimalt; (250) 384–4889.

Lake Days, Lake Cowichan; second weekend, festival.

Jazzfest International, Victoria; ten days of sixty concerts and workshops featuring cool jazz, blues, and world music, sponsored by Victoria Jazz Society; (250) 388–4423; www.vicjazz.bc.ca.

Victoria Flower and Garden Festival, third weekend; Juan de Fuca Recreation Centre, 1767 Island Highway; (250) 382–3658.

Folk Fest, last week; at the Inner Harbour, which is transformed into a bazaar of ethnic food booths, arts, and crafts, with music, dance, and community theater performances from 11:00 A.M. to 10:00 P.M.; (250) 388–4728.

July

Canada Day, July 1 holiday; fireworks at Inner Harbour, stage shows at bandshell and huge cake and clowns in Beacon Hill Park, (250) 382–2127; Sidney has three-day celebration with parade and other events, including fireworks at Tulista Park, (250) 656–4365; Salt Spring Island, fireworks at Ganges, (250) 537–4223.

Sidney Build a Boat Competition, July 1; bottom of Beach Avenue, near bandstand; build a boat and sail it on prescribed course; (250) 656–1125.

Fifth Regiment Band Concert, Victoria; every Sunday in July, 2:00–4:00 P.M. at Fort Rodd Hill Historical Park, 603 Fort Rodd Hill.

Folkfest, Victoria; first week of July; intercultural folk celebrations, Centennial Square, sponsored by International Cultural Association of Greater Victoria; (250) 388–4728.

All Sooke Day, Sooke; third Saturday; logging sports competition and salmon BBQ, Sooke Community Park; (250) 642–6351.

Moss Street Paint In, Victoria; third Saturday; in the Art Gallery of Greater Victoria block, with more than sixty local artists, sculptors, and illustrators showing and practicing their art; dancing and samples of local beer in the evening; (250) 384–4101.

Latin Music Festival, Victoria; three-day Latino music and folklore celebration, Market Square, sponsored by Victoria Immigrant and Refugee Centre; (250) 361–1909.

Victoria Shakespeare Festival, starts approximately second week of July through first ten days of August; tent in Inner Harbour; professional quality with wide range of plays and events, tickets around $10; (250) 360–0234; www.island net.com/-tinconnu.

Duncan-Cowichan Summer Festival, third weekend; downtown Duncan.

Ladysmith Celebration Days, Ladysmith; the weekend closest to B.C. Day (first Monday of August); parade, logger sports, entertainment, fireworks; (250) 245–2112.

Vancouver Island Blues Bash, Victoria; fourth weekend; free in the afternoon, fee at night, Market Square; (250) 388–4423.

King's Cup Maritime Festival, Sooke; last weekend; longboat races and boat building, Sooke Harbour; (250) 642–6351.

Islands Folk Festival, Duncan; third full weekend; more than one hundred dancers, workshops, children's activities, constant entertainment; at Providence Farm, Tzouhalem Road near Duncan; (250) 748–3975; www.folk fest.bc.ca.

August

Symphony Splash, Victoria; first Sunday of August (B.C. Day weekend); Victoria Symphony plays pop concert from barge in Inner Harbour, huge audience on lawns of Parliament; bring a dinner in basket, folding chair or blanket; (250) 385–9771.

Victoria Western Communities Summer Festival, Colwood; Juan de Fuca Recreation Centre; (250) 474–6003.

Cowichan Bay Sailing Regatta, first full week, at Cowichan Bay.

Victoria International Airshow, two days, Victoria International Airport; (250) 656–3337.

Victoria International Comedy Festival, three days, primarily at Market Square, but also at other sites.

Sunfest, Victoria; weekend of world music, Market Square; (250) 388–4423.

Sooke Fine Arts Show, twelve-day juried art exhibit of artists from greater Victoria, starting first full weekend; light lunch available; at Sooke Arena, 1 block up from corner of Sooke Road and Phillips; (250) 642–6351.

First Peoples' Festival, Victoria; second full weekend; three-day free event at Heritage Court and Thunderbird Park with art and cultural activities of Vancouver Island's three First Nations—Coast Salish, Nuu-chah-nulth, and Kwakwaka'wakw—sponsored by the Victoria Native Friendship Centre (250–384–3211) and Royal British Columbia Museum (250–387–2134).

Dragon Boat Festival, Inner Harbour, Victoria; third weekend; local groups form teams to compete in racing traditional Chinese dragon boats; food, health, educational, and souvenir booths around Inner Harbour; (250) 472–2628.

Fringe Theatre Festival, Victoria, starts next to last Saturday of August and runs for ten days; more than forty different acts, music, and alternative theater presentations at various Victoria locations, many of high quality, some indoors and some on the street; most require a purchased entrance badge; (250) 383–2663.

Vancouver Island Blues Bash, last weekend; free and ticketed concerts and performances featuring blues and R&B indoors and outdoors all over town; (888) 672–2112.

September

Classic Boat Festival, Victoria; first weekend; a great display of boats of all sizes in and around the Inner Harbour on Labor Day weekend, including a schooner race, sponsored by the Victoria Real Estate Board; (250) 385–7766.

Cowichan Exhibition, first full weekend; Duncan Exhibition Grounds; (250) 748–0822.

October

Royal Victoria Marathon, marathon, half marathon, and 8-kilometer run start and finish in front of the Parliament buildings; (250) 382–8181.

November

Great Canadian Beer Festival, second weekend; Victoria Conference Centre, 4:00–9:00 P.M.; features only all-natural beers, samples $1 each; (250) 595–7729.

Festival of Lights, Ladysmith; last Thursday; (250) 245–2112.

NANAIMO TO PORT HARDY, PORT ALBERNI, WEST COAST

January

Sea Lion Festival, Nanaimo; last weekend; celebrates the migrating sea lions; (250) 754–8474.

February

Trumpeter Swan Festival, Courtenay; first weekend.

March

Pacific Rim Whale Festival, Ucluelet/Tofino; middle of March through first week of April; whale watching and varied events; (250) 726–7742.

April

Brant Wildlife Festival, Parksville/Qualicum; second weekend; celebrates Brant geese migration; (250) 752–9171.

Spring Art Show, Cowichan Native Village, 200 Cowichan Way, Duncan; 250 native artists; (250) 746–1633.

Saanich Peninsula Arts & Crafts Society Show & Sale, Saanich Fairgrounds, 1528 Stelly's Crossroad, Brentwood Bay; last weekend; (250) 652–3314.

May

Comox Valley Highland Games, Lewis Park, Courtenay; third Saturday; (250) 897–1822.

June

Great Walk, Gold River to Tahsis; 62½-kilometer (37½-mile) marathon walk sponsored by Tahsis Lions Club; (250) 934–6570.

Chemainus Daze, Chemainus; last weekend; pancake breakfast, hamburger bake, parade, family fun, Waterwheel Park and Old Town; (250) 246–4701.

Steam Train Rides, Port Alberni; last weekend in June through August; along the waterfront from Alberni Valley Museum; (250) 723–2181.

Nanaimo's Heritage Days, last ten days of month; various locations in Nanaimo; (250) 753–5868.

Cumberland Miners Memorial, next to last Sunday of month; services and all-day honor to labor martyr "Ginger" Goodwin, evening barbecue, downtown Cumberland; (250) 336–2445.

Comox Valley Annual Pow Wow, Comox; last weekend, Comox Valley Exhibition Grounds; (250) 334–9591.

July

Canada Day, July 1, Parksville; pancakes, bazaar, entertainment, fireworks (250–248–3613); Port McNeill, airshow and fireworks at airport (250–956–4708 or 250–956–4130); Port Hardy (250–949–6665); Port Alberni, three days of events at E & N Railway Station (250–723–2181); Ucluelet, family picnic on Village Green (250–736–7744).

Annual Festival of the Arts, Salt Spring Island; four weeks starting first weekend, at Activity Centre, Ganges; (250) 537–4223.

Comox Valley Folk Festival, Comox; second weekend; blues, folk, bluegrass, R&B; Courtenay Fairground, Headquarters Road; (250) 334–2352.

Pacific Rim Summer Festival, Ucluelet and Tofino; last two weeks; chamber music and multicultural concerts, various venues; (250) 726–7572.

Sandcastle Competition, Parksville; second weekend; parade, Masters Invitational, Saturday night dance; Beach Community Park off Highway 19; (250) 954–3999.

Comox International Airshow, Comox; third weekend; air acrobatics, stunt flying; (250) 339–8201.

Marine Festival, Nanaimo; last weekend; street fair, fireworks, laser show, silly boat regatta, Jet Ski races; (250) 754–8474.

International Bathtub Races, Nanaimo; final Sunday of Marine Festival; race from Nanaimo across the strait to the mainland.

Ukee Days, Ucluelet; third weekend; salmon bake, Village Green; (250) 726–7742.

August

Vancouver Island Brewery Annual Pacific Rim Retreat, Tofino; first weekend; beach volleyball, clambake; Cox Bay; (250) 721–3280.

Filberg Festival, Comox; long weekend at beginning of month; arts, crafts, entertainment, food; put on by Fore & Aft Foods, Heritage Lodge & Park, 61 Filberg Road; (250) 334–9242; www.filbergfestival.com.

Summer Festival, Campbell River; second weekend; arts and crafts, loggers sports, parade, downtown; (250) 287–2044.

Mill Bay Fishing Derby, second weekend; Mill Bay marina.

Nanaimo Realty Salmon Fishing Derby, second weekend; Qualicum Beach.

Volleybash, Parksville; last weekend; Canadian Beach Volleyball Championships at all levels, including professionals; Saturday barbecue; Sunday finals; (250) 721–3280.

September

Port Alberni Salmon Festival, four days starting first Friday; Clutese Haven Marina; (250) 723–8165.

Dixieland Jazz Festival, Nanaimo; first full weekend; Dixieland jazz and vintage car rally; (250) 754–8474.

Gyro Boat Show, Nanaimo; first three-day weekend; exhibit of boats from throughout Northwest; Cruiseship Dock in downtown; (800) 663–7337.

Islander Days, Gabriola Island; first long weekend; exhibitions and activities at various locations.

Alberni District Fall Fair, four days over second weekend; Alberni Fairgrounds; (250) 723–9313.

Ladysmith Fall Fair, second weekend; Jameson Community Center.

Salt Spring Island Fall Fair, third weekend; Farmers' Institute, 351 Rainbow Road; (250) 537–4755.

Index

A

AAA Stamp, Coin, Jewellery Inc., 83
accommodations
    Bamfield, 241
    Bowser, 219
    Brentwood Bay, 168
    Campbell River, 222–23
    Comox, 221
    Cormorant Island, 258
    Cortes Island, 257
    Courtenay, 221
    Cowichan Bay, 203
    Denman Island, 255
    Duncan, 207
    Gabriola Island, 254
    Galiano Island, 252–53
    Hornby Island, 256
    Malahat, 203
    Malcolm Island, 259
    Mayne Island, 251
    Nanaimo, 215
    Parksville, 216–17
    Pender Islands, 247
    Port Alberni, 230
    Port Hardy, 225–26
    Port McNeill, 225
    Port Renfrew, 185
    Quadra Island, 256–57
    Qualicum Bay, 218
    Qualicum Beach, 219
    Saanich, 168
    Saanichton, 168
    Salt Spring Island, 246–47
    Saturna Island, 250
    Sidney, 169
    Sonora Island, 257
    Sooke
        bed-and-breakfasts, 180–81
        hotels, motels, and inns, 180
    Sproat Lake, 230
    Tofino, 238–39
    Ucluelet, 240
    University of Victoria, 132
    Victoria
        bed-and-breakfasts, 157
        hotels, 155–57
Adrienne's Tea Garden, 33
Adventure Clothing Ltd., 77
Aerie, The (resort & restaurant),
    190–92
African Rifles, 297
airlines, 11, 12–14
AKAL Airport Shuttle Bus, 14
Alberni Inlet, 277, 300, 304, 315
Alcheringa Gallery, 79, 82
Alderlea Vineyards Ltd., 205–6
All Fun Water Slides & Recreation
    Park, 188–89
All in Bloom, 96
Amos & Andes Imports, 82
Amtrak, 16
Angela Fashions, 84
annual events and festivals (list),
    335–42
Anthony's Old Time Portraits, 56
Antique Row, 83
antiques shops (list), 323–24
Applewood Antiques, 89

April Point Lodge & Fishing Resort, 256
Arbutus Cafe, 205
Arbutus Ridge Farms, 195
Arca Nova, 84
Architectural Walking Tours, 273
Art Gallery of Greater Victoria, 144
Artina's Jewellery, 63
Artisan Wine Shop, 46–47
auto rental, 19–20
Avalon Restaurant, 87
Aviation Museum, B.C., 145
Azuma Sushi, 101

B

B.C. Aviation Museum, 145
B.C. Ferries, 12
B.C. Forest Discovery Centre, 206–7
B.C. Shavers & Hobbies, 94
B.C. Transit (buses), 18
Baan Thai, 134
Babe's Honey Farm, 161
Baden-Baden, 78
Bamfield, 240–41
Barb's Place Floating Seafood Restaurant, 137
Barkley, Charles William, 277
Barkley, Frances, 277
Barkley Sound, 277
Bastion (Nanaimo), 211
Bastion Square, 54
Bay Centre, 48
Beach House Cafe, 217
Beacon Avenue (Sidney), 163
Beacon Books, 166
Beacon Hill Park, 145–46
Beacon Landing Pub & Restaurant, 165
Beagle Pub, 125
Bean Around the World, 118
Bear Mountain, 189
Bear Mountain Golf and Country Club, 189
Bear Mountain Victoria Golf Resort & Spa, 189
Beaver, 281, 282, 283

Beaver Lake, 162, 272
Begbie, Matthew Baillie, 294–96
Belfry Theatre, 130
Bennett, W. A. C. "Wacky," 321
Bent Mast, 124
Bernstein & Gold, 102
Best Western Tin Wis Resort and Conference Centre, 234
bicycle shops, 24
biking, 24, 261
Birdcages, 296
Birks Jewellers, 47
Bistro Suisse, 166–67
Black Ball Transport (ferries), 15
Blanshard, Richard, 287
Blethering Place Tearoom & Restaurant, 33, 128
Bligh, William, 276–77
Blinkhorn, Thomas, 286
Bliss Clothing Co., 107
Bloedel, J. H., 315
Blue Carrot Café, 67–68
Blue Fox Cafe, 85
Blue Grouse Vineyards, 197–98
Blue Peter Pub & Restaurant, 167
Blueberries Bakery Cafe, 239
bookstores (list), 324–26
Boomtown, 108
Botanical Beach Provincial Park, 184
Bowser, 219
Brasserie L'Ecole, 132–33
Breakers Cafe, 182
Breeze, 58
Brentwood Bay, 168
Brentwood Bay Lodge, 149–50
Brentwood Seagrille & Pub, 150
Britannia & Co. Antiques, 85
British Candy Shoppe, 101
British Colonist (newspaper), 293
British Columbia Act of Consolidation, 302
Broad Street, 75
Broughton, William, 279
Broughton Street Café-Deli, 73
Bubble Tea Place, The, 118
Bubby Rose's Bakery & Café, 126

Bun Shop, 70
Bungy Zone Adrenaline Centre, 209–10
bus destination stops, popular (list), 329–31
bus lines, 11–12, 18
bus tours, 18–19
Butchart Gardens, 33, 146–47
Butchart, Jenny, 314
Butchart, Robert, 314

C

Cadboro, 282, 283
Cadboro Bay, 283
Cafe Brio, 90–91
Café Madrid, 72–73
Cafe Mexico, 68
Cairo Coffee Merchants, 93
Calibre for Men, 108
Camille's Fine West Coast Dining, 56
Campbell River, 221–22
Canadian Pacific Railroad, 309
Canadian Princess Resort, 239
Cannery Building, 165
Canoe Club Brewhouse and Restaurant, 134
canoeing, 269–70
Captain Cook's Bakery Ltd., 86
car rentals, 20
Carr, Emily, 152–57, 319–20
carriage tours, 22
carriages, 21
Cary, George H., 293
Celebration Carriage Services, 162
Century Antiques and Collectibles, 83
Chandler's Seafood Restaurant, 66–67
Charelli's Deli, 141
Charles Baird Antiques, 88
Charles Dickens Pub, 42
Chatham, 279
Chemainus, 207–8
Chemainus Valley Museum, 208
Cherry Point Vineyards, 192
Che-wech-i-kan, 290–91

China Beach Provincial Park, 182
Chinatown, 115
Chinatown Trading Company, 116–17
Chinese-Canadian Cultural Association, 118
Chocolate Tofino, 236
Chocolatier Bernard Callebaut, 72
Church & State Winery, 148
Churchill, Winston, 314, 318
Classic Silverware, 93
Clayoquot Sound, 237
Cobble Hill Orchard, 196
Cobble Hill Pottery, 196
Coho ferry, 15
Colin Campbell Village Butcher, 128
Colonist (newspaper), 293, 301
Columbia, 278
Columbia River, 278
Colwood, 171
Command Post Militaria & Antiques, 52–53
Comox, 219–20
Comox Valley, 219
Comox Valley restaurants, 220
Connolly, William, 281
Constance, 285
Cook, James, 276, 277
Cook Street Fish and Chips, 125
Cook Street Market Place, 125
Cook Street Village, 125–26
Cook Street Village Wines, 125
Cook'n'Pan Polish Delikatessen, 142
Coombs, 227
Cooper, James, 286, 287, 289, 294
Cormorant Island, 258
Cortes Island, 257
Country Cupboard Cafe, 179
Courtenay, 219, 220
Cowichan Bay, 196, 198, 203
Cowichan Bay Maritime Centre Museum, 199
Cowichan Chemainus Ecomuseum, 200
Cowichan Trading Company, 51
Cox, William, 301
Craigdarroch Castle, 155, 273

Craigflower School, 291
Cridge, Edward, 303
Crocker, Charles, 309
Crofton, 206
Crosby, Thomas, 304
Crystal Pool and Fitness Centre, 272
Cumberland, 220
Cup a Joe, 124
Curious Comics and Image, 113
currency exchange, 4
Currie, Arthur, 317–18
Cuthbert, Herbert, 314
Cycletreks, 261

D

Da Tandoor, 90
Daily Times (newspaper), 309
Dale's Gallery, 118
Dallas, Alexander, 293
Dallas Road, 152
Dannsu Gifts, 110
Dan's Farm and Country Market, 160
D'Arcy McGee's, 65
D'Arcy's Pub, 56
Dark Horse Books, 112
DeCosmos, Amor (William Smith),
    293, 301–2, 307
Deep Cove Chalet, 167
Demers, Father Modeste, 303
Denman Island, 255
Details, 74
Dig This, 109–10
Discovery, 276, 279
Discovery Islands, 256–59
dive shops, 262–64
diving, 261–64
Domus Antica Galleries, 88
Don Mee's Seafood Restaurant, 119
Douglas, Amelia, 282, 288
Douglas, David, 304
Douglas, James, 281–83, 285,
    287–94, 300
Dragon Song Music Company, 122
Duchess of San Lorenzo, 289
Dufferin, Lord Frederick, 308
Duncan, 203, 204

Dunsmuir, Joan, 151, 310
Dunsmuir, Robert, 151, 305, 309–10
Dutch Bakery & Coffee Shop, 95

E

E & N railway, 23, 309
Eagle Aerie Gallery (Tofino), 236
Eagle Feather, 71
Earl's, 48
Earthly Delights, 193
East Sooke Regional Park, 175
Eastern Food Market, 119
Ebizo Sushi, 74
Eco Cruising Tours, 163
Eliza, Francisco, 279
Elizabeth, Queen, 314
Elk Lake, 162, 272
Elk Lake Park, 162
emergencies, 4
Emily Carr House, 152–53
Empress of India, 314
Engeler Farm, 195
English Inn & Resort, 140
English Sweet Shop, 101
Esquimalt, 282
Estevan Village, 133
Eugene's Greek Restaurant on
    Broad, 99
events (list), 335–42
eyeglass repair, 4

F

Fairburn Farm, 160–61, 198
Fairfield, 126
Fairmont Empress Hotel, 31, 32,
    34–35
Fan Tan Alley, 121
Fan Tan Cafe, 117
Fan Tan Gallery, 117–18
Fanny Bay Inn, 219
farms, 161–62
F.A.S. Seafood Producers Ltd.,
    136–37
Fernwood, 126–27
ferries, 12, 14–15
Ferris' Grill, 103

Fields Shoe Outlet, 102
Fields Shoes, 53
Fine Arts Festival, 173
Finest at Sea. *See* F.A.S. Seafood
   Producers Ltd.
Finlayson, Roderick, 283
Fisgard, 171, 285
Fisgard Market, 120
fishing, 264–66
Flag Shop, 92
Flavour, 109
Flowers on Top, 76
Floyd's Diner, 135
Foo Hong Chop Suey, 120–21
Footloose Leathers, 79
Forbidden Plateau, 272
Fort Rodd Hill Historic Park, 171
Fort Rupert, 286
Fort Vancouver, 282
Four Mile Roadhouse, 33
Foxglove Toys, 110
Franklyn, William, 301
Fraser, Simon, 280
Freedom Kilts Company, 126
French Beach Provincial Park, 179

G

Gabriola Island, 253–54
Galiano Island, 252
Galleon Books & Antiques, 166
galleries (list), 326–27
Galloping Goose Trail and Park, 170
Gamboa Greenhouses, 193
Games Workshop, 112
Garlic Rose, 65–66
Garrick's Head Pub, 57
Garry Oaks Winery, 246
Gate of Harmonious Interest, 115
George V, 279
George VI, 314
Gibbs, Mifflin, 297
Glendale Gardens Greenspace and
   Pacific Horticulture College, 153
Glenterra Vineyards, 193–95
Global Village Store, 114
Godfrey-Brownell Vineyards, 202

gold rush, 292–94
Golden Chopsticks Restaurant, 78
Goldstream Provincial Park, 172, 189
golf, 266
golf courses, 266–69
Goodfellow's Cigars Ltd., 69
Gorge Tour, 30
Gossips, 205
Government House, 153
Graciella Shoes, 108
Grafton Bookshop, 130
Grant, Ulysses S., 302
Grant, Walter, 285
"Graveyard of the Pacific," 315
Gray Line of Victoria, 18–19
Gray, Robert, 278
Great Depression, 320
Greater Victoria Public Library, 72
Green Cuisine, 110–11
Grey, Earl, 287
Gulf Islands, 243–56

H

Habit, 115
Hanna, James, 277
Harbour Sweets, 71
Harmon, 277
Harris, Lauren, 319
Haunted Bookshop, 166
Haute Cuisine Cookware, 97
Heart's Content, 121–22
Hector, James, 306
Helijet Airways, 12
Helmcken, John S., 35, 288–89,
   301, 302
Helmcken House, 35–36
Hemp & Co., 107
Heritage Farm & Vineyard, 161
Heritage Walking Tour, 163
Hernandez, Juan Perez, 276
Heron Rock Bistro, 124–25
hiking, 269
Hilary's Fine Cheeses, 200
Hills, George, 303
Hillside Farm, 161
Hill's Native Art, 63

Hime Sushi, 73
Hornby Island, 255
hospitals, 5
hot lines, 5
Hudson's Bay Company, 164, 281,
    282, 283, 285, 286, 287, 288, 289,
    290, 291, 293, 296, 305
Hughes Ltd., 102–3
Hugo's Grill and Brewhouse, 70–71
Hunan Village Cuisine, 119

I

Il Terrazzo Ristorante, 106
Imperial Eagle, 277
Inner Harbour, 28
Insideout Home and Garden Ltd., 70
Instinct Art and Gifts, 97
Interactivity Games, 82
Irish Linen Stores, 47
Irish Times, 53–54
Island Butterfly World (Coombs), 228
Island Spirit, 63

J

J & J Watch and Clock Repair, 87
J & J Wonton Noodle House, 89–90
James, Chief Wilks, 321
James Bay, 123–25
James Bay Coffee & Books, 124
James Bay Inn, 123
James Bay Tearoom and Restaurant,
    32, 124, 134–35
James Bay Trading Company, 61–62
James, Percy, 318
Jan K Company, 116
J. Burke & Sons Tobacconists, 164
Jean Hutton Custom Framing, 86
Jeune Brothers Outdoor
    Equipment, 111
Jewish community of Victoria, 303
Jia Hua Trading, 116
JJ's Coffee, 164
John's Place, 135–36
Johnson Street, 107
J. R.'s India Curry House, 65
Juan de Fuca Regional Park, 182

Juan de Fuca Strait, 277
Juan de Fuca Trail, 182
Jubilee Window, The, 39
Judy Hill Gallery & Gifts, 205

K

Kaboodles, 51
Kabuki Kabs, 21
Kanakas (Hawaiians), 287
kayaking, 269–70
Kay's Korner, 125
Keg Steakhouse & Bar, 65
Kennedy, Arthur, 300
kid stuff, 271
Kimbo Restaurant, 117
Knightsbridge Gift Shop Ltd., 78
Kopti, 277
Koto House, 77
Kwagiulth Museum, 256
Kwong Tung Seafood Restaurant,
    119–20

L

La Cache, 95
Lady Washington, 278
Ladysmith, 208–10
Langford, Edward, 288
Langford, 172
Lantern Tours in Old Burial
    Grounds, 273
Lasqueti Island, 254
Laundromats (list), 327
Le Coteau Farms & Garden
    Centre, 160
Le Petit Saigon, 71
Leather World, 102
Legends, 113
Lens & Shutter, 78
Lester & Gibbs, 297
Lester, Peter, 297
library, public, 5
Lifestyle Markets, 125
Lighthouse Pub and Restaurant, 184
liquor sales, 5
Little Qualicum Falls Provincial
    Park, 228

Loft, 235
Loi Sing Restaurant & BBQ
   Bakery, 120
Lola's Pizza, 66
London, Jack, 311
Long Beach Unit, 232
Lotus Pond Vegetarian
   Restaurant, 112
Lund's Auctioneers & Appraisers,
   91–92
Lunn's Pastries Deli & Coffee
   Shop Ltd., 164
Lush, 45–46
Lyle's Place, 100
Lytton, Bulwer, 293

M

Macdonald, Alexander, 300
Macdonald, John A., 303, 306
Macdonald's Bank, 300
Mackay, John, 277
Mackenzie, Alexander (explorer),
   279–80
Mackenzie, Alexander
   (prime minister), 306
MacMillan, H. L., 315
MacMillan Provincial Park, 228
MacMillan-Bloedel Company,
   228, 315
Mahle House, 214
Malahat Restaurant & Mountain
   Inn, 190
Malahat, 188, 190, 203
Malahat (people), 190
Malaspina, Alejandro, 279
Malcolm Island, 258–59
Maple Bay, 206
maps
   downtown Victoria, 27
   greater Victoria, viii
   Nanaimo, 212
   Vancouver Island, iv
   Victoria neighborhoods, 26
Maquinna, Chief, 277
Margaret, Princess, 314
Marina Coffee House, 139–40

Marina Restaurant (Oak Bay), 138–39
Maritime Museum of British
   Columbia, 54–55
Market Square, 68, 109, 110
Marley Farm Winery, 150
Martinez, Estaban Jose, 278
Maynard, Hannah, 309
Mayne Island, 250
McBride, Richard, 316
McCreight, John Foster, 303
McKay, Joseph, 290–91
McLoughlin, John, 281
McNeill, William H., 282
Meadowbrook Farm, 161
Meares, John, 278
Meares Wharf (Tofino), 237
medical care, 5
medical insurance, 3
Menzies, Archibald, 279
Merridale Ciderworks, 193
Metchosin, 171
Michell Brothers Farm, 159–60
Milestone's, 64
Mineral World and Scratch Patch
   (Sidney), 167
Miniature World, 42
Mirage Design, 93
Mirage Home & Garden, 93
Miroirs, 92
Moka House, 125
Mo:Lé, 114
Mom's Cafe (Sooke), 174–75
money, 4
Moon Key Groceries, 117
Moonstruck Organic Cheese—
   Makers of Fine Organic
   Cheeses, 245
Moose Crossing, 63
Mouat Provincial Park, 244
Mount Arrowsmith Ski Area, 228
Mount Royal Bagel Factory, 141
Mount Washington Ski Resort, 271
Mt. Newton Blueberries, 161
Muffet & Louisa, 68–69
Muir, Annie, 286
Muir, John, 286, 291

Mungo Martin House, 35
Munro's Books, 60–61
Murchie's Tea and Coffee, 32, 59–60
Museum at Campbell River, 222
MV *Lady Rose*, 229
MV *Frances Barkley*, 229
MVP Sports Cards, 83

N

Nanaimo, 210–15
Nanaimo Art Gallery, 213
Nanaimo Bastion, 211
Nanaimo District Museum, 211
Nanaimo restaurants, 214–15
Nautical Nellies Restaurant &
    Oyster Bar, 64
New Caledonia, 280
New England Square, 111
New Saigon Vietnamese
    Restaurant, 93–94
New Town Barber, 122
Newcastle Island, 254
newspapers, 5
nightclubs (list), 327–29
Nootka incident, 278
Nootka people, 277
Nootka Sound, 277
North Island Forest Tours, 273
North West Fur Company, 279,
    280, 281
Not Just Pretty, 88

O

Oak Bay Explorer, 19
Oak Bay Marina, 17
Oak Bay Village, 127–28
Oak Bay Village Wines, 131
Ocean Garden Restaurant, 121
Ocean Pointe Resort, 137
Ocean Pointe Resort Wine
    Shoppe, 138
Ocean River Sports, 270
Oceanwood Country Inn, 250
Ogden Point Cafe, 136
Oh Gelato!, 44, 47
Old City Quarter (Nanaimo), 213

Old Country Market (Coombs), 227
Oldfield Orchard & Bakery, 161
Old Morris Tobacconist, 58–59
Old 'n' Gold, 86
Old Nick's Emporium, 113
Old Spaghetti Factory, 35
Old Time Deli, 47
Olde Town Shoe Repair, 111
Olympia Restaurant, 164
Onderdonk, Andrew, 309
One-Hour Photo Express, 82
O'Reilly, Peter, 295
Original Christmas Village, 50–51
Ottavio Italian Bakery &
    Delicatessen, 128
Otter Point Bakery & Tea Room, 174
Out of Ireland, 62
Outlooks for Men, 103

P

Paboom, 79
Pacific (ship), 315
Pacific Antiques, 83–84
Pacific Coast Lines (PCL), 11–12
Pacific Editions, 91
Pacific Rim National Park, 231
Pacific Trekking, 50
Pagliacci's, 76–77
Panama Canal, 316
Pandora, 285
Pantages, Alex, 312
Paprika Bistro, 133
parking, 20–21
Parksville, 216
Parliament building, 38–40
Patisserie Daniel, 94
Pearse, Benjamin, 296
pedal cabs, 21
Pemberton, August, 294
Pemberton, Joseph Despard, 290
Pemberton, Phoebe, 309
Pender Islands, 247
Penny Farthing Olde English Pub, 130
Periklis Restaurant, 106
Pescatore's Fish House & Grill, 42–43
pharmaceuticals, 5

pharmacies (list), 329
Phoenix Restaurant, 163
Pier Bistro, 166
Pig War, 296–97
Plenty Epicurean Pantry, 88–89
Point Ellice Bridge disaster, 312
Point Ellice House, 30, 33
Point-No-Point Resort, Restaurant
    & Tearoom, 33, 181
Polk, James K., 284
popular bus destinations
    (list), 329–31
Port Alberni, 228–30
Port Hardy, 215, 225
Port McNeill, 224–25
Port Renfrew, 183–85
Port Renfrew Hotel, 183
Port Sidney Marina, 16–17
Princess liners, 314
prohibition, 318
prostitution, 310–11
public restrooms (list), 331–32
Puget Sound Agricultural
    Company, 286, 287–88

Q

Quadra, Juan Francisco de la
    Bodega y, 279
Quadra Island, 256
Qualicum Bay, 218
Qualicum Beach, 217–18, 219
Queen Charlotte Islands, 225
Quimper, Manuel, 279
Quonley's Gifts and Grocery, 115
Quw'utsun' Cultural and Conference
    Centre, 203–4

R

Rattenbury, Alma Pakenham, 318–19
Rattenbury, Francis Mawson, 313,
    318–19
Re-Bar, 54
Receptor Shoes, 102
recipes
    Basic Risotto with Parmigiano, 129
    Braciole del Vinaio, 98

Caesar Salad Easy Blender
    Dressing for Ten, 218
Charcoal-Grilled Seafood
    Steaks, 15
Chocolate Covered
    Tarantulas, 154
Crab Chowder, 235
Gingerbread Squares, 197
Green Curry, 57
Jicama Salad, 105
Lamb Pot Roast, 194
Lavender Honey Cheesecake, 178
Mushrooms and Cream, 196
Pagliacci's Famous Tomato
    Sauce, 76
Quick Coffee Cake, 251
Red Bandit Rockfish, 177
Sesame-Citrus Dressing, 58
Sole-wrapped Lingcod, 176
Spicy Honey Walnuts, 65
Tarte aux Pommes au Fromage
    Blanc, 244
Vinoteca Almond Torte, 248
Winter Vegetable Lasagna, 246
Recollections Antique and
    Collectibles Mall, 83
Red Cedar Moon, 162
Reef, 104–5
Resolution, 276
Restaurant Matisse, 104
restrooms (list), 331–32
Rhineland Bakery, 94–95
Ringo, Sam, 297
Rising Star Bakery & Cafe, 100
Robert Shaw Specialty Pies, 141–42
Roberta's Hats, 51–52
Robinson's Outdoor Store, 100
Roche Cove Llamas B&B, 175
Rock Cod Cafe, 198–99
Rogers' Chocolates, 45
Roger's Juke Box Records, 87
Rogers' Tudor Sweet Shoppe, 130
Romanoff & Company
    Antiques, 84–85
Room by Room by Room, 90
Roosevelt, Franklin D., 314

Roots, 49
Rosemeade Farms, 162
Rosemeade Dining Room, 140–41
Rosie's Diner, 125
Ross, Charles, 283
Royal British Columbia
 Museum, 37–38
Royal London Wax Museum, 40–41
Royal Roads University, 171
Ruckle Provincial Park, 244
Russell Books, 94

S

Saanich, 168
Saanich Historical Artifacts
 Society, 160
Saanich Peninsula Visitor's Guide, 163
Saanich People, 164
Saanichton, 168
Saanichton Christmas Tree & Ostrich
 Farm, 162
Salt Spring Island, 243–46
Salt Spring Vineyards, 245
Saltspring Soapworks, 109
Sally Bun, 89
Sam's Deli, 43–44
San Juan Island, Pig War and, 296–97
San Remo Restaurant, 143
Santiago, 276
Santiago's Cafe, 135
Sasquatch Trading Company
 Ltd., 49–50
Saturna Island, 249–50
Saturna Island Vineyards, 249
Sayward, 224
Scallywags, 95
Scandia Restaurant, 165
Scaramouche Gallery, 79
Schooner Restaurant and Motel, 235
scooters, 24
Seed of Life Natural Foods, 52
Seeing Is Believing, 62
Senzushi, 93
Serious Coffee, 163
Seward, William, 301
Seymour, Frederick, 300

Shabby Tiques, 89
shopping, hours, 4
Siam, King of, 314
Siam Thai Restaurant, 77
Side Street Bistro, 130
Sidney, 159, 169
Sidney Bakery, 163
Sidney Candy Man, 166
Sidney Historical Museum, 164
Silver Rill Corn, 162
Silverside Farms, 196
Silverwood, 101
Simply the Best Fine Clothing &
 Accessories, 75
Simpson, George, 281
Six Mile Pub, 170–71
skiing, 271–72
slaves, 275, 310
Sluggett Farms, 162
Small City Bistro, 131
Smyth's Market Garden, 162
Snowden's Books, 112
Songhees, 282, 283
Sonora Island, 257–58
Sonora Resort and Conference
 Centre, 257
Sooke, 172, 173–81
Sooke Harbour House, 175–77
Sooke Region Museum and Tourism
 Information Centre, 172–73
Sour Pickle Cafe, 70
Special Teas, 83
SpiceJammer, 92
Spinnaker's Brewery Pub &
 Restaurant, 143
Spirit of Victoria, 44
Spitfire Grill, 167–68
Sproat, Gilbert Malcolm, 304
Sproat Lake, 229, 230
Staines, Emma, 285
Staines, John, 285, 288, 289
Standard (newspaper), 301
Starbucks Coffee, 53, 125, 163
Starling Lane Winery, 149
Steamer's Pub, 102
Sterling Farm, 162

Stevenson's Shoe Clinic, 95
Still Life, 108
Stone Pipe Grill, 174
Stone's Fine Jewellery, 44
Store Street, 68
Stormtech & Edinburgh Tartan
    Shop, 45
Strathcona Hotel, 157
Strathcona Provincial Park, 223–24
Street, 50
streetcars, 311, 321
Sun & Surf Swimwear, 99–100
Sun Wing Greenhouses, Ltd., 162
Swans Cafe & Pub, 69
Swans Hotel, 69
Sweet Memories, 52
swimming, 272
Sydney Reynolds, 43

T

Tahsis, 277
Tally Ho horse-drawn carriages, 314
Tallyho Carraige Tours, 22
Tamami Sushi, 118
Tanner's Books, 166
Tapa Bar, 96
Tattoo Zoo, 66
taxes, 6
taxis, 19–20
tea, 32–33
Temple Emanuel (San Francisco), 303
Temple Emanuel (Victoria), 303
Temptations, 163
theaters, live (list), 332–33
Theo's Greek & Western Cuisine
    Restaurant, 166
Thompson, David, 280
Tod, John, 287
Tofino, 227, 228, 231, 235–38
Tolmie, Simon Fraser, 320
Tony's Trick & Joke Shop, 73
Tourism Victoria Centre, 28
Tradewinds, 119
trains, 16, 23
Triple Spiral Metaphysical, 122–23
True Grain Bread, 200

Trutch, Joseph, 295, 303
Trutch, Julia, 295
Tugwell Creek Honey Farm &
    Meadery, 178–79
Turntable, 122
Turtle Express, 123
Tuscan Kitchen, 97
Tyee Coal, 291

U

Ucluelet, 231, 239
Undersea Gardens, 41
Universal Tattoo, 99
University of Victoria (UVic), 9, 321
Upstairs Gallery, 104
UVic Housing and Conference
    Services, 132

V

Valencia (ship), 315
Valerianos, Apostolos, 277, 278
Valhalla Pure Outfitters Factory
    Outlet, 72
Van Isle Coin & Stamp, 84
Vancouver, George, 276
Vancouver Island Brewery, 144
Vancouver Island Soup, 87
Vanity Fair Antique Mall, 88
Venturi-Schulze Vineyards, 195
VIA Rail Canada, 16
Victoria Bug Zoo, 154
Victoria Butterfly Gardens, 148
Victoria Clipper, 14
Victoria Golf Club, 311
Victoria Harbour Ferries, 22–23, 29
Victoria Inner Harbour Marina, 17
Victoria International Airport, 13
Victoria International Hostel, 104
Victoria Regent Hotel, 67
Victoria Regional Transit
    System, 18
Victoria Theatre, 311
Victoria Yacht Club, 311
Vignetti Zanatta Winery and
    Vinoteca Wine Bar, 201–2
Vinoteca Restaurant, 202

Vitamin Shop, 99
Volume One, 205

W

W. & J. Wilson Clothiers, 49
Waddington, Alfred, 305
Walkem, George A., 308
walking tours, 272–73
Warren, George, 319
Wendy Russell Jewellery, 84
Wesley Street Restaurant, 214
West Coast Crab Bar, 235
West Coast Trail, 183–84
West Coast Trail Motel, 184
West End Gallery, 97
West Pacific Traders, 63–64
Whale Store, 75
whale watching, 273–74
Wharf Street, 64
Wharfside Eatery & Decks, 68
Whirled Arts, 123
White Heather Tea Room, 33, 131
Wickaninnish Beach, 232
Wickaninnish Inn, 233–34
Willie's Bakery, 107
Willows Gallery, 133–34
Winchester Galleries, 75
Wine Barrel, 74
wine shops
    Cook Street Village Wines, 125
    Ocean Pointe Resort Wine
        Shoppe, 138
    Wine Barrel, 74

wineries
    Alderlea Vineyards Ltd., 205–6
    Blue Grouse Vineyards, 197–98
    Cherry Point Vineyards, 192
    Church & State Winery, 148
    Garry Oaks Winery, 246
    Glenterra Vineyards, 193–95
    Godfrey-Brownell Vineyards, 202
    Marley Farm Winery, 150
    Merridale Ciderworks, 193
    Salt Spring Vineyards, 245
    Saturna Island Vineyards, 249
    Starling Lane Winery, 149
    Tugwell Creek Honey Farm &
        Meadery, 178–79
    Venturi-Schulze Vineyards, 195
    Vignetti Zanatta Winery and
        Vinoteca Wine Bar, 201–2
Wooden Shoe Dutch Groceries
    & Delicatessen, 142
Woofles—A Doggie Diner, 110
Work, John, 286
World of Flowers, 125

Y

Yates, James, 289
Yellow Jacket Comic Books
    & Toys, 113
Yuquot, 277

Z

Zinnia World Notions, 108
Zydeco, 108

About the Authors

Kathleen and Gerald Hill are native Californians who divide their time between Sonoma in the northern California wine country and Victoria, British Columbia. As a team the Hills wrote *Northwest Wine Country: Wine's New Frontier; Sonoma Valley: The Secret Wine Country; Victoria and Vancouver Island: A Personal Tour of an Almost Perfect Eden; Napa Valley: Land of Golden Vines; Monterey & Carmel: Eden By the Sea; Santa Barbara & the Central Coast: California's Riviera; The Encyclopedia of Federal Agencies and Commissions; Facts on File Dictionary of American Politics; The People's Law Dictionary;* and an international exposé, *The Aquino Assassination.* Together they have written for *National Geographic Traveler* and *Wine Spectator.* Kathleen authored *Festivals USA* and *Festivals USA—Western States* and has written for the *Chicago Tribune, San Francisco Magazine, Napa/Sonoma Magazine, Cook's Magazine,* the *San Francisco Examiner Magazine,* and other publications.

Kathleen is Food and Wine Editor of the *Sonoma Valley Sun,* where both she and Gerald are columnists. They host radio shows on KSVY radio, the "Kathleen Hill Show" and "Hill on History," respectively. The Hills have also co-taught American government and politics at University of British Columbia, University of Victoria, and Sonoma State University. They often comment on American politics on Canadian radio.